STANLEY BALDWIN
CONSERVATIVE LEADERSHIP AND
NATIONAL VALUES

Stanley Baldwin is one of the most significant modern British politicians, but also one of the most controversial and puzzling. As Conservative leader 1923–1937 and three times prime minister, Baldwin presided over the beginning of his party's long twentieth-century dominance. He did so in new and difficult conditions: the onset of modern democratic politics, the rise of Labour, chronic economic depression, the General Strike, persistent newspaper attacks, imperial discontent, the Abdication, and the threats from Mussolini and Hitler. He retired amidst wide public acclaim, from opponents as well as his own party. Yet after 1940 his reputation collapsed, and he was blamed for many of the supposed shortcomings of interwar British government, especially failure to deter the European dictators. More recently he has been held to symbolise the backwardness of British national culture. The reasons for his ascendancy and the nature of his contribution to public life have remained elusive.

This book provides a new understanding of Baldwin's career, including the first serious analysis of the moral and intellectual influences in his early life. Its main concerns are investigation of a Conservative mind, and its communication with the various audiences that constituted the political nation. It considers the construction of 'public character' and a distinctive Conservative doctrine and language, and assesses Baldwin's part in Conservative electoral success and the performance of interwar governments. This is not a conventional biography, rather an examination of the nature of political leadership, Conservative politics, and 'national values'.

PHILIP WILLIAMSON is Reader in History, University of Durham, having previously studied at Peterhouse, Cambridge, and as a research fellow at Nuffield College, Oxford. He is the editor of *The Modernisation of Conservative Politics: The Diaries and Letters of William Bridgeman, 1904–1935* (1988), and author of *National Crisis and National Government: British Politics, the Economy and Empire, 1926–1932* (1992). He is also co-editor, with Edward Baldwin, of a forthcoming selection from Stanley Baldwin's letters and recorded conversations.

STANLEY BALDWIN

Conservative leadership and national values

PHILIP WILLIAMSON

CAMBRIDGE
UNIVERSITY PRESS

PUBLISHED BY THE PRESS SYNDICATE OF THE UNIVERSITY OF CAMBRIDGE
The Pitt Building, Trumpington Street, Cambridge CB2 1RP, United Kingdom

CAMBRIDGE UNIVERSITY PRESS
The Edinburgh Building, Cambridge, CB2 2RU. UK   http://www.cup.cam.ac.uk
40 West 20th Street, New York, NY 10011–4211, USA   http://www.cup.org
10 Stamford Road, Oakleigh, Melbourne 3166, Australia

First published 1999

Printed in the United Kingdom at the University Press, Cambridge

Typeset in Bitstream Baskerville No. 2 11/12.5 [WV]

A catalogue record for this book is available from the British Library

Library of Congress Cataloguing in Publication data
Williamson, Philip, 1953–
    Stanley Baldwin: conservative leadership and national values / Philip Williamson.
        p.   cm.
    Includes bibliographical references and index.
    ISBN 0 521 43227 8 (hardback)
    1. Baldwin, Stanley Baldwin, Earl, 1867–1947.   2. Conservatism –
Great Britain – History – 20th century.   3. Great Britain –
Politics and government – 1910–1936.   4. Conservative Party (Great Britain) –
Biography.   5. Prime ministers – Great Britain – Biography.
I. Title.   DA566.9.B15W56   1999
9451.083′092 – dc21   [B]   98–43633   CIP

ISBN 0 521 43227 8 hardback

For Joseph

For fourteen years I preached . . . up and
down Great Britain, attempting to achieve
a national unity of spirit and a high
conception of what democracy may be, and
calling for unselfish service to that ideal.

> Earl Baldwin of Bewdley, *An Interpreter of
> England* (1939), p. 10

S.B. was always an idealist; they tell me also
he was quite a cunning politician.

> Lady Baldwin in Cazalet journal, 1940
> (R. Rhodes James, *Victor Cazalet* (1976), p. 223)

. . . a statesman who has gathered to himself a
greater volume of confidence and goodwill than
any public man I recollect in my long career.

> Winston Churchill speaking of Baldwin at the
> 1935 Conservative party conference

Contents

Illustrations

Tables

Acknowledgements

The central feature of this book is an examination of political leadership in its widest public aspects, and the use of public statements as its main source. Nevertheless the interpretation offered could not have been developed without information obtained from a large number of private records. I am especially grateful to the 4th Earl Baldwin and Lady Baldwin for their hospitality and assistance, and to Lord Baldwin for permission to consult and quote from his family's papers and publications.

For access to collections of Baldwin papers I am indebted to the Syndics and the staff of the manuscripts room of Cambridge University Library, and to the staff of Worcester County Record Office and the manuscripts section of the University of Sussex Library. Andy Burns of the British Steel East Midland Regional Records Centre was especially helpful in unearthing material on the Baldwin firms. I am also most grateful to Lord and Lady Crathorne for permitting me to consult the papers of the 1st Lord Crathorne, and to Richard Oldfield and Lord Davidson for enabling me to read material in the personal papers of the 1st Lord Davidson and Joan, Lady Davidson.

In Stourport Pauline Annis provided me with much information about the history of the Baldwin family and companies, helped with illustrations, and gave me a fascinating tour around local Baldwin sites. Mrs F. Llewellyn of Stourport Library and Mrs M. Sanders of Worcester City Library provided further information. At Wilden I am grateful to Nic Harvey for the gift of his history of Wilden School, and to his wife for showing me Wilden Church.

I thank the archivists in the libraries and record offices listed in the primary sources section on pp. 362–5 for answering my inquiries and supplying documents and copies, and numerous others who were helpful, if only in establishing that no Baldwin material had survived. I received particular help or information from Larry Bruce at Middlesbrough Central Library; C. P. Atkins at the National Railway Museum Library, York; David Beasley, the Librarian at Goldsmiths' Hall, London, and Jonathan Smith of Trinity College Library, Cambridge. Oliver Brett, the Librarian at Windsor Castle, gave permission to consult the 'Royal' volumes in the Baldwin papers. Material from the Royal Archives is used with the gracious permission of Her Majesty the Queen.

Maurice Cowling and Professor John Vincent first suggested that I write this book, though its format has changed since its original conception. I am also grateful to them for research material, information on sources, and much intellectual stimulation.

Further information about sources was kindly provided by Anne Jenkin, Alistair Cooke, Professor David Dilks, and Professor Cameron Hazlehurst. Christina Bussfeld, Matthew Grimley, and Lindsay Edkins sent me copies of useful documents. Peter Claus supplied information on the City and further materials, and asked hard questions. I thank Stuart Ball for copies from the Headlam diary, and Geoffrey Channon for copies of his articles on railway history. I am grateful to David Jarvis for the loan of his important doctoral thesis.

For answering specific questions I thank Chris Brooks, Catriona Burness, Duncan Bythell, Barry Doyle, Alan Heesom, Anne Orde, and Oliver Westall. Ranald Michie has given advice on business issues, and created a price series for conversion of various sums into modern values. Jonathan Parry gave me the benefit of his Victorian expertise in commenting on Alfred Baldwin. William Davies has been a most patient and tolerant editor.

I am grateful for support from the University of Durham – from colleagues in the History Department and from staff of the University Library, and for assistance from the University research and travel funds. I am especially grateful to the University for electing me to a Sir Derman Christopherson Research Fellowship in 1994–5.

Michael Bentley, Duncan Bythell, and Christine Woodhead read the whole book in draft and made many valuable comments. To Helen and Peter Ghosh and their family I owe particular debts of hospitality. Peter has throughout been a source of ideas and a rigorous reader and commentator.

Abbreviations and conventions

Unless otherwise mentioned, the place of publication is London.

AC	Austen Chamberlain papers
AWB	A.W. Baldwin, *My Father. The True Story* (1956)
Berrows	*Berrow's Worcester Journal* (the principal Worcestershire newspaper)
BF	Baldwin family papers
BLtd	Baldwin Ltd papers
BT	Board of Trade records
B/WCRO	Baldwin papers, Worcester County Record Office
Cabinet	Cabinet conclusions (minutes, from PRO CAB 23)
CP	Cabinet Papers (memoranda, from PRO CAB 24)
CRD	Conservative Research Department papers
CUL Add.	Cambridge University Library, Additional manuscripts
DBB	*The Dictionary of Business Biography*, ed. D. J. Jeremy (5 vols., 1984–6)
DBFP	*Documents on British Foreign Policy 1919–1939*
DGFP	*Documents on German Foreign Policy 1918–1945*
DNB	*Dictionary of National Biography 1941–1950* (Oxford, 1959)
GMY	G. M. Young, *Stanley Baldwin* (1952)
HCDeb, HLDeb	*House of Commons* – or *Lords* – *Debates*, 5th series, unless otherwise stated (c., cc. indicate column numbers)
Interpreter	Earl Baldwin of Bewdley, *An Interpreter of England* (1939)
JCCD	J. C. C. Davidson (1st Viscount Davidson) papers
JD	Joan Davidson (Lady Davidson, née Dickinson) papers

Jones diary	unpublished diary in the Thomas Jones papers (like the published extracts, actually a compilation of diary, memoranda, and letters, but 'diary' is used here as a convenient shorthand)
Jones *DL*	Thomas Jones, *A Diary with Letters 1931–1950* (1954)
Jones *WD*	Thomas Jones, *Whitehall Diary*, ed. K. Middlemas (3 vols., Oxford, 1969)
M&B	K. Middlemas and J. Barnes, *Baldwin. A Biography* (1969)
NC	Neville Chamberlain papers
OE	Stanley Baldwin, *On England and other Addresses* (1926)
OI	Stanley Baldwin, *Our Inheritance. Speeches and Addresses* (1928)
PRO	Public Record Office
SB	Stanley Baldwin political papers
SOL	Stanley Baldwin, *Service of Our Lives. Last Speeches as Prime Minister* (1937)
TTF	Stanley Baldwin, *This Torch of Freedom. Speeches and Addresses* (1935)
WCRO	Worcester County Record Office
WSC Comp	*Winston S. Churchill, Companion* parts to vols. IV–VI, ed. Martin Gilbert (1976–94): references are by volume number, then part number and page number, e.g. *WSC Comp* IV/iii.2107–8

SPEECHES AND NEWSPAPERS

For non-parliamentary speeches before May 1923, newspaper and date of publication are given. From May 1923 such speeches and addresses are cited by place or audience and by date of delivery, e.g. 'Birmingham, 9 Oct. 1931' or 'Primrose League, 6 May 1932', as the texts are available in bound volumes in the Baldwin papers and were normally published verbatim in *The Times* (in the edition of the day following the date given here, except for Saturday speeches, printed on Monday). Certain newspapers were searched selectively for comment, but most references in the notes are not to the originals but to the press cuttings in the Baldwin papers at Cambridge.

PRIVATE PAPERS AND EDITIONS

The locations of manuscript collections of letters, diaries, and memoranda and the full titles of and publication details of editions of such papers, organised by the subject's name, are given in the list of primary sources, pp. 362–5. References to these editions in the notes are by shortened titles.

FURTHER PUBLISHED WORKS

Most secondary sources are identified in the notes only. The Bibliographical essay, pp. 366–71, is intended as a reader's guide to contemporary and historical writings about Baldwin, and is arranged accordingly.

Introduction: the historical problem

Few British political leaders have been so successful and significant as Stanley Baldwin. Yet few have suffered so much belittlement and abuse in retirement, and later biographers and historians have had considerable difficulty in producing plausible explanations for his ascendancy. More nonsense has been written about him than about any other modern prime minister. This has had consequences for wider understandings of twentieth-century Britain, as interpretations of his politics are integral to several major debates: on the Conservative party's long-term electoral dominance, on constitutional issues, on 'national culture', and on Britain's industrial, imperial, and international decline.

This book is not concerned primarily with recounting Baldwin's life. Rather, it concentrates upon defining the nature of his politics, identifying its sources, examining its expressions, and assessing its impact. It aims to contribute to a fuller grasp of larger issues, especially the character and success of modern Conservatism. In doing so, it suggests a method for creating new understandings of British political leaders, by directing attention towards their widest public functions – not just to their particular party and ministerial roles, but to their relationships with the electorate, opposing parties, and the media, and to their interaction with 'political culture'.

I

Baldwin was Conservative leader for fourteen years from 1923 to 1937, and prime minister three times, from 1923 to 1924, 1924 to 1929, and 1935 to 1937. He led his party to larger electoral victories than any other twentieth-century party leader. If his four years, from 1931 to 1935, as deputy to MacDonald within the

1

'National' government are included, he also led it for a longer period in office than anyone except Thatcher. What makes his career still more significant is that these successes were achieved in new and difficult conditions. Aside from Bonar Law's brief (seven-month) tenure in 1922–3, Baldwin was the first Conservative prime minister to preside over a truly mass democracy, with universal suffrage – female as well as male, and overwhelmingly working class. He was certainly the first to feature on the modern mass media of radio and sound film. He was the first to bear the political impact of prolonged economic depression and mass unemployment in the traditional manufacturing and mining areas, and the first to face a major socialist party and highly politicised trade-union leadership. He became the first leader of opposition to a Labour government, and the only prime minister to confront a general strike. His reputation was made in 1922 by helping to free the Conservative party from a coalition government, yet in 1931 he led it into another and more enduring coalition. During his leadership the British overseas dominions moved from Empire to Commonwealth, and Indian nationalists mounted their greatest civil-disobedience campaigns. The last great struggle between free trade and protection was fought, and sterling suffered its first and most spectacular devaluation. Baldwin was also the first Conservative leader to be confronted by Stalinist and fascist ideologies, and the first who had to justify rearmament to an electorate apprised of the horrors of modern aerial bombardment, steeped in anti-war feeling, and placing its trust in international peace-keeping. He remains the only prime minister to have superintended a royal abdication.

Such were the hazardous conditions for the leader of a party long identified with hierarchy, privilege, monarchy, property, sound finance, imperialism, and the armed services. Not simply Conservative party interests but the very structures and values which sustained those interests seemed under threat, and there were sharp disagreements among Conservatives about how best to react. In these circumstances Baldwin's resilience and success were remarkable. Few political careers have veered so often between such high peaks and such low troughs. He survived several party rebellions, and two attempted coups by senior colleagues. He suffered sustained criticism from conservative mass-circulation newspapers, and the most serious organisational and electoral challenges ever mounted by newspaper owners. He defeated or out-manoeuvred many of the leading public figures of his time – Lloyd George, Asquith, MacDonald, Birkenhead, Austen and Neville Chamberlain, Beaverbrook, Bishop Temple, King Edward VIII, and Churchill. He lost two general elections, in 1923 and 1929, but on both occasions Conservatives retained the largest share of the popular vote and denied their opponents an overall parliamentary majority. Those defeats were amply recouped in the landslide victories of 1924, 1931, and 1935, when Conservatives secured majorities of over 200 seats, and in the last two elections the largest popular support of modern times. Baldwin also enjoyed more personal parliamentary triumphs than any other twentieth-century party leader. In the mid 1920s and again in the mid 1930s he commanded an extraordinary national ascendancy, surpassed only by Churchill from 1940 to 1945. To criticise him at Conservative meetings during the 1930s was said to be 'little short of blasphemy'. If an MP interrupted him while speaking in the House of Commons 'it seemed almost like brawling in church'.[1] During the 1937 Coronation he shared the popular applause with the new King and Queen. Unusually for a party leader he retired at a time of his own choosing, amidst warm tributes not just from his own party but from his opponents – in Churchill's words, 'loaded with honours and enshrined in public esteem'.[2]

II

The problems in interpreting Baldwin's career have generated a succession of unusually unpleasant, divided, and amorphous historical reputations. His contemporaries had been perplexed by him. His rise to high office was rapid and unexpected, a surprise magnified by his own insistence that he was just an ordinary, simple, man. A jocular public statement a week before he became prime minister – that he looked forward to retiring to his native Worcestershire 'to read the books I want, to live a decent life, and to keep pigs'[3] – came to define an image, but also a problem. He

---

[1] C. Petrie, *Chapters of My Life* (1950), pp. 165, 171; T. Jones, 'Stanley Baldwin', *DNB* p. 50.
[2] J. Ramsden, *The Age of Balfour and Baldwin* (1978), p. 351; Attlee and Sinclair in *HCDeb* 324, cc. 682–4 (31 May 1937); Cripps to Baldwin, 31 May 1937, SB 152/170; W. S. Churchill, *The Second World War*, vol. I: *The Gathering Storm* (1948), p. 18.
[3] Belatedly reported in *The Times*, 25 May 1923.

had been an industrialist, yet seemed to be a countryman. He was a politician who could appear to be non-political. He had literary and cultural interests yet paraded a dislike of intellectuals; he disdained oratory yet made impressive speeches. Dramatic decisions and sharp reversals of fortune during his first two years as leader deepened the mystery. He could seem both sedate and impulsive, appear ineffective yet transform the political landscape. He made serious mistakes, only to rebound with great successes. He often looked vulnerable but proved to be irremovable, a political innocent yet able to beat the most formidable opponents. Contemporary commentators described him as an 'enigma', and searched for the 'real' Baldwin. Profile-writers and memoirists predicted that he would 'puzzle the future historian'.[4]

Within four years of his ministerial retirement many thought there was no puzzle at all, as he became a principal victim in an enduring denigration of the dominant elements of interwar public life. No other former prime minister's reputation has collapsed so completely and so swiftly, nor turned upon so few sentences.[5] Munich, the outbreak of war, and Dunkirk created an atmosphere in which earlier criticisms by Conservative 'anti-appeasers' of Baldwin's reactions to German rearmament became widely accepted across the political spectrum, and were expanded into a comprehensive indictment. A misjudged passage in a November 1936 speech was seized upon as proof that, following a severe by-election defeat at East Fulham in 1933, he had minimised the German danger and delayed British rearmament until the 1935 election had been won – resulting in ineffective deterrence, diplomatic humiliation, and military reverses. Most vividly in *Guilty Men* by 'Cato' (Michael Foot, Peter Howard, and Frank Owen) and most savagely in an article by A. L. Rowse and in the popular press, it was asserted that Baldwin had deceived and betrayed the nation because his preference, sustained by ruthless party management, had always been for doing nothing except retaining power. He seemed ordinary and simple precisely because he was ordinary and simple; for 'Cato' a 'little man', for George Orwell

---

[4] E.g. A. G. Gardiner, *Certain People of Importance* (1926), pp. 1–8; W. Steed, *The Real Stanley Baldwin* (1930); B. Roberts, *Stanley Baldwin: Man or Miracle?* (1936); L. S. Amery, *My Political Life*, 3 vols. (1953–5), II. 505.

[5] For fuller examination, see P. Williamson, 'Baldwin's Reputation', forthcoming.

'simply a hole in the air'.[6] A legitimate attempt to preserve his own property – the ornamental gates to his home, requisitioned for scrap metal – brought violent public abuse and hate mail.[7]

Much of the criticism came from writers on the left who preferred to forget Labour and Liberal opposition to government rearmament during the mid 1930s; it became a standard anti-Conservative weapon for radical publicists preparing for the post-war general election.[8] Yet criticism was also fostered by a Conservative newspaper proprietor and minister – Beaverbrook (employer of the *Guilty Men* authors) – seeking revenge in a quarrel that long pre-dated rearmament, and it went largely unchallenged by other Conservatives now cloaking themselves in the Churchillian mantle. By 1945 Baldwin had been erased from the party's public memory, his name avoided in election literature and speeches.[9] Passages from his addresses, quoted or anthologised in innumerable interwar celebrations of English politics and culture, vanished from the equally numerous celebrations published in the 1940s. After his death in 1947 his principal memorial was a simple monument by the roadside near his Worcestershire home – a poignant contrast to his national acclaim in 1937 (plate 15). The critical verdict now received the imprimatur of Churchill's war memoirs, the index of which encapsulated the indictment: 'great party manager', 'aversion to foreign problems', 'excludes Churchill from office' and, famously, 'confesses putting party before country'.[10] To this was added a Keynesian historiography which, forgetting that Baldwin was not a social democrat and discounting imperial protectionism as an alternative – even credible – political economy, extended the charges of neglect and failure to the issues of economic depression and mass unemployment. A broad consensus, Labour–Churchillian–Keynesian,

[6] A. Salter, *Security* (1939), pp. 194–7; 'Cato', *Guilty Men* (July 1940), pp. 17–21, 25–7, 35–7; A. L. Rowse, 'Reflections on Lord Baldwin', *Political Quarterly* 12 (1941), 305–17, reprinted in Rowse, *The End of an Epoch* (1947), pp. 77–89; press extracts in M&B pp. 1056–7; G. Orwell, *The Lion and the Unicorn* (1941: Penguin edn, 1984), p. 56.
[7] For the story of the Astley Hall gates and examples of the abuse, see M&B pp. 1056–63.
[8] E.g. 'Gracchus', *Your M.P.* (1944), p. 18; T. L. Horabin, *Politics Made Plain* (Penguin special, 1944), pp. 49–50.
[9] J. Ramsden, *The Age of Churchill and Eden* (1995), p. 80, and see pp. 171–2. An exception was Q. Hogg, *The Left Was Never Right* (1945), pp. 54, 57–65.
[10] Churchill, *Gathering Storm*, p. 697, and see pp. 30, 80, 161, 181, 194–5, 198, 199. Churchill nevertheless contributed to the Baldwin memorial, and spoke at its unveiling in 1950: M&B p. 1072.

became entrenched. It entered the textbooks, and it remains a common impression, perpetuated even by some of the better historians.[11] Forty years after the war Michael Foot, by then Labour party leader but still brandishing *Guilty Men*, was able to block a proposal to place a statue of Baldwin alongside those of other prime ministers in the Houses of Parliament.[12]

So compelling were the perspectives of the 1940s that they were accepted by Baldwin's official biographer, G. M. Young, and – almost as damagingly – did not seem to be contested by his friend and chief obituarist, Tom Jones,[13] nor by his surviving Cabinet colleagues.[14] In mitigation Young argued that, during the General Strike and the Abdication especially, Baldwin had preserved the constitution and national unity. But his 'explanations' of the main points of censure only added further criticisms: indolence, irresolution, inattention to foreign affairs, even negligence of official duties, underlain by an inordinate personal need to retain public affection.[15] Baldwin, a reluctant biographical subject but stung by critics who in his view lacked 'historical sense', had been persuaded by friends to commission Young because he thought a historian who had written *Portrait of an Age* (1936) and seemed to share his own distaste for 'the modern psychological approach in biographies' would be well equipped to 'picture the mentality' of

[11] E.g. B. Pimlott, 'Many More Pygmies than Giants', *The Independent on Sunday*, 4 April 1993: 'Baldwin neglected to rearm against Hitler'.

[12] J. Critchley, 'Why Baldwin Deserves a Place in the House', J. Haviland, 'Baldwin Must Wait for his Commons Statue', and 4th Earl Baldwin letter, *The Times*, 27 Feb., 5, 10 March 1982. *Guilty Men* was re-published in 1998 as a Penguin 'Twentieth Century Classic' (*sic*), with a new preface by Foot. The introduction, by John Stevenson, gives only the slightest indication of how little the book has withstood subsequent scholarly scrutiny.

[13] Jones drafted his obituary in 1937, but when revising it in 1941 felt unable to 'appraise' the rearmament controversy (Jones papers A7). What stuck – and was adopted by Young – was the suggestion of 'indolence'. Only a shortened version was published in *The Times*, 15 Dec. 1947, but the full text appeared as a pamphlet, *Lord Baldwin. A Memoir* (1947). Jones's review of Young's book, in *The Observer*, 16 Nov. 1952, left its central charges intact, and Young's interpretation influenced Jones's article on Baldwin in the *DNB*, written 1953–4. Yet as 'P.Q.R.' in *The Spectator*, 7 June 1935, Jones had praised Baldwin for making possible the 'drastic' air rearmament 'now in operation'.

[14] E.g. reviews of GMY by L. S. Amery, *The Spectator*, 14 Nov. 1952; Lord Norwich (Duff Cooper), *The Daily Mail*, 14 Nov. 1952; W. Elliot, *Time and Tide*, 15 Nov. 1952. Amery's criticisms in *My Political Life* became particularly influential.

[15] GMY, esp. pp. 23, 56–8, 61–3, 72, 100, 106, 120–2, 126, 128, 167, 182, 200, 204. In June 1935 Young had shown himself markedly less worried about Germany than Baldwin had already been for two years: see AWB pp. 349–50.

the interwar years.[16] Young, however, approached his task in exactly the manner Baldwin had feared, one which encouraged the substitution of speculation and innuendo for what Young considered to be the inadequacies of his private papers as source material. Finding 'the psychology of the subject ... so absorbing that the history ... mov[ed] further and further into the background',[17] Young initiated another persistent strand of interpretation – where psychological or temperamental supposition replaces adequate historical explanation.

However, a reaction to this historiography had already begun, with Bassett's demonstration that Baldwin's alleged 'confession' on the difficulties of rearmament had been misrepresented. Baldwin's November 1936 statement had in fact referred to conditions well before the 1935 election, and at that election he had sought a mandate to expand a rearmament which was already under way.[18] The reaction was pursued most vigorously by Baldwin's second son who – after a private rebuke to an embarrassed Jones[19] – published a biographical counterblast. Against Young's psychological speculations he presented Baldwin's formative experiences, religion, and values – although his candour about his father's parents and a schoolboy scrape unintentionally stimulated the appetite for yet more psychological interpretations. Against the Churchillian–Labour account of the 1930s he deployed the best available historical source – at that time *Parliamentary Debates* – which those claiming historical authority had signally ignored.[20] In these ways he anticipated conclusions from later academic research, and enabled Robert Blake to produce the first detached (if plainly Conservative) assessment.[21]

---

[16] Jones *DL*, pp. 482, 527 (21–22 Jan. 1941, 23 Dec. 1944); M&B pp. 1059, 1063; Baldwin in H. Pearson and H. Kingsmill, *Talking of Dick Whittington* (1947), p. 189.

[17] GMY p. 11; Young to Duff Cooper, 22 Sept. 1946, Cooper papers 2/1.

[18] R. Bassett, 'Telling the Truth to the People. The Myth of the Baldwin "Confession"', *The Cambridge Journal* 2 (1948–9), 84–95, also 239–42.

[19] A. W. Baldwin-Jones letters, 29, 31 March 1953, CUL Add. 7938: Jones wrote that 'in a long life I can't recall receiving a letter which has so shaken me'.

[20] A. W. Baldwin, *My Father. The True Story* (1955). Another notable riposte was D. C. Somervell, *Stanley Baldwin. An Examination of Some Features of Mr. Young's Biography* (1953), and there was a lesser-known pamphlet defence, D. H. Barber, *Stanley Baldwin* (1959).

[21] R. Blake, 'Baldwin and the Right', in J. Raymond (ed.), *The Baldwin Age* (1960). Blake had earlier accepted Young's and Churchill's interpretations in reviews for Beaverbrook's *Evening Standard*, 'The Disastrous Mr. Baldwin' (14 Nov. 1952) and 'Was Winston Fair to Baldwin?' (25 Sept. 1953).

With the opening of government, party, and personal records from the late 1960s, understandings of the interwar period became more properly historical. The new evidence brought specialist party and policy studies which stimulated fresh and more complicated interpretations, and in 1969 the first comprehensive, fully documented, biography by Keith Middlemas and John Barnes. It became possible to transcend naive criticism or defence in favour of understanding, and led in time to such a rehabilitation of Baldwin's reputation that in the 1990s a Conservative prime minister could publicly claim him as a model, and a Labour prime minister could speak at the dedication of a memorial to him in Westminster Abbey.[22]

Some recent historical studies have been perceptive about Baldwin.[23] Nevertheless, the general effect of interpretations since the 1960s has been to re-cast him as an elusive figure. His public position notwithstanding, the official and private records display no firm and persistent imprint of him as a commanding figure. Contemporaries at a loss to explain his dominance frequently ascribed it to 'character', and subsequent accounts – from Jones and G. M. Young onwards – have not always been more substantial or precise. Middlemas and Barnes's 'new style' of leadership turns out to be little more than basic man-management.[24] Various versions of an interpretation that Baldwin himself chose to project – 'my worst enemy would not say of me that I did not know what the reaction of the English people would be to a particular course of action'[25] – are less explanations than evasions. To say that he

---

[22] John Major on becoming prime minister in 1990 and Tony Blair in his address on 18 December 1997 – marking the fiftieth anniversary of Baldwin's death – both invoked him as a 'consensual' politician, plainly drawing parallels with their own public stances. Earlier, in 1967, Sir Edward Heath had spoken at a private House of Commons luncheon to commemorate the centenary of Baldwin's birth. The organising committee included Lord (R. A.) Butler, Sir Geoffrey Lloyd, Lord and Lady Davidson, and Baldwin's surviving private secretaries.

[23] Notably M. Cowling, *The Impact of Labour 1920–1924* (Cambridge, 1971), pp. 297–300, 407–8, 421–2, and *The Impact of Hitler. British Politics and British Policy 1933–1940* (Cambridge, 1975), pp. 259–71; B. Schwarz, 'The Language of Constitutionalism: Baldwinite Conservatism', in *Formations of Nation and People* (1984), 1–18; D. Jarvis, 'Stanley Baldwin and the Ideology of the Conservative Response to Socialism, 1918–1931' (PhD thesis, University of Lancaster, 1991: hereafter cited as 'Jarvis thesis'), to be published as *Conservative Ideology and the Response to Socialism 1918–1931.*

[24] M&B ch. 18, esp. pp. 488–91; K. Middlemas, 'Stanley Baldwin', in H. van Thal (ed.), *The Prime Ministers*, 2 vols. (1975), II. 255–6.

[25] E.g. Abdication speech, in *SOL* p. 73 (10 Dec. 1936); GMY pp. 54, 129.

embodied 'Englishness' overlooks the extent to which Englishness has always been diverse and contested: what did Durham miners, Worcestershire farmers, and City financiers share? It also overlooks a rare period of Conservative success in Scotland.[26] Attributing his power to some special ability to interpret and reflect public opinion[27] assumes that 'public opinion' formed something homogeneous, easily identifiable, and intrinsically Conservative, rather than divided, diffuse, and in substantial degrees reactionary, Liberal, Labour, or socialist. Over 45 per cent of electors were always non- or anti-Conservative. It also assumes that 'public opinion' existed as an independent entity, rather than developing in dynamic relationship with what was said by the competing political parties, let alone the media. Ascribing Baldwin's success simply to the occupation of the 'centre' or 'middle' of politics presumes that a political 'centre' pre-existed in some manifest and stable form, rather than having repeatedly to be defined and constructed. To describe him unambiguously as 'consensual', moderate, or conciliatory is to disregard periods when he deliberately sharpened differences, notably over the General Strike and at the 1924 and 1931 elections.[28] A still grander or (depending on perspective) more dismissive view, that he encapsulated the spirit or will of the interwar age[29] begs similar if larger questions. All these interpretations imply that Baldwin's conception and practice of leadership was essentially passive, neutral, or hollow – 'not to create popular feeling', but to 'react to the mood of the people'[30] – in effect, non-leadership. Then again, it is certainly significant that he was considered sincere and trustworthy, and had skills of communication on the platform and in the new mass media.[31] But these

---

[26] Blake, 'Baldwin and the Right', p. 26; Ramsden, *Balfour and Baldwin*, pp. 212–13. For the indicative significance of the Scottish vote, see R. McKibbin, *The Ideologies of Class* (Oxford, 1990), p. 264.

[27] Ramsden, *Balfour and Baldwin*, pp. 207–8; S. Ball, *Baldwin and the Conservative Party. The Crisis of 1929–1931* (New Haven, 1988), p. 8.

[28] A point well made in C. L. Mowat, 'Baldwin Restored?', *Journal of Modern History* 27 (1955), 171–2. See also B. Malament, 'Baldwin Re-restored?', *ibid.* 44 (1972), 95, and Jarvis thesis, pp. 12–14 and ch. 6.

[29] E.g. Blake, 'Baldwin and the Right', pp. 25–6; epigraph to M&B, p. viii; D. Cannadine, 'Politics, Propaganda and Art. The Case of Two Worcestershire Lads', *Midland History* 4 (1977), 107: Ramsden, *Balfour and Baldwin*, p. 207; S. Ball, '1916–1929', in A. Seldon (ed.), *How Tory Governments Fall* (1996), p. 260.

[30] Ball, *Baldwin and the Conservative Party*, p. 8.

[31] J. Ramsden, 'Baldwin and Film', in N. Pronay and D. W. Spring (eds.), *Propaganda, Politics and Film 1918–45* (1982), pp. 126–8; J. Ramsden, *An Appetite for Power. A History of the*

describe forms of delivery, empty in themselves, rather than the qualities for creating a believing audience: substance and purpose.

There are other lines of inquiry – structural, organisational, sociological, ideological – which suggest that Baldwin himself mattered very little, and that his long period of prominence owed as much to fortunate circumstances as had his original rise to the premiership. The 1918 redistribution of parliamentary seats, the 1921 partition of Ireland, and the efficiency of the Conservative party machine; the Conservative preference of newly enfranchised women voters, the broader social composition of direct tax-payers, the steady rise in real incomes; the division of the anti-Conservative vote, Liberal party disintegration, the troubles of the first two Labour governments: together these certainly explain a great deal about interwar Conservative success. So, more recently, do important analyses of interwar Conservative propaganda, seen as promoting anti-collectivist and anti-inflationary 'conventional wisdoms' and hostile stereotypes of the trade-unionised working class.[32] Plainly enough, Baldwin's power and success were no more his own unaided creation than were those of any other political leader. Yet these approaches do not register the large and distinctive impression he made upon the public mind. Nor do they accommodate the widespread contemporary belief that he constituted a political force and an electoral asset in himself.

The nature of writing about Baldwin is so peculiar that it can produce verdicts which are, in the strict sense of the word, incredible. Although now properly discounted as a specific explanation for Baldwin's calling of the 1923 election, it is still asserted as general interpretation that his chief political aim, an 'obsession' which 'sustained his career', was to exclude Lloyd George from office[33] – this when he was confronted by the rather more fundamental challenges of newly emergent socialism, direct-action

Conservative Party since 1830 (1998), pp. 253–6; Ball, *Baldwin and the Conservative Party*, pp. 11, 16.

[32] The seminal essay is R. McKibbin, 'Class and Conventional Wisdom: The Conservative Party and the "Public" in Interwar Britain', in his *Ideologies of Class*, pp. 259–93. See also D. Jarvis, 'British Conservatism and Class Politics in the 1920s', *English Historical Review* 111 (1996), 59–84.

[33] R. Blake, *The Conservative Party from Peel to Churchill* (1970 edn), pp. 220, 222, 227, 236; J. Campbell, 'Stanley Baldwin', in J. P. Mackintosh (ed.), *British Prime Ministers of the Twentieth Century*, 2 vols. (1977), I. 191 and *passim*; M. Pugh, *The Making of Modern British Politics 1867–1939* (Oxford, 1982), pp. 229, 274; Ball, *Baldwin and the Conservative Party*, p. 8. This interpretation originated with Jones and Amery.

trade unionism, and aggressive totalitarian regimes. Again, we are told that Baldwin's party was engaged in a 'retreat from Empire' back to 'English nationalism', and that he himself had little interest in the Empire or even the rest of Britain;[34] yet Conservatives still defined themselves as imperialist and unionist, and Baldwin came to be regarded as the leading imperial statesman of his time. A recent claim that his contribution should be understood chiefly in terms of economic and social policies[35] is interesting in contradicting earlier interpretations, but it would have surprised Baldwin almost as much as the Cabinet colleagues actually responsible for those policies – Neville Chamberlain and Churchill. Equally curious conclusions result when a couple of passages from his speeches about old-fashioned industrial paternalism and the English countryside – the last now as often quoted and anthologised as it had been in the interwar years – are taken to encapsulate his essential themes. Martin Wiener, in a book influential among politicians and publicists in the 1980s, made him symbolic of a supposed English culture of backward-looking 'anti-industrialism';[36] yet his party was supported by most industrialists, he himself had spent twenty years helping to create a modern industrial firm, and he continued to own large holdings of industrial shares. Others have similarly presented Baldwin's vision as 'unrealistic, irrelevant and escapist'. It is claimed that he had 'no ideas', and 'never ... could be bothered to go to the heart of his country's problems';[37] yet this was a leader who not only survived intense public scrutiny for fourteen years, but commanded widespread respect. Such has been the poverty of the interpretative tradition that it could produce Robert Skidelsky's glib paradox: 'the most interesting thing about Stanley Baldwin is that he was completely uninteresting'.[38]

[34] M. Pugh, *The Tories and the People 1880–1935* (Oxford, 1985), pp. 184, 185, also Pugh, *Making of Modern British Politics*, pp. 277–8, 296; Campbell, 'Baldwin', p. 210; Ramsden, *Balfour and Baldwin*, pp. 211–13.
[35] A. Seldon, 'Conservative Century', in A. Seldon and S. Ball (eds.), *Conservative Century* (Oxford, 1994), pp. 32–4.
[36] M. J. Wiener, *English Culture and the Decline of the Industrial Spirit 1850–1980* (Cambridge, 1981), pp. 100–2, and index p. 211.
[37] D. Cannadine, 'Politics, Propaganda and Art', pp. 104–7; Campbell, 'Baldwin', pp. 210, 216.
[38] R. Skidelsky, *Interests and Obsession. Selected Essays* (1993), p. 152, from his review of R. Jenkins, *Baldwin* (1987).

III

The present study proceeds from the view that so dominant a politician cannot be uninteresting; that on the contrary study of Baldwin raises central historical questions which if intelligently addressed can reveal much about Conservatism and the broader political culture of the interwar years. It contains an account of Baldwin's mature career, and an examination of his early life. It is not, however, a biography, in the conventional sense of being structured as the chronicle of a life. This is not simply because Baldwin already has numerous biographers, but rather because of scepticism about the value of biography – certainly as applied in the relentless flow of biographies on twentieth-century British politicians. Indeed, the unusual character of Baldwin's leadership makes him an especially difficult subject for traditional biography, in ways which expose the shortcomings of the genre.

Biographical information is manifestly important for under-standing political leadership, and full-scale biographies may be valuable in opening the study of recent periods and subjects where documented research has not previously been undertaken. But once more broadly researched historical studies have proceeded, biography rarely brings further illumination. Narration of a life is easy on the mind of author and reader, but it is not obviously a powerful or even an effective form of explanation. Too often it is a substitute for such explanation. All accounts of the past are abstractions of some kind, but the tendency of political biography is to abstract in particularly misleading ways. For all political leaders are enveloped and entangled within a mass of pressures and expectations – from colleagues, civil servants, their own party acti-vists, and their opponents; from Parliament, the media, sectional groups, voters; from different and sometimes conflicting policies, and from the unpredictable and often irresistible force of events. In reacting to such pressures, they cannot escape being substan-tially diverted and shaped by them. Their careers lose the linear and self-propelled trajectory assumed by biography. It is a com-monplace that Baldwin's political eminence could never have been predicted from his life before October 1922; but it is equally true that if he could have substantially controlled his own career it would on several occasions have taken quite different courses from those it actually took between May 1923 and May 1937.

Then again, the imperative task of political persuasion and the weight of party and electoral expectations mean that political leaders partly create for themselves, and partly have imposed upon them, a *public* personality. This constructed or imagined persona has unusual properties. It may have only tenuous links with the politician's private personality; yet it becomes a force in itself, which the individual feels he must respect or try to exploit, and which in some sense he becomes. Quite literally, the lives of leading politicians are not their own. It is not, therefore, self-evident that examination of psychological development – aside from the obvious evidential problems it raises – reveals much of genuine significance for a public career. Moreover, as few politicians are able to impose themselves sufficiently and for long enough to affect the course and character of a political system, so only a few deserve more biographical attention than can be supplied by a good *Dictionary of National Biography* entry. The limitations of the genre are indicated by the way that all extended political biographies – notably the thousand pages of Middlemas and Barnes on Baldwin – are drawn inexorably into descriptions of the 'times', in attempts to supply meaning for their accounts of the 'life'.

In principle, the most complete understanding of major politicians would seem to require two complementary approaches. One is the study of 'high politics' – in the interpretative, not simply descriptive, sense, where the narrative is not of one politician nor even of one party, but rather of the whole system of political leadership. Here individuals are placed within the full multi-party and multi-policy contexts which properly explain the details of their careers. Such high-political accounts now exist for almost the whole period of Baldwin's leadership.[39] Their insights – the remorseless situational and tactical pressures, the chronic uncertainties, and the short horizons which afflict all political leadership – are taken for granted here.

The second approach, followed in this book, is that appropriate for the small number of politicians who, by their originality as well as importance, merit extended individual attention. It seeks to go beyond biographical narrative, in order to ask questions about the

---

[39] Cowling, *Impact of Labour 1920–1924*; P. Williamson, *National Crisis and National Government. British Politics, the Economy and Empire 1926–1932* (Cambridge, 1992); Cowling, *Impact of Hitler 1933–1940*. The best statement of 'the character of high politics' is in the first, pp. 3–12.

nature and practice of political leadership. The qualities that really distinguish and explain a politician's effectiveness are manifested less in the linear succession of particular events than in longer-term consistencies or patterns which, as the narrative suspensions in the best biographies indicate, are revealed more effectively by an analytical, rather than narrative, structure. More particularly, these qualities are likely to be revealed in speeches – in public presentation and argument.

Attention to speeches is part of the originality claimed here. Speech – political rhetoric – has rarely been the main source material for recent historical work.[40] This is partly because insufficient thought is given to matching sources and questions: questions are addressed to inappropriate sources, or else particular sources are approached with questions to which they cannot supply answers. It is also because the 'reality' of political leadership is presumed to reside overwhelmingly among the private or organisational evidence of letters, diaries, memoranda, and minutes, so that – except for the occasional major pronouncement – speeches or other public statements are treated as supplementary or inferior sources. Where the questions are to do with policy formation, decision-making, party tactics, private opinion, and detailed motivation, this is obviously correct. Here public statements will not yield answers. Historians do not assume that a politician's speech – or article or book – states the complete or even partial grounds for a particular action, nor that it reveals his full, or even any, belief about a specific issue. For these aspects of politics, the problematic nature of speeches and publications as public and rhetorical statements – necessarily concerned more with persuasion and concealment than with description and explanation – is well understood.

Yet amidst the rich private evidence it can be forgotten that politicians are not just policy-makers, tacticians, and administrators. They are also public figures for whom speech-making and publication is a principal function, precisely because politics is a *public* activity and because they need to win support for them-

[40] For suggestive comments on the significance and possibilities of such material, see M. Bentley, 'Party, Doctrine and Thought', in M. Bentley and J. Stevenson (eds.), *High and Low Politics in Modern Britain* (Oxford, 1983), pp. 123–53, and H. C. G. Matthew, 'Rhetoric and Politics in Great Britain, 1860–1950', in P. J. Waller (ed.), *Politics and Social Change in Modern Britain* (Brighton, 1987), pp. 34–58.

selves, their parties, and their causes. It can as easily be forgotten that while historians can observe the inner workings of party and government, these were hidden from all except a tiny number of contemporaries. Everyone else could only 'know' and respond to political leaders through their constructed and projected public characters, especially as revealed by speeches and media presentation. For this reason, those politicians who work only at their correspondence and only in committees will not usually go far. What distinguishes political leaders from backbenchers or officials are the party, public, or parliamentary reputations acquired by public utterance. This is what creates their ability to become policy-makers and strategists; and their power to affect party and national affairs continues to be largely dependent upon this capacity for public persuasion.

So, in an important sense, politicians are what they speak and publish. What they say may often be the collective party line, but leaders are normally such because they add something distinctive and persuasive, causing particular importance to be attached to themselves not just by their own party and supporters but by opposing parties and other bodies too. These things most obviously consist of observations on issues and policies, and challenges or replies to opponents and rivals. But speeches also have a deeper function. They place the issues and tactics of the moment within the wider interests and values, the fears and antipathies, the histories and the purposes that constitute both a party's claims for support and an individual's claim to significance – which have variously been called ideology, doctrine or, more recently, 'language'.[41] These may be intellectually rigorous and original, though normally they are not. Their function is not to satisfy academic tests as theory, but to attract and hold the support of diverse audiences possessing a range of conventional beliefs and present interests, as well as hopes for the future. Nevertheless, in these utterances political leaders may well be imaginative and creative. They seek to form particular understandings of current conditions, and to

---

[41] Some social and electoral historians, disillusioned by structural and especially class analyses, have recently taken the so-called 'linguistic turn', offering examination of political 'language' – and hence the creative role of politicians and the state in political culture – as a major advance in understanding. Yet such emphases had been central to the earlier 'high politics' studies, so often disparaged by such historians. See esp. Cowling, *Impact of Labour*, pp. 5–10, and Bentley, 'Party, Doctrine and Thought'.

define issues in certain ways. They aim to persuade their audiences to want, expect, or fear new things – or old things for new
reasons, or new things for old reasons. They encourage them to
adopt new beliefs and detect new friends or enemies – or else to
hold fast to familiar values, allies, and enmities. By these means
they not only shape opinions on particular issues, but create more
lasting political identities and electoral alliances. It is by these
means that a political 'centre' or 'consensus' may come into existence – not simply from the momentum of events or structural
change, but by the constructive and collective efforts of successful
politicians, forming areas of agreement and selecting points of
difference.

Given that speeches have these persuasive and instrumental
functions, they may or may not express aspects of the speaker's
private belief. In judging how far private belief may be a likely
and significant component, personal correspondence and diaries
can provide assistance. But private records concerned with the
stream of events do not in themselves necessarily or even usually
contain extended evidence about belief, because by their very
nature as private statements any belief is chiefly left implicit, a
matter of silent assumption. Belief is more likely to be indicated
in underlying and consistent themes, in the wider framework and
texture of responses to particular events, as revealed where the
politician is compelled to make concessions towards explicitness –
in long series of speeches and publications.

British party ideologies or doctrines have almost invariably been
investigated through examination of 'thinkers' and 'writers' who
produced quasi-academic theoretical tracts. As Conservatives have
generated few major 'thinkers' and as Conservative politicians
rarely acknowledge the influence even of lesser 'thinkers', there
has been widespread acceptance of their routine insistence that –
with, perhaps, the exceptional case of 'Thatcherism' – Conservatism has no ideology or theory, but is unique (and they would
claim superior) in being 'empirical', 'instinctive', 'practical', or
'realistic'. This has been compounded by many political historians
having a depleted conception of what is 'political', which is
reduced to programmes, policies, and organisation. It has been
further aggravated by limited assumptions about the elements in
'electoral behaviour', narrowed to the structural determinants of
'class' or, most recently, gender. The broader character of political

activity and electoral choice, the context of argument and imagery
derived from a rich and varied political culture, remains under-
explored.[42] Insofar as the existence of Conservative ideas has been
acknowledged, these have usually been presented as large abstractions, unrelated to specific political cultures and arguments, and
so appearing to be bland, banal, and toothless. Accordingly histories of the Conservative party rarely consider 'ideas' or 'thought' a
worthwhile subject for study. Yet the notion that Conservatism
was just an empty container filled and re-filled by the expediencies
of the moment is inherently implausible. It has been well said
that the party's claim to be non-ideological is itself an ideological
statement.[43] But what must also be understood is that party doctrine or ideology has always been generated much less by 'thinkers' than by politicians themselves; that within the Conservative
party its collective leaders and Central Office staff were those who
most publicly and persistently sought to persuade large audiences
that Conservative ideas and values were superior to those of their
various opponents.

This book therefore makes considerable use of Baldwin's
speeches – both the large number which are obviously political
statements, and his many ostensibly 'non-political' addresses. The
precise extent to which he expressed a distinctive political message is hard to assess, because no other leading interwar politician
has been examined in this manner. A historical literature which
would allow adequate comparison does not yet exist. Nevertheless
it has always been plain that Baldwin possessed a public character
quite unlike – and much more widely admired than – that of any
other contemporary politician. The argument here is that its
essential elements lay in two features: the unusual emphasis his
speeches and addresses gave to deeper, doctrinal, concerns, and
the particular substance and tone of this doctrine. Together these
gave Baldwin an ability to appear free from party interests and

[42] See, however, F. O'Gorman, *British Conservatism. Conservative Thought from Burke to Thatcher*
(1986) – an anthology which includes passages by Baldwin, with sensible commentary,
pp. 42–7, 81–3, 179–84 – and the recent work in M. Francis and I. Zweiniger-
Bargielowska (eds.), *The Conservatives and British Society 1880–1990* (Cardiff, 1996), and
J. Lawrence and M. Taylor (eds.), *Party, State and Society. Electoral Behaviour in Britain since
1820* (Aldershot, 1997).
[43] E. H. H. Green, *The Crisis of Conservatism. The Politics, Economics and Ideology of the British
Conservative Party 1880–1914* (1995), p. 312.

high-political pressures – a position with great potential strengths, but also liable to cause difficulties.

Baldwin's speeches have not been wholly ignored by biographers and historians. As four volumes of his addresses were published and as several of his phrases and passages remain well known, it has long been recognised that they indicate something important. Yet even apart from the general undervaluation of speeches as historical evidence, Baldwin has suffered from remarkably naive, selective, and uncontextualised readings of his words.[44] His November 1936 reference to rearmament is just the most obvious instance. Other persistent sources of misunderstanding are those of May 1924 on the English countryside, and March 1925 on the Baldwin ironworks. Even catch phrases – such as 'dynamic force' or 'Safety First' – have been misconstrued or misattributed. Another, lesser, example is indicative of the obstacles facing serious discussion of Baldwin. It has long been a social-historical 'fact', derived from his own words, that as an old Harrovian he determined to pack his first Cabinet with former Harrow pupils. Yet what should have been evident from such an improbable statement is confirmed by any intelligent reading of the reprinted address containing the statement, and proven by the original newspaper report punctuated throughout with the words 'laughter' and 'cheers' – that the comment was, quite simply, a joke.[45]

IV

The principal aim of this book is to examine a Conservative political mind, and a particular form of party leadership. It is an investigation of political power considered not simply in terms of decisions in Cabinet or party councils, but as relationships established with various public audiences, including the opposing parties. The approach is therefore deliberately selective. Tactical activities now familiar from the 'high politics' accounts are noted where appropriate, but the emphasis is upon a political rhetoric and the presentation of a public personality. As these constituted

---

[44] Exceptions are Schwarz, 'The Language of Constitutionalism', and Jarvis thesis, ch. 6; also P. Williamson, 'The Doctrinal Politics of Stanley Baldwin', in M. Bentley (ed.), *Public and Private Doctrine* (Cambridge, 1993), pp. 181–208.

[45] *OE* p. 267; *The Times*, 20 July 1923. Omission of audience reactions in Baldwin's collected addresses has contributed to other misreadings.

a major attempt to elevate Conservative leadership into an articulation of 'national' values, this book is also a study of a Conservative public doctrine.

Nevertheless, because Baldwin's career has attracted so much controversy and misunderstanding, a necessary preliminary – the first chapter – is to re-examine its course and its chief episodes. Here as elsewhere specific misconceptions and factual errors have been addressed in the notes, in order to avoid cluttering the text. The second chapter begins the task of defining the qualities of Baldwin's leadership, chiefly by a process of elimination but with the effect of emphasising its peculiarities. Because he displayed such an unusual combination of political characteristics, chapters 3 and 4 investigate their sources – in what is intended as a model of how examination of an interwar politician's early life can genuinely and effectively illuminate his career. Chapter 5 describes Baldwin's public assessment of the situation he thought it was his task to address, in order to indicate his purposes and his practice. The next five chapters then analyse more fully the various aspects of his form of Conservative doctrine. These chapters proceed largely from Baldwin's own perspective and quote extensively from his speeches, because this enables his intentions, meanings, and 'tone' – the texture of its presentation – to be most clearly understood. It also allows the substance and range of Conservative arguments to be more fully explicated, reaching beyond familiar emphases on 'economics' and 'class' to the constitution, to family, local and patriotic loyalties, to empire, ethics, and religion. The conclusion considers why Baldwin came to occupy a pre-eminent national position, and assesses his contributions to the Conservative party's interwar success and to public life more generally.

The starting point is to place Baldwin in his contemporary contexts. If this procedure seems obvious, it must be said that these contexts are neither those of the 'Baldwin' constructed during the 1940s and early 1950s, nor those of the 'Baldwin' that has confounded late twentieth-century social-democratic, statist, and secularised sensibilities. The actual Baldwin of the 1920s and 1930s must be understood as a man formed by a particular Victorian and Edwardian culture – comprising not just narrowly 'political' experiences but also industrial, moral, religious, and literary influences – who responded in a distinctive manner to the shocks and challenges which that culture suffered during the Great War and its aftermath. He must also be understood by grasping the full implications of a truism: that what has since 1940 become known and familiar was in the interwar period new and unknown; that mass democracy, the Labour party, and trade unions could seem to threaten property, private enterprise, and national cohesion; that a second war of mechanised slaughter was feared as Armageddon, yet believed to be avoidable.

CHAPTER 1

Public career

I

The circumstances of Baldwin's political rise were crucial to his
leadership style and public reputation. A relatively late start in
Parliament and a short ministerial apprenticeship contributed to
one of his persistent characteristics, a sense of detachment from
'professional politics'. Propelled to high office by the successive
disruptions of war, party rebellion, divided leadership, and a fatal
illness, he was acutely conscious of having been specially favoured
by events and – far from disguising the fact – made this central to
his public character. Nevertheless he had acquired some relevant
experience, although he did not always choose to emphasise it.
Nor could events have swept him forward had he really been such
an 'obscure' backbencher and 'insignificant' minister as would
later be claimed.

Baldwin succeeded his father as Unionist MP for West Worcestershire (Bewdley) in 1908, at the age of forty, during the long
Edwardian period of Liberal government. An unassuming man at
a time when Unionist opportunities for promotion were scarce, he
had little incentive but to follow his father's example as a permanent backbencher, concentrating his energies more on his industrial and commercial career than on politics. Until 1917 he
continued to expand his family's business interests, speaking
infrequently in the House of Commons and then mostly on matters relating to his constituency or to commerce. Nevertheless he
attended regularly, and moved on the fringes of London political
society.[1] He was in the mainstream tariff-reform section of his
party, and participated in backbench movements. He joined the

---

[1] M&B pp. 50–1; Baldwin to his mother, 1909–14 *passim*, BF.

council of the Anti-Socialist Union (ASU), and became a member and financial sponsor of the Unionist Social Reform Committee (USRC), associating with many future Conservative ministers.[2]

The Great War brought a gradual increase in his political involvement, as his priorities shifted and as demands upon MPs increased. In early 1915 he was among the founders of the Unionist Business Committee, a precursor of the 1922 Committee of backbench MPs. After the formation of the Asquith Coalition government in May 1915, he joined a group of Unionist and Liberal MPs pressing for military conscription, but later helped organise backbench resistance to critics of the Unionist leadership.[3] Much of his time became taken up by appointment to departmental committees – for the Home Office, interviewing large numbers of interned foreign citizens and later Sinn Fein prisoners; for the Board of Trade, on trade relations after the war; for the War Office on expenditure control and for the Treasury on War Loans for the Small Investor, which recommended the creation of the National Savings scheme.[4] By 1916 he was known in government circles as a respected and diligent MP with useful commercial and financial experience. These qualities explain his appointment as Parliamentary Private Secretary to the Chancellor of the Exchequer, Bonar Law, when the Lloyd George Coalition government was formed in December 1916, and his promotion a

[2] For ASU: F. Coetzee, *For Party or Country* (Oxford, 1990), pp. 156–7. For membership of USRC and its agricultural, industrial unrest, and health sub-committees: J. W. Hills *et al.*, *Industrial Unrest. A Practical Solution* (1914), preface; A. Ashley, *William James Ashley* (1932), p. 114; J. Ridley, 'The Unionist Social Reform Committee 1911–1914', *Historical Journal* 30 (1987), 396–7. Lord Birkenhead, the former USRC chairman, in 'Mr Baldwin's Power', *Britannia*, 4 Jan. 1929, described Baldwin as its 'life and soul' and having 'largely financed our activities'. The first statement is plainly dramatised by hindsight, but the latter is possible.

[3] W. A. S. Hewins, *Apologia of an Imperialist*, 2 vols (1929) II. 11, 63, 66 (diary, 27 Jan. 1915, 11 Feb., 24 March 1916); A. Marrison, *British Business and Protection 1903–1932* (Oxford, 1996), pp. 223–4; backbench Liberal and Unionist MPs' letter to Asquith, *The Times*, 15 Sept. 1915.

[4] Respectively: (a) McKenna to Baldwin, 22 May 1915, BF, warning that the work would be heavy; *HCDeb* 72, cc. 4, 189, 923 (3, 17, 23 June 1915); Baldwin's extensive log-books of cases in JCCD 25–6, 65; Jones *DL* p. 524; (b) Runciman minutes, 2 Nov. 1915, 11 Jan. 1916, SB 26/1–2, 5; committee papers in Ashley papers 42245, with ff. 38–41 recording that Baldwin was so hard worked elsewhere that he might not have time to serve; (c) *HCDeb* 92 c. 347 (27 March 1917); (d) Reports, 28 Dec. 1915, 26 Jan. 1916 in *Parliamentary Papers* 1914–16 (Cd 8146) XXXVII. 473, and 1916 (Cd 8179) XV. 649. He also served on the Home Office Committee on the Use of Cocaine in Dentistry: report, *Parliamentary Papers* 1917–18 (Cd 8489), VIII. 151.

month later to Junior Lord of the Treasury and again in June 1917 to Joint Financial Secretary.

The Financial Secretaryship was a senior non-Cabinet post, but for Baldwin's career it had still further significance. As Law was also Unionist party leader and Leader of the Commons, Baldwin learned about party management and benefitted from his patronage. As he now had responsibility for the Treasury tasks of supervising the civil service and controlling government expenditure, he acquired knowledge of other departments and much experience in conducting Commons business. Moreover, at that time the Treasury had a vast increase of new, technical work. It needed a second Financial Secretary because the original appointee had been sent to Washington to obtain United States assistance in the chronic wartime financial crises. Baldwin became engaged in the domestic aspects of these crises, representing Law at the daily Bank of England Exchange Committee and helping to introduce massive War Loans and two war budgets. He was in fact one of the work-horses of the government, and within Whitehall and Westminster one of its most familiar members.[5]

The work demanded quiet efficiency rather than the kinds of political display that attracted public notice and rapid promotion. Baldwin's re-appointment as sole Financial Secretary after the post-war election in 1918 registered this solid but unobtrusive success, since with Austen Chamberlain replacing Law as Chancellor of the Exchequer he supplied ministerial continuity in addressing the almost equally formidable work of financial reconstruction. As chairman of 'the Baldwin Council' and member of numerous other committees, he was among the architects of the new systems of Treasury control imposed on other departments during this period.[6] Even so, approaches from Law about Dominion governorgeneralships and speculation that he might become Speaker of the House of Commons indicated modest Westminster expectations of his domestic political prospects.[7]

When Baldwin did enter the Cabinet, in April 1921, it was

---

[5] See indexes to *HCDeb* for 1917–21; Baldwin to his mother, 1917–19 BF; and 1917 letters to Joan Dickinson, in *Memoirs of a Conservative. J. C. C. Davidson's Memoirs and Papers 1910–37*, ed. Robert Rhodes James (1969), pp. 78–80.

[6] E. O'Halpin, *Head of the Civil Service* (1989), pp. 26, 47–51.

[7] M&B p. 75. Some journalists did tip him as a possible Chancellor of the Exchequer: see e.g. J. Green, *Mr. Baldwin* (1933), p. 82; A. Bryant, *Stanley Baldwin* (1937), pp. 62–3. But they did not reflect the views of the government leadership at this time.

because the retirement of Law had created a Unionist vacancy. As a new member of an intimate and supremely confident group which had presided over victory in war and negotiation of the peace, on matters of general policy he was diffident, and rarely consulted by the inner Cabinet leadership. His performance as President of the Board of Trade revealed other qualities. According to Chamberlain, the new Unionist leader, the minister would require 'great knowledge, great skill in debate and perfect ... tact', because he had responsibility for 'by far the greatest Parliamentary fence' before the government – the Safeguarding of Industries Bill, which by allowing anti-dumping tariffs threatened to divide the Unionist and Liberal wings of the Coalition.[8] In the event the Bill passed comfortably, as Baldwin smothered controversy with good humour and undoctrinaire argument. When dispute did arise, in spring 1922, over the application of the safeguarding duties to German fabric gloves, he displayed considerable toughness, resisting all-party pressure from Lancashire cotton interests, reversing an adverse Cabinet decision by threatening resignation, and defeating Liberal ministerial opposition led by Churchill.[9] Conservative MPs were impressed by what seemed an increasingly rare phenomenon within the Coalition government: a Conservative minister taking a stand for Conservative policies.

Baldwin's next threatened resignation involved a much greater disagreement, one which he initially expected would end his political career. Yet the outcome was a giant-killing exploit that catapulted him to the front rank: the overthrow of Lloyd George, Churchill, and the Conservative leadership of Chamberlain, Birkenhead, Balfour, and Horne. During 1921 Baldwin had continued to affirm the Coalition line that the 'old political labels' were 'extinct'.[10] But with the Cabinet losing touch with much Conservative and 'moral' opinion, he became increasingly uneasy. While still defending Lloyd George's leadership of the Coalition,

---

[8] A. Chamberlain to Lloyd George, 19 March 1921, AC 24/3/62. Chamberlain thought the bill so sensitive that he wanted its author, Horne, to remain at the Board of Trade – though without denying Baldwin promotion to another Cabinet place.

[9] Cabinets 19, 24, 34, 35, 37, 38 (22); Baldwin to A. Chamberlain, 10 April 1922, AC 24/4/2, and to Lloyd George, 5 July 1922, Lloyd George papers F/3/1/16. For Churchill's resentment, see *WSC Comp* IV/iii.2107–8.

[10] *HCDeb* 142, c. 1573 (6 June 1921), with earlier statements in *Berrows*, 30 Nov., 7 Dec. 1918.

by March 1922 he had shifted to saying that 'there was no more important duty at present than to preserve the Tory party'.[11] In early October he decided to leave the government, if necessary alone. Within the alarming context of growing popular support for the new socialist Labour party, Baldwin was appalled both by the Coalition leaders' readiness to contemplate war in the Near East, and by the Conservative leaders' determination to perpetuate Lloyd George's premiership at the risk of alienating much of their own party. Unionist/Conservative discontent with the Coalition had been mounting for two years, and ultimately only the reluctant return of Bonar Law as alternative leader supplied the certainty of success. Nevertheless Cabinet divisions precipitated the rebellion, and Baldwin was the first of its members to call for the end of the Coalition. It was he, rather than the other, more politically experienced, Cabinet dissentients Griffith-Boscawen and Curzon, who had the resolve and reputation to supply the focus for the final manoeuvres of Conservative junior ministers and backbench MPs, and on 19 October 1922 to open the attack at the party meeting at the Carlton Club.[12]

The rebellion and the refusal of most defeated Coalition Conservative leaders – the 'Chamberlainites' – to assist Law placed Baldwin among the three leading figures in the new Conservative government, and his Treasury experience made him a natural choice as Chancellor of the Exchequer. Initially he complicated matters by proposing that the post should instead go to McKenna, who had been a Liberal but who as a wartime Chancellor and now a major City figure had special qualifications for tackling a looming crisis in international finance.[13] After McKenna refused and

---

[11] *The Manchester Guardian*, 18 March 1922. Lloyd George as early as November 1921 sensed that Baldwin might be unreliable in a major crisis: Jones *WD* III. 156 (8 Nov. 1921).

[12] 'The Break Up of the Coalition', Griffith-Boscawen papers c. 396/119–23; *The Crawford Papers*, ed. John Vincent (Manchester, 1984), pp. 450, 451 (10, 16 Oct. 1922); *The Leo Amery Diaries*, ed. John Barnes and David Nicholson, 2 vols. (1980, 1988) I. 294–5, 297, 299 (12, 14, 16, 17, 18 Oct. 1922); *The Austen Chamberlain Diary Letters 1916–1937*, ed. Robert Self (Cambridge, 1995), p. 205 (20 Nov. 1922); Lord Templewood, *Empire of the Air* (1957), pp. 23–5, 28–30. Cf. Lucy Baldwin, 'Recollections of a Cabinet Breaker's Wife', SB 42/3–10, partly in AWB pp. 114–17; Baldwin's own accounts in D. Maclean memo, 25 July 1923, Maclean papers c. 467/52–4, and in Jones *DL* pp. 60–2 (18 Sept. 1932).

[13] AWB p. 117; Jones *DL* p. 62; R. S. Churchill, *Lord Derby* (1959), p. 454 (diary, 19 Oct. 1922). McKenna had been Chancellor in the Asquith Coalition 1915–16, but was now Chairman of the Midland Bank and no longer an MP. As originator of the 1915

after the November 1922 general election had vindicated the insurgents' insistence that Conservatives could win an independent majority, Baldwin had two main tasks as Chancellor. In both he considerably enhanced his standing. The United States government's demand for settlement of the British war debt took him to Washington in January 1923. Law regarded the negotiated terms as harsh and an excessive burden upon the British economy, and the Cabinet recalled Baldwin for consultation. The chronic financial problems of the late 1920s and early 1930s would reveal Law's wisdom, but at this time Baldwin shared the Treasury and City view that early settlement was vital to restore British credit and to obtain American assistance in European financial reconstruction. For the second time in twelve months he persuaded a Cabinet to reverse its position – this time even in the face of a prime-ministerial resignation threat.[14] Then, in his April 1923 budget, he won further City, business, and Conservative approval in his determined efforts to consolidate the restoration of stable and 'sound' finance. Assisted by expenditure cuts achieved under the Coalition he was able both to reduce income tax and to establish a new Sinking Fund for redemption of the government's internal debt. An impression of strength and integrity was completed by growing parliamentary admiration for his straightforward, conciliatory, and amiable manner.

The illness that forced Law's final retirement in May 1923 created an extraordinary problem over the succession to the premiership. Austen Chamberlain and others who just months earlier would have been obvious contenders remained separated from the Cabinet, and were for most Conservative MPs still tainted by their loyalty to the Coalition. This left two otherwise improbable candidates: Curzon, the Foreign Secretary and acting prime minister, but a member of the House of Lords – and Baldwin. The circumstances of the King's choice of Baldwin are notoriously tangled, largely because a small group of Baldwin's personal (and mostly

McKenna import duties, he could have been made acceptable to Conservative protectionists.

[14] It is commonly stated that Baldwin pre-empted Cabinet discussion by naively or cunningly revealing the proposed terms to the press on his arrival at Southampton. In fact they had been revealed by the Americans ten days earlier (see *The Times*, 17, 18 Jan. 1923). Baldwin's solecisms were more precise: to publicise his own support for them, and to claim that the US government was compromised by the need to conciliate ignorant Mid-Western opinion.

non-ministerial) supporters, possibly with his knowledge, side-stepped Law's refusal to offer formal advice to the King. They submitted a powerfully argued case in Baldwin's favour, though they may not have intended it to be interpreted as Law's own opinion.[15] It is nevertheless clear that the memorandum did indicate Law's private preference; that even those who recommended Curzon admitted his faults of arrogance and tactlessness; and that these faults strongly influenced the recommendation of Baldwin by Balfour, the other living Conservative ex-Prime Minister. Balfour and the King were also right to fear damaging political and constitutional complications from the appointment of a prime minister who sat in the House of Lords, which then contained not a single representative of the new Labour opposition. It is clear too that most Conservatives, and indeed most wider political and press opinion, thought Baldwin the better choice. Curzon's bitter description of him as 'a man of no experience, and of the utmost insignificance' revealed more about his own wounded vanity than Baldwin's actual stature. In larger perspective, however, there is no gainsaying Chamberlain's verdict: that Baldwin's emergence had been an 'accident of an accident'.[16]

II

Even for a man with a string of recent political successes to his name, Baldwin began his premiership with a confidence remarkable in both degree and effect. In part this reflected his inexperience at the highest political levels, but it was also the first manifestation of a distinctive outlook. He made a strength of being little known outside Westminster and Whitehall by addressing his party and the public with a new note of purposefulness, idealism, and sensitivity towards labour. Simple deductions from

---

[15] See Cowling, *Impact of Labour*, pp. 258–67, and C. Hazlehurst, 'The Baldwinite Conspiracy', *Historical Studies* 16 (1974–5), 167–91. Joan Davidson, 'Diary of 2nd crisis in Government', JD, adds circumstantial details which suggest that Baldwin at least knew that a memorandum was being prepared. On the evening of 19 May Baldwin met Joan Davidson and Waterhouse at dinner, then joined Davidson and Amery at 10 Downing Street. Davidson later had a long talk with Sykes. On the following morning, the 20th, Baldwin had breakfast with the Davidsons before Davidson left for Downing Street to complete the memorandum, which Sykes and Waterhouse then took to the King. Joan Davidson herself believed the memorandum had been 'of great use'.

[16] H. Nicolson, *Curzon. The Last Phase* (1934), p. 354; *A. Chamberlain Diary Letters*, p. 364 (28 Feb. 1931).

his business and Treasury background were belied. In seeking policies to support his messages, he nevertheless began with a perspective from his departmental experience: that the root of Britain's post-war economic problems lay in the financial and
commercial chaos in continental Europe, turning upon the Franco-
German dispute over German reparations and, since January
1923, on the French occupation of the Ruhr. He was, he said,
'going to try and settle Europe, though he failed and failed
again'.[17] It was for this reason that he again attempted, unsuccess-
fully, to recruit McKenna, and even thought of Grey, another Liberal, but the most eminent ex-Foreign Secretary, as a possible
replacement for Curzon.[18] In the autumn, however, Baldwin
abruptly changed direction. Sceptical Cabinet colleagues were persuaded to allow him to announce, during the Conservative party
conference at Plymouth on 25 October, his personal belief in tariff
protection for domestic industries. By emphasising Bonar Law's
pledge at the 1922 election against fundamental fiscal change in
the current Parliament he also signalled his intention to seek a
fresh electoral mandate while, under Cabinet pressure, avoiding
any suggestion of an imminent dissolution. But in mid-November
Baldwin again precipitated events and overcame considerable
Cabinet opposition to call an immediate election.

The underlying *policy* imperative in Baldwin's adoption of industrial protection was reduction of unemployment, which remained
stubbornly persistent and which even an eventual European settlement might worsen in the short term, by increasing German
exports. Yet most of the specifics might have been obtained by
quieter extension of existing forms of import duties – the
McKenna, safeguarding, and revenue duties. The dramatic shift
and its linkage to an election must be understood in *political* terms.
Baldwin's mission to 'settle Europe' had been obstructed by
French obstinacy and Curzon's ill-tempered diplomacy, and in
September the sole foreign-policy 'summit' meeting of his career –
with the French premier, Poincaré – was embarrassingly incon-
clusive, confirming that no early success could be expected. For a

---

[17] Baldwin in Trevelyan to Ponsonby, 30 May 1923, in Cowling, *Impact of Labour* pp. 306–
7; cf. Jones *WD* I. 237–8 (28 May 1923).
[18] McKenna declined when a City of London seat could not be made available for him. For
Grey, Dawson memo, 17 June 1923, Dawson papers 70/16–23; Jones *WD* I. 243 (30
Sept. 1923).

new and inexperienced prime minister without his own parliamentary majority, the resulting criticism from several directions – not just from Labour and Liberals but from Chamberlainites, the Conservative right, and Conservative newspapers – was peculiarly unsettling. More fundamentally, a policy vacuum and continuing criticism during a fourth winter of high unemployment might cause severe long-term damage to Conservative interests, undermining his efforts to evoke a more sympathetic presentation of his party, whetting Labour's most radical ambitions, and assisting its already rapid electoral advance. By reviving a version of tariff reform, the creed of most Conservative activists, and by raising expectations of an early election, he aimed to establish his own authority, restore impetus, and suggest to the working classes that Conservatism offered a constructive and 'national', classless, alternative to socialism. Dividing the former Coalition leaders and regaining co-operation from Chamberlainite Conservatives was an incidental benefit – pursued actively only when Baldwin wished to show his more recalcitrant Cabinet colleagues that they were not irreplaceable – while a desire to pre-empt Lloyd George's rumoured plan to call for imperial economic initiatives may have influenced the precise timing of his announcement. Baldwin then decided upon an immediate election because the party's Central Office was confident of victory, because it would foreshorten Conservative disagreements and hostile parliamentary manoeuvres by the opposition parties, and because it seemed best to proceed before the Liberals, now reunited in defence of free trade, could complete the amalgamation of their Lloyd Georgeite and Asquithian organisations.[19]

The general election on 6 December 1923 was disastrous (table 1). Baldwin had made a major miscalculation: free-trade opinion was even more entrenched than he had supposed. Although

---

[19] The best examination remains Cowling, *Impact of Labour*, chs. 15–16; it is confirmed by R. Self, 'Conservative Reunion and the General Election of 1923: A Reassessment', *Twentieth Century British History* 3 (1992), 249–73. Jones's well-known report of Baldwin saying *twelve years later* that he adopted protection in order to 'dish' Lloyd George (Jones, *Lord Baldwin*, p. 8; M&B p. 212), was coloured both by Baldwin's current (1935) concern at a renewed Lloyd George challenge, and by Jones's admiration for Lloyd George. Baldwin later corrected himself (Baldwin to Jones, 25 Nov. 1940, Jones papers A6/2), but when Jones subsequently published his obituary notices he preferred Baldwin's earlier, more dramatic, version. Another common view, that his primary concern was reunion with the Chamberlainite leaders, is also unsupported by contemporary evidence.

Table 1. *General elections 1922–1935*

Date of election	Percentage of poll	MPs
1922: 15 November		
Conservative	38.5	344
Independent Liberal	18.9	62
National Liberal	9.9	53
Labour	29.7	142
outcome: Conservative government (74 majority)		
1923: 6 December		
Conservative	38.0	258
Liberal	29.7	158
Labour	30.7	191
outcome: minority Labour government January 1924		
1924: 29 October		
Conservative	46.8	412
Liberal	17.8	40
Labour	33.3	151
outcome: Conservative government (210 majority)		
1929: 30 May		
Conservative	38.1	260
Liberal	23.5	59
Labour	37.1	287
outcome: minority Labour government		

National government formed 24 August 1931

Date of election	Percentage of poll	MPs
1931: 27 October		
Conservative	55.0	470
Liberal (Samuelite)	6.5	32
National Liberal (Simonite)	3.7	35
National Labour (MacDonaldite)	1.5	13
National	0.5	4
[total National government	67.2	554]
Independent Liberal	0.5	4
Labour	30.9	52
outcome: National government (492 majority: Conservatives alone had a 418 majority over Labour, and 145 over the total of all other groups)		
1935: 14 November		
Conservative	47.8	387
National Liberal (Simonite)	3.7	33
National Labour (MacDonaldite)	1.5	8
National	0.3	1
[total National government	53.3	429]
Liberal (Samuelite)	6.7	21
Labour	38.0	154
outcome: National government (242 majority)		

Note: Minor parties and independent MPs omitted, hence apparent arithmetical discrepancies in the size of majorities.
Source: Adapted from F.W.S. Craig, *British Electoral Facts 1832–1980* (Chichester, 1981).

Conservatives remained the largest party, the overall Commons majority for which most of their organisers and MPs had repudiated the Coalition only fourteen months earlier was now lost. The Labour advance had not been halted but accelerated to the brink of entering government; the Liberal party had regained potential by winning the parliamentary balance of power. As Baldwin's personal responsibility was complete and conspicuous, he initially thought he should – and would have to – resign both the premiership and the party leadership. He survived the immediate aftermath largely for negative reasons. Despite his colleagues' anxieties about the prospect of a 'socialist' government, many remained anti-Coalitionists and considered his retention of the leadership the best obstacle to Chamberlainite-organised efforts at alliance with Liberals. It also became widely accepted that the least embarrassing way out of the predicament of an indecisive election result would be for the existing government to await the verdict of the Commons. Nevertheless, even in defeat Baldwin had acquired positive assets, which counteracted doubts about his judgement. Conservative protectionists credited him with a heroic fight for a great cause, while bold decisions, submission to a popular verdict, and forthright speeches had secured him a public reputation for unusual – almost non-political – honesty and directness. Once Baldwin had been persuaded that to face Parliament would seem as honourable and constitutional as it was expedient, such opinions helped sustain his leadership as party manoeuvres continued to operate in his favour.

On 18 December the Liberal leaders announced their intention of voting against the Conservative government, allowing the Labour party to take office for the first time. In angry reaction, the Chamberlainites finally abandoned coalitionism and reconciled themselves to full Conservative reunion. They accepted a developing Cabinet view that a minority Labour government could do little harm, and that successful anti-socialism now demanded the demolition of the Liberal party and attraction of anti-Labour Liberals into the Conservative party. After the Conservative government's defeat in the Commons on 21 January 1924 and its resignation the following day, Baldwin invited the Chamberlainite leaders into his new shadow cabinet. In return, they helped him withdraw from his protectionist commitment and at a party meeting on 11 February supported his continued leadership.

Baldwin's position nevertheless remained weak. Although residual tensions between anti-Coalitionists and Chamberlainites meant that no widely acceptable rival could emerge, he had to accept a more collective style of leadership. Baldwin's principal contributions as first Leader of the Opposition to a Labour government were to maintain a constructive Conservative stance to supplement the obvious anti-socialist attacks, and to expound his colleagues' proposals for a programme consisting of reversion to industrial safeguarding duties, imperial economic co-operation, measures against food 'profiteering', improved housing, and a new emphasis upon extended social insurance. He helped re-open Liberal party divisions by encouraging Churchill to lead a 'constitutionalist' rebellion, though at first this backfired and created renewed Conservative disagreements when Churchill stood as an Independent against the Conservative candidate at the Abbey, Westminster by-election.[20] He also took much trouble to ensure that the next election would be fought on the Conservatives' most advantageous ground. In August he travelled to Belfast to persuade the Northern Ireland prime minister to accept a proposed Labour government bill appointing an Irish Boundary Commission, helping to remove the danger that Ireland or House of Lords obstruction to the bill could be made into a leading election issue.[21] The shadow cabinet's original intention was to defeat the Labour government by obtaining Liberal support against its proposed treaty with Soviet Russia, until the Campbell case – a bungled dispute over the prosecution of a communist editor – presented them with the tactical gift of forcing responsibility for the fatal Commons vote upon the Liberal leadership. In the subsequent general election on 29 October, a Liberal collapse – the penalty for successively voting out Conservative and Labour governments – helped Conservatives obtain a huge Commons majority, expunging Baldwin's misjudgement of just ten months earlier.

---

[20] Baldwin wanted Churchill to stand with Conservative support – against the wishes of protectionist colleagues – but was thwarted by the local Conservative association: *WSC Comp* v/i.113–15, and see R. Boothby, *I Fight to Live* (1947), p. 36.

[21] Baldwin to Joan Davidson, 14, 21 Aug. 1924, *Davidson Memoirs*, p. 196, and to Wood, 6 Sept. 1924, Halifax papers A4.410.14.1; *Amery Diaries* I. 386 (19 Sept. 1924). M&B p. 270 mistakenly places the meeting in London.

III

The 1924 election was dominated by the prevailing anti-socialist 'red scare', heightened during the campaign by the 'Zinoviev letter'. Many Conservatives nonetheless believed the scale of their victory – an unexpected demonstration that even within mass democracy Labour could be decisively defeated – owed much to Baldwin's attractiveness to moderate voters. In contrast to his position on first becoming prime minister, he now also had his own parliamentary majority and the freedom to construct his own government. He used this new authority to consolidate Conservative reunion on his own terms, and according to his conception of a 'national' Conservatism. He disregarded the resentments of anti-Coalitionist colleagues by giving high office to Austen Chamberlain, Birkenhead, and other Chamberlainites. On the other hand he refused to treat the Chamberlainites as a group or Chamberlain as their leader, ignoring the latter's unwelcome suggestions on ministerial appointments. As the election had proved that the party could win many working-class and former Liberal votes, few senior Conservatives now doubted that anti-socialism could be best advanced by 'progressive' rather than reactionary means, and by accommodation of Liberal 'constitutionalists'. Baldwin made sure the strategic lessons were preserved by re-appointing Neville Chamberlain as Minister of Health, and by the surprising choice of Churchill as Chancellor of the Exchequer – intended to be so generous as to guarantee his loyalty, but so tied to financial detail as to curb his belligerence against Labour.[22] By these means Baldwin created a government almost as comprehensive as the Lloyd George Coalition, yet both more attuned to Conservative opinion and less offensive to most Liberal and Labour sensibilities.

In opposition Baldwin had accepted a highly collective leadership because his position had been weak. Now he continued it because his own position had become so strong, because his pro-

---

[22] Jones *WD* II. 303 (8 Nov. 1924); *Self-Portrait of an Artist. From the Diaries and Letters of Lady Kennet*, ed. Lord Kennet (1949), p. 229 (18 Nov. 1924). Baldwin had originally intended Chamberlain for the Treasury and Churchill for Health, but the political effects would have been similar to those of the eventual appointments. His plans were changed by Chamberlain asking for Health.

tectionist phase had taught him caution, and because with a reunited Conservative leadership most of his Cabinet colleagues had considerable experience and initiative. After ten years of international, economic, and political dislocation, and amid general expectations of a strong economic recovery, the Cabinet's principal objective was to restore stability. This would be done by the traditional Conservative methods of efficient and economical administration, sound finance, prudent tax relief, preservation of imperial interests, and consolidation of well-established official policies. In deference to post-war democratic conditions it would also be achieved by appropriating the radical style of sustained legislative activity, in the Conservative forms of financial and administrative rationalisation, significant yet cheap and uncontroversial social reform, adjustments to reflect the changed social and political status of women, and encouragement to economic competitiveness and working-class self-reliance. There would also be sensitivity towards the League of Nations. Aside from the vital prime-ministerial task of presenting the government's actions in the most broadly attractive terms, Baldwin's normal role was to adjudicate between his colleagues' proposals and to facilitate their acceptance by the Cabinet, including Churchill's return to the gold standard and Churchill's and Neville Chamberlain's major expansion of the state pensions scheme in 1925. He was decisive in winning Cabinet endorsement for Austen Chamberlain's four-power guarantee of Germany's western frontiers, the 1925 Locarno pact; for the establishment of the Central Electricity Board in 1926; and for the equalisation of the parliamentary franchise for women at the age of twenty-one in 1928. He brought Northern Ireland and Irish Free State ministers together to settle their boundary in late 1925. He also arbitrated in the usual disputes between stubborn ministers with strong departmental interests. In 1925 he produced a compromise between Churchill and Bridgeman of the Admiralty over cruiser construction, and reluctantly accepted Churchill's argument that safeguarding duties on iron and steel would breach the commitment against general tariffs.

Baldwin's greatest influence was upon the government's treatment of a developing industrial relations problem. The fundamental economic need for industrial co-operation had long been among his leading themes, but during early 1925 a highly personal decision and a series of speeches had a major public impact. In February he persuaded the Cabinet to resist intense Conservative party pressures for restrictive legislation against trade unions. At Birmingham on 5 March he appealed for a 'truce of God' to help 'pull the country into a better and happier condition'; in the House of Commons on the 6th he obtained the withdrawal of Macquisten's bill attacking trade-union financial support for the Labour party, as a symbol of Conservative commitment to his prayer of 'Give peace in our time, O Lord'; and then in three speeches at Leeds on the 12th and 13th he invoked the moral and spiritual support of social responsibility, sacrifice, selflessness, and Christian ideals.[23] Although these efforts failed to tranquillise the two sides of the coal industry and the leaders of other trade unions, they gave Baldwin a remarkable command over Conservative and public feeling when confrontation came. After making unsuccessful attempts during July 1925 to reconcile coal owners' and miners' leaders, and in the face of threatened strikes by transport unions in support of the miners, he took the large political risk of offering a temporary government subsidy and a Royal Commission of Inquiry. When the Samuel Commission Report of March 1926 also failed to bring the miners and owners together, Baldwin resumed mediation – persisting beyond a point which most Cabinet members thought prudent – until apparent trade-union interference with newspaper freedom made it politically impossible for him to continue negotiations. By then, however, Baldwin's appeal for industrial peace and his attack upon what he presented as the 'unconstitutional' methods of trade unions had stiffened opinion among much of the public while weakening the resolve of many Trades Union Congress (TUC) leaders, and helped bring the May 1926 General Strike to an unexpectedly early end. Baldwin tried to settle the remaining coal industry lockout. He presented his own proposals on the basis of the Samuel Report two days after the Strike ended. In June the Cabinet sanctioned both a mines-reorganisation bill and a miners' eight-hours bill, and into the autumn he continued to offer mediation to the miners either personally or through Churchill. But between the owners' absolute rejection of voluntary reconstruction and the miners leaders' absolute rejection of wage cuts no agreement was

[23] Four of these speeches are in *OE* pp. 23–40, 40–52, 61–9, 202–11.

possible. As Baldwin and the Cabinet would not contemplate imposing what would have been effective nationalisation – seen as an unacceptable concession to trade-union pressure and social-ism – by November desperate hardship forced the miners to return to work on the owners' terms.

The General Strike and prolonged coal stoppage temporarily disrupted Baldwin's hopes of social reconciliation and co-operation in industrial regeneration. Added to the earlier coal subsidy they imposed large financial and economic costs, exacerbating what had proved to be only a weak and patchy recovery which left over a million unemployed. During 1927 further awkward problems accumulated. The credit which the Locarno pact had created with peace and internationalist opinion was dissolved by armed defence of British interests in China, by the Arcos raid and the consequent diplomatic breach with Soviet Russia, and by the breakdown of the Geneva naval disarmament conference, which led to Lord Cecil's resignation from the Cabinet and strained relations with the United States. The General Strike had made it impossible for Baldwin to continue resisting his party's demand for a Trades Dis-putes Bill, the introduction of which further embittered relations with the Labour movement. After he reluctantly yielded to party and Cabinet pressures to strengthen the House of Lords by mod-ifying its composition, the resulting proposal aroused so much Labour and Liberal outrage and Conservative division that he was relieved at having to abandon it. In April 1927 he suffered a slight physical collapse, and for a long period was tired, depressed, and uncertain. His procrastination affected the whole Cabinet, with individual ministers complaining of their collective indecision. The government was clearly losing initiative and public support.

Hindsight coloured by eventual election defeat in 1929 created an impression that the decline continued inexorably, weakening Baldwin's authority and reputation. The reality was more compli-cated. From early 1928 the Cabinet regained momentum with new policies, and Baldwin reasserted himself and dominated the Conservative election campaign. Churchill reduced the financial burden upon agricultural and industrial production by rating relief, and Baldwin convinced a piqued Neville Chamberlain that this 'derating' scheme was compatible with his large-scale reform of local government. With voluntary re-organisation by private industry and agriculture thought to be the fundamental remedy for economic stagnation, assistance for 'labour transference' and training was provided to ease redistribution of the workforce. Baldwin encouraged discussions between employers' representatives and the TUC on industrial co-operation, the Mond–Turner talks. He quelled Cabinet divisions and an incipient backbench rebellion to preserve the 1924 position on tariffs before the election, but a large extension of industrial safeguarding was promised for the future. He also persuaded a reluctant Churchill to accept a colonial development fund as a further stimulus to trade, and other lesser economic, social, and health measures were prepared.

Many Conservatives shared Baldwin's own belief that his reputation would be decisive at the election, and the Cabinet and Central Office readily entrusted overall strategy to him. The principal threat to the Conservative ability to defeat the Labour party was a Liberal recovery, with Lloyd George using his personal political fund to help finance over 500 candidates and in March 1929 pledging his party to reduce unemployment dramatically through unorthodox forms of loan finance and public works. Baldwin decided the best response both to this and to the Labour challenge was to understate his government's new proposals and instead emphasise its substantial past record, in order to contrast responsible and sound Conservative 'performance' with irresponsible and specious radical 'promises'. The subsequently much-derided slogan, 'Safety First', taken by critics to characterise Baldwin's whole politics – indeed, an entire phase of British political culture – as passive and complacent, was not chosen by him nor by the Conservative Central Office. It was, rather, the inept attempt by the party's advertising agents to summarise for an election poster (plate 10) what was, in context, a calculated counterattack, underpinned by Conservative confidence in Baldwin's leadership and popular appeal – 'The man you can trust'.[24]

---

[24] P. Williamson, ' "Safety First": Baldwin, the Conservative Party, and the 1929 General Election', *Historical Journal* 25 (1982), 385–409. The Central Office's preferred poster slogan was 'the man you can trust', which more appositely expressed the election strategy. It remained the secondary message, but party officials allowed themselves to be persuaded by supposed experts: Jones *WD* II. 186 (1 June 1929); Gower notes, 22 June 1953, Jones papers AA1/38.

IV

The general election of 30 May 1929, like that of December 1923, gave neither Conservatives nor Labour an overall parliamentary majority and left Liberals with the numerical balance of power. But while Conservatives again polled the largest number of votes, for the first time since 1918 they no longer formed the largest House of Commons party. Against most of his colleagues' advice Baldwin decided not to follow the 1923–4 precedent of meeting Parliament but to resign immediately, avoiding any risk of the Cabinet being accused of seeking unfair means to exclude Labour from office, or of suffering parliamentary humiliation from Lloyd George. He also came to think that Labour should be allowed longer in government than in 1924. The more MacDonald's Cabinet faced the limitations of minority government as well as the usual complications of office, the more its idealistic followers might become disillusioned and divided. The Liberal party might again be split over the dilemma of how to wield the balance of power, this time with still more fatal effects. Conservative positions could be patiently re-adjusted and developed in step with the resulting reaction of popular opinions. Meanwhile a 'hung' Parliament might constrain conflicts over the imminent, and delicate, issue of Indian constitutional reform. At the Conservative shadow cabinet on 17 July Baldwin on the one hand smothered Churchill's soundings for a revived anti-socialist alliance with Liberals, and on the other resisted Amery's and Neville Chamberlain's desire for an early re-adoption of imperial protectionism.[25] In the autumn he supported the Labour Cabinet in accepting proposals by the Conservative Viceroy of India, Lord Irwin, to call a Round Table Conference and to promise India ultimate self-governing 'dominion status' within the Empire – what became known as the 'Irwin Declaration'.

Cumulatively, all this generated one of the Conservative party's most severe and prolonged internal crises, yet also a remarkable feat of political survival on Baldwin's part.[26] As the election stance had depended so much on confidence in his leadership, defeat badly damaged him. Many constituency and backbench Conserva-

---

[25] *Amery Diaries* II. 45 (17 July 1929); Williamson, *National Crisis*, pp. 118–19.
[26] The fullest account is Ball, *Baldwin and the Conservative Party*.

tives had disliked aspects of the 1924–9 government's accommodation with post-war realities, and now had difficulty understanding anything less than persistent all-out opposition to 'socialist' ministers. Baldwin had lost the enthusiastic support of the protectionists which had sustained him after the 1923 election – indeed most of them blamed the latest defeat on his rejection of their appeals for further tariffs. His continued reluctance to risk another electoral rebuff over the re-adoption of general tariffs provoked a revival of protectionist organisation and agitation. 'Diehards' – the Conservative right – were also angry at Baldwin's acquiescence in what they regarded as the Labour Cabinet's abdications of imperial power, in Egypt, over naval disarmament, and especially in India. As discontent spread from autumn 1929, members of the shadow cabinet and its inner 'Business Committee' – themselves exasperated by Baldwin's stoical acceptance that he could not be a good, attacking, opposition leader, and shaken by his assent to the Irwin Declaration – came to doubt whether he could continue. Fearing that his collapsing reputation might damage their own positions, some wondered how far they should continue to support him.

Discontent was exacerbated by the 'press lords', Beaverbrook and Rothermere, though paradoxically their interventions eventually helped Baldwin. As owners of the chief mass-circulation newspapers read by Conservatives – respectively the *Express* and *Mail* groups – and as prominent political figures in the early 1920s, they had resented Baldwin's refusal to accord them the respect they thought they deserved. Since 1923 their newspapers had frequently criticised his leadership, and after the 1929 defeat they saw opportunities to recover their own power and perhaps force his removal. Beaverbrook proclaimed his own version of imperial protectionism, 'Empire Free Trade', which attracted so much interest from frustrated protectionists that he created an 'Empire Crusade' campaign organisation. After Baldwin denounced inaccurate *Daily Mail* reports about his acceptance of the Irwin Declaration, Rothermere allied himself to Beaverbrook and from early 1930 they each sponsored parliamentary candidates, and even formed their own 'United Empire' party. Their newspapers inflamed constituency criticism of official Conservative policies, and their recruitment of substantial memberships and interventions in by-elections restored them as serious political forces.

Control of the Conservative party became extremely difficult. The Labour government's inability to prevent rising unemployment and the onset of economic depression improved the electoral prospects for imperial protectionism, but Baldwin could not easily satisfy Conservative protectionists without creating an impression that party policy was being imposed by newspaper owners. For months he shifted uneasily between his own desire to fight the press lords, and Business Committee and Central Office advice to conciliate at least Beaverbrook. There was a series of increasingly fraught party meetings. At the Albert Hall on 21 November 1929 he embraced imperial economic unity; at the Coliseum on 5 February 1930 he offered more detail. At the Hotel Cecil on 4 March he proposed a national referendum on the most sensitive question, tariffs on food imports. Faced by intense pressure to drop the referendum in favour of a 'free hand' in applying tariffs, at the Caxton Hall on 24 June he discovered his best defence by switching the issue to resistance to 'press dictation'. Nevertheless, by the autumn Baldwin faced a party revolt of similar proportions to that of 1922, and there was no shortage of candidates for the role he had then played. Neville Chamberlain especially had emerged as a crucial figure, removing one of the malcontents' main targets, Davidson, the party chairman closely identified with Baldwin, and taking the chairmanship himself. He and other Business Committee members came close to asking Baldwin to resign, until Dominion proposals at the Imperial Conference supplied an opportunity to adopt the 'free hand' without appearing to submit to Beaverbrook. This enabled Baldwin at another party meeting at Caxton Hall on 30 October to defeat a motion of no confidence in his leadership.

Even now dissent subsided only briefly. A substantial minority of MPs, candidates, and peers had voted against Baldwin, and in early 1931 Beaverbrook resumed the Empire Crusade to challenge him directly by contesting by-elections against Conservative candidates. Divisions had now also widened over Indian policy, following the first session of the Round Table Conference. During late 1930 Churchill placed himself at the head of die-hard resistance to significant concessions towards Indian nationalism. In January 1931 he resigned from the Business Committee to attack Baldwin's acceptance of the Conference's proposal to go beyond the Simon Commission Report and establish a representative All-

India federal government. Supported by Rothermere's newspapers, the Beaverbrook and Churchill campaigns together exposed such continuing doubts about Baldwin's leadership that the Business Committee and Central Office now succumbed. On 1 March Neville Chamberlain sent Baldwin a report by the party's principal agent on the extent of discontent, and intimated that most of his colleagues thought he should resign.[27]

In the first shock, Baldwin agreed to go. But he quickly changed his mind. He suspected that Chamberlain and his staff had been motivated by personal ambition, and he refused to resign under what he again chose to treat as primarily a matter of 'press dictation'.[28] Aided by the Irwin–Gandhi pact of 5 March, which ended the nationalist civil-disobedience campaign, but amid much ill-feeling within the collective party leadership, Baldwin then mounted a spectacular political recovery. In two speeches he offered such reassurance on India that on 16 March Churchill suffered a humiliating defeat at a Conservative backbench meeting. During the St George's Westminster by-election he execrated Beaverbrook and Rothermere for seeking 'power without responsibility'. On 19 March the Conservative candidate defeated the Empire Crusade candidate, demonstrating that newspaper owners could not convert large readerships into decisive votes. Ten days later Beaverbrook publicly submitted to the Conservative leadership. Baldwin had worn down his critics over nearly two years by sheer persistence and by a combination of policy adjustments and defences of party integrity which deflected attacks upon his alleged shortcomings as leader.

V

National politics as a whole were now passing through a chaotic period, due to the severity of the economic depression, the strain upon public finances, a paralysed Labour government, and divisions within all three parliamentary parties. During 1930 a wide-

[27] The report is printed in I. Macleod, *Neville Chamberlain* (1961), pp. 139–41. Ball, *Baldwin and the Conservative Party*, pp. xvi–xvii, 96–7, 124–7, 141–3, argues that the position was more serious in October 1930 than in March 1931. Williamson, *National Crisis*, pp. 130, 184, re-affirms the traditional emphasis.
[28] *The Modernisation of Conservative Politics. The Diaries and Letters of William Bridgeman 1904–1935*, ed. Philip Williamson (1988) (cited hereafter as *Bridgeman Diaries*), pp. 243–5 (March 1931); Jones *DL* pp. 3–6 (11, 16 March 1931).

spread sense of national crisis and desire for strong government
had produced some suggestions for a cross-party 'national government'. Against this, and despite their own difficulties, Baldwin
and his colleagues had insisted that Conservatism constituted the
'national party', and instead encouraged various Liberal dissentients, headed by Simon, to join them in opposition to the Labour
government. However, during July and August 1931 a sterling and
budget crisis demanded extraordinary and potentially unpopular
action, and the Labour Cabinet asked for all-party assistance.
Conservative leaders offered broad support, provided large expenditure cuts were imposed. But Baldwin was determined both that
Labour ministers should bear full responsibility for the crisis, and
that his rehabilitated leadership should not suffer from renewed
suspicion of truckling to Labour. Accordingly, after briefly breaking his holiday for consultations with ministers and Bank of England directors in London, he physically distanced himself by
returning to the south of France. However, Neville Chamberlain –
acting as Baldwin's deputy – had with other Business Committee
members come to see possible advantages in 'national government'. When the sterling crisis worsened and the Labour Cabinet
became divided over cuts in social-service expenditure, an
unpleasant prospect opened: a precarious Conservative-led
government reducing working-class incomes against a vigorous
Labour party opposition defining the issue as 'the rich versus the
poor'. In these circumstances Chamberlain obtained Liberal support in persuading the Labour Prime Minister, MacDonald, to
head an emergency all-party Cabinet. On Baldwin's recall to
London, he offered to form a mainly Conservative government.
But on 24 August he acquiesced in the desire of his Conservative
colleagues – and of Liberal leaders and the King – for the National
government.[29] He himself took a managerial role as Lord President of the Council.

Baldwin's doubts rapidly dispersed. The new government's formation initially eased the sterling crisis, and it perpetuated the
split in the Labour leadership. It spread political responsibility for
tax increases and, most importantly, for expenditure cuts – now
elevated from Conservative partisan demands into patriotic 'sacrifices' for the 'national interest'. The financial crisis appeared so

---

[29] Williamson, *National Crisis*, chs. 4, 8–9.

grave that almost all Conservatives overcame their worst suspicions of 'coalition', Liberals, and MacDonald to support their
leaders' participation in the government, with the effect of sealing
Baldwin's recovery of his party's confidence. Despite the original
declarations that the National government would be just a short-
lived emergency arrangement, over the following weeks its attractiveness to Conservative leaders increased. In mid-September
Baldwin proposed to MacDonald that it should be reconstituted to
fight a general election as a permanent coalition. The Indian
Round Table Conference and the pressures of economic
depression and financial crisis had enlarged the areas of common
ground between Conservatives, many Liberals, and MacDonald's
followers, while as the National government's largest component
the Conservative party was assured of ultimate control. The new
government had received unusually wide public approval, and
seemed to fulfil Baldwin's ambition since 1924 of making the Conservative party the magnet for all non-socialist opinion. This
ambition acquired special urgency because under trade-union
pressure the Labour opposition had shifted sharply towards the
left, and because in resisting cuts in wages and benefit payments
it appeared capable of securing sufficient popular support to deny
a decent majority to Conservatives – even perhaps to defeat
them – if they fought the election alone.

The danger increased when enforced devaluation – departure
from the gold standard – on 21 September destroyed the original
public justification for the government and its drastic budgetary
measures. In defending its past actions and current policies by
stressing continued financial strains and a balance-of-payments
crisis, the Cabinet created further arguments for its own perpetuation. The chief obstacle was a fundamental difference over trade
policy between its protectionist Conservative and the free-trade
Liberal members, now supported by MacDonald's Chancellor,
Snowden. Baldwin's answer was to propose a reconstructed coalition, replacing the free-trade ministers with Simon's dissident
Liberals. Another problem was MacDonald's fear of appearing to
be merely a Conservative prisoner. Very few Labour ministers and
MPs had followed him, but Conservatives thought MacDonald
retained much working-class support and considered him the vital
symbol of the government's 'National' character. Here Baldwin's
answer was to guarantee MacDonald's position by again

relinquishing his own claim to the premiership, and pledging Conservative ministers to continue serving under him in the next Parliament.

Armed with this assurance, MacDonald forced an unwelcome compromise on the Conservatives. The free-trade ministers stayed in an un-reconstructed Cabinet, and the government fought the election not on an agreed trade policy, but on a 'doctor's mandate' to undertake whatever measures it considered appropriate in the national interest. This left the main National government partners in open dispute over protection. But the chief point was gained: they fought the election as a comprehensive and full-blooded anti-socialist alliance. Baldwin declared privately that 'the great thing this time is to give Socialism a really smashing defeat'.[30] On 27 October 1931 this aim was amply achieved, inflicting on the Labour party a repulse even more severe than that suffered by the trade unions in 1926. Apart from the huge collective National government majority, Conservatives alone had a majority of 418 over a demolished Labour opposition, reduced to just 52 MPs.

The National government is often treated as a Conservative government in disguise, or even without disguise. It was not considered to be so by Churchill and the diehards, by Amery and 'whole-hog' protectionists, and by anti-statists and isolationists, all of whom thought that Conservatism had been compromised. Nor, on the other hand, was it considered to be so by the many Conservative MPs who owed their election to local pacts with Liberals and to non-Conservative votes. Nor was it by Baldwin. He presented the election as a 'national' and non-party victory, and besides bringing the Simonite Liberals into the government worked hard over the next five years to preserve and even extend its non-Conservative composition. By diluting the influence of those reactionary and doctrinaire Conservative sections which had been so troublesome to him in opposition, the coalition election consolidated his version of a modern, permeable, and 'national' Conservatism. In the short term this included sound budgets, tolerance of high unemployment, and restricted social expenditure.

---

[30] A. Chamberlain to his wife, 8 Oct. 1931, AC 6/1/826. M&B p. 651 gives a misleading impression of Baldwin's restraint during this election. For the momentous Cabinet politics of autumn 1931, see Williamson, *National Crisis*, chs. 10–12.

But it also came to mean sterling management, cheap money, a house-building boom, agricultural marketing, industrial reorganisation and, as the economy slowly recovered, resumed social reform. Like other leading Conservatives, Baldwin even hoped for the coalition's fusion into a 'National party', which might permanently check the alarming Labour advance of the 1920s, and deal so conclusively with the most sensitive national problems that these could be placed 'out of party politics' – that is to say, beyond successful socialist challenge.[31] Conservative ministers insisted upon the adoption of protection, but proceeded by negotiation and so far accommodated free-trade ministers as to agree in January 1932 to suspend collective responsibility, allowing them to dissent publicly from the majority Cabinet decision – the 'agreement to differ'. Baldwin was unusually angry when, despite this, the free-trade ministers resigned in September over the Ottawa Imperial Economic Conference resolutions, but he again declined the opportunity to create a purely Conservative government. He renewed his pledges to MacDonald and committed his party to continued alliance with the National Labour and Simonite Liberal National groups.[32]

As Lord President, and additionally as Lord Privy Seal from September 1932 to December 1933, Baldwin had a roving commission. He chaired or attended the key Cabinet committees, acting as effective (though not official) leader of the Commons, deputised for MacDonald or other ministers absent at international conferences, and himself led the British delegation at the Ottawa conference. He undoubtedly welcomed the relief from prime ministerial or departmental responsibility for innumerable decisions on detail. But in his mind the arrangement enabled him to concentrate upon the larger responsibilities of government policy and political strategy. In declining to return to the Chancellorship of the Exchequer or to take any other departmental office, he also anticipated that ministerial and party management would require special attention, given the prime minister's tiny personal

---

[31] Jones *DL* pp. 25–6 (28 Jan. 1932). Cf. Aberdeen, 4 Dec. 1931, and *HCDeb* 261, c. 803 (9 Feb. 1932), and other Conservative views in Williamson, *National Crisis*, p. 484; T. Stannage, *Baldwin Thwarts the Opposition* (1980), pp. 25–6.

[32] Jones *DL* pp. 55–6 (14 Sept. 1932); Baldwin to MacDonald, 12 Sept. 1932, SB 167/189–90; Baldwin in Cabinet 48(32), 28 Sept. 1932; party conference speech, 7 Oct. 1932.

following and the possibility that the greatest parliamentary difficulties might come not from the depleted Labour opposition, but
from under-employed and discontented Conservative MPs.[33]

The most serious Conservative dissent was that on India, led by
Churchill. Since 1929 Baldwin had become deeply committed to
Indian constitutional reform. Having already staked his own leadership on the issue while in opposition, he now made it a test of
confidence in the National government.[34] For him, the three-
pronged strategy of promising India ultimate Dominion status,
winning the co-operation of moderates, Muslims, and Princes, and
obtaining their assent to an Indian federation limited by British
'safeguards' and 'reservations', was the only means of keeping
India within the Empire. For Churchill and the diehards, Indian
responsibility in central government – however circumscribed or
constrained – was a fatal concession to the Indian Congress
demand for full Indian independence. What made the diehard
attack so dangerous was that it became entwined with the issue
of Conservative party identity, particularly among constituency
activists in southern England and Lancashire. Although in the
event the diehards never mustered more than seventy-nine Commons votes, their campaign against the March 1933 White Paper
obtained much support within the Conservative National Union,
where success might have converted many more MPs and jeopard-
ised the party leadership. Baldwin had to provide considerable evidence that the policy had support from specifically *Conservative*
Indian experts and was not, as the diehards alleged, the consequence of insidious influence from the 'socialist' (National
Labour) and Liberal members of the government.[35] By pronounc-
ing in June that the White Paper would be *sub judice* during its
scrutiny by a parliamentary Joint Select Committee, he gained
time to obtain endorsements from further key Conservative figures and for the instruments of party management to operate.
When the Committee reported, enough reassurance had been
generated to secure a decisive victory within the National Union

[33] Baldwin in Wigram memos, 2, 4 Nov. 1931, in M&B pp. 653–4, 655–6.
[34] Jones *DL* p. 128 (28 April 1934). For the Indian policy disputes, see R. J. Moore, *The Crisis of Indian Unity 1917–1940* (Oxford, 1974); C. Bridge, *Holding India to the Empire. The British Conservative Party and the 1935 Constitution* (Delhi, 1986).
[35] E. g. Worcester, 29 April 1933; National Union Central Council, 28 June 1933, 4 Dec. 1934.

in December 1934 and to ensure the Government of India Bill's passage through both Commons and Lords by August 1935. However, the divisions had killed all prospect of Conservative assent to a fused 'National party'.

VI

The area of government strategy which now occupied Baldwin most was that where foreign policy, armaments, and domestic peace opinion became inextricably linked. As the international situation deteriorated from 1931, the Cabinet's consistent objectives were to preserve European stability, avoid war, and prevent attacks upon British territories. Within this context the threat of aerial bombing became Baldwin's particular concern, initially as an issue in disarmament. British experts expected air attacks to be directed against civilians, and to be not just horrific in themselves but the decisive feature of any future war. Fear of such a 'knock-out blow' underpinned the deep public attachment to peace and the League of Nations. With the 1932 Disarmament Conference almost immediately entangled in detail, Baldwin argued in Cabinet for the bold, if highly optimistic, course of proposing international abolition of air forces. When this became lost in the departmental and diplomatic jungle, he tried to revive it by a Commons speech on 10 November. If air warfare were permitted, he warned, 'the bomber will always get through'. At the same time, however, he declared that Britain could not continue its own unilateral disarmament.[36]

During 1933 Hitler's accession to power, indications of German rearmament, and German withdrawal in October from the Disarmament Conference and League of Nations, persuaded the whole Cabinet that British rearmament was unavoidable. Allowing for the complexity of the situation, Baldwin and his colleagues did not 'delay', still less 'neglect', rearmament. Planning started with the appointment of a Defence Requirements Committee in November, by which time Baldwin had begun to prepare the public with warnings of the possible failure of disarmament talks, a resumption of foreign rearmament, and 'deficiencies' in Britain's

[36] *HCDeb* 270, cc. 630–8 (10 Nov. 1932). For further details on Baldwin's proposal, see U. Bialer, *The Shadow of the Bomber. The Fear of Air Attack and British Politics 1932–1939* (1980), ch. 1; S. Roskill, *Hankey, Man of Secrets*, 3 vols. (1970–4), III. 62–4.

own defences.[37] But Hitler's objectives remained uncertain. Even
while ordering rearmament and demanding revision of the peace
treaty, he seemed prepared to proceed by peaceful means and
to negotiate arms limitation agreements – as achieved with the
Anglo-German naval treaty in June 1935. It was difficult to obtain
accurate and agreed estimates of the scale and speed of German
military production. Even in strategic and economic terms the
issues were far from straightforward, as conflicting priorities
needed decision and re-decision within shifting conditions:
between Japanese and Italian as well as German threats, between
domestic and imperial defence, between the demands of airforce,
navy, and army, between the prospects of deterrence, arms limitation, or war, between re-direction of industrial resources as
against continued economic recovery, and between immediate
expenditure or long-term financial strength.

Attention became still more focused upon air policy as the Cabinet decided to concentrate on expanding the RAF, and as Churchill identified air defences as the chief area of Britain's – and the
Cabinet's – vulnerability. With the Air Minister in the House of
Lords, Baldwin made himself the government's chief Commons
spokesman on the issue. A series of poor by-election results, beginning with a striking Conservative defeat at East Fulham on 25
October 1933, intensified the Cabinet sense that rearmament
needed very careful public presentation. For it was popularly
believed that rearmament would precipitate an arms race, leading
inexorably to war – the belief which underpinned the faith placed
in international disarmament and collective security.[38] After Baldwin had announced in July 1934 a large expansion of the RAF
(forty-one extra squadrons by 1939) against outright Labour and
Liberal opposition, he stressed several points. In an age of aerial
warfare, British isolation from continental affairs was impossible.
The government intended only to repair gaps in national defences.
The best defence against an aerial 'knock-out blow' would be the

[37] Conservative party conference, 6 Oct. 1933; *HCDeb* 283, cc. 1013–17 (29 Nov. 1933).
The best account of rearmament is N. H. Gibbs, *Grand Strategy* I: *Rearmament Policy*
(1976).
[38] For a revived debate on this notorious episode, after the appropriate records became
available, see M&B pp. 744–7, 764; C. T. Stannage, 'The East Fulham By-election',
Historical Journal 15 (1972), 165–200; M. Ceadel, 'Interpreting East Fulham', in C. Cook
and J. Ramsden (eds.), *By-Elections in British Politics* (1973), pp. 118–39; J. P. D. Dunba-
bin, 'British Rearmament in the 1930s', *Historical Journal* 18 (1975), 587–609.

deterrence of a British bomber force. The commitment to collective security remained, but the fulfilment of British obligations to the League of Nations required armed strength. None of this indicated a weakened attachment to peace nor, if circumstances allowed, to mutual arms limitation and ultimate international disarmament. Against Churchill's accusations of inadequate rearmament Baldwin had already promised in March 1934 that British air power would not be inferior to that of 'any country within striking distance of our shores'. With rearmament in progress, in November he denied Churchill's assertion that Germany was rapidly approaching equality with Britain in military aircraft, but nevertheless acknowledged the suspected acceleration in German rearmament by announcing that completion of the new RAF squadrons would be brought forward to 1937. However, the March 1935 Defence White Paper, intended to assist the justification of rearmament to the British public, provoked Hitler to repudiate all military limitations imposed by the peace treaty and to claim that Germany had already achieved air parity. The claim was false, but the Cabinet could not ignore the larger threat. In May Baldwin admitted being 'completely wrong' in his earlier forecast of *future* German aircraft production, a statement which Churchill chose to present as a 'confession' of error and a vindication of himself on *current* air strengths.[39] Baldwin announced a further RAF expansion (a further thirty-nine squadrons for 1937), and the Defence Requirements Committee was re-constituted not just to strengthen the air deterrent, but to prepare for the possibility of war by planning a general rearmament, including the navy and army. Armaments would plainly become a major, and highly delicate, issue at the next general election.

By early 1935 the National government seemed generally to be in difficulties. An ageing, weary MacDonald remained effective in Cabinet discussions, but his speeches had become embarrassingly prolix and confused, and he obviously could not remain prime minister at the election. Baldwin, now aged sixty-seven, also thought of retiring,[40] but when MacDonald finally agreed to step down the political situation had deteriorated so much that he decided he

---

[39] See M&B pp. 786–9, 814–20, and, for a more critical account, Gibbs, *Rearmament Policy*, pp. 138–41, 174–5.
[40] Baldwin to Oliver Baldwin, 24 Aug. 1934, CUL Add. 8795/17; MacDonald diary, 10 Feb. 1935; Roskill, *Hankey* III. 162–3 (diary, 24 Feb. 1935).

should return to the premiership. By-election results had remained poor, and in February Wavertree was lost to Labour through the intervention of Churchill's son, fighting on the Indian issue. New, often reduced, rates for unemployment benefits had provoked revolt even among Conservative MPs, and had to be suspended. The League of Nations Union and other peace organisations were conducting a national 'Peace Ballot', implicitly critical of the government. Lloyd George had launched a 'new deal' economic and social programme, and threatened to mount a movement to secure the parliamentary balance of power at the next election. After the Wavertree defeat there were even rumours that the Cabinet was breaking up, which shook financial confidence and caused such a marked fall in government securities that Baldwin had to make a public denial.[41]

In reality the Conservative leaders became, if anything, even more attached to their coalition partners. The political threat was not that the Labour party might win the next general election; it was rather that the government's existing majority might be so far reduced that the credibility and authority of the 'national' alliance, and with it those of the collective Conservative leadership, would be severely damaged. This could occur from a loss of the Liberal and wider moderate voters who had supported the National government in 1931, and who now constituted much of the peace and League of Nations opinion or who seemed likely to be attracted by Lloyd George's agitation.[42] As Baldwin himself believed and as his non-Conservative colleagues also thought, he would be better able to recapture parts of this 'liberal' opinion – as well as reconcile Conservative rebels – than the only other serious candidate for the premiership, Neville Chamberlain. For a long period Baldwin hoped that 'national' credentials could be refreshed by obtaining new Liberal, even Labour or trade-union, recruits to the government, and from February the Cabinet entered into elaborate negotiations with Lloyd George.[43] But

[41] City notes, *The Times* 12, 13, 14 Feb. 1935; *HCDeb* 297 c. 1711 (11 Feb. 1935), and see Chelsea, 21 Feb. 1935; Simon diary, 14 Feb. 1935.

[42] For the political problem and government responses in 1934–5, see Cowling, *Impact of Hitler*, chs. 1–3.

[43] Jones *DL* p. 123 (27 Feb. 1934), for Bevin; W. P. Crozier, *Off the Record. Political Interviews 1933–1943*, ed. A. J. P. Taylor (1973), p. 26 (12 June 1934); Dawson memo, 6 May 1935, Dawson papers 78/101–2, for Samuelites and 'responsible Labour'; Jones diary, 1 June 1935, for A. V. Alexander. For Lloyd George, Cowling, *Impact of Hitler*, pp. 37–40, 55–8.

Chamberlain's hostility towards Lloyd George proved conclusive, and after Baldwin became prime minister for the third time on 7 June 1935 the negotiations lapsed.

Instead Baldwin adopted an alternative method of regaining liberal sympathies. In July he presented the results of the Peace Ballot as supporting the government's commitment to the League of Nations, which he now described as the 'sheet anchor of British policy'. Although from August the Abyssinian crisis brought the anxieties of a possible war against Italy, it assisted the recovery of the Cabinet's political position. It created conditions which strengthened its new identification with the League, winning approval from the League of Nations Union and undercutting Lloyd George's attempt to combine critics of the Cabinet's foreign and domestic policies in a cross-party 'Council of Action for Peace and Reconstruction'. It provided good public arguments for rearmament, particularly for its extension to the Royal Navy. It also caused important changes within the Labour party in early October – a leadership crisis and the removal of its pacifist leader, Lansbury, and an acceptance, if necessary, of military sanctions to make the League of Nations effective, even though the party continued to oppose the government's rearmament programme.

Baldwin was now able to square the political circle, and promptly called a general election. Chamberlain had proposed that the fight should primarily be on the rearmament programme, cushioned by its presentation as an employment policy. Baldwin chose a different, more subtle, strategy, with wider resonances. He encased rearmament within the larger theme of British support for collective security and League-based attempts to settle the international crisis, now made still more dangerous by the outbreak of open Italian–Abyssinian war. With the passage of the India Act, Churchill and other Conservative critics publicly rallied to Baldwin's leadership and the commitment to continued rearmament. Support for the League of Nations consolidated the re-attachment of much liberal and peace opinion to the government, while the Labour movement could be presented as agreeing with the Cabinet's foreign policy. In promising 'no great armaments' Baldwin was not defining a limitation on the physical *scale* of rearmament. Rather, he was offering reassurance of its restricted (because peaceful) *purpose*, by confronting Labour accusations of 'war-mongering' and the crucial text of peace opinion – Lord

Grey's statement that 'great armaments lead inevitably to war'.[44]
Nine months after the government seemed to have 'alienated . . .
every section of the population',[45] on 14 November 1935 it
obtained a 242-seat majority.

VII

Even more than after the 1924 election, the size of the victory
was thought to represent a personal triumph for Baldwin. Yet four
weeks later his and the Cabinet's reputations plummeted, as an
anxious yet over-confident foreign secretary, a clever French minister, and a newspaper leak exposed inconsistencies in their policy
aims, and between these and their public presentation.[46] Baldwin
and the Cabinet wanted to concentrate British deterrence and
diplomacy upon containing the German threat to European peace,
and to preserve the possibility of co-operation with both Mussolini
and the French glimpsed in the 'Stresa front' of April 1935. They
regarded Italian aggression in Abyssinia as unpleasant but nonetheless a distraction from the major problem. They hoped that
Mussolini could be stopped by collective League of Nations pressure, to the point of agreeing to economic sanctions. But they also
wished to avoid a situation where these sanctions escalated into
war against Italy, especially a war in which they feared Britain
would receive no armed assistance from France. No British preparations existed for a Mediterranean war, and the naval base at
Malta was practically defenceless against air attack. As Baldwin
repeatedly said in public, Britain would take 'no isolated action'.

---

[44] Viscount Grey, *Twenty-Five Years 1892–1916*, 2 vols. (1925), I. 91, also II. 271–9. The
extent to which Baldwin sought a mandate for rearmament has been debated. Baldwin
naturally spoke on other subjects, as British elections are never fought on one issue
alone. His speeches also shifted towards industrial issues as the campaign proceeded
because his advisors anticipated that Labour would concentrate on these, as more advantageous to themselves than the international issue: Ball memo, 8 Nov. 1935, CRD 1/7/
24. But irrespective of the relative proportions of words, everyone understood that
defence and foreign policy were the central questions. Precisely because Baldwin wanted
a large majority to facilitate rearmament, he enveloped it in other issues and presented
it in the best and most guarded manner.

[45] R. A. Butler to Brabourne, 22 Feb. 1935, Brabourne papers F97/20A. cf. M&B p. 809.

[46] For diplomatic, political, and public contexts see R. A. C. Parker, 'Britain, France and
the Ethiopian Crisis 1935–1936', *English Historical Review* 89 (1974), 293–332; Cowling,
Impact of Hitler, pp. 76–102; D. Waley, *British Public Opinion and the Abyssinian War 1935–
6* (1975).

It alone should not bear the burdens of being the League's policeman.

The French-inspired 'Hoare–Laval pact' to carve up Abyssinia went further than Cabinet ministers liked in meeting Italian claims. Nevertheless, because it promised to prevent a British–Italian war they would have used it as a basis for a League-brokered settlement, had not its premature public disclosure generated a political crisis. By seeming to give Mussolini a 'reward for aggression' and still more by appearing to betray the election commitment to the League, it produced shock and outrage across great swathes of public and parliamentary opinion, including Conservative. Baldwin had publicly expressed concern about the effect of sanctions, but he was nevertheless caught by his invocation of League of Nations idealism. His attempt to calm the situation in a House of Commons speech on 10 December was further vitiated by his efforts to protect Hoare, and by a collision between his instinct for frankness and the diplomatic need for reticence on a major Cabinet concern – that the French government could not be trusted to fulfil its League obligations and come to Britain's military aid. The phrase he used – 'my lips are not yet unsealed'[47] – was inept, sharpening the sense that something shameful had occurred. The Cabinet now faced what Baldwin described as the 'worst situation in the House of Commons he had ever known', with estimates that its majority could fall to a hundred – a humiliating and, therefore, probably crippling three-fifths reduction. Ultimately, after carefully taking the views of each Cabinet member, he decided that the pact had to be repudiated and Hoare persuaded to resign and take most of the blame.[48] Baldwin's own retraction and apology on 19 December was his worst parliamentary moment. That the crisis caused severe disappointment without discrediting him completely indicated the depth of

---

[47] The explanation offered here of the phrase in *HCDeb* 307 c. 856 (10 Dec. 1936) best fits the context, and the evidence of Cabinet minutes and Baldwin's statement to a League of Nations Union deputation on 13 Dec. 1935, PREM 1/195. Baldwin suspected Laval of secret intrigues with Mussolini (Don diary, 19 Dec. 1935), and even of being in his pay: Baldwin to Davidson, 27 Feb. 1943, JCCD 289; P. Howard, *Beaverbrook* (1964), pp. 114–15; T. Cazalet-Keir, *From the Wings* (1967), p. 102. In Jones *DL* p. 160 (7 Jan. 1936), and a meeting in June 1936 (Waley, *British Public Opinion*, p. 142), he stressed concern that an Italian war would have seriously weakened Britain militarily against Germany. The common element was doubt about French reliability.

[48] 'Most secret' annex to Cabinet 56(55), 18 Dec. 1936, reprinted in *DBFP* 2s., xv. 756, 760.

public respect upon which he could now draw. Nevertheless his authority had suffered and critics tended to become harsher. His own self-confidence had been dented, making him still more cautious about policy and less sure in his judgement of public reactions.

The lessons he drew from the crisis were that collective security required a collective readiness by all League powers to apply immediate military sanctions, and that this was a further reason for Britain needing increased armaments.[49] In practice, the first was subverted when German forces re-occupied the demilitarised Rhineland in March 1936. In a reverse of the Abyssinian crisis Baldwin and the Cabinet refused to support the French, even though this meant the end of the Locarno treaty, which was supposed to guarantee security along Germany's western frontiers. They did so because a widespread public view that Hitler's action removed a legitimate grievance reinforced their own opinion that it was not an issue on which to risk a European war.[50] Baldwin himself hoped that the end of the grievance and new offers of negotiation from Hitler might instead clear the way for a general European settlement. With this purpose, after Abyssinia had been defeated the government reconciled itself to fresh criticism from liberal opinion by abandoning sanctions against Italy, in effect acknowledging the failure of the League of Nations, at least in its current form. The incident also exposed a shift in Cabinet power when, to Baldwin's embarrassment, Neville Chamberlain used a public speech to precipitate the decision.

Rearmament did proceed, but it brought Baldwin further embarrassments. The election result was treated as a mandate for a free hand to expand all three armed services, and he played an important part in shaping and presenting the new programmes, now accompanied by industrial preparations, which were announced in March 1936 and again in February 1937. On becoming prime minister again he had appointed Swinton and the businessman, Weir, to invigorate aircraft production, but rearmament was now becoming so extensive, and faced such complex organisational and resource difficulties, that in early 1936 he

[49] Jones *DL* p. 160 (7 Jan. 1936); Baldwin in Cabinet Committee, 13 Jan. 1936, M&B pp. 900–1; *HCDeb* 309, cc. 1830–1 (9 March 1936); Worcester and Albert Hall, 18 April, 14 May 1936.
[50] Cowling, *Impact of Hitler*, pp. 105–8; Gibbs, *Rearmament Policy*, pp. 227–54.

accepted backbench suggestions that it should be supervised by new government machinery. The political effect was to revive the problem of Churchill. Contrary to some Conservative expectations, including Churchill's, Baldwin had not restored him to ministerial office during 1935, believing he would be disruptive in Cabinet and a provocation to the German government.[51] Now, although Churchill had been invited to join a secret technical committee, Baldwin resisted backbench pressure to give him ministerial charge of the larger defence committee. For administrative and industrial as well as political and diplomatic reasons, what he and the Cabinet wanted was not Churchill's capacity for initiating new departures and igniting public disputes, but steady, quiet, implementation of the already agreed medium-term programme. The purpose of rearmament remained precautionary, because the main government aim continued to be diplomatic reconciliation, leading to eventual arms limitation. Baldwin's choice of Co-ordinator of Defence was constrained by refusals from other ministers, but even so his appointment of Inskip, the Attorney-General, was a misjudgement. Although Inskip did the job competently, the choice was so improbable as to be politically counter-productive – reducing, not increasing, Conservative backbench confidence in the rearmament programme. Concern about the relative military strengths of Britain and Germany now reached well beyond Churchill, and in July 1936 and again in November a deputation of Conservative privy councillors impressed their anxieties on Baldwin and Inskip. In these circumstances, Baldwin's efforts to defend the Cabinet's policies became so strenuous and so confiding that on 12 November he spoke in the Commons with what he called 'appalling frankness', but in practice doing injustice to the government's record by leaving an impression that he had delayed rearmament for the sake of electoral advantage. His technique of dramatic candour, so often a strength, had now badly miscarried. Once more he had caused puzzlement and drawn criticism upon himself.

Even as Baldwin became prime minister in 1935, he had given some thought to when he might retire.[52] After the Hoare–Laval

---

[51] Dawson memo, 6 May 1935, Dawson papers 78/101–2; R. A. Butler memo, July 1935, Butler papers G6/57.
[52] N. Chamberlain diary, May 1935; Baldwin to Edith Macdonald, 22 June 1935, and to Monica Baldwin, 4 Aug. 1935, BF.

crisis he reconciled himself to Chamberlain becoming his successor, and wavered between two or three years as his time of departure. He wished to avoid what he considered to be MacDonald's – and, he even added, Gladstone's – mistake of 'overstaying your utility' and remaining in office too long. Yet because he also wished to avoid any impression of being pushed by his critics, especially the 'press lords', and therefore wanted to wait until his reputation was again secure and his 'Party in good heart',[53] he was at some risk of repeating the mistake. He began to leave more decisions to an exasperated Chamberlain, and postponed ministerial reshuffles for him to settle when he formally took over.[54] His inability to restore new momentum for the government after the Hoare–Laval crisis began to arouse wider dissatisfaction, and a growing sense that he ought to retire.[55] During summer 1936 Baldwin became so tired, depressed, and run down that he had to take almost three months' rest. He now decided to retire at the coronation, which since King George V's death in January had been in preparation for the following year.

The Abdication of Edward VIII in December 1936 confirmed his decision.[56] This was not just because his firm yet sensitive handling of the King, his command over political opinion, and his parliamentary explanations were almost universally regarded as personal triumphs. It was also because the royal crisis became a remarkable expression of national and imperial unity in support of the public values he had always sought to express and embody. This enabled him to retire in May 1937 – shortly before his seventieth birthday, and almost exactly fourteen years after he first became prime minister – on the highest note. He delivered a series of much admired re-statements of his political creed, received warm valedictions from the Cabinet, Commons, and Con-

[53] N. Chamberlain diary, 8 Feb. 1936; Baldwin to Oliver Baldwin, 1 Jan., 25 Feb. 1936, CUL Add. 8795/21–2; Jones *DL* p. 175 (21 Feb. 1936); R. Rhodes James, *Victor Cazalet* (1976), p. 184 (diary, 18 May 1936); 'The Reminiscences of Clement Davies', ed. J. Graham Jones, *The National Library of Wales Journal* 18 (1993–4), 411–13, at p. 412.
[54] E.g. Jones *DL* p. 228 (7 July 1936); *Amery Diaries* II. 427–8 (1 Oct. 1936); Dawson diary, 26 Oct. 1936.
[55] E.g. *The Diaries and Letters of Robert Bernays 1932–1939*, ed. Nick Smart (Lampeter, 1996), p. 252 (4 April 1936); A. *Chamberlain Diary Letters*, pp. 509–10 (20 June, 4 July 1936).
[56] In *Harold Nicolson. Diaries and Letters*, 3 vols., ed. N. Nicolson (1966–8), I. 286 (10 Dec. 1936) and in Davies, 'Reminiscences', p. 411, Baldwin gave a misleading impression of a sudden decision. Cf. Jones *DL* p. 209 (23 May 1936), and Baldwin to Mrs Gwynn Brown, 26 Aug. 1936, CUL Add. 8770.

servative party, and amid the public acclamation surrounding George VI's coronation was honoured with a Garter knighthood and earldom.

VIII

Baldwin's public career did not end with his ministerial retirement. At his last Cabinet meeting he said that 'he still had some good work in him and he hoped that his services to the State would not entirely cease'.[57] His great public prestige meant that he received many offers from national, imperial, and foreign institutions. He remained a chancellor of two universities and governor of four schools,[58] and collected further honorary degrees and city freedoms. The City of London formally thanked him for his career. He continued as a trustee of the Rhodes Trust, British Museum, and Pilgrim Trust (of which he had been the first chairman, 1930–5), and a member of the Imperial War Graves Commission. Having been given a fund 'anonymously' to promote closer ties with the Dominions in thank-offering for his role during the Abdication, on departmental advice he established and became chairman of an Imperial Relations Trust.[59] After a long rest, he accepted the presidency of Dr Barnardo's Homes and spoke for several other charities, and became president of the MCC for 1938–9 and in 1940 chairman of the Garton Foundation, which was mainly concerned with promoting industrial co-operation.

What Baldwin did mean to withdraw from was parliamentary politics, in order to avoid causing complications for his successor and former colleagues. He even hesitated before accepting elevation to the House of Lords.[60] Nevertheless during 1938 he

---

[57] Cabinet 22(37), 26 May 1937.
[58] Chancellor of St Andrews and Cambridge universities; governor of Malvern, Hartlebury, Charterhouse, and Harrow schools.
[59] Jones diary, 26 Jan., 3 May and 14 May 1937; press statement and first annual report in *The Times*, 22 June 1937, 26 June 1939. The donor was Sir Henry Strakosch, a prominent City financier of South African origin. He gave £250,000, and a second donor gave a further sum for travelling scholarships.
[60] Roskill, *Hankey* III. 278; *Crawford Papers*, p. 576 (15 Jan. 1937); Dawson diary, 26 Jan. 1937. Having been sensitive to the issue of House of Lords reform (p. 219–20, below) at one point he said he did not want to go to the Lords unless life peerages were created: N. Chamberlain diary, 8 Feb. 1936. Baldwin to Monica Baldwin, 27 March 1937, BF, says the King persuaded him to take an earldom; Jones *DL* p. 349 (30 May 1937), thought his wife was responsible.

regained close contact with Westminster and Whitehall opinion, and was drawn into an active elder statesman's role. Privately he intimated anxiety at what he considered to be Neville Chamberlain's insensitivity towards moderate, liberal, and Labour opinion, resulting in a loss of the fundamental 'national' cohesion required to withstand the German threat. When Eden resigned as foreign secretary in February 1938, it appeared for a time that Baldwin might become a political kingmaker. Both Eden and Chamberlain sought his approval, but Baldwin's sympathies lay with Eden as best representing his own conception of a broad-based Conservatism. He became Eden's mentor and regarded him as the 'next P.M.', for which purpose he urged him to develop a wide 'Baldwinite' popular appeal and advised upon – even contributed to – his speeches.[61] Nevertheless he supported Chamberlain's efforts to avoid war with Germany over Czechoslovakia, and on his pressing invitation became president of the British Association for International Understanding, a publicity machine for appeasement.[62] During the Munich debate in October 1938, in his sole speech in the House of Lords, he aimed to help rally 'wobbling' Conservative opinion behind Chamberlain's agreement with Hitler.

Baldwin was not deluded about the increasing danger and unpleasantness of the Nazi regime. After consulting Eden, his speech also called for national, cross-party, co-operation and for industrial mobilisation to accelerate rearmament.[63] Already, in March 1935, Baldwin had with other university chancellors appealed for funds to help Jewish scholars fleeing from Germany.[64] After the *Kristallnacht* pogrom of November 1938 he assisted church and Jewish organisations aiding refugees from Central Europe by heading and broadcasting an appeal in Britain and North America for a 'Lord Baldwin Fund for Refugees'. The broadcast – made after consultation with government officials –

[61] Baldwin to J. P. L. Thomas, March 1938, and Thomas to unknown 12 April 1938, Cilcennin papers; *The Diplomatic Diaries of Oliver Harvey 1937–1940*, ed. John Harvey (1970), 115, 124, 126–31, 132, 150 (12, 25 March, 13, 22, 25–26 April, 7 June 1938); M&B pp. 1042–4.
[62] N. Chamberlain to Baldwin, 7 Dec. 1938, SB 174/19–21; Baldwin to Londonderry, 11 Nov. 1939, Londonderry papers D3099/2/17/56.
[63] *HLDeb* 110 cc. 1390–4 (4 Oct. 1938); *Nicolson Diaries* I. 375 (4 Oct. 1938). For advance sounding of party opinion, see Eden to Baldwin, 31 Sept. 1938, and J. P. L. Thomas to Fry, 3 Oct. 1938, SB 124/136–7, 140–5.
[64] *The Times*, 13 March 1935.

attracted German newspaper attacks and diplomatic protests, but it also generated one of the great British charitable responses of the early twentieth century, organised with *The Times* and aided by arrangements for donations to be made at bank and Post Office branches. In seven months the Fund raised over £522,000 (about £17 million in modern terms) from more than a million donors, and assisted, among many others, some 10,000 Jewish children.[65]

As Baldwin had planned before his ministerial retirement, his main efforts were directed towards non-party political 'education', meaning resistance to communist and fascist ideas. His earlier collected addresses were reprinted in popular forms, and his new addresses continued to be published verbatim and to receive editorial comment in the quality newspapers. He became the founding president of the National Book Association, conceived as a 'Baldwin book club' to rival – and enlarge the middle ground between – the Left and Right Book Clubs, and in order to help recruit subscribers he co-operated in Arthur Bryant's writing of a tribute to himself.[66] He remained chairman of governors of the Bonar Law Memorial College at Ashridge, and became an active president of the Association for Education in Citizenship. Well aware that in any European war Britain would need North American support, he travelled to Canada in April 1939 to lecture and broadcast across the continent on British political values, and to meet Canadian politicians and newspaper controllers.[67] In August he went to New York to evoke the shared Anglo-American commitment to freedom in a nationally broadcast address to a Congress on Education for Democracy. During the first nine months of the Second World War he made further speeches for various war-related causes, drafted King George VI's first Christmas Day broadcast to the Empire,[68] and contributed a booklet on *The*

[65] *The Times*, 9, 10 Dec. 1938, with daily subscription lists printed from 13 Dec. 1938 into January 1939, and the Fund's final report on 28 Sept. 1939; *Harvey Diplomatic Diaries*, p. 228 (14 Dec. 1938); Jones *DL* pp. 425–6 (20 Jan. 1939); A. J. Sherman, *Island Refuge. Britain and the Refugees from the Third Reich 1933–1939* (2nd edn, 1994), pp. 184–5; A. Gottlieb, *Men of Vision. Anglo-Jewry's Aid to Victims of the Nazi Regime 1933–1945* (1998), pp. 119–21; Lord Reading letter, *The Times*, 20 Dec. 1947.

[66] Bryant–Davidson correspondence, 18 April–23 June 1937, JCCD 230, 232; Bryant to Baldwin, 28 May 1937, SB 73/26.

[67] Baldwin to Tweedsmuir, 23 Jan., 6 April 1939, Buchan papers Acc. 7214 mf. 309.

[68] Hardinge to Baldwin, 29 Nov., 16 Dec. 1939, SB 178/313–14; *The Times*, 27 Dec. 1939, for the broadcast.

Englishman to a British Council series directed towards international opinion.

From autumn 1938 into early 1940 Baldwin continued to be consulted periodically by Eden, other Conservative dissidents, and Labour politicians, who sought his support for their various efforts to have the Chamberlain Cabinet reconstructed into a broad 'government of national unity'.[69] But the intensification of the war and formation of the Churchill coalition government in May 1940 made his views redundant within high politics, and produced public attacks upon his supposed responsibility for the outbreak and early defeats of the war. He continued to visit London and Cambridge several times a year for meetings of the organisations with which he remained associated, and to meet friends and former colleagues, including Churchill, Eden, Halifax, Labour leaders, and a loyal group of younger Conservative MPs. But he finally withdrew from public life, declining invitations to speak or broadcast because he did not want to risk arousing unnecessary controversy during wartime.[70] He died on 14 December 1947, aged eighty. His ashes and those of his wife were interred in the nave of Worcester Cathedral.

[69] *Harvey Diplomatic Diaries*, pp. 211, 213, 249, 256 (10, 13 Oct. 1938, 29 Jan., 22 Feb. 1939); Jones *DL* pp. 418–19 (30 Oct. 1939); Cripps to Baldwin, 13 June 1939, SB 124/153; Cripps diary, 19 June 1939, in *WSC Comp* v/iii. 1525; Baldwin to Davidson, 18 Jan. 1940, JD; M&B pp. 1053–4.
[70] Baldwin to Jones, 24 Aug. 1941, Jones papers A6/178, and to Curtis, 30 Sept. 1941, in Jones *DL* pp. 491–2. For moving accounts of Baldwin's final years, see AWB pp. 313–34, and M&B pp. 1054–72.

CHAPTER 2

Political leadership

Biographical narrative goes only a short way towards understanding political leaders, because it does not address the vital questions. What gave Baldwin his dominance? What were the sources of his power, and how did he exercise it? What *kind* of politician was he, and what constituted his 'leadership'? Political leadership is not a single, undifferentiated, activity, conducted by all its practitioners in the same manner. If its essence is the acquisition and retention of sufficient authority to command support or acquiescence, its performance is nevertheless a complicated matter. Support and acquiescence may derive from several sources, each with its own demands – Cabinet or shadow cabinet, Parliament, party organisation, or wider public groups. The materials are correspondingly various: policy, legislation, or administration; strategy or tactics; parliamentary opinion, party management, the media, sectional interests, or public attitudes. These can be used to achieve or to resist different kinds and different degrees of change. If an individual leader is to be properly understood, the specific qualities of his leadership must be identified. With Baldwin the difficulty has been that for many activities which, since 1945, have been regarded as intrinsic to successful leadership, the evidence is unfavourable, mixed, or ambiguous. The historical task is not just to reassess this evidence – the purpose of this chapter – but to consider other possible criteria for success.

I

At first sight there is much circumstantial material and contemporary statement – including comments by Baldwin himself – to support post-war charges that in the internal conduct of government or opposition he was indolent, complacent, negligent, and

indecisive. He rarely wrote or dictated political or official letters
and never, when leader, a memorandum. Nor did he annotate the
letters and memoranda he received. In Cabinet and committees
he seldom dominated discussion. He initiated few acts of state,
and did not supervise legislation. He took only spasmodic interest
in the details of policy-making, still less in those of execution and
administration. He could be reluctant even to discuss ministerial
or party matters, let alone take decisions: he might listen without
comment, suggest that a minister make up his own mind, propose
time for further consideration, or switch the conversation to books,
the countryside, any subject except politics.[1] Some successfully
interpreted his silence or laconic comments as approval, but
others were surprised and angry when their advice was later
ignored.[2] Complaints even from colleagues and friends could be
numerous and sharp. While some inferred that he was secretive,
more assumed an absence of understanding, ideas, or application.
Amery wrote of his 'molluscous inertia', Hoare of his 'slipshod,
happy-go-lucky quietude', the two Chamberlains of his being 'stu-
pid', 'useless', and 'self-centred', without 'the qualities of a leader'.[3] It seemed symptomatic that he was occasionally observed on
workdays reading novels or magazines.[4] He much enjoyed
Chequers as a weekend retreat, and took long holidays in south-
eastern France – usually a month when in government, seven
weeks after the 1929 election defeat. In private he sometimes
spoke of his 'many weaknesses as a PM', and took it for granted –
even confided to his Labour opponent – that he could not be a
good opposition leader.[5] Among friends he cheerfully declared
himself 'a lazy devil by nature'.[6]

[1] E.g. N. Chamberlain diary, 5 Oct. 1925, 30 July 1928; Jones *WD* II. 99, 194 (12 April
1927, 21 June 1929); Jones *DL* p. 57 (14 Sept. 1932); *Amery Diaries*, I. 543, II. 74–5 (7
May 1928, 25 June 1930); *The Reith Diaries*, ed. Charles Stuart (1975), p. 117 (2 March
1934); Crozier, *Off the Record*, p. 46 (12 June 1935).
[2] E.g. *Amery Diaries*, I. 367, 563–4 (7 Feb. 1924, 24, 27 Sept. 1928).
[3] *Amery Diaries*, II. 65, 197 (3 March 1930, 4 Sept. 1931); Hoare to N. Chamberlain, 17
March 1937, NC 7/11/30/74; N. Chamberlain diary, 8 June, 20 July 1929; *A. Chamberlain
Diary Letters*, pp. 252, 256, 364, 370, 422, 497, 502, 510 (29 June, 19 July 1924, 28
Feb., 12 June 1931, 18 Dec. 1932, 28 Dec. 1935, 15 March, 4 July 1936).
[4] *Parliament and Politics in the Age of Baldwin and MacDonald. The Headlam Diaries 1923–1935*,
ed. Stuart Ball (1992), p. 37 (13 Dec. 1923); *Crawford Papers*, p. 506 (27 March 1925);
Chips. The Diaries of Sir Henry Channon, ed. Robert Rhodes James (1967), p. 116 (11
March 1937); GMY p. 72.
[5] E.g. M&B p. 807; Jones *WD* II. 137–8 (17 May 1928); MacDonald diary, 7 May 1929;
N. Chamberlain to his sisters, 13 Oct. 1929, 26 Oct. 1930, NC 18/1/672, 714.
[6] Jones *WD* II. 143, 167 (13 Sept. 1928, 17 Jan. 1929); Baldwin to Margesson, 13 July
1932, Margesson papers 1/1/14.

Baldwin's 'lethargy and complacency' have become clichés,[7] but such evidence should not be accepted at face value. No modern political leader could have survived long if the unreflective conclusions drawn from it by some contemporaries and by numerous biographers and historians were substantially true. It is not just that this evidence is incomplete, and relates only to certain aspects of his leadership. If juxtaposed to other, more positive, evidence, it suggests an improbably fractured and capricious personality – according to G. M. Young, Jones, and their successors, that of a psychological misfit alternating between immobility and action, guided by 'instinct' and given to 'impulse'. This is not to deny that Baldwin was a complicated man, over-protective of his nervous constitution, conscious of difficulties when faced with decisions and so liable to procrastinate. Nor is it to pretend that he worked as hard and methodically as Neville Chamberlain or MacDonald, or with the agility and drive of Lloyd George or Churchill. But Baldwin could never have achieved what he did without resources of method, ideas, and will.

The man who described himself as 'lazy' also described himself as a simple, ordinary, English countryman with no oratorical gifts. The first self-characterisation had as little substance as the others; all projected a modesty which was partly authentic but partly intended to charm and disarm. Other evidence shows that Baldwin had an elevated conception of personal duty, was by his own lights conscientious in its performance, and found his work and responsibilities a great strain. He cannot seriously have considered himself a 'scrimshanker'.[8] He was not slothful in manner and mind. He was physically vigorous, and had a pent-up nervous energy which found release in compulsive pacings, fidgeting hands, and facial twitches.[9] His private conversation was 'often rapid and pungent', and could display an imaginative and robust sense of humour.[10] He also had the strength of a reflective if cautious mind – and the common sense to seize moments of relaxation during long, busy

---

[7] For continuing, relentless, centrality see e.g. Ball, *Baldwin and the Conservative Party*, pp. 13–14, 28, 54, 92, 134, 207.

[8] Jones *DL* p. 163 (24 Jan. 1936), and see pp. 69, 111, 267 (10 Nov. 1932, 30 May 1933, 17 Sept. 1936); Jones *WD* I. 326–7 (5 Aug. 1925). Eustace Percy, *Some Memories* (1958), pp. 131, 134–5, offers a general verdict.

[9] Jones *DL* pp. 4, 27, 207 (11 March 1931, 27 Feb. 1932, 23 May 1936); Kennet, *Self-Portrait*, p. 229 (18 Nov. 1924); AWB pp. 50–1.

[10] Jones, *Lord Baldwin*, p. 21. Cf. Jones *DL* pp. 27, 93 (27 Feb. 1932, 19 Feb. 1933); Percy, *Some Memories*, p. 192; M&B pp. 505–6.

days – together with 'the humility which admits mistakes'.[11] In the 1930s a new acquaintance familiar only with the 'mellow look' of his photographs found that in the flesh he revealed surprising 'determination and shrewdness', indeed a 'deep rustic craftiness'. A highly experienced ex-minister was struck by an unsuspected force: 'a powerful man who so far as I know has never yet put out his full strength'.[12] The former Coalition leaders, so contemptuous towards him in 1922–3, amply learnt their mistake. Lloyd George eventually judged him 'shrewder than Asquith' – a high accolade – and Churchill considered him 'the most formidable politician I have ever known'.[13]

Nor did Baldwin lack executive and administrative experience and ability, despite becoming prime minister after just two years heading government departments. He had spent twenty-five years as a large-scale employer and managing director, and four years in the administrative treadmill as Financial Secretary of the Treasury. As a businessman he had been energetic and 'crisp', with a 'quiet faculty for bossing men and things'.[14] As a departmental minister, civil servants admired his efficiency and some Cabinet colleagues thought him 'exceedingly capable and business-like'.[15] Following wartime and post-war reforms, he inherited sophisticated government and party bureaucracies which he knew how to use for their intended purposes – provision of advice and relief from unnecessary paperwork and administration. His own sense of good organisational practice led him in 1923 to admonish Cabinet colleagues with an 'ABC of business procedure', and in 1924 to initiate the creation of a shadow cabinet secretariat.[16] He was also capable of considerable decision, tenacity, and ruthlessness. Even in the Coalition Cabinet he had not really been 'silent'. Before his contribution to the Cabinet's collapse, he had intervened effectively on detailed financial, Ulster, Russian, and trade

[11] Jones *DL* p. xxx, and e.g. p. 5 (11 March 1931).
[12] Crozier, *Off the Record*, pp. 24–5 (12 June 1934); *Crawford Papers*, p. 558 (19 Feb. 1935).
[13] Jones *DL* p. 470 (5 Sept. 1940); Churchill in *The Times*, 22 May 1950. Similarly, *A. Chamberlain Diary Letters*, p. 497 (28 Dec. 1934).
[14] Dore (former works manager at Wilden) memoirs, 18 July 1948, BF; Kipling to Louisa Baldwin, undated (early 1900s), Kipling papers 11/2; AWB pp. 68, 83.
[15] AWB pp. 34–5; A. Griffith-Boscawen, *Memoirs* (1925), pp. 262–3.
[16] CP150(23), 16 March 1923; *Amery Diaries*, I. 365–6 (23–24 Jan. 1924).

matters, and wanted to threaten British retaliation against United States shipping subsidies.[17]

His statement when attacking Lloyd George at the Carlton Club meeting that 'a dynamic force is a very terrible thing' has been taken as emblematic of his politics, yet there have been few more dynamic exertions of prime-ministerial will than his pitching a reluctant Cabinet into the protectionist election just thirteen months later. He was not repelled – at least not between 1924 and 1929 – by Churchill's 'hundred-horse-power mind',[18] nor by Neville Chamberlain's relentless legislative and administrative activity, on which he came to rely during the 1930s. His chief objection to dynamic forces was rather – to complete his Carlton Club sentence – that they were 'not necessarily right'.[19] On Ireland during 1924, the political levy and coal subsidy in 1925, the General Strike, female suffrage, resistance to the 'press lords', perpetuation of the National government in 1931, Indian policy, the Abdication, and even rearmament, he acted with determination and firmness.

On close examination it becomes clear that in internal party and ministerial processes his style of leadership had more to do with choice and context than temperamental deficiency. Baldwin was a *Conservative*, in a fundamental manner which subsequent political developments have obscured. He was not reactionary or diehard, indeed in some respects – towards mass democracy, female citizenship, the Labour movement, and Empire – he was in his own party's terms modern, even progressive. But neither was he a Conservative radical, in the sense of regarding politics as primarily concerned with programmes and legislation, with a continuous exercise of state power to achieve change. In this he differed not only from several of his Conservative colleagues – let alone the Liberal and Labour members of the National government – but

---

[17] M&B p. 106; *Crawford Papers*, p. 424 (30 June 1922); Cabinets 36, 42 (22) 30 June, 3 Aug. 1922. Jones *WD* II. 23 (26 April 1926), has Baldwin denying his 'silence' (cf. I. 256). D. Dilks, *Neville Chamberlain*, vol. I (Cambridge, 1984), p. 284, reports Baldwin described in 1922 as 'disappointing' and lacking 'decision'. But the original Lloyd George–A. Chamberlain letters, 16–17 March 1922 (Lloyd George papers F/7/5/11–16) reveal these as less considered verdicts than instrumental statements arising from disagreement over a reshuffle – in which Baldwin, given his 'considerable share of good sense', was not to be demoted but moved or even *promoted*.

[18] GMY p. 106.

[19] Carlton Club speech, 19 Oct. 1922.

also from the Conservatism which has prevailed in varying forms since statism triumphed in the 1940s. True, he had been a tariff reformer before 1914, and briefly revived this form of radicalism in 1923. He was also resigned to increased legislation as 'a necessary concomitant to democracy',[20] and felt obliged by circumstances to welcome programmatic initiatives from colleagues. But he was normally 'against action for action's sake', and had little belief in state solutions *per se*.[21] 'There are some people who have a craze for making laws. They believe that human nature is going to be made better by making laws. I believe the cause is deeper.'[22] He wanted less to set the policy agenda than to limit it: to prevent or restrain many proposed changes, whether pressed by reactionaries, Liberals, or – most obviously – by Labour. Overt legislative competition with socialists, conceding their demands for state direction, was among the things he most wished to avoid.

The point is important evidentially, given that Baldwin did not leave the kind of private papers that historians have come to expect: voluminous, detailed, and chronologically precise. Instead most historical impressions – where not drawn from the disappointed or aggrieved (like Austen Chamberlain) – have been strongly influenced by the extensive diaries and letters of the Conservative radicals Amery and Neville Chamberlain and the social-democratic official Tom Jones, who in this particular were largely unsympathetic or oblivious to Baldwin's perspectives. Their testimonies must not be accepted uncritically. If the evidence from other ministers or from Baldwin's secretaries – let alone Baldwin himself – were as substantial, conventional historical understandings of Baldwin would be different. More plainly, the point has interpretative implications. For example, in social and economic matters Baldwin considered the energies and disciplines of civil society – private enterprise, personal morality, voluntary organisation – to be more effective and healthier than those of the state. So, to take a specific case, the enduring belief that Baldwin failed through negligence or lethargy to prevent the General Strike and subsequently to settle the coal dispute is dissolved once the extent

[20] Select Committee on the Hours of Meeting and Rising of the House: *Evidence* (*Parliamentary Papers* 1929–30 V. 711), q. 630 (30 April 1930).
[21] Davidson, 'Stanley Baldwin', *Cambridge Review*, 24 Jan. 1948; Jones *DL* p. xxxii.
[22] Select Committee on Procedure on Public Business, *Special Report* (*Parliamentary Papers* 1930–1, VIII. 203), q. 189 (18 Feb. 1931).

of his hostility to state participation in industrial relations is understood.[23]

To Baldwin the Conservative must be added his methods of delegation, his assiduous committee attendance, and his deliberate adoption of a synoptic view.[24] These derived partly from business experience – his father's trust in his works managers, and his own membership of company boards where chairmen presided over managing directors.[25] It derived also from a reaction begun by Bonar Law against Lloyd George's supposed subversion of the responsibilities of both individual ministers and the Cabinet,[26] especially after he abandoned tariffs – his one concession to using policy as a personal instrument – in early 1924. For him leadership did not lie in the details; these were properly matters for colleagues and officials. Even while pressing protection in autumn 1923 and feeling he had to 'lead, guide and decide all the time', he thought the policy details could wait until later.[27] He expected ministers or party spokesmen to exercise their own initiative and reach their own conclusions, under sustained Cabinet or committee scrutiny and with collective decision on important or general issues.[28]

For Baldwin political leadership was rather, in part, a matter of co-ordination, arbitration, and trouble-shooting. Here he followed his earlier business trait of being 'not much interested in how the wheels went round', but 'always deeply concerned to see that they did revolve and in supplying the lubricating oil'.[29] His biographers have emphasised his care over ministerial appointments, and ability to preserve a 'fraternal spirit' within Cabinets – not inconsiderable achievements from 1924, after the bitterness of the 1922–3 leadership splits, and again from 1931, given the mixed character of the National government.[30] Yet there were both

[23] See ch. 6 below.
[24] This is now well recognised: e.g. M&B pp. 483–7, 944; Ramsden, *Balfour and Baldwin*, pp. 266, 268.
[25] Dore to A. W. Baldwin, 16 July 1948, CUL Add. 7938; Dore memoirs, 18 July 1948, BF.
[26] R. Blake, *The Unknown Prime Minister* (1955), pp. 446, 476–7.
[27] Baldwin to his mother 27 Oct. 1923, BF; Dawson memo, Oct.–Dec. 1923, Dawson papers 70/71.
[28] E.g. Percy, *Some Memories*, p. 128; Brown in Somervell, *Baldwin*, pp. 14–15; M&B pp. 343, 482–4.
[29] Dore to A. W. Baldwin, 16 July 1948, CUL Add. 7938.
[30] M&B pp. 481–91; J. Campbell, *F. E. Smith* (1983), pp. 805–6; Simon to Tweedsmuir, 27 May 1937, Tweedsmuir papers mf MSS 308.

harder and softer edges to these qualities, which could create difficulties. Some appointments were successfully calculated for party
or public effects (for example the ex-coalitionists in 1924, and
Eden's promotions in 1935), but the choice of Inskip in 1936 damaged confidence. Cabinet harmony became a major argument
against Churchill's appointment in 1935–6. He was capable of
dangling prospects of office to suppress criticism (the Chamberlainites in 1923, and perhaps Austen Chamberlain during the
Hoare–Laval crisis) and, it appears, of securing refusals from
those he did not really want (Horne in 1924, and again Austen
Chamberlain in 1935).[31] Even given the importance of maintaining good coalition relations and even granted the policy-
making by committee, it remains surprising that during the
international and political deterioration after 1932 Baldwin did
not earlier replace a foreign secretary (Simon) he considered
'unable to take a decision', and a prime minister so obviously
entering his dotage.[32] This self-confessed 'inability to be a
butcher'[33] aggravated the embarrassments of the Hoare–Laval
crisis, as initial loyalty to Hoare gave way to him being required
to sacrifice himself to save the government.

In the conduct of government and party business he followed
another businessman's practice. While masses of incoming letters
and memoranda kept him well informed, he himself worked far
less on paper than by word of mouth – 'in constant conference'
and like 'a consulting physician', spending most of the week 'at the
beck and call of everyone for 14 hours a day'.[34] He met colleagues
individually to settle lesser matters directly, to hear their problems and proposals, to resolve disputes, and to prepare important

[31] Cowling, *Impact of Labour*, pp. 268–71, 315–25, 414. It is not certain (as is now often
assumed) that in December 1935 Baldwin hinted to Chamberlain that he might succeed
Hoare as Foreign Secretary, in order to silence criticism from him in a crucial Commons
debate on the 19th. The supposed evidence is a much later and second-hand recollection;
Chamberlain's own contemporary papers do not record such a hint. The recollection
could be a transposition from a well-documented conversation on the 20th, after the
debate, when Baldwin informed Chamberlain that Eden would be appointed. Chamberlain had had hopes, and when he reacted badly to disappointment Baldwin tried on the
following day to neutralise him by offering a lesser post, but without conviction and only
increasing his resentment: see D. Dutton, *Austen Chamberlain* (1985), pp. 316–18.

[32] *A. Chamberlain Diary Letters*, p. 445 (3 July 1933); Jones *DL* pp. 128, 175 (28 April 1934,
21 Feb. 1936), and see pp. 448, 482; M&B pp. 802–3.

[33] 1936 comment in M&B p. 807.

[34] Baldwin to his mother, 9 July, 24 Aug., 27 Oct. 1923, BF. Cf. Lord Vansittart, *The Mist
Procession* (1958), p. 353; AWB p. 11.

committee or Cabinet decisions – reconciling departmental, party, and personal interests, and often making it unnecessary for him to say much at formal meetings.[35] Beyond these ministerial consultations was a further range of private meetings, as likely to be in non-official contexts or at Chequers as in Whitehall and Westminster. Few other prime ministers have made such wide contacts among officials, imperial pro-consuls, ambassadors, bankers, businessmen, trade unionists, churchmen, cultural leaders, writers, academics, newspaper editors, Dominion statesmen, backbench MPs, and Liberal and Labour leaders.[36]

These contacts not only eased government or party business, but provided an extended range of information and opinion for a greater function, one inherent in what he called 'the essential and ultimate loneliness' of the prime ministership. For Baldwin, the political leader was distinct from even his most senior colleagues in bearing the responsibilities for strategy, broad political effects, and trying 'to look far ahead'[37] – assessing issues not just on the basis of substantive merits, departmental interests, or a balance of Conservative attitudes, but also on the possibilities existing in opposition statements, parliamentary atmosphere, tendencies within the 'public mind', and – not least – his own conception of longer-term purpose. He spoke of the need for a statesman to 'possess his soul in patience' and harden himself against 'ephemeral criticism', and of the danger of becoming 'consumed in an infinity of detail' and losing the vital 'sense of proportion, perspective and direction'.[38] Percy described this as Baldwin's concern less for particular or immediate policies than for 'the *tone* of government' and 'the middle distance'. Churchill, both more critically and less comprehendingly, called it his 'phlegmatic capacity of putting up with a score of unpleasant and even humbling

---

[35] A. Eden, *The Eden Memoirs. Full Circle* (1960), p. 269. See Cowling, *Impact of Labour*, pp. 308–11, for extensive preparations before bringing protection to the Cabinet in 1923; and Williamson, 'Safety First', pp. 393–4, for another, technically excellent, instance, on derating in 1928.

[36] The evidence lies in the Baldwin, Davidson, and Jones papers, and those of Dawson, Crawford, Henson, Weir, and many other correspondents. Insofar as a description of Baldwin as 'the most isolated man in the country' – Jones *WD* II. 100 (2 May 1927) – is not exaggeration, it indicates an exceptional condition, symptomatic of his difficulties during that year.

[37] Lord Oxford and Asquith, *Memories and Reflections*, 2 vols. (1928), II. 243–4; *OI* pp. 307–8 (8 Jan. 1927).

[38] *OI* p. 308 (8 Jan. 1927), and *TTF* p. 197 (15 Aug. 1932).

situations in order to be master of something very big at the end of a blue moon'.[39] A simpler description would be that Baldwin possessed political judgement. This was the product of long thought – his familiars described the process as 'rumination' – which came easiest to him in the detachment of Chequers or Aix-les-Bains. It was the quality he exerted against colleagues when he opposed the Macquisten Bill in 1925, was 'dictatorial' in resisting protectionist agitation in 1928,[40] supported Irwin on India in 1929 to 1931, and in 1933 identified the problem of totalitarianism. It was the difference between Amery or Neville Chamberlain drafting election manifestos, and his deciding the campaign theme. It was also a quality which his colleagues usually respected, so that however little he said in Cabinet or committee his interventions were normally decisive.

Where Baldwin created misunderstanding and sometimes got into trouble was in keeping his various advisors separate, failing to report conversations, and rarely revealing his deeper thoughts or offering private explanations. During the 1931 sterling crisis, for instance, Neville Chamberlain was shocked when Baldwin declared an interview with Bank of England directors 'a pure waste of time' – unaware that he had already been briefed by them and by American bankers.[41] At the 1932 Ottawa Conference Chamberlain, encouraged by Baldwin to believe he was running the British delegation, was taken aback when seeking to resolve a dispute to find that Baldwin had settled it two days earlier – just as it was Baldwin who, when Chamberlain and Runciman made rival resignation threats, negotiated a compromise and held the delegation together.[42] Some of his intimates noted that he gave an *'impression* of inertia' which was 'certainly not due to any lack of interest or industry', and that 'occasional flashes . . . showed him to have taken in far more than anyone would have supposed'.[43] His silences and evasions were partly the product of a native shyness and reticence in exchanges with individuals, but they were

[39] Percy, *Some Memories*, pp. 127, 131–3; Jones, *Lord Baldwin*, p. 22.

[40] *Amery Diaries*, I. 560 (1 Aug. 1928).

[41] N. to A. Chamberlain, 14 Aug. 1931, AC 39/3/26; Williamson, *National Crisis*, pp. 277, 300–1.

[42] C. Edwards, *Bruce of Melbourne* (1965), pp. 209–10; N. to I. Chamberlain, 21 Aug. 1932, NC18/1/795; Jones *DL* p. 50 (29 Aug. 1932).

[43] Dawson to Irwin, 17 June 1930, Halifax Indian papers C152/19/80 (my italics); Vansittart, *Mist Procession*, p. 445. Cf. P. J. Grigg, *Prejudice and Judgment* (1948), p. 107.

also protection against the importunate and inquisitive, avoidance of inexpedient unpleasantness and – given tensions within his party, and later the different perspectives within a coalition – an effect of caution and calculation.[44] He spoke privately of the need for 'guarding every word', and said that he 'told nobody his political ambitions and trend'.[45]

In reality Baldwin did have confidants, but although he felt close to Bridgeman and Halifax, others were not top-ranking politicians – or even politicians at all. Like other prime ministers Baldwin relaxed and corresponded most easily with younger women who lacked inconvenient public ambitions, notably Kathleen Hilton Young[46] and Joan Davidson. However, the unlikely impression from his affectionate letters to Mrs Davidson – beginning 'Little Maid' and ending 'your loving S.B.' – of closer similarity to Asquith's and Lloyd George's dalliances is dispelled by their obviously being intended to be read by her husband too.[47] The Davidsons formed an extended or second family for Baldwin, almost an adoptive son and daughter, the more so as in various ways his own family did not share his political concerns.[48] His eldest son – after appalling experiences in the Great War and the Near Eastern wars of 1920–1 – led an unsettled life, broke with his parents and publicly declared himself a socialist in 1923, and became a Labour MP from 1929 to 1931;[49] his younger son chose a business career, in 1937 rejecting invitations to succeed his father as Conservative candidate at Bewdley. Davidson was Baldwin's principal lieutenant, not just as party chairman from 1926 to 1930 but from the early 1920s onwards as his confidential fixer, sharing his higher aims yet also handling the murkier matters of organisation, patronage, and money. Baldwin also particularly

[44] Vansittart, *Mist Procession*, p. 354; AWB p. 106; 'Gentleman with a Duster' [Harold Begbie], *The Conservative Mind* (1924), p. 15.
[45] *The Diary of A. C. Benson*, ed. P. Lubbock [1926], p. 303 (2 Feb. 1924); Kennet, *Self-Portrait*, p. 233 (10 March 1925).
[46] Kennet, *Self-Portrait*, pp. 227, 229, 232–3, 244–5, 251, 253. Lady Hilton Young (later Lady Kennet) had earlier, as Kathleen Scott, been one of Asquith's confidants.
[47] Extracts from the Baldwin–Joan Dickinson/Davidson letters in *Davidson Memoirs* omit the endearments, but accurately indicate their content. An edition of these letters is in preparation.
[48] G. M. Young, and A. W. Baldwin, to Davidson, 8 March [1946], 14 Jan. 1956, JCCD 302, 310. Cf. *Davidson Memoirs*, pp. 76–84.
[49] See Oliver Baldwin, *The Questing Beast* (1932). The breach was partially repaired later: see Baldwin's warm letters to Oliver in CUL Add. 8795.

valued Tom Jones, whom he first knew as assistant Cabinet secretary, for his wide knowledge and contacts, and Geoffrey Dawson,
editor of *The Times*, for a different span of information and his
independent influence. With both Jones and Dawson, as their diaries testify, he discussed issues, tactics, personalities, and appointments with greater freedom than he felt possible or prudent with
any Cabinet colleague.

Yet even with Jones and Dawson, Baldwin clammed up or
changed the subject if they were too unsympathetic to his own
opinions, or intruded on sensitive questions.[50] Grasp of the context
is still more vital for understanding his relations with his colleagues, and for assessing their verdicts about him. Undoubtedly
there were periods when he vacillated between conflicting pressures or became exhausted and depressed, losing direction and
impetus. This was especially true for some months during 1927 –
when Salisbury thought him 'almost a pure passenger' in
Cabinet[51] – and repeatedly during mid-1936, until he was persuaded to take a long rest.[52] But more often what some interpreted
as vacancy or indecision can be shown from other evidence or later
outcomes to have been unspoken disagreement, or preference for
alternative advice. Whatever individual colleagues might have
said, it can never be presumed that Baldwin lacked cogent and
firm views of his own on issues, strategy, or persons. He could be
as sharp about them as they were about him: Horne a 'Scotch cad',
Austen Chamberlain 'the stupidest fellow he knew', Amery not
adding 'a gram to the influence of the Government', Hoare 'a
timid rabbit', Winterton 'no more use . . . than a daisy', Churchill
'denied judgment and wisdom'.[53] It is also notable that his colleagues' opinions about him fluctuated sharply between criticism
and admiration, in ways which turned less on variations in his own
performance than on how far he was receptive to their opinions.

---

[50] Baldwin consulted Dawson about protection in October 1923 (before raising it in
Cabinet), but after Dawson expressed doubts did not see him again until after the election defeat: Dawson memo, 20 Dec. 1923, Dawson papers 70/71–91. Other examples
are M&B p. 498; Jones *WD* II. 98–9 (12 April 1927); Jones *DL* pp. 56–7, 161 (14 Sept.
1932, 14 Jan. 1936).

[51] Salisbury to Irwin, 24 April 1927, Halifax Indian papers c. 152/17/209; Williamson,
'Safety First', p. 392.

[52] Jones *DL* pp. 175, 189–90, 228–30 (21 Feb., 26 April, 7, 15, 24 July 1936); M&B pp.
929–30, 960, 962–3.

[53] M&B p. 282; *Amery Diaries* I. 330 (19 June 1923); Jones *WD* II. 180 (14 April 1929);
Jones diary, 11 March 1931, 23 May 1936; Jones *DL* p. 204 (22 May 1936).

Amery and Neville Chamberlain, especially susceptible in this respect, were among his most enthusiastic supporters on protection in late 1923 yet considered him hopeless in early 1924 – failing to understand that he ignored their advice because their dogmatic protectionism had become an embarrassment to him. Those who thought Baldwin lost and incommunicative from late 1929 to early 1931 under-estimated his resistance to the 'press lords' and support for Indian constitutional reform, and his well-founded doubts about the loyalty of some of his colleagues. His self-estimation in this period was expressed when defending his position on India: 'no man is so strong as he who is not afraid to be called weak'.[54]

On party management – the Churchillian explanation for Baldwin's dominance – the record is again mixed. Against the victory over Churchill's prolonged campaign on India within the party's institutions from 1932 to 1935, can be set the major difficulties of 1930–1. Here, once more, the evidence is far from adequate. Baldwin wrote that there was 'no relationship between men so close as that of a Prime Minister and his Chief Whip',[55] yet little material relating to his two chief whips, Eyres-Monsell and Margesson, or to any other whips of this period, appears to have survived. Although there is much evidence about the Central Office and successive party chairmen, Baldwin's preference for word of mouth – aggravated, here, by the absence of any diarist – makes his contribution within the party machinery hard to detect, let alone assess. Only a few glimpses emerge. For the first Caxton Hall party meeting in 1930, Baldwin forestalled any effective attack upon himself by summoning only MPs and candidates, knowing that decisions on the leadership would also have required the presence of Conservative peers. The second Caxton Hall meeting did include the peers and was allowed to debate the leadership, but now he had Bridgeman and Neville Chamberlain to devise the tactics that minimised the rebel vote.[56]

Three things are clear. Various elements in the Conservative party, from constituency associations through the National Union

[54] *HCDeb* 247, c. 748 (26 Jan. 1931). The phrase was a quotation from Lord Minto, supplied by Minto's biographer, Buchan.
[55] Baldwin to Margesson, 30 Oct. 1935, Margesson papers 1/3/11.
[56] Baldwin to Salisbury, 23 June 1930, SB 165/303; Bridgeman–N. Chamberlain letters, 13 Oct., 1 Nov. 1930, Bridgeman papers.

to the parliamentary backbenches, were frequently unhappy with the collective leadership and especially with Baldwin. But satisfaction of party opinions was not for him the only or even the first criterion of success, and this did not supply the momentum for his leadership. The whips' office was efficient and exercised subtle supervision of the 1922 Committee and other backbench parliamentary committees, while the Central Office was a sophisticated machine which supplemented its own activities with various subsidiary or 'front' bodies, notably the mid-1930s' 'Union of Britain and India'.[57] Except on trade-union legislation in 1927 and during the 1929–31 period in opposition – when the Central Office itself briefly caved in to rank-and-file dissatisfaction with Baldwin – the party's central institutions combined sufficient responsiveness with intelligent manipulation to ensure that the leadership preserved effective control. The best that can be deduced is that party management was a collective affair conducted by Baldwin with senior colleagues, whips, and party officials; that he usually received excellent advice, and that his own contribution lay chiefly in well-timed delivery of well-pitched speeches.

II

Another basis of Baldwin's authority was the House of Commons. Tributes from across the political spectrum on his retirement and again on his death emphasised his stature as a 'great parliamentarian'. He was renowned for the amount of time he spent in the Commons, his long attendance through even private members' debates, and his approachability in the Smoking Room and Lobby. He was punctilious over the courtesies of the House, ensured that backbenchers had opportunities to speak, made himself known to new members, and endeared himself to MPs of all parties – even the communists – by words or acts of congratulation, kindness, or familiarity.[58]

For a senior politician, let alone a prime minister, such attentiveness was exceptional. Critics, then and later, thought the expla-

[57] S. Ball, 'The 1922 Committee', *Parliamentary History* 9 (1990), 129–57; Ramsden, *Balfour and Baldwin*, chs. 10–11; Seldon and Ball, *Conservative Century*, chs. 3, 5–7, 9.
[58] Baldwin to Churchill, 21 Nov. 1929, *WSC Comp* v/ii. 116; R. Bernays, *Special Correspondent* (1934), p. 115; *Nicolson Diaries*, I. 233 (19 Dec. 1935); Gallacher (communist), *HCDeb* 445, cc. 1473–4 (15 Dec. 1947); M&B pp. 491–5; Jenkins, *Baldwin*, p. 66n.

nation to be his desire to avoid other work, to escape from his papers and colleagues.[59] Part of his own explanation would have been that the prime minister was still Leader of the House – and as Lord President from 1931 to 1935 he was effectively acting Leader – to which attached a further duty of being seen to support his whips, and setting an example for his backbench MPs. For these reasons he thought it 'politic', after a morning of meetings and committees in Downing Street, to spend a further eight or nine hours each day – from around 2.30 pm to 11 pm – based in the Commons, for some of the time sitting on the government bench but also working in his room beside the chamber, reading official papers, dealing with correspondence, and conducting interviews, while remaining on instant call if needed during debates.[60] During the 1930s he was sensitive to the danger that a huge coalition majority could under inattentive leaders breed serious Conservative backbench discontent, especially while the non-Conservative MacDonald remained prime minister. The disintegration of the Lloyd George Coalition remained an awful warning.[61] Beyond that, as we shall see, he had a deep Conservative sense of the House of Commons's importance – not just from lingering traditionalism, but from belief that the onset of mass democracy and independent working-class politics gave the Commons renewed significance. His central strategic concerns included the preservation of Parliament as the ultimate focus of national tensions, because it was there, in its cloistered, institutional yet personalised forms, that these tensions could be most easily resolved or contained.

In tactical terms, Baldwin's familiarity with many MPs and the admiration and trust he commanded even among opponents – the force of his 'character' – yielded large political rewards. His uncanny ability, on numerous occasions, to sense and shape the mood of the House is well attested. He was capable of disarming

[59] Somervell, 'Politics' f. 39, Somervell papers; *The Times*, 28 May 1937; Jones, *Lord Baldwin*, p. 20; GMY pp. 57–8.
[60] Jones *WD* II. 14 (14 April 1926); Jones *DL* p. 128 (28 April 1934); *Davidson Memoirs*, p. 406 (29 Jan. 1935); Downing Street memo, 'Specimen Day of Rt. Hon. S. Baldwin', prepared for Canadian prime minister 1927, and addendum c. 1936, Mackenzie King papers, memoranda C41776–9, C108379–82.
[61] Baldwin to Lady Londonderry, 6 Nov. 1931, Londonderry papers D3099/3/15/17; Jones *DL* pp. 25, 228 (28 Jan. 1932, 7 July 1936).

the most bitter opposition, as during the 1931 crisis.[62] He had a remarkable record of commanding parliamentary speeches, notably those on the Macquisten Bill, the General Strike, India, and the Abdication. He could also achieve the rare feat of admitting and apologising for mistakes without fatal damage to his reputation, as over the scale of German rearmament and the Hoare–Laval pact.

Yet even here Baldwin's record was not consistent, and contrary testimony can be adduced. Some MPs found him aloof or inattentive.[63] During the 1924–5 session he was considered a 'strangely silent Prime Minister', taking 'less part in debate than any occupant of his office in modern times'.[64] In 1928 Neville Chamberlain complained not only that he seldom spoke, but that when 'unable to resist the demand' to participate he 'fails again and again to make the speech that is wanted'.[65] He could completely lose the House, and his first speech on the Hoare–Laval pact was nearly disastrous. The complaints were most numerous during the two periods in opposition, when he was criticised for lack of punch, ignorance of procedure, and even poor attendance.[66] Austen Chamberlain thought he had 'no House of Commons gifts', and lacked 'conspicuously one of the most necessary qualities in a parliamentarian – readiness in debate'.[67]

Again the evidence becomes so contradictory as to suggest deliberate method and purpose more than defects of temperament and application. In the Commons as in Cabinet Baldwin believed in delegation. In 1927 he provoked an uproar and suspension of proceedings by refusing Labour demands that he rather than the relevant departmental minister should reply to a debate.[68] His own preferred techniques in addressing the House were deliberate understatement; the narrative or downright tedious statement to reduce tempers; elevated digression to carry the House away from

[62] *HCDeb* 256, cc. 67, 1494. Baldwin to Reith, 31 Jan. 1940, in M&B, pp. 494–5, gives his conception of successful parliamentarianism.
[63] *Bernays Diaries*, p. 30 (16 Dec. 1932); *Channon Diaries*, p. 420 (15 Dec. 1947).
[64] *Christian World* and *British Weekly*, both 13 Aug. 1925.
[65] N. Chamberlain to Irwin, 12 Aug. 1928, Halifax Indian papers c. 152/18/114a.
[66] N. to I. Chamberlain, 11 Oct. 1930, NC 18/1/712; *Bridgeman Diaries*, pp. 236–7 (July 1930); *A. Chamberlain Diary Letters*, pp. 250–1, 367, 370 (18 April 1924, 21 March, early June 1931).
[67] A. Chamberlain, 'Stanley Baldwin', published posthumously in *The Daily Telegraph*, 28 May 1937; Ball, *Baldwin and the Conservative Party*, pp. 15, 79.
[68] *HCDeb* 210, cc. 1080–4, 1125 (17–18 Nov. 1927).

controversial particulars; humorous comment to deflate, or 'staggering candour' to disarm, criticism.[69] He made many adequate debating speeches and was good at repartee during question time, but the forensic demolition, magnifying of differences, 'thrusts, innuendos and half-truths' which constituted conventional debating styles were alien to his sense of appropriate parliamentary relationships, to the honest and amiable public personality that he wished to project, and to his broader political strategies, particularly towards the Labour party. His paradoxical advice to new MPs was 'never criticise the opposition', and he was especially concerned to avoid 'jibes' against Labour speakers.[70] In these senses, his perceived shortcomings as a Commons opposition leader were almost deliberately self-induced. But they also resulted from a belief that minority Labour governments were best left to create or suffer their own embarrassments, and that much of his work properly lay outside Parliament, in preparing public opinion for the next general election.

The striking feature about Baldwin the parliamentarian, as in much else, was his singularity. Even in his most impressive moments, he did not conform to the grand forms of parliamentary oratory. He had little physical presence, and used few deliberate gestures. He spoke in an 'ungainly' manner, and had a 'curious habit of rolling his tongue around his mouth and grimacing'.[71] He also tended to use a 'low ... voice of a kind calculated to cause despair to an elocutionist'.[72] The surprising incongruity between delivery and content was caught in some journalists' comments. One wrote that 'by a speech which has scarcely one Parliamentary quality he captivates the House and regains authority'.[73] Another – a puzzled Liberal – noted after his speech on the Macquisten Bill that he was 'probably ... the worst speaker of the Prime Ministers of the last thirty years', yet 'when he sat down he was received with tumultuous cheers'.[74] His failure to fulfil conventional expec-

---

[69] Jones *WD* II. 56, 157 (13 May 1926, 13 Nov. 1928); Jones *DL* pp. xxx, 227 (7 July 1936); *HCDeb* 220, c. 2372 (2 Aug. 1928); R. Menzies, *Afternoon Light* (1967), p. 98.

[70] Nicolson reported in annotation to Lord Somervell's copy of his brother's book, Somervell, *Baldwin* (in present author's possession); Jones *DL* p. 382 (14 Dec. 1937); and see below p. 237.

[71] *Headlam Diaries*, p. 63 (19 May 1925). Cf. *Crawford Papers*, p. 482 (21 May 1923).

[72] L. Masterman, *C. F. G. Masterman* (London, 1939), p. 355.

[73] *Christian World*, 13 Aug. 1925.

[74] Masterman, *Masterman*, p. 355.

tations about parliamentary leadership sometimes caused difficulties, yet his distinctiveness, even oddity, was also among his greatest strengths – and in all probability he knew this perfectly well.

Nevertheless, Baldwin's parliamentary position cannot alone explain his considerable reputation outside Parliament, nor his resources of support during his periods of poor parliamentary performance and criticism among Conservative MPs. Here his leadership had other novel aspects.

III

Baldwin came to political leadership during the early years not just of mass democracy, but of the modern mass media. The British Broadcasting Company was formed the day before Baldwin's success at the Carlton Club meeting in October 1922, and during the 1924 general election he made the first Conservative political broadcast. By the time he retired in 1937 the BBC had a potential audience of around 33 million, or about 70 per cent of households. With moving films already popular, in the 1920s Baldwin featured in the first party-made films and then became the first Conservative leader to appear in sound newsreels and election films, which by the mid 1930s were seen by cinema audiences of up to 20 million. Baldwin was not just a passive beneficiary of these changes. His prominence in national consciousness cannot be fully understood without appreciating how he and his advisors pioneered new forms of political communication – devices now so commonplace that their early impact is easily under-estimated. This is a further area where, contrary to some other features of his public personality, Baldwin was a consciously modern politician.[75]

Responsiveness to new media was an obvious development from familiar party connections with newspapers, and the need to reach the expanded electorate. But it was also stimulated by major changes in the press, which made the political value even of ostensibly 'Conservative' newspapers more problematical. The spread

---

[75] See Ramsden, 'Baldwin and Film', pp. 126–43, and *Appetite for Power*, pp. 253–6; S. Nicholas, 'The Construction of a National Identity. Stanley Baldwin, "Englishness" and the Mass Media', in Francis and Zweiniger–Bargielowska (eds.), *Conservatives and British Society*, pp. 127–46.

of newspaper chains and mass-circulation popular papers had created powerful proprietors – above all Beaverbrook and Rothermere – promoting a populist or 'sensational' style of political comment, more independent of party allegiance if not downright critical of the Conservative leadership. The Beaverbrook–Rothermere 'persecution of Mr. Baldwin' became one of the most striking and incalculable features of interwar politics. By October 1925 some political commentators were even asking: 'Can a political party possibly survive when the most popular newspapers which nominally support it are engaged day and night in ridiculing its leader?'[76]

Baldwin often declared his indifference to press opinion: the praise of newspapers, he would say, had no more effect upon him than their blame.[77] During his first bout of press criticism he claimed that 'I don't mind it one little bit. All in the day's work.'[78] By the 1930s this attitude had become integral to his public style: his further advice to a new MP included 'if you belong to a press cutting agency, cancel your subscription'. Even parliamentary reporters came to believe that 'never once did he court Fleet Street'.[79] After surviving Beaverbrook's and Rothermere's assaults in 1930–1, Baldwin had some cause to feel relaxed about press criticism or blandishments. Yet like other political leaders this insouciance was partly affected, as defence against the vacillations and violence of newspaper comment. He simply could not afford to ignore the press, and some attacks hurt him: he considered David Low, who drew many cartoons of him for Beaverbrook's newspapers, 'evil and malicious'.[80] His very antipathy towards the 'press lords' and distaste for 'sensational' journalism testified to great concern about the character of newspapers. Nor was he so aloof from press manipulation as he appeared to be.

Baldwin was himself a newspaper proprietor, if in a small, passive, and unpublicised manner. He inherited shares in *Berrow's Worcester Journal*, the chief Worcestershire newspaper group, which

---

[76] *The Spectator*, Oct. 1925, quoted in T. Driberg, *Beaverbrook* (1956), p. 194.

[77] Jones *WD* II. 59, 99 (14 May 1926, 2 May 1927); M&B p. 499.

[78] Baldwin to his mother, 8 Aug. 1923, BF.

[79] Lord Somervell annotation in Somervell, *Baldwin*; J. Margach, *The Abuse of Power* (1978), pp. 23, 25.

[80] A. Christiansen, *Headlines All My Life* (1961), p. 154.

his father and other local Conservatives had bought in 1894 to secure it for their party's interest.[81] Part of the function of national party leadership was to encourage such favourable newspaper control on a larger scale, and the persistent criticism from the Beaverbrook and Rothermere press made this still more imperative. His close relationship with Dawson of *The Times* has already been mentioned. Gwynne, editor of *The Morning Post*, was a long-standing friend, and in 1924 Baldwin supported the party chairman's efforts to prevent the newspaper's purchase by Rothermere.[82] As takeover battles for provincial newspapers intensified in the late 1920s, Baldwin and Davidson cultivated and assisted Rothermere's chief rivals, the Berry brothers, owners of *The Daily Telegraph* and *The Sunday Times*.[83] In early 1931 they even persuaded the Berrys to plan a new paper to challenge Beaverbrook's and Rothermere's domination of the London evening press – a proposal eventually made redundant by Baldwin's oratorical counterattack.[84] His old-fashioned faith in provincially owned newspapers, as counterweight to the 'bad' London press,[85] was manifested in his cordial relations with Mann, editor of *The Yorkshire Post*.[86] During run-ups to elections and at other critical periods Baldwin consulted most of these newspaper controllers – Dawson, Gwynne, the Berrys, Mann – and probably others.[87] Despite his criticism of Lloyd George's methods he even used, if more sparingly, that controversial prime-ministerial instrument, the honours system. Gwynne and Mann declined knighthoods, but Baldwin created his own press lords in the two Berry brothers, Camrose and Kemsley.[88]

[81] Obituary notice, *Berrows*, 20 Dec. 1947. For Alfred Baldwin's shares, 'Summary of Estate Duty Account', B/WCRO 8229/6.

[82] S. Koss, *The Rise and Fall of the Political Press in Britain*, 2 vols. (1981, 1984), II. 435–7. The Baldwin and Gwynne papers contain friendly exchanges from the early 1920s.

[83] Davidson memos, 5 May, 13 Dec. 1928, 6 March 1929, JCCD 182, 183, 186; *Davidson Memoirs*, pp. 294–5; Jones *WD* II. 181 (14 April 1929); Lord Hartwell, *William Camrose* (1992), pp. 187–8.

[84] Jones diary, 11 March 1931; *Davidson Memoirs*, pp. 359–60; Hartwell, *Camrose*, p. 170.

[85] Baldwin to Churchill, 15 May 1928, in *WSC Comp* v/i. 1287; Jones diary, 16 Nov. 1935. Contrast N. Chamberlain's attitude, in Koss, *Political Press*, II. 3.

[86] There is significant Baldwin–Mann correspondence in their respective papers. For *The Yorkshire Post* see Koss, *Political Press*, I. 7, II. 3, 387–8, 439.

[87] For Bruce, editor of *The Glasgow Herald*, recalling a summons from Baldwin in early 1930, see Riddell diary, 4 Aug. 1934.

[88] Lady Bathurst to Baldwin, 18 Feb. 1924, SB 159; Koss, *Political Press*, II. 414. Baldwin privately admitted an uneasy feeling about conferring three peerages on one family – Buckland (cr. 1926, d. 1928), Camrose (cr. 1929) and Kemsley (cr. 1936): Baldwin to Oliver Baldwin, 14 July 1938, CUL Add. 8795/33. For Camrose pressure, see *Davidson Memoirs*, pp. 296–7, and Hartwell, *Camrose*, pp. 173–4.

It was because Baldwin believed there was a 'conspiracy' by the Beaverbrook and Rothermere press to ignore his speeches that in May 1924 he gave a notorious interview to another popular newspaper, *The People*, in which he embarrassingly let slip his bitter private opinions towards the 'press lords' and former Coalition leaders.[89] Thereafter he avoided formal interviews, but he continued occasionally to give off-the-record briefings to trusted journalists, even non-Conservative ones, and he remained friendly towards parliamentary correspondents, bound by the lobby convention of discretion.[90] He also encouraged the Conservative Central Office's remarkable press office – in effect a covert news agency – which fed 230 provincial newspapers with political stories, even leading articles.[91]

If Baldwin was not much at ease with reporters, he certainly accepted the importance of visual presentation in the popular press. In May 1923 he and his wife co-operated with advisors' efforts to establish a strong image for a new prime minister with little national prominence, as they would later co-operate with his first, popular, biography.[92] On the day after his appointment family photographs appeared in the newspapers, and Baldwin himself was later photographed in the Downing Street garden and walking around Chequers. Subsequently he was projected by a vast stream of photographs: at political meetings, civic receptions, sporting events, factories, and agricultural shows; with his family at Christmas, greeting the Hunt at Chequers, on holiday in France. Often these were not casual snapshots, but the product of staged occasions. For example, during the 1923 election Tom Jones found himself captured in a now familiar image as Baldwin posed for two photographers who had specially made the long journey from London to Astley (plate 7).[93]

---

[89] Baldwin in A. Chamberlain memo., 21 May 1924, AC 14/6/3. The supposed interview appeared as the main story in *The People*, 18 May 1924. For assessments, Jones *WD* I. 280 (25 May 1924); Margach, *Abuse*, pp. 26–7.

[90] *Davidson Memoirs*, p. 170; Crozier, *Off the Record*, pp. 24–7 (12 June 1934); A. Baker, *The House is Sitting* (1958), pp. 33–5; Margach, *Abuse*, pp. 24, 27–8. For his secretaries trying to help, see *Bernays Diaries*, p. 29 (15 Dec. 1932).

[91] R. Cockett, 'The Party, Publicity and the Media', in Seldon and Ball, *Conservative Century*, pp. 549–53, with Baldwin's endorsement on p. 552.

[92] Mrs Baldwin gave interviews. Both Davidsons gave off-the-record briefings: Mrs Davidson, 'Diary of 2nd crisis in Government', JD. A. Whyte, *Stanley Baldwin* (1926), pp. 11–12, indicates an interview as one source.

[93] Jones *WD* I. 255 (25 Nov. 1923): 'the P.M. stood or walked for [the photographers] as directed'. Other photographs taken that day are in M&B plates 41–2.

In an age of rapid improvements in pictorial journalism, what a later generation would call 'photo-opportunities' were an effective way not merely of becoming 'known' to the mass electorate but of evoking useful impressions. His depiction in a variety of roles implied a man of wide sympathies, while (despite his wing collars) his very styles of dress – those variously of the modern businessman or even 'respectable mechanic',[94] of the suburbanite and the countryman, more often than the stiff formality of the traditional political elite – suggested someone 'ordinary', accessible, in touch with 'the people', and at ease with power. With similar effects, his pipe became established in public iconography. It provided a cartoonist's motif; presentations of new pipes were occasions for public merriment; his unusual choice of tobacco became a news story, and tobacco and match manufacturers used his name and image for advertisements. Sometimes he felt compelled to produce a pipe for photographers and audiences.[95] Although the story of him practising poses before a mirror is a case of retrospective malice, a supporter did comment good-humouredly after the 1923 election that he could 'forgive Baldwin his impetuosity in matters political but I can never forgive him for his vulgarity in being photographed *with intention* on the steps of 10 Downing Street with that accursed pipe in his hand!'.[96]

Despite Baldwin's and the Central Office's efforts and even after the great election victories of the 1930s, Conservative party managers remained worried about adverse newspaper coverage.[97] Yet while press criticism certainly aggravated problems of internal party management, their anxiety was excessive. Most newspapers were anti-socialist, and even the Beaverbrook and Rothermere newspapers tended to assist the party at elections – *The Daily Mail*'s publication of the 'Zinoviev letter' was only the most crude example. Nevertheless the anxieties were important, because they

[94] R. Blumenfeld, *All in a Lifetime* (1931), p. 156. See also B. Lenman, *The Eclipse of Parliament* (1992), p. 93 for his 'marvellously evocative image': he was 'born baggy'.

[95] S. Salvidge, *Salvidge of Liverpool* (1934), p. 255 (diary, Dec. 1923), and see Cannadine, 'Politics, Propaganda and Art', pp. 101–3. Among the Baldwin ephemera in Bewdley Museum there are advertisements for 'Dr White's Glasgow Presbyterian' tobacco and Swan Vestas matches.

[96] Hamilton to Hoare, 4 Jan. 1924, Templewood papers V:1. The growth of the supposed 'fact' of Baldwin practising poses can be traced back from GMY pp. 56–7, to Rowse, *End of an Epoch*, p. 84, which garbled what was simply a *speculation* in Salter, *Security*, p. 196.

[97] E.g. Stonehaven, and Ball, to Baldwin, 10 May 1934, 6 Dec. 1935, SB 48; Jones diary, 16 Nov. 1935.

added to the impulses which made a well-financed Conservative
Central Office the most productive and innovative interwar party
organisation in other forms of propaganda.[98] Baldwin was for
example able to make early use of the new electrical media. He
first spoke through microphone and loudspeakers at a party meeting in July 1924, and in the election that year could be heard by
larger audiences than had ever been possible before. Before the
next election, further improvements in relay systems enabled him
to address simultaneously several meetings scattered across different towns and counties.[99]

Baldwin's chief contribution was to become the first politician to
master radio broadcasting. When political broadcasts first began,
during the 1924 election, he was the only party leader to seek
advice from Reith, the BBC's managing director. He immediately
grasped the medium's distinctive characteristics. The audience
was large yet fragmented, consisting of small groups or individuals
usually listening at home, and a political broadcast intruded into
their evening entertainment. Many listeners were not committed
Conservatives nor even particularly interested in party disputes.
On the other hand because the BBC was a 'national' and ostensibly independent monopoly, its broadcasts implied a special
degree of authority. MacDonald as prime minister misjudged the
opportunity by being broadcast speaking to a Labour party meeting, where the platform techniques of sharp vocal modulation,
physical movement, and prolonged harangue created such a poor
radio impression that the BBC felt obliged to issue a public explanation. With the benefit of this example, three days later Baldwin
spoke sitting in a studio, reading from a short and specially written
script, and adopting an intimate, conversational, and seductively
'non-party' tone. The first-ever Conservative political broadcast
began as follows:

You have had the advantage last time of listening to an orator. I am no
orator, and I merely propose to say a few words to you and apologise
for interfering with the ordinary programme . . . I can undertake at the

[98] Ramsden, *Balfour and Baldwin*, pp. 231–3, 236; Cockett, 'Party, Publicity and the Media',
pp. 548–57; Jarvis, 'Conservatism and Class Politics', pp. 63, 73–4.
[99] Baldwin to Mrs Davidson, 30 July 1924, in *Davidson Memoirs*, p. 196; *The Times*, 28 July
1924, 3, 18, 29 Oct. 1924; 26 Jan., 28 Feb., 22 March 1929. Speaking at Leicester on
the last occasion, he was also heard at meetings in Nottingham, Northampton, Mans-
field, Retford, and Grantham.

beginning that in no case will I go on so long as to interfere with your
hearing of the Hallé concert, for I cannot imagine anyone who would
prefer to listen to a speech on politics to listening to a Hallé concert. I
am not going to waste your time with discussing the programmes of the
parties . . . I merely wish to take this opportunity of addressing a few
words to you as man to man.

In what was immediately recognised as a 'broadcasting triumph'
he dilated mainly on the nature of democracy and its responsibilities, but seamlessly developed this into assertions about Labour
'class hatred' and economic disruption before ending with a gentle
and courteous 'I thank you all for listening to me and I wish you
and everyone good-night.'[100]

Thereafter Baldwin confirmed his lead, aided during his 1924–
9 government by being asked as prime minister to broadcast to
and for the nation and the Empire on great public occasions – and
during the General Strike by becoming the first political leader to
broadcast during a national crisis. By the late 1920s he had
become what he remained until Churchill's broadcasts in 1940,
the most experienced, most respected, and most popular politician
on radio – indeed the supreme 'wireless personality'.[101] He continued to seek advice from Reith, whether on wordings or on the
social composition and circumstances of his listeners. He refined
such techniques as relaxing with small talk before broadcasts,
then speaking as if 'addressing 2 or 3 people round a fire'.
Together with radio's effect of concealing the nervous awkward-
ness of his delivery yet amplifying his rich and 'musical' voice,
public impressions of calmness, sympathy, straightforwardness,
and likeability were reinforced.[102]

Baldwin also established a rapport not just between himself and
Reith, but between his version of Conservative leadership and the
Reithian ethos of public service broadcasting, which aimed to
shape the BBC as a national, unifying, institution. This relation-

---

[100] Transcript and comment, *The Times*, 17 Oct. 1924. Cf. MacDonald's broadcast and BBC
statement, *ibid.*, 14 Oct. 1924. See also *Reith Diaries*, p. 90 (11–17 Oct. 1924); A. Briggs,
The History of Broadcasting in the United Kingdom, 4 vols. (Oxford, 1961–79), I. 271.
[101] Roberts, *Baldwin*, p. 152. Briggs, *Broadcasting*, II. 141, has estimates comparing audiences
for each of the 1935 election broadcasts.
[102] *Reith Diaries*, pp. 95, 102, 103, 120, 185 (8 May 1926, 13 and 22 April, 29 May 1929,
5 Feb. 1935, 21 Jan. 1936); J. Reith, *Into the Wind* (1949), p. 97; Robertson Scott memo,
28 Jan. 1938, CUL Add. 8770. For voice, Christiansen, *Headlines*, p. 155; Vansittart,
Mist Procession, p. 356.

ship survived its first and vital test during the General Strike, when Baldwin decided that the government should not take formal control of the BBC, while maintaining covert supervision.[103] His credibility as a 'national spokesman' – and therefore his ability to deliver political messages subliminally – was assisted by his attention to ostensibly non-partisan addresses, which enabled him to speak outside the strict quotas imposed on party-political broadcasts. For example he was broadcast commemorating Sir Walter Scott, unveiling Mrs Pankhurst's memorial, lecturing on 'Democracy', speaking to schools on 'Political Freedom', and opening a series on 'National Character'. Some of his broadcasts, especially that on King George V's death, sold well as gramophone recordings. From such a position, he could maintain his winning way with party broadcasts. 'I am afraid', he opened during the bitter 1931 election campaign, 'that you must be growing tired of listening to political talks, but I hope you will listen to me for a few moments.' It was during a broadcast on Indian policy in early 1935 that he said 'I sometimes think that, if I were not the Leader of the Conservative Party, I should like to be leader of the people who do not belong to any Party.'[104] His technique reached its perfected form in the first broadcast of the 1935 election campaign. He opened by effortlessly implying his own eminence above mere politics, yet suggesting a personal intimacy: 'I do not propose to make to you tonight the ordinary sort of fighting electioneering speech. I want to talk to you quietly before my voice is lost in the din of conflict.' He drew towards his close by simulating still more personal contact: 'I have been talking to you in your own homes as if I were with you there.'[105] According to impressions collected by Conservative party managers, such broadcasts had a considerable persuasive effect upon electors. Baldwin himself had no doubt about their impact. In retirement he observed privately: 'Give me a wireless a week before a General Election, and anybody can have the papers.'[106]

As with radio so with film, 'Baldwin was the first British poli-

---

[103] *Reith Diaries*, pp. 92–7 (1–28 May 1926); Briggs, *Broadcasting*, I. 360–84. Generally, Nicholas, 'Construction of a National Identity', pp. 138–9.
[104] Broadcasts, 22 Oct. 1931, 5 Feb. 1935.
[105] 25 Oct. 1935.
[106] Robertson Scott memo, 28 Jan. 1938, CUL Add. 8770. For party managers' views, Gower to Baldwin, 2 Nov. 1935, and G. Lloyd memo, 8 Nov. 1935, SB 203/40–1, 55–8.

tician to give the new medium . . . his serious attention.'[107] Newsreel cameras as well as newspaper photographers were present when he made himself available in Downing Street and Chequers as the new prime minister in 1923, as they would be at innumerable other prepared occasions.[108] Here, as with other forms of publicity, he was more attuned to modernity than some of his colleagues. A proposal to film Cabinet ministers at work brought a protest from a shocked Austen Chamberlain: 'Bovril does this sort of thing, but ought Baldwins to do it?'[109] Baldwin himself was largely guided by Central Office advisors, who from 1925 developed party films, cinema vans, formed good relationships with newsreel companies, and created the Conservative and Unionist Films Association. These guaranteed him not just wide exposure but the best production values (see plate 12). Once reliable film sound systems became available from 1931, he united his qualities and experience developed on radio and before cameras, and with his advisers became skilled in devising attractive short sentences or passages. They would have understood the modern technique of 'sound-bite' as much as that of 'photo-opportunities'.

Baldwin was plainly attentive to media presentation, and there is no doubt that its quality was significant in his success. No previous party leader and prime minister had been photographed, heard and 'seen live' as much as he was, nor were any of his contemporaries able to present themselves so attractively. Especially with radio and cinema audiences, an initial advantage of novelty was followed by one of long familiarity. His understanding of these qualities gave him the confidence to close important broadcasts and films with direct personal appeals: 'cannot you trust me?', 'you trusted me before, I ask you to trust me again', 'I give you my word – and I think you can trust me by now'.

Some historians go further, implying that Baldwin's dominance was produced by artifice, through media projection of his 'charac-

[107] Cockett, 'Party, Publicity and the Media', p. 559.
[108] Ramsden video compilation, 'Stanley Baldwin', item 1. For this paragraph see Ramsden, 'Baldwin and Film'; the booklet accompanying his film compilation, and T. J. Hollins, 'The Conservative Party and Film Propaganda between the Wars', *English Historical Review* 96 (1981), 359–69.
[109] A. Chamberlain to Baldwin, 23 July 1926, SB 161/45. Until overruled by Baldwin, Chamberlain had earlier refused to allow photographers to record the signing of the Locarno Treaty.

ter' – by presentation rather than political substance.[110] Yet the extent of admiration and the types of response he evoked across parties, and among the educated elites as well as the wider public, cannot just have been a propaganda construction. The medium was not the message. Even if successful use of new communication techniques is added to the other facets of Baldwin's leadership considered so far – ministerial co-ordination, political judgement, good advice on party management, and unsteady yet strong parliamentary reputation – the sum is hardly exceptional or luminescent. He was manifestly more than, in his own self-deprecating phrase, 'just a wheel-greaser'.[111] While political judgement can be a narrow matter of tactical manoeuvres, his capacity to command favourable opinion suggests the presence of a deeper purpose and an unusual ability to create receptive audiences. Nor were his performances in Parliament and on radio and film somehow independent of the things he said. It must be asked what he considered the purposes of media presentation to be, and what effects he hoped to achieve. Baldwin had other conceptions of leadership, and what he said was significant because it constituted the substance of that leadership. If these conceptions and this substance are to be understood, their sources need to be investigated.

[110] Esp. Cannadine, 'Politics, Propaganda and Art', pp. 97–107.
[111] Jones, *Lord Baldwin*, p. 22.

CHAPTER 3

Influences: business and ethics

Baldwin's 'early life' before he entered government in 1917 – his first fifty years – remains largely unknown, and what little is known has mostly been misunderstood. Here the biographical tradition has been remarkable for its lack of serious curiosity, its condescension towards non-political and non-metropolitan activities, and its perpetuation of factual errors. It consists largely of psychological assertion, which – ignoring his son's sensible cautions[1] – has become a kind of morality tale, purporting to explain Baldwin's supposed personal peculiarities and deficiencies: an inherited mixture of English 'solidity' and Celtic 'mysticism'; an only child, thereby assumed to have suffered unusual 'loneliness'; a 'secluded' and – worse, it seems – 'provincial' upbringing by an overbearing yet highly strung father and a withdrawn, psychosomatically stricken mother; a diffident, submissive, young man, conscious of disappointing his parents, forced into business against his will, and distanced from modern industrial and political realities. Parts of this are manifestly false, while other parts are contradicted by the ample family evidence of loving, proud, parents and an affectionate, contented, son. Some parts may be true, but these have dubious significance for understanding his later career. The principal assertion, that Baldwin's early life left him cripplingly reticent, might have surprised Jones, Dawson, Bridgeman, Halifax, and the Davidsons, or indeed the public audiences who heard much autobiography and personal witness from him.

Understanding will be found less in attempted revelation of Baldwin's inner 'psychology' than in the formative experiences

---

[1] AWB pp. 19, 33–5, and cf. p. 61. The psychological emphasis is evident in M&B pp. 10–13, 19, and rampant in F. Williams, *A Pattern of Rulers* (1965), pp. 5–59, and I. Taylor, *Victorian Sisters* (1987), pp. 108, 110, 190.

which have largely escaped study – his business career and moral and intellectual education, as well as his early political activities. Precisely because his emergence in 1923 was so unexpected and his triumph over defeat during 1924 so extraordinary, he himself came to feel that his early life had been a special preparation for national leadership: he 'knew that what had been instilled in his childhood had now come to life and found an outlet', and that his many years in industry had given him a rare and valuable form of political knowledge.[2] The half-truth that his family 'straddled the artistic and intellectual climate of Victorian England' must not merely be stated but investigated.[3] So too should the undoubted truth that his father was the chief influence on him, for Alfred Baldwin was himself a considerable figure yet has received little historical attention.[4]

I

The Baldwins are usually categorised simply as 'Worcestershire ironmasters', with the prime minister's self-effacing descriptions of early years in a 'backwater'[5] and his well-known 1925 evocation of the family ironworks at Wilden taken as sufficient indication of his background and business career.[6] These characterisations are at best incomplete, and if interpreted literally – to mean sequestered, modest, sluggish, antiquated, oblivious to new technology, and confined to manufacturing – they are positively misleading. Nor should Baldwin's later presentations of himself as a countryman be used to measure his attitudes towards urban commercial life. For the Baldwins were in fact among the more substantial and dynamic businessmen of the late Victorian and Edwardian periods, and contributed to a great wave of industrial modernisation. Alfred Baldwin was not just one of 'the kings of British

[2] 1925 conversation in E. Palmstierna, *Atskilliga Egenheter* (Stockholm, 1950), translated extract in Jones papers AA1/27; and see below pp. 189–90, 278. Palmstierna was Swedish ambassador in London for much of the interwar period, becoming one of Baldwin's friends.
[3] M&B p. 8.
[4] It is indicative that Alfred was listed in *Who's Who*, yet omitted from *Who was Who*. Useful accounts are A. W. Baldwin, *The MacDonald Sisters* (1960), ch. 10, and C. Baber and T. Boyns, 'Alfred Baldwin', in *DBB* I. 116–18.
[5] E.g. *OE* p. 101.
[6] Most influentially in GMY p. 22.

manufacturing industry'; he was also 'one of the most commanding figures in commerce'[7] (see table 2). These regional, metropolitan, and international business interests were extended by his son
(table 3).[8] This background not only illuminates Stanley Baldwin's
opinions about the interwar economy; it also challenges historical
stereotypes about pre-1914 British businessmen.

At least six firms at some time bore the Baldwins' family name,
and they came to own, control, or chair a further set of industrial
companies. In the late 1850s the young Alfred Baldwin had
inherited a place in three overlapping business partnerships
between his uncles, brothers, and cousins, who were important in
the wider commercial life of the upper Severn valley.[9] In the
parent firm, Baldwin, Son & Co. of Stourport, Alfred became a
managing partner in an iron-casting business which by the 1880s
'command[ed] the trade' in door hinges, exported tinned and
enamelled hollow-ware, and had created a subsidiary, the Anglo-
American Tin Stamping Co. So successful were the two companies
that when amalgamated with the West Bromwich firm of Archibald Kenrick & Sons Ltd – which had family associations with
the prime minister's future colleagues, the Chamberlains[10] – their
original names and management were retained, the Baldwins
received Kenricks shares and directorships, and Alfred for some
years chaired the enlarged Kenrick's board.[11] Stanley inherited,
and in 1920 added to, his father's shares in Kenrick's, and with
these enabled his own second son to become from the 1930s an

[7] *The Daily Chronicle* and *The Birmingham Despatch*, both 14 Feb. 1908.
[8] The following account is derived from numerous sources, but chiefly: family papers in
B/WCRO 6385, 8229; Baldwins Ltd papers, WCRO 12382; Alfred Baldwin & Co. Ltd
and Wright, Butler & Co. Ltd files, BT 31/3592/22068, 31/4018/25588; Baldwins Ltd
prospectus, 1902; Bowesfield Steel Co. Ltd papers; annual *Directory of Directors* and *Stock
Exchange Official Intelligence*. For detailed references to these and additional sources, see
Philip Williamson, 'The character of British business: the case of the Baldwin family
1820–1960', forthcoming.
[9] For involvement in the creation of the regional railway system, see G. Nabarro, *Severn
Valley Steam* (1971), pp. xv, 16, 21, 23, 44, 48–9. The three main Baldwin firms in 1880
were described in William Curzon, *The Manufacturing Industries of Worcestershire*
(Birmingham, 1881), pp. 41–5, 98–106.
[10] Three Chamberlains married four Kenricks, of whom Joseph Chamberlain's first wife
was mother to Austen, and his second mother to Neville: K. Feiling, *The Life of Neville
Chamberlain* (1947), pp. 4–6.
[11] R. A. Church, *Kenricks in Hardware. A Family Business 1791–1966* (Newton Abbot, 1969),
pp. 70, 79–80, 93–4, 110–11, 127, 133, 140–1 (on occasion mis-naming the firm as
'A & E Baldwin'). For Alfred as chairman, see *Directory of Directors*, 1887–94.

Table 2. *Alfred Baldwin (1841–1908): business interests*

A. Baldwin firms and associates
  1. *Baldwin, Son & Co.*, Stourport, established *c*.1813, ironfounders and
     (1824–65) gas suppliers: partner 1857–86
     [Became limited company 1886, and amalgamated – while retaining
     its name and own board – with no. 4 for shares worth £40,000]
  2. *Baldwin Bros.*, Stourport, established 1858, worsted spinners and (from
     1863) carpet makers at Bridgnorth: partner 1858 to ?late 1870s
     [Partnership dissolved]
  3. *Anglo-American Tin Stamping Co. Ltd*, Stourport, established 1877: director
     and sometime chairman 1877–98
     [Amalgamated 1898 with no. 4 – while retaining its name – for
     shares worth £25,000]
  3a. *Baldwin & Baldwin*, Stourport, established 1885, malleable ironfounders
     and enamel signmakers: partner
     [Merged with no. 3 before 1898]
  4. *Archibald Kenrick & Sons Ltd*, West Bromwich [amalgamating with nos. 1
     and 3]: director 1886–1908, chairman 1886–?94
  5. *E. P. & W. Baldwin*, Wolverhampton, later Wilden near Stourport,
     established 1849, tinplate and sheet-iron manufacturers: partner
     1857, proprietor 1870, later senior partner, and on incorporation,
     chairman 1898–1902
     [Worth about £20,000 in 1870. Comprising Horseley Fields Iron
     Works, Wolverhampton 1850–85; Wilden Iron Works, from 1854;
     Swindon Iron Works, near Dudley, from 1866; Falling Sands Iron
     Works, near Wilden, from 1896; and – by purchase of Knight &
     Crowther Ltd, 1901 – Cookley Iron Works, Brierley Hill, and Stour
     Vale Iron Works, near Kidderminster: company valued 1902 at
     £220,000]
  6. *Blackwall Galvanized Iron Co. Ltd*, London: director and sometime
     chairman 1883–1902
  7. *Alfred Baldwin & Co. Ltd*, Panteg, Monmouthshire, established 1886,
     tinplate and sheet metal manufacturer: chairman 1886–1902
     [Nominal capital 1886 £50,000. Acquired Albion Slope Colliery, and
     1888 Lower Sheet Mills, 1892 Pontymoile Tinplate Works and
     Phoenix Galvanizing. Co. Ltd, all Pontypool: company valued 1902
     at £350,000]
  8. *Wright, Butler & Co. Ltd*, Panteg and Swansea, established 1882, iron and
     steel manufacturers: director ?late 1880s–?1902
     [Comprising in 1902 Landore Blast Furnaces and Steel Works,
     Swansea; Elba Steel Works and Colliery, Gowerton; the Steel Works
     and Golden Vale and Oakwood Collieries, Cwm Avon; Aberbaiden
     Colliery, near Port Talbot, all Glamorganshire; and the Primitiva
     and Monges Iron Ore Mines, north Spain]
  9. *Baldwins Ltd*: chairman 1902–8
     [Amalgamating nos. 5, 6, 7, 8 and the Bryn Navigation Colliery Co.
     Ltd, Swansea: assets valued at £1 million, with share capital of
     £850,000. In 1905 acquired the goodwill of the tinned sheet
     business of S. J. Thompson & Co., Wolverhampton, and share in
     Beaufort Works Ltd, Swansea]
  10. *Port Talbot Steel Co. Ltd*: director 1906–8
     [Jointly owned by Baldwins Ltd. and Gloucester Railway Carriage &
     Wagon Co. Ltd]

Table 2. *(cont.)*

B. Other firms

11. *Aldridge Colliery Co. Ltd*, near Walsall: chairman 1874–98, director 1898–1905, chairman 1905–8
12. *Bentong Straits Tin Co.*: director 1888–91
      [Company liquidated 1891]
13. *Berrow's Worcester Journal Co. Ltd*: chairman 1894–?1908
14. *Bowesfield Steel Co. Ltd*, steel-sheet manufacturers and galvanisers, Stockton-on-Tees: chairman 1896–1904
15. *Golden River Quesnelle Co. Ltd*, London: director 1896–8
      [Gold prospecting in British Columbia; company liquidated 1901]
16. *Allen Everitt & Sons*, copper and brass tube manufacturers, Smethwick: director 1897–1905
17. *Metropolitan Bank (England and Wales) Ltd*, London: director 1898–1901, chairman 1901–8
18. *Great Western Railway*: director 1901–5, chairman 1905–8
18a. *Fishguard & Rosslare Railways & Harbour Co.*: chairman 1905–8
19. *Central Insurance Co. Ltd*, Birmingham and London: deputy-chairman 1903–5

C. Business memberships

Severn Commission
London Chamber of Commerce, from early 1880s
Iron and Steel Institute
Institute of Mechanical Engineers
Goldsmiths' Company, City of London: freeman April 1893, elected to the Livery 1897, and to Court of Assistants 1901
British Iron Trade Association: board of management 1896–?, president 1897–9

D. Shares and property

At death, estate duty account totalled £198,346, including:
a. *Shares*, total value £188,215, in Aldridge Colliery Co. Ltd; Baldwins Ltd; Bowesfield Steel Co. Ltd, Stockton; Berrows Worcester Journal Ltd; Beaufort Works Ltd, Swansea; Cynon Colliery Co. Ltd; Droitwich Canal Co; Duffryn Rhondda Colliery Co. Ltd; Allen Everitt & Sons Ltd; Gloucester Railway Carriage & Wagon Co. Ltd; Great Western Railway; Archibald Kenrick & Sons Ltd; La Magona d'Italia; Legeh Concessions Syndicate Ltd; Metropolitan Bank (England and Wales) Ltd; Parkinson & W. & B. Cowan Ltd; Standard Bank of South Africa; Union Bank of Australia
b. *Land*: 37 acres, under tenant farmer

Sources: see note 8 on p. 90; further details from obituaries in B/WCRO (owing to some discrepancies and obscurities in the sources a few details are conjectural, and there may be omissions).

Table 3. *Stanley Baldwin (1867–1947): business interests*

A. Baldwin firms

1. *E. P. & W. Baldwin*: partner 1890, and after incorporation 'governing director' 1898–1902
2. *Alfred Baldwin & Co. Ltd*: director ?*c.* 1896–1902
3. *Baldwins Ltd*: managing director responsible for Midland division 1902–17; vice-chairman 1908–17
   [1909 acquired the goodwill of the tinning business of W. P. Burnley & Co., Manchester, and erected Kings Dock Tin Plate Works; 1915 acquired Port Talbot Steel Co. Ltd, erected Margam steel works, and took share in United Tube Corporation]

B. Other directorships

4. *Gloucester Railway Carriage & Wagon Co. Ltd*: 1906–17
5. *Beaufort Works Ltd*, Swansea, tinplate makers: 1905–?
6. *Legeh Concessions Syndicate Ltd*, London: 1906–13
   [Tin prospecting in Siamese province of Legeh, and in Cornwall; company liquidated 1913]
7. *Metropolitan Bank (England and Wales)*: 1908–14
   [Bought by what became the Midland Bank]
8. *Great Western Railway*: 1908–17
   As GWR representative, also:
   8a. *Alexandra (Newport and South Wales) Docks & Railway Co.*: 1908–17
   8b. *West London Extension Railway Co.*: 1910–14
   8c. *Port Talbot Railways and Docks Co.*: 1916–17
9. *Aldridge Colliery Co.*: 1909–17
10. *South Wales Mineral Railway Co.*: 1914–17
11. *Port Talbot Steel Co.*: 1914–17
    [Baldwins Ltd became sole owners 1915]
12. *United Tube Corporation Ltd*: vice-chairman 1916–17
    [On Baldwins Ltd acquiring a financial stake]
13. *Grand Trunk Railway Co. of Canada*, London board: 1916–17
14. *Grand Trunk Pacific Railway Co.*, London board: 1916–17
[15. *Scottish Equitable Life Assurance Society*: vice-president from *c.*1926]

C. Related positions

Association of the Manufacturers of Tinned Sheets: E. P. and W. Baldwin representative from 1890, treasurer 1896–9, chairman 1899–1908, president 1909–?
Goldsmiths' Company, City of London: freeman June 1904, elected to the Livery 1907, and Court of Assistants 1915
British Iron Trade Association: member, board of management 1909–?

Note: In accordance with ministerial rules, Baldwin relinquished all his directorships in March 1917. But for no. 15 see *Directory of Directors* from 1927. Baldwin's family had long connections with the Society; vice-presidencies of such societies were honorific, their main purpose being a symbolic guarantee of their probity; and mutual insurance offices owned by the policy-holders and paying no dividends could be regarded as public institutions. Hence the position was not regarded as a 'directorship' as such, and his appointment seems to have aroused no public comment. Even so, a prime minister's name might be thought to have given a society an advantage over its rivals.
Sources: see note 8; further details from BF (again, obscurities in the sources mean some dates are conjectural).

active, reforming, director of the firm.[12] Here as in other respects, Stanley Baldwin did not conform to the claimed 'anti-industrial' pattern of 'gentrification', by which the heirs of successful manufacturers withdrew from participation in manufacturing.

Alfred Baldwin's main interest lay in an offshoot of the original family firm, E. P. & W. Baldwin. This began not in Worcestershire but in the Staffordshire Black Country, where by the late 1860s it had two works, although its main base had now become Wilden, just outside Stourport.[13] When the firm suffered financial difficulties in 1870, Alfred bought out his elder brothers and as sole proprietor made it a leading competitor in its trade (its prosperity indicated by the scale of his extensions to Wilden House: plate 2). This was the firm that Stanley Baldwin entered in July 1888, becoming a partner, initially with a one-tenth share, two years later. Overcoming the early pains of adjustment from student life to adult work, he quickly became 'quite the man of business' and 'almost as keen on it as his father'. Suggestions that he felt a persistent 'distaste for business' are conjectural – and hard to reconcile with his continuing in it for twenty-eight years – as are those that his 'faculty of independence' was especially frustrated by his father.[14] He learnt his trade properly, took a metallurgy course at Mason College, Birmingham, and was soon given important responsibilities. In autumn 1890, aged twenty-three, he visited the firm's customers in the critical North American market, and afterwards dealt personally with their orders – trying to cement their loyalty amidst mounting American protectionism. When his father accepted wider work which took him away from Wilden for prolonged periods, Stanley's responsibilities grew. From the mid

[12] Church, *Kenricks*, pp. 183, 202–3, 215–17, 240–1, 248–50. A. W. Baldwin (the 3rd Earl Baldwin) spent a period as works manager at Wilden before joining Kenricks and the boards of at least six other, mainly manufacturing, companies by 1939. Stanley also helped a cousin, Hugh Poynter (an artist's son), to become a successful Baldwins Ltd executive: Taylor, *Victorian Sisters*, pp. 189–90.

[13] All published sources incorrectly give the firm's origin as Wilden. The details in table 1 are established by 1850 partnership deed and 1854 Wilden lease, in B/WCRO 6385/5(i) and 4/iv.

[14] Harold Baldwin letters, 1888 and 1891, in AWB pp. 58–9. The claimed 'distaste' may be accurate, but the sources are questionable. Harold Baldwin's comments are ambiguous, and their complaints perhaps reflect his own feelings towards business more than Stanley's. AWB's other source, Dore, is a recollection by a man who became works manager at Wilden only after Baldwin's activities had widened well beyond those works. Windham Baldwin himself, b. 1904, as an adult knew his father only as a politician.

1890s he effectively ran the whole firm, becoming its 'governing director'[15] rather than simply his father's agent.

E. P. & W. Baldwin was one of a group of West Midlands firms using local materials to make iron, tinplates, and metal sheets, originally for the Birmingham and Black Country metal-finishing trades (plate 3). From the 1870s the industry faced major changes. Overseas sales increased rapidly, steel became an alternative to iron, and for some products zinc galvanisation competed with tinning. Together these developments made the inland location and iron ores of the West Midlands seem less favourable. Then in 1891 the chief export market for tinplate collapsed when the United States imposed the McKinley tariff, resulting in protracted sectoral depression and numerous business failures.[16] The Baldwins recognised these new realities earlier than most and reacted with unusual initiative – diversifying, re-organising, opening new markets, not merely surviving but growing. Alfred Baldwin entered the large London-based trade for galvanised products by taking control of the Blackwall Galvanized Iron Co. After closing his unprofitable Wolverhampton works, he joined the most advanced and best-located sections of flat-metal manufacture, in Monmouthshire. With J. R. Wright and Isaac Butler, pioneers in the development of Siemens steel, he formed Alfred Baldwin & Co. to open new works for tinning and galvanising steel. After the tinplate trade collapsed in 1891, their firms moved further into the still-profitable sheet trade: the Monmouth works converted from plate manufacture, the Midland works concentrated on high-quality iron sheets, and Alfred Baldwin led a syndicate to start steel-sheet manufacture in a new area, the burgeoning Cleveland iron district in north-east England. The Baldwins also followed metallurgical and technical developments closely, buying the latest machinery and rights for new processes, and taking out international patents for innovations developed in their own works.[17] In the 1870s and 1880s they confirmed their international reputation by winning awards at overseas trade fairs.

---

[15] His position as described in E. P. & W. Baldwin Ltd share ledger in B/WCRO 8229/17.

[16] W. E. Minchinton, *The British Tinplate Industry* (Oxford, 1957), ch. 2; J. C. Carr and W. Taplin, *History of the British Steel Industry* (Oxford, 1962), ch. 13; K. Warren, *The British Iron and Steel Sheet Industry Since 1840* (1970), chs. 1–7.

[17] E.g. Church, *Kenricks*, p. 133; 1864 indenture for rights to tinplate innovation, and 1895–6 Stanley Baldwin letters on patents, B/WCRO 6385/4, letter-book 8229/17.

Later, in contrast to rivals who continued to rely upon merchants for their orders, they also sought out new markets for themselves. They hired their own travelling agents within Britain and in continental Europe, and in the depth of the tinplate depression in 1897–8 Stanley Baldwin himself visited possible customers in long journeys around northern and eastern England and through Germany and Austro-Hungary.

However, Baldwins were like almost all other metal firms in one respect: their membership of defensive trade associations. Contrary to a common view of Victorian industry as highly individualistic, associations became common in most manufacturing sectors from the 1860s as firms co-operated to preserve profits, particularly in the face of mounting foreign competition.[18] As was usual, the various Baldwin firms belonged to several associations according to their different products, but they became most dominant in the Association of Tinned Sheet Manufacturers, comprising the English producers of top-quality iron sheets. For almost twenty years from 1890, and as chairman of the Association from 1899, Stanley Baldwin took a leading part in its quarterly meetings at Birmingham, fixing prices, standardising products, negotiating sales quotas, and arranging the purchase and destruction of redundant plant.[19]

The Baldwins were also prominent in another major manufacturing development – the shift, around the turn of the century, from family firms towards large-scale, 'corporate', companies.[20] Alfred Baldwin had participated in attempted combinations among West Midlands sheet-makers in 1889, and of the various Wright and Butler interests in South Wales and Monmouthshire in 1890. Thereafter, Baldwins took the lead. Stanley Baldwin supervised E. P. & W. Baldwin's conversion into a limited company in 1898, and its raising of new capital for the purchase in 1901

[18] A petty cash book in BLtd records subscriptions to the 'Tinned Plate Trade' from 1864 and an 'Ironmakers Association' in 1870; B/WCRO 6385/4 reveals periodic attempts between firms from 1869 to concert changes in wage-levels, and references to tinplate makers' associations from the 1880s; Church, *Kenricks*, records Baldwins' membership of hollow-ware makers' associations.

[19] Association of the Manufacturers of Tinned Sheets, minute books 1887–1913, BLtd; Baldwins membership indenture, 31 March 1890, and Tinned Sheet Association Letter Book 1894–1901, B/WCRO 6385/2, 8229/17.

[20] H. Macrosty, *The Trust Movement in British Industry* (1907), chs. 1–2; P. L. Payne, 'The Emergence of the Large Scale Company in Great Britain 1870–1914', *Economic History Review* 20 (1967), 519–42.

of another leading West Midlands sheet firm.[21] In the following year a great vertical and horizontal integration of Baldwin and Wright and Butler companies, from raw material extraction to semi-manufactured and manufactured products, was achieved with the formation of Baldwins Ltd. (details in table 2). Valued at £1 million (around £55 million in 1990s prices), with shares quoted on the stock exchange and employing about 4,000 persons, this was probably among the largest hundred industrial companies of the time.[22] Alfred Baldwin was the original chairman, with his son as one of four managing directors (plate 4), responsible for its Midland division and the employment of a thousand men. After Alfred's death his senior ally, J. R. Wright, became chairman, and Stanley Baldwin added the vice-chairmanship to his managing directorship.[23]

The new company became a notable success during the rest of the Edwardian period and the Great War. It had been formed amidst a new trade crisis, as cheap American and German steel imports damaged many Welsh steelworks.[24] But Baldwins' combination of steel-making with plate, sheet, and galvanisation works meant that the firm suffered less than most, steadily increased its profits, and continued to grow and modernise. It bought further shares of Black Country sheet and Glamorgan steel production, and invested in improved, larger-scale, plant – leading the industry in opening new tinplate works and a massive integrated steelworks. Alfred and Stanley Baldwin had always been more than just Worcestershire ironmasters, but in the 1900s they helped create a major manufacturing business with several regional centres and large overseas sales. Although still mainly owned by the Baldwin,

---

[21] Share certificate book 1898–1901, BLtd; summary of capital shares and shareholders list, 5 Sept. 1901, B/WCRO 8229/17. 'Swindon Works. A Historical Note' at British Steel Archives, Irthlingborough, describes him as 'directly responsible for the purchase of Knight and Crowther Ltd'.

[22] In Payne, 'Emergence of the Large-scale Company', the top 52 industrial firms in 1905 were valued at over £1.9 million (most were under £5 million). In C. Shaw, 'The Large Manufacturing Employers of 1907', *Business History* 25 (1983), the largest 100 firms have over 3,000 employers, but this excludes mineworkers. Neither lists Baldwins Ltd, but on capitalisation and total employment together it obviously qualifies among the big companies, certainly within heavy industry.

[23] Given the contemporary emphasis on seniority, Stanley, aged forty, did not expect to replace his father immediately as chairman. He thought the new appointments 'quite the proper thing': Baldwin to his mother, 1 March 1908, BF. Wright was 65, and remained chairman until 1925.

[24] See Alfred Baldwin at Baldwins Ltd annual meeting, *The Times*, 22 Oct. 1904.

Wright, and Butler families and allies, it was no longer a 'family firm' but had moved towards a recognisably modern shareholder-owned, managerial, multi-divisional, company.

The Baldwins had other, broader, business interests. There were some exotic touches, with (unsuccessful) involvement in companies prospecting for tin in South East Asia and gold in Canada. But the investments and directorships were mostly sensible developments from their original business, a diversification common among ironmasters into other metal manufacture and collieries, and into railways, banking and insurance, where their industrial and regional experience were most relevant. Nevertheless several features deserve comment (see tables 1 and 2). Far from remaining provincials, from the early 1880s the Baldwins became established in London too – at first in connection with their own export business, but later with other commercial activities – in ways which not only qualify Stanley Baldwin's later self-portrayals but also subvert interpretations of a separation in British economic life between a provincial 'industrial capitalism' and a metropolitan commercial 'gentlemanly capitalism'.[25] For the Baldwins these were not exclusive worlds. Alfred and Stanley became successively directors, and Alfred became the chairman, of both the Great Western Railway and the Metropolitan Bank. The first, by market value, employment, and operation a truly giant company, had always been London-based and was closely associated with the City's financial institutions. The second, though formed largely of amalgamated Birmingham and South Wales banks, had moved its headquarters to London and gave Alfred a seat on the Committee of London Clearing Banks. Even before they became MPs, Alfred Baldwin and Stanley Baldwin spent much of their time in London, joined London clubs and established second family homes there,[26] an arrangement eased by Baldwins Ltd opening a London office. Alfred joined the London Chamber of Commerce as early as 1885, and the integration of both father and son into the City was demonstrated by their membership of its central form of association, a livery company. When Stanley Baldwin signed a joint public letter

[25] The literature is summarised and assessed in M. Daunton, ' "Gentlemanly Capitalism" and British Industry 1820–1914', *Past and Present* 122 (1989), 119–58.
[26] Stanley Baldwin at first stayed at his father's London home, but on his death in 1908 took a house in Queen's Gate, before buying the lease on 93 Eaton Square – a fashionable and expensive address – in 1912.

protesting against the Lloyd George 'people's budget' of 1909, it was neither as an MP nor as a Midlands industrialist but as one of the 'bankers, merchants and businessmen' of London, alongside some of the biggest names in City finance.[27]

Alfred Baldwin was evidently as impressive in commercial administration as in industrial enterprise. He helped rescue the Metropolitan Bank from nearly crippling losses, and from his 'immense ability' as Great Western chairman a fellow director and Unionist Cabinet minister, Walter Long, judged that if he had concentrated on politics instead of business he might have become Chancellor of the Exchequer.[28] As within the Baldwin companies, in these wider business spheres Stanley Baldwin plainly owed much to Alfred's work and reputation. His new directorships in 1905–6 reflected their shared investments, and those of 1908–9 were inherited from his father. Some of his later directorships were as a Great Western or Baldwins Ltd representative. Even so, his appointment to so many company boards indicates that he was well regarded as a businessman in his own right. On his resignation as a Great Western director in 1917, the board expressed its 'unanimous wish' that he should return whenever he left government office.[29] These additional directorships also show that his father's death and his election to Parliament were far from bringing his withdrawal from business. Although he did invest more in property, financial trusts, and government stock, he did not adopt economic 'gentrification' by becoming simply a leisured *rentier* – let alone doing what later interpretation suggests he would have wanted, becoming an actual country gentleman. From 1902 he rented Astley Hall (plate 5) as an appropriately substantial residence for a prosperous businessman with a growing family, within easy reach of his Wilden office, but when he bought the property in 1912 he did not increase his modest hundred acres

[27] Letter in *The Times*, 15 May 1909, also signed *inter alia* by Rothschilds, Barings, Gibbs, Hambros, Glyn Mills, Goschen, and Avebury. (I am grateful to David Jarvis for this reference.)

[28] Overheard 1913 comment in AWB p. 27. For the Metropolitan Bank, W. F. Crick and J. E. Wadsworth, *A Hundred Years of Joint Stock Banking* (1936), pp. 99–106, 311, 319–20, and references to Alfred Baldwin at annual general meeting, *The Economist*, 2 Feb. 1907.

[29] Baldwin to his mother, 30 March 1917, 8 Jan. 1918, BF. Strictly, Stanley succeeded not to his father's place on the GWR Board, but to that of another deceased director: *Great Western Railway Magazine*, Nov. 1908, p. 235.

into what might properly be called a 'landed estate'.[30] Although he
no longer personally supervised production at Baldwins' Midlands
works, this was a consequence of the new structure of a large-
scale company. He remained a *managing* director, and continued
until 1917 as an active member of his various boards and to
acquire new directorships.[31] In addition to the Baldwins vice-
chairmanship, he then had a second vice-chairmanship and nine
other directorships. Even before the iron, steel, and coal boom of
the Great War, his wealth must have substantially exceeded the
almost £200,000 (about £10 million in modern prices) left by his
father.

Stanley Baldwin had, then, already enjoyed one successful – and
highly remunerative – career before he became a leading politician. This had an important effect upon his attitude towards
political life. When on entering the Coalition government in early
1917 he observed ministerial rules and resigned all his directorships, it was in a spirit of wartime service which – given his
minor office, the uncertain tenure of governments, and his fall in
income – left him undecided whether to devote himself in the long
term to 'commerce or public life'.[32] After he joined the Cabinet,
and even after he became party leader and prime minister, he
continued to regard resumption of business as a possible alternative to full-time politics[33] – and to contrast himself to the 'professional parliamentarians' who surrounded him.[34] Here was one
root of a leading Baldwin characteristic: his remarkable ability to
stand apart from, and appear to rise above, the party fray.

No one was adequately prepared for the severity and duration

[30] AWB p. 69. Some of this land was acquired, perhaps inherited, from his uncle, another
Stanley Baldwin: schedule of deeds to Solhampton estate Astley, B/WCRO 6385/1.
[31] Share ledgers and board minutes in Bowesfield Steel Co. papers record his unsuccessful
efforts in 1907–8 to gain full control of the company (he, Wright, and Butler eventually
sold their shares to Dorman Long in 1912). His London directorships of Canadian railways were acquired on his own account, not as a GWR director: Baldwin to his mother,
Ladyday 1916, BF. His pre-war appointment diaries in BF, like his father's journals,
record a busy business schedule, travelling between Wilden, Birmingham, Gloucester,
Pontypool, and Paddington, as well as attendance in the House of Commons. But M&B
pp. 25, 43, overstates his position within Baldwins Ltd, since Wright remained its active
chairman and its head office was moved from Wilden to his base at Swansea: cf. 'J. R.
Wright' in *DBB* v. 899.
[32] Baldwin to his mother, 11 Feb. 1917, BF.
[33] Baldwin to Bonar Law, 2 April 1921, in *Davidson Memoirs*, p. 104; Jones *WD* II.138 (17
May 1928); MacDonald diary, 7 May 1929; N. Chamberlain diary, 1 March 1931.
[34] Stamfordham memo, 2 June 1929, RA GV K2223/30.

of the interwar economic depression, but Baldwin certainly thought that his business career had given him relevant experience. He had known two earlier periods of bad trade, with the loss of a major foreign market in the 1890s and then foreign competition in the domestic market in the 1900s. He had seen both followed not just by recovery but by renewed growth, as supply and demand re-adjusted and new markets were opened. This may well have given him initial confidence in the restorative capacities of the mid-1920s economy. From his father's example of careful financial administration, with the firm's requirements as the first call on profits and by the creation of large reserves, he had concluded that the businesses which survived and prospered were those conducted on the most prudent financial principles[35] – and acquired a businessman's belief that these were equally appropriate for the whole nation. His pre-1914 parliamentary speeches display great concern with the preservation of investment capital from erosion by direct taxation. As Chancellor of the Exchequer in 1923 he spoke of the 'two or three rules that I always held by in bad times, and I always pulled through. They were these – cut your losses; cut down your expenditure; enter into no new commitments; and hope for the best.'[36]

Nevertheless Baldwin believed that businesses should and could respond positively to economic depression, exercising the kind of enterprise which had enabled the Baldwin firms to adjust to new conditions. As Iron Trade Association president in the 1890s his father had spoken of British disadvantages as the 'first in the field' when faced with rising American and German competition, but he also emphasised the opportunities for finding new markets and adopting new techniques. After Alfred's death, Stanley remained 'progressive'-minded within Baldwins Ltd, supporting continued improvement of plant and method.[37] It is also significant that the Baldwins were among the pioneers of large-scale industrial

---

[35] Early Baldwin ledgers in BLtd show relentless ploughing back of profits into the firms. The original Baldwins Ltd shareholders were required to apply two years' profits to plant renewal, and by 1913 the company had reserves of over £400,000. A. R. Holmes and E. Green, *Midland. 150 Years of Banking Business* (1986), pp. 126–7, records that the Metropolitan Bank acquired 'very well constructed' financial control systems.

[36] *HCDeb* 2, cc. 1147–52 (17 March 1909); 5, cc. 442–6 (19 May 1909); 31, cc. 1788–90 (9 Nov. 1911); Birmingham speech, 3 Feb. 1923.

[37] *Iron and Coal Trades Review*, 14 May 1897, 6 May 1898; A. Dore to A. W. Baldwin, 16 July 1948, CUL Add. 7938.

combination, and had long experience of collective regulation by trade associations. In the industrial 'rationalization' movement which his government encouraged in the late 1920s and in the National government's efforts in the 1930s to promote co-operation and 'self-government' among manufacturers and farmers, Baldwin would have seen a natural development of familiar and successful practices. He did not regard these as devices to cushion old-fashioned and inefficient production, but as the necessary means to build stronger units capable of matching foreign, especially American, producers who had already achieved the competitive advantages of larger scale.

Most obviously, Baldwin's industrial experience influenced his preference for tariff reform – though it is important to understand that the link was not wholly straightforward. Like other businessmen with interests spread across several sectors, the Baldwins were subject to conflicting pressures within the fiscal controversy. Nevertheless, after momentary hesitation the arguments for tariff reform arising from their own firms prevailed over the free-trade influences dominant among their City connections.[38] As early as 1898 Alfred Baldwin had argued that American and German competitiveness in tinplate and steel resulted from their tariff protection, which by allowing stronger price regulation stimulated investment in improved plant. When in 1903 he became a supporter of Joseph Chamberlain's campaign and helped form an Iron Trade Tariff Committee, his emphasis upon retaliation plainly referred to the damage inflicted on his own business by the McKinley tariff. But he also generalised from his firms' experience of growing imperial markets to argue that 'the greater question' was imperial preference, as the means 'to develop the Empire, to strengthen the Empire, and to unite the Empire'. Accordingly he subscribed to Chamberlain's Imperial Tariff Committee rather than his Tariff Reform League.[39] By the 1906 election, following the foreign dumping of steel bars in the British market, both Baldwins gave more support to domestic protection. Stanley nonethe-

[38] Kipling to A. Baldwin, 6 June 1903, Kipling papers 11/1; A. Baldwin journal, 9 June 1903. For problems in relating economic interest to fiscal attitudes, see Marrison, *British Business and Protection*; and for divisions within the Baldwins' own trade, Minchinton, *Tinplate Industry*, pp. 84–6.

[39] *Iron and Coal Trades Review*, 6 May 1898; A. Baldwin journal, 25 June, 7 July 1903; *Worcester Daily Times*, 5 Oct. 1903; J. Chamberlain to A. Baldwin, 13 Oct. 1903, CUL Add. 8812/218, and 26 Oct. 1903, B/WCRO 8229/1(iii).

less continued to present the advantages of a more consolidated Empire as an economic bloc which would enable Britain to match foreign competition, modernise its industrial structure, and restore balance between its manufacturing, agricultural, and financial sectors.[40]

II

Stanley Baldwin was unquestionably a 'big businessman'. In his maiden House of Commons speech he spoke as an hereditary industrialist – belonging to a 'class which he and his family had represented for four or five generations . . . the class once called masters, then employers of labour, and now capitalists' – and his other parliamentary speeches before the Great War were chiefly on business matters.[41] Membership of the Anti-Socialist Union council seems to complete the profile. In the timeless businessman's manner he called in 1914 for a 'business' rather than a 'political' approach to commercial and financial issues: 'I always feel that the greatest need in this House is for men with a practical business knowledge on both sides to combine to keep their Leaders in order.'[42] During the interwar years, with the name 'Baldwins' continuing to signify a great iron, steel, and coal conglomerate, contemporaries were more conscious of the prime minister's industrial associations than later biographers and historians have been. In economic position there was little to distinguish him from Lloyd George's 'businessmen in government' recruited in 1916–17, or from the Conservative businessmen who into the 1920s formed various pressure groups to espouse a 'business politics' – or, for that matter, from Neville Chamberlain, except in the bigger scale of Baldwin interests. Yet Baldwin differed a good deal from these men; indeed he contrasted himself as much to businessmen politicians as he did to professional politicians, most famously in his description of the 'hard-faced' MPs elected in 1918.[43] The difference lay in the religious, moral, and social values

[40] *Worcester Daily Times*, 3 Jan. 1906; S. Baldwin election address, 1 Jan. 1906, SB 35/2–3; *Berrows*, 1, 8, 15 Jan. 1910, 8 March 1913.

[41] *HCDeb* 4s. cxc, c. 1433 (22 June 1908), and see his further Commons speeches of 17 March, 19 May, 15 July 1909, 13 July 1911, 10 April 1913, 5 March 1914.

[42] *HCDeb* 63, cc. 2093–4 (25 June 1914).

[43] See below p. 139; also his contemptuous comments on 'plutocratic' members of the Geddes committee, in Davidson to Bonar Law, 13 Jan. 1922, Law papers 107/2/2a.

he inherited from his father, reinforced by other family influences and by his education, and then intensified by the experience of the Great War.

The Baldwins, father and son, are known to have been devout Christians, but the character of their religion requires specification. They have been classified as 'High Anglicans', but if this had been the case the prime minister would not have commanded such widespread public admiration. The identification arises from a misunderstanding. When in 1865 Alfred Baldwin wrote of himself as 'what is called an extreme High Churchman', the description was not absolute but relative – that of a former Nonconformist addressing the daughter of a Nonconformist minister – and he immediately qualified the phrase.[44] Alfred was a familiar mid-Victorian type, one who self-consciously experienced a loss of faith and with equal self-consciousness set about discovering a new faith. The extended Baldwin family were Wesleyan Methodists. Alfred's maternal grandfather had been President of the Wesleyan Conference, and he had been reared in 'the full power of [his mother's] inheritance and connexion'. But as a young man he renounced Methodism, while retaining its moral seriousness and sense of struggle against 'worldly maxims' and 'deceits of the devil'. Like another former evangelical, Gladstone, he always kept a journal accounting before God for his every waking hour. He sampled various spiritual alternatives – other forms of 'dissent', Roman Catholicism, rationalism, freemasonry – and searched for renewed belief in books.[45] By his late twenties he had settled for the Church of England, within which – at a time when earlier ecclesiastical factions were breaking down – he adopted an eclectic and deliberately open-minded position.

---

[44] A. Baldwin to Louisa Macdonald, 14 Oct. 1865, B/WCRO 8229/6(ii), partly in AWB pp. 29–30. With qualification ignored, this was glossed as 'high Anglican' in M&B p. 7, from whence the mis-identification entered other accounts. Around this time even some Nonconformist divines accepted the description 'High Churchman': see the Congregationalist R. W. Dale quoted in J. P. Parry, *Democracy and Religion. Gladstone and the Liberal Party 1867–1875* (Cambridge, 1986), p. 208 n. 59.

[45] Baldwin, *Macdonald Sisters*, pp. 184–5, 186–7; AWB pp. 29–30; A. Baldwin to Louisa Macdonald, *passim* late 1865 and early 1866, B/WCRO 8229/6(ii) (unless otherwise stated, subsequent letters to Louisa are at this location). Alfred Baldwin's journals, seven volumes 1868–1908 in B/WCRO 8229/2–5, are plainly time-accounting exercises, with concise narrative but little description or reflection. Extended prose is mostly confined to appeals to, or thanks for, God's help, or else determinations to lead a better life: see AWB pp. 30–1.

Alfred admitted high-church sympathies only 'in some points'. He was impressed by Keble's spirituality and interested in church decoration and sacred music, but disliked Anglo-Catholic liturgical practices and 'ornate ritual'. If the young Stanley Baldwin seemed 'full of High Church culture' this was just a youthful enthusiasm, soon discarded.[46] What Alfred meant was attachment to tradition and the apostolic succession, and an emphasis upon the Church of England's special role and responsibility as *the* national church.[47] Both he and his son were firm supporters of Church Establishment, and of the special place of church schools within the national educational system.

The larger influences upon Alfred Baldwin were F. D. Maurice and especially Charles Kingsley, Maurice's ally and populariser. The 'principles which [Kingsley] first spoke to my heart' became Alfred's 'mainstay'.[48] In place of his inherited evangelical sense of fundamental sin and emphasis upon atonement, Maurice and Kingsley gave Alfred a more hopeful incarnational belief – that in Christ God had revealed His presence within the world, and that in order to reveal the Kingdom of Christ on earth all men had 'to realize' in their 'daily life' the truth that 'Christ is King'.[49] From Maurice's conception that 'Christ is in every man' it followed that all men and women were naturally capable of goodness, and were members one of another; all deserved the utmost respect and had solemn obligations towards each other. Here was a source – conveyed to his son – of an ultimate trust in and love of the people, and a faith in national 'character'. From here, too, came emphasis on the great value of the individual, but equally of the great importance of social solidarity.

Maurice and Kingsley had been the leading figures of mid-Victorian Christian Socialism. This 'socialism' must not be interpreted in its subsequent senses. Although later forms of Christian Socialism became important within the Labour movement, most

<hr/>

[46] A. Baldwin to Louisa, 8 Dec. 1865, 15 April 1871; S. Baldwin at Wilden Church, *Kidderminster Shuttle*, 11 May 1940; Bernard Pares in Jones, *Lord Baldwin*, p. 4; AWB p. 48. It is noteworthy that Stanley Baldwin allowed his low-church wife to prevail in the religious education of their children: O. Baldwin, *Questing Beast*, p. 7.
[47] A. Baldwin to Louisa, 24 Dec. 1865, enthusing over Pusey's *Eirenicon*.
[48] A. Baldwin to Louisa, 26 Feb. and two undated 1866 letters, for Maurice; and 14 Oct. 1865, 2 Nov. 1865, 8 April 1866, for Kingsley.
[49] A. Baldwin to Louisa, 14 Oct. 1865. The following account of Maurice and Kingsley draws upon E. Norman, *The Victorian Christian Socialists* (Cambridge, 1987), chs. 1–3, 10.

of its early adherents were Liberals while Maurice and Kingsley themselves were hardly distinguishable from Tory paternalists. They did not question the essentials of property, political economy, the social structure, or political institutions, and they were sceptical about state action, critical of trade unions, and hostile to 'socialism' in its radical political forms. Their principal objections were to the deleterious social and moral effects of economic competition: poverty, ignorance and squalor, materialism, selfish individualism, class division, and the treatment of labourers as mere factors of production. Their aims were primarily religious and moral: on the one hand to recall the wealthy, the privileged, and employers to Christian social responsibilities, on the other to show the working population the virtues of Christian conduct, independence, and self-help. They placed special emphasis upon education and co-operation among the poorer classes, as helping to raise them to moral responsibility and fulfilment of their higher qualities: Kingsley's Christian Socialist manifesto spoke of education as making the people 'fit to be free'. Insofar as they had economic and political aims, these lay in the belief that mutual sympathy and performance of duties would create a fellowship between the classes which would improve production, raise living standards, and restore respect for social leaders and government.

Maurice's doctrines of the essential brotherhood of mankind and the organic unity of the nation led him to dislike not just class tensions but also parties and theoretical systems, as divisive and likely to manifest only partial truths. He also expressed a strong understanding of the nation as being under direct divine guidance. Alfred Baldwin similarly thought that 'a man to be a good man must be a lover of his country and hold above all things to the purity of life', and described himself as 'prouder of being one of this country than of any thing else'. Within this national community he not only drew from different schools of thought, but – as did his son – attached special importance to remaining independent of any church party or 'clique'.[50] He had, that is to say, a sense of profound unities underlying the divisions of national life. This helps to explain the cast of mind which caused Stanley

---

[50] A. Baldwin to Louisa, 20 Oct. 1865, in Baldwin, *Macdonald Sisters*, p. 187, and 14 Oct. 1865, in AWB pp. 29–30. For Stanley, see below ch. 9.

Baldwin to find significance in an unidentified passage he copied
out sometime in the early 1920s:

When you have lived longer in this world and outlived the enthusiastic
and pleasing illusions of youth, you will find your love and pity for the
race increase tenfold, your admiration and attachment to any particular
party or opinion fall away altogether ... This is the most important
lesson that a man can learn – that opinions are nothing but the mere
result of chance and temperament; that no party is on the whole better
than another; that no creed does more than shadow imperfectly forth
some one side of the truth; and it is only when you begin to see this that
you can feel that pity for mankind, that sympathy with its disappoint-
ments and follies ... Nothing but the Infinite pity is sufficient for the
infinite pathos of human life.[51]

Alfred Baldwin also learnt from Maurice and Kingsley that
religion and secular activity were not distinct spheres. The properly
Christian life was one of engagement with the ordinary everyday
world, because this was where God's purposes and the fellowship
of man would be achieved. He admired the Church of England for
being 'so practical in her teaching', and declared his own 'exal-
tation of practice over theory'. The vital point was to 'be in the
world' yet not 'of the world', by performing useful and honest work
'thoroughly and well, simply because it is your duty to do it' – not
primarily from concern for personal gain.[52] The outcome of this
effort must not, and could not, be calculated with exactness,
because all lay in the hands of a Divine Providence at once universal, national, and personal. Those who enjoyed wealth, rank,
power, or special gifts held them in stewardship from God, and
had particular obligations to serve their fellow men. Nevertheless
all honest work by all men and women, whatever their position or
abilities, was of equal value: there was as much nobility in the
labour of working people as there was in the business of their
social and intellectual superiors. Alfred's own account of the creed
he had derived from his books and thought – an expression of
practical Christian idealism – deserves extensive quotation:

I call that man worldly who forgets what I hope is the very root of all my
belief, that GOD is really and indeed the King of this earth; that He as
truly governs this England of ours as He did the Jews of old: – and then

[51] AWB p. 128.
[52] A. Baldwin to Louisa, 8, 24 Dec. 1865, undated 1866.

by forgetting this great truth, supposing GOD prospers him, he is led into imagining that his goods and riches are his own; got by his own skill. Whereas my belief is that all is GOD's. That we are holding all that we have for the advancement of His glory and the good of His Church. That every good gift comes from above and that we are bound to use every gift whatever it may be, as in His sight. That is my belief; I wish my practice were better. Hence it seems to me to follow that a man's daily labour, whatever it be if only honest, is holy; that work is what every man should do; and as to the results he should not trouble himself much about them. I mean that he should strive to do his duty in that state of life in which GOD has placed him: then whether his work be prospered with this world's increase or otherwise will matter little to him. I do not believe in anyone shirking the duties of his station, whatever it be. The thing is to do the small things, the common things if you will, of everyday life on broad principles; never letting the mind get narrowed by attention to details; but always trying to do everything well, because it is our plain duty . . . So the harm is not in riches nor in influence but in the way they are used: and if GOD does give a man either one or the other that man is to me a coward who refuses to accept them and do GOD duty thereby. If only we hold to right principles I think it matters little whether we are rich or poor.[53]

What is so striking about these and similar statements by Alfred Baldwin in the 1860s is how much of the faith, attitude, language, and teaching re-appeared fifty and more years later in the conduct and speeches of his son, the prime minister.

III

Stanley Baldwin's mother and her family expanded the range of influences upon him. Louisa Macdonald joined her husband in the Church of England, but like him she came from a strongly Wesleyan family. She was a granddaughter, daughter, and sister of Methodist ministers; one of Stanley Baldwin's uncles was President of the Wesleyan Conference in 1899. She was also sister-in-law to the painters and designers Edward Burne-Jones and Edward Poynter, and aunt to Rudyard Kipling. Through Burne-Jones the Macdonald sisters had in their formative years been closely associated with the circles of William Morris and Rossetti.[54] After her

[53] A. Baldwin to Louisa, 13 Oct. 1865, in AWB pp. 28–9.
[54] See Baldwin, *Macdonald Sisters*, and – for the information, not the judgements – Taylor, *Victorian Sisters*. Louisa and her sisters modelled for Burne-Jones pictures and inspired references in Morris's poems.

marriage Louisa remained in contact with Morris and Alfred Baldwin became a minor art patron, commissioning work from Poynter and Burne-Jones and arranging for Wilden church to be decorated with Burne-Jones and Morris stained-glass windows.[55] Stanley Baldwin did 'not remember a time when he did not know' Morris, and retained 'sacred recollections' of their last meeting in 1896. As prime minister in 1927 he subscribed to a Morris memorial hall at Kelmscott.[56]

The socialism which Morris adopted in the 1880s was commonly treated as separable from his art. The elder Baldwins retained their commissions with him and, in a 1934 centenary tribute, their son made no mention of his politics. Nevertheless Stanley Baldwin experienced some of the cultural and moral atmosphere which had generated this form of socialism. Louisa had immersed herself in Scott, Carlyle, Ruskin, and the 'medievalist' literature which had inspired Burne-Jones and Morris with an emphasis upon honour, truthfulness, social sympathy, and respect for skill and dignity among working people. Although Alfred Baldwin disliked some of the medievalism, baulked at Ruskin's economic views and rejected the criticism of industrialism, he accepted other aspects of his wife's enthusiasms.[57] At the very least their son learned that socialist beliefs could be held by admirable and intelligent people, and to that extent must not be dismissed with contempt. Aside from Morris he had the example of his aunt, Georgiana Burne-Jones, who during the time he frequently stayed with her in Sussex had become a radical member of the parish council, preaching the socialism of Ruskin and Morris to local servants and labourers.[58] When Kipling much later wrote of his cousin that 'S.B. is a Socialist at heart. It came out of the early years when he was in that sort of milieu among some of the academic socialist crowd –

[55] *The Collected Letters of William Morris*, ed. N. Kelvin, vol. 1 (Princeton, 1984), pp. 129–30, 136, 143, 149–51, 155, 162, 198–200, 203–4, 218–19, 239, 247–8; Taylor, *Victorian Sisters*, p. 106; N. Pevsner, *The Buildings of England. Worcestershire* (1968), p. 290.
[56] *TTF* pp. 180–2; Baldwin to May Morris, 6 March 1927, Bodleian Library MS Top. Oxon. c. 369/50. In 1921 Baldwin paid a thousand guineas for Burne-Jones's designs for Morris's edition of Chaucer, and donated them to the Fitzwilliam Museum: GMY p. 21. The youthful Baldwin is said to have had a romantic interest in May Morris: P. Henderson, *William Morris* (1967; 1971 edn), p. 352.
[57] A. Baldwin to Louisa, 2 Nov. 1865, Whit Monday and undated 1866.
[58] A. Thirkell, *Three Houses* (Oxford, 1931), pp. 78–9; Taylor, *Victorian Sisters*, pp. 157–8, 169, 180. Baldwin met his future wife while visiting Lady Burne-Jones at Rottingdean, and often stayed with her family there.

unconsciously but none the less effectively', he was bitter at the formation of the National government, and exaggerated the 'socialist' connection.[59] Nevertheless he expressed an element of truth, for while remaining impervious to its economic and political implications Baldwin had absorbed something of the values and language of the 'higher' ethical socialism. After reading a collection of his addresses in 1937, R. A. Butler wrote in terms strikingly similar to those of Kipling but with a more astute political conclusion: 'His springing from the milieu of intellectual socialists to lead . . . the Conservative party has been a great stroke of fortune for us.'[60]

Baldwin's family environment was full of books and literary effort. His father had a large library not just of theology but of history and fiction, and subscribed to literary as well as business reviews. His mother's clerical brother, most of her sisters, and three of her nephews published prose or verse. Her youngest sister, Edith, a strong presence in Baldwin's childhood, was among Kipling's 'earliest and most sympathetic critics'.[61] Between 1886 and 1911 Louisa herself published volumes of verse, ghost and children's stories, and four novels. Shortly after her son became prime minister for the second time she had an Armistice Day poem printed in the newspapers. None of her work is of great distinction, but by her example and teaching she nurtured in her son a feeling for words and a knowledge of English literature which helped his speeches to touch the imaginative worlds of his audiences and to evoke bonds of shared emotions.[62] She also transmitted what became another of his marked characteristics, a love of colloquial sayings and quaint anecdotes – further stimulated by the family's devotion to Dickens's novels – which, if usually taking the poorer classes for their subject, always did so with

---

[59] Kipling to H. A. Gwynne, 26 Aug. 1931, Kipling papers 15/15: see Lord Birkenhead, *Rudyard Kipling* (1978; 1980 edn), p. 341. Kipling knew something of the family environment, but only came to know the Baldwins and Burne-Joneses well after his return from India and America in 1896.

[60] Butler to Brabourne, 19 April 1937, Brabourne papers Eur F97/21, after reading *TTF*, containing Baldwin's address on Morris.

[61] *OI* p. 286; *The Letters of Rudyard Kipling*, ed. Thomas Pinney, 3 vols. and continuing (1990–), 1.9n, 38n.

[62] *OI* p. 287, and *The Times* obituary, 18 May 1925, written at her son's request. Her last poem was published in *The Morning Post*, 11 Nov. 1924. For Baldwin's sense of the popular resonances of literature, see e.g. Jones *DL*, pp. xxvi–xxvii.

admiration for popular wisdom or affectionate tolerance of human frailties.[63]

Baldwin's relationship to Kipling is often noted but never given the significance it deserves. Their political – though not personal – breach after 1930, primarily over Indian policy, has obscured their closeness during the previous three decades. Before 1914 Kipling advised the Baldwins on imperial matters, invested in Baldwin companies, and made Stanley Baldwin his children's co-trustee.[64] He helped in Stanley's early election campaigns, and in 1919 predicted that he would 'go very very far' in his ministerial career. During the 1920s he agreed with most of the Baldwin government's big decisions, including (surprisingly) that to allow Labour into office after the 1923 election. He shared Baldwin's antipathy towards Lloyd George, Beaverbrook, and 'gangster journalism', and regarded Conservative successes as largely triumphs of Baldwin's 'character and personality'.[65] Baldwin's sense of affinity with his cousin is exemplified in a conversation about the Asquith Coalition in late 1916:

I was highly pleased to find that Kipling had come to the same conclusion about the government that I had, and by the same road, after almost as long and anxious a cogitation. We have common puritan blood in us and he said a thing I have so often said and acted on. 'When you have two courses open to you and you thoroughly dislike one of them, that is the one you must choose for it is sure to be the right one.'[66]

The Kipling whom Baldwin first came to know well from 1897 was making a huge public impact with his self-appointed mission of national admonition and exhortation. In such poems as 'Recessional', 'The White Man's Burden', and 'The Lesson' he

[63] Baldwin, *Macdonald Sisters*, pp. 194–7. BF contain two volumes entitled 'Worcestershire rustic anecdotes & sayings collected by S. B.' (1891) and 'Anecdotes from Worcestershire Petty Sessions by S. B.' (1897–1901).

[64] Kipling to A. Baldwin, May 1893, 4 Sept. 1900, in *Kipling Letters* II.98–9, III.30–1, and 1900–3 letters in Kipling papers 11/1; shareholders' list, 6 Aug. 1901, B/WCRO 8229/17; Kipling to S. Baldwin, 21 July 1900, 16 Dec. 1901, Kipling papers 11/3; trusteeship details in Kipling papers 9, 10.

[65] Kipling to Louisa Baldwin, undated [early 1900s], 3 July 1919, 31 Jan. 1923, Kipling papers 11/2; Kipling–S. Baldwin letters 1904–1927, in Kipling papers 11/3, Baldwin (Sussex) papers 2/21, and SB 162/100. Their disagreement is pre-dated in C. Carrington, *Rudyard Kipling* (1955; 1970 edn), pp. 562–3, and Birkenhead, *Kipling*, p. 301, while Taylor, *Victorian Sisters*, pp. 104, 116–17, 190–1, uses the small change of family life to invent a trans-generational Baldwin–Kipling 'feud'.

[66] Baldwin to Joan Dickinson, 16 Nov. 1916, JD. See also *Kipling Letters*, III.30, 200, 324–5, 378, 407; Pearson and Kingsmill, *Talking of Dick Whittington*, pp. 188–9.

warned against complacency and arrogance, preached humility and reverence before God and past generations, and taught the pressing obligations of sacrifice and service. He also recommended an appropriate personal code. 'If –' can be read as a commentary upon how Baldwin conducted and presented his political career: calmness and patience, truthfulness and generosity, realism and fortitude, detachment and modesty; the ability to 'talk with crowds and keep your virtue', and to 'walk with Kings' without losing 'the common touch'. For Baldwin, the inspiration – or most likely, a confirmation of his own sensitivities – did not lie in Kipling's values alone, but also in the form and tone of their expression. As Nobel prize-winner and unofficial poet laureate, Kipling demonstrated how a compelling phrase or prophetic utterance could more profoundly crystallise the public mind than any political programme and party catchword. Baldwin denied that he was 'a rhetorician or an orator', claiming to have been cured of attachment to 'fine language' by Froude's dictum that 'oratory is the harlot of the arts'.[67] But this was disingenuous, indeed the denial was itself a rhetorical strategy. From the Carlton Club meeting onwards Baldwin displayed a similar facility to Kipling's for impressive and evocative statement. Kipling polished some of his early addresses – even, once, a diplomatic statement[68] – and supplied him with his famous rebuke to the 'press lords' in 1931. Baldwin occasionally borrowed lines or metaphors from Kipling's verse and stories – allusions with considerable resonance among audiences still close to those works. Nevertheless, Baldwin himself clearly possessed that 'literary creativity which lies at the heart of politics'.[69] However ironically intended, it is significant that Kipling could observe that 'the real pen in our family is Stan's'.[70]

There was a further inspiration or confirmation. The Baldwins had a well-developed love of nature as well as the simple virtues

---

[67] *OE* pp. 93, 155.

[68] Davidson memo, 12 July 1923, JCCD 153, records Kipling adding a prologue to a Baldwin re-draft of an important note to the French government.

[69] J. Vincent, *Disraeli* (Oxford, 1990), p. 46. Some of Baldwin's allusions to Kipling's poems and stories will be noted in later chapters. There were obvious similarities between Baldwin's and Kipling's collected addresses: see the latter's *A Book of Words* (1928), with what would later be considered Baldwinesque sentiments on pp. 18–19, 36–7, 177–87.

[70] *Davidson Memoirs*, p. 173: Kipling added that he 'spoke such good English because he had absorbed in his youth the best prose and poetry which the country produced'. For Baldwin's own comments on his literary ability, Jones *WD* II.13 (14 April 1926).

of the common man; and in the early 1900s, after long periods overseas, Kipling also 'discovered England' and English rural working people, to great literary effect. In numerous stories and verses he used the countryside and rural life to evoke a particular conception of England and the English character, one that appealed to immemorial values and ancestral roots as forces against present social, political, and imperial dangers. In *Puck of Pook's Hill* and *Rewards and Fairies* the past literally sprang from the landscape, as a device to teach the continuity and stability of the English nation, the instinctive skill of its leaders in internal reconciliation and external resistance, and – a persistent theme – the inherited wisdom, independence, and resourcefulness of its common people. Elsewhere, Kipling used the English countryside to represent authenticity and tranquillity, an antidote to the shallow chatter of urban intellectuals and a restorative for the 'fevered breath and festered soul'. 'Prophets at Home' and 'Sussex' identified spiritual health with attachment to one's locality or county, while 'An Habitation Enforced' – Baldwin's favourite Kipling story, which he read 'over and over again' – invested 'home' with great power and reach.[71] Kipling's Sussex, Baldwin's Worcestershire, and each man's 'England' are hardly distinguishable, and had much the same meanings and purposes.[72]

IV

Baldwin's biographers have shown little interest in his education, except to search for supposed psychological clues. It has been characterised as 'blighted' by punishment at Harrow for juvenile pornography, leading to his withdrawal into 'indolence' and ending in failure at Cambridge, which in further disappointing his father destroyed his self-confidence. Although these accounts invariably contain factual inaccuracies,[73] there may be some truth in them.

---

[71] Jones, *WD* II.13 (14 April 1926); Jones *DL* p. 165 (24 Jan. 1935). For 'An Habitation Enforced', see *Actions and Reactions* (1909).
[72] The similarities are noted in Ramsden, *Balfour and Baldwin*, p. 213, but the interpretation put on both seems to me to be misleading.
[73] The biographies place much interpretative weight on these matters: see AWB pp. 39–48; M&B pp. 14–18, 20; Hyde, *Baldwin*, pp. 16–22; Young, *Baldwin*, pp. 5–7; Jenkins, *Baldwin*, pp. 34–6. Yet the factual basis is shaky. The decision to send Baldwin to Harrow rather than Eton (a supposed cause of unhappiness) was not made at the last moment, but three years earlier: A. Baldwin to Louisa, 1 Nov. 1878. The Harrow headmaster, Butler (who, after punishing Baldwin, is said to have remained a discouraging presence

After Baldwin became a public figure he himself spoke of having wasted his educational opportunities. Even so, the conclusions drawn from these episodes are exaggerated. The evidence could as easily suggest that neither his teachers, nor his father, nor he himself considered that he had been disgraced. In taking the Honours degree he was more ambitious than the many students who still took only the ordinary pass degree, while some of his teachers disliked the emphasis placed upon examination results – and clearly an 1880s degree should not be judged by modern academic standards.[74] Baldwin also retained strong attachments to both Harrow and Cambridge, becoming a Governor of the first and Chancellor of the second. Over fifty years later he did recall that his father had written 'I hope you won't get a Third in life', but if this did occur the context might have been that of encouragement more than rebuke. Certainly his father's surviving letter on his twenty-first birthday was one that any son would be proud to receive, and the very point of Baldwin's story was that he had *not* got a 'Third in life'.[75]

The important historical question lies elsewhere: in what Baldwin might have gained from his education. For those Victorian sons who like him were not hoping to enter the civil professions,

for him) became Master of Trinity College in his second year, not his first or second term. Descriptions of his two or even three Tripos (Honours) examinations at Cambridge, and a change from Classics to History, are nonsensical. He read History throughout, but like all Cambridge undergraduates had in his first term to take the two-part 'Previous', the qualifying examination in classics, scripture, and mathematics, in which he obtained first and second classes. His next *university* examination was the final-year Historical Tripos (not divided into two parts until 1899), in which he was placed in the third class. But this was hardly the shock his biographers have assumed, since he had already obtained a third in his second-year *college* history examination. Details in *The Cambridge University Reporter*, 1885–8.

[74] The emphasis in A. Baldwin journal, 16 June 1888, is that his son had passed the Tripos; the third class is reported without comment. The following entries – on a five-day Cambridge visit to attend the degree ceremony and meet his son's friends and teachers, then a four-week family holiday in France – contain no hint of disappointment. To put his degree in perspective: in the 1880s the third class was the most common Historical Tripos result (aside from those taking just the lesser Ordinary degree). For scepticism about examinations, see D. Wormell, *Sir John Seeley and the Uses of History* (Cambridge, 1980), pp. 55–6, 73, 113–17; A. Cunningham, *William Cunningham* (1950), pp. 30, 71.

[75] Jones *DL* pp. 154–5 (18 Sept. 1935), repeated in Jones, *Lord Baldwin*, p. 4 – the apparent source for GMY p. 21, and AWB p. 48. If there was such a letter it has not survived. AWB pp. 44, 53–4, 61, give Alfred's contemporary verdict that the Harrow incident was 'much exaggerated' and was 'now over and done with', together with his remarkable 21st birthday letter and the 1891 journal comment that Stanley was 'a satisfactory son in every way'.

the main purpose of public school and university was less a 'good degree' than acquisition of the attributes and connections of a 'gentleman'. Contrary to much historical literature about 'gentlemanly values', the Baldwins did not regard these as a distraction or escape from industrial values, but as perfectly complementary to them. Their expectations were of a successful business career providing sufficient financial independence to become also a 'public man' – to participate in public life – while remaining 'in all things a Christian gentleman'.[76] At the minimum, Baldwin's education supplied the self-assurance, codes, and acquaintances giving passage from provincial wealth into the governing elites. Two friends from this time, Sanders and Bridgeman, were significant for him as Unionist party whips before 1914, then as fellow 1922 party rebels and Cabinet ministers. But there was a further aspect. His time at Harrow (1881–5) and Trinity College, Cambridge (1885–8) coincided with important moral and intellectual developments which gave more articulate form to what he absorbed at home, and immersed him in a distinctive version of national culture.

The post-Arnoldian public schools and reformed universities promoted a new and arresting ethos, drawn from the now mainstream Christian Socialist and Broad Church influences, and reinvigorated in the mid 1880s by the conclusions of philosophical Idealism, the cults of T. H. Green and Arnold Toynbee, and the revelations of Andrew Mearns's *Bitter Cry of Outcast London*.[77] They taught a social Christianity and an organic conception of society, which demanded active citizenship, disinterested commitment to public service, and an obligation to help and seek fellowship with the poor – chiefly manifested in the wave of university 'settlements' in London slums. Baldwin may not have read hard for his examinations or spoken at debating societies, but he was serious about such non-curricular concerns. During his first week in Cambridge he expressed a wish to take Holy Orders. If his father

---

[76] A. Baldwin to S. Baldwin [Aug. 1888], in AWB pp. 53–4; Jones *DL* p. 539 (5 Jan. 1946). Stanley gave his own second son the same kind of education (though at Eton, not Harrow), before starting him in industry.

[77] If Alfred Baldwin's decision to send his son to Harrow was indeed influenced by admiration for its headmaster, this was because Butler was a follower of Maurice and Kingsley, and part of this movement. He was a considerable public figure: see E. Graham, *The Harrow Life of Henry Montagu Butler* (1920), and J. R. M. Butler, *Henry Montagu Butler* (1925).

dissuaded him, the underlying motives were certainly not discouraged. He was active in his college's Sunday Essay Society, and spoke on church reform. He spent an Easter at, and took his father to visit, the Trinity College mission at St George's, Camberwell.[78] Four decades and more later he still invoked this spirit of the 1880s, presented as a practical ethic not just for privileged students but for all social classes.

To claim that Baldwin's political attitudes were generated by books and lectures – still more that he had some intellectualised 'philosophy', or expected policy to be determined by 'theory' – would plainly be absurd. Yet it is also implausible that he remained untouched by the prevailing ideas and idioms of his student years. His later public disdain for the 'intelligentsia' should be seen for what it was: political and moral criticism of Liberal, Labour, and secularised intellectuals – not dismissal of intelligence and learning in themselves. Engagement with books became one of his most familiar and most admired characteristics. His deployment of English literature has already been mentioned. His school Greek and Latin nurtured an enduring love for classical texts which, used in his addresses to suggest his resources of clarity and wisdom, also gave his public character an attractive scholarly patina which impressed even academics and *literati*, including G. M. Young.[79] With their further references to Carlyle, Ruskin, Froude, Morley, Lecky, Arnold, and other Victorian sages, these addresses displayed a sense of historical and ethical works as constituents of the 'public mind', one which he sustained through his political career by continued reading of serious books.[80] If what he read and heard at Cambridge did not give him an intellectual approach to politics, it helped shape his attitudes and language; and if what he acquired was in late-Victorian terms unremarkable, even commonplace, this in itself might later be a form of power,

---

[78] AWB p. 48, and A. Baldwin journal, 21 July 1888. The Sunday Essay Society, formed 1884, was addressed by Baldwin in his own rooms on 6 Nov. 1887. I am grateful to Jonathan Smith of Trinity College Library for details on the Society.
[79] See esp. Classics Association address, *OE* pp. 99–118, which produced press comment along the lines of 'our Scholar Prime Minister' (*The Spectator*, 16 Jan. 1926). For admiration, Gosse and Gilbert Murray to Baldwin, 9, 11 Jan. 1926, SB 161/107–8, 182; GMY pp. 20, 107–8; Young to Murray, 26 Jan., 5 March 1948, Murray papers 99/8–9, 45.
[80] Some addresses, notably his Edinburgh Rectorial, *OE* pp. 75–92, with its footnotes, betray assistance from speech-writers, but for his own reading see numerous references in Jones diaries, e.g. *DL* pp. 29, 33, 124, 191, 314.

in enabling what he said to resonate across party boundaries. In fact the particular context was significant. Baldwin went to the Trinity College of William Cunningham, author of *The Growth of English Industry and Commerce* (1882) and to the wider History school headed by J. R. Seeley, author of *The Expansion of England* (1883) and *Introduction to Political Science* – lectures initially delivered to Baldwin's first-year classes. And he was there as Cambridge academics responded anxiously and noisily to the 1884 Parliamentary Reform Act and 1886 Irish Home Rule crisis.

Largely under Seeley's influence, the Cambridge history syllabus was designed as a training not so much in historical scholarship as in citizenship and statesmanship.[81] It therefore included not just British and European history, but political science, law, and economics – though studied by historical not abstract methods, in keeping with the practical purpose. Even the strictly historical courses assumed that understanding the past had moral and political significance for the resolution of future national issues. In its central constitutional and institutional aspects, the most influential texts were Stubbs and Maine: the latter, Baldwin recalled, had 'complete' authority during his Cambridge years.[82] The syllabus taught British exceptionalism and superiority in the achievement of liberty, stability, and unity, an achievement derived from an island location, sturdy national character, ancient traditions of self-government and voluntary association, excellent institutions, and responsible leaders who trusted in experience and exercised patience, all sustained by a manifest Divine dispensation. It presented the British constitution as the foundation of national greatness and prosperity, and the source of those evolving individual freedoms and opportunities described in Maine's 'movement from Status to Contract' – a phrase Baldwin later used when commending Conservative over socialist attitudes towards the

---

[81] The most recent examinations of 1880s Cambridge historical and political studies is R. Soffer, *Discipline and Power. The University, History and the Making of an English Elite 1870–1930* (Stanford, 1994).

[82] F. Pakenham, *Born to Believe* (1953), pp. 71–2, quoted and commented upon in Ramsden, *Balfour and Baldwin*, pp. ix–x. Both writers take Baldwin's further comments as evidence of his chronic haziness and innocence of intellectual influences. Yet it is hardly surprising that after fifty years he recollected Maine's thought in its conventional aphoristic form (and got it right), and both fail to spot the characteristic Baldwin tease. Nor is it surprising that a shy man should be disconcerted by cross-examination from the future Lord Longford.

working population.[83] It valued parliamentarianism also as the guarantee for peaceful adaptation, because it sustained a fundamental national consensus by absorbing and accommodating internal differences, and preserved the vital balance between stability and change.

Baldwin's later answer to a question from his children on the English Civil War indicates much about the history he had absorbed, and its connection with his larger political values. He would, he said, have supported neither the Cavaliers nor the Roundheads, but 'would have been like the squire who, aloof from the trouble, drove his hounds between the opposing armies . . . and passed on to his hunting'.[84] Wisdom did not lie in the extremes of ideological preoccupation but in a *via media* and a detachment preserved by respect for the habitual and the practical. Yet if this late-Victorian account of the British past was one of steady progress, it also taught that stagnation or worse could follow if the delicate balances were disturbed. This seemed to be occurring during Baldwin's Cambridge years, with political power extended to the uneducated masses and national policy hijacked by radical enthusiasm. In the aftermath of the 1884 extension of the parliamentary franchise, Maine's *Popular Government* described democracy – in terms which Baldwin would use after the 1918 enfranchisement – as 'by far the most difficult' form of government. It had no necessary connection with progress and was characterised by 'great fragility', because excessive popular expectations and the evils of demagoguery produced a persistent tendency towards despotism. When the Reform Act was followed by the supposed threat to national unity and imperial greatness created by the Irish Home Rule issue, many Cambridge professors and Trinity Fellows who had not, like Cunningham, already become Conservatives, now publicly declared for Unionism – initially a Liberal Unionism, but nevertheless becoming Conservative allies.[85]

Baldwin could never have doubted that Unionism and Conservatism had secure intellectual and academic credentials. In 1927 he spoke of Seeley and Cunningham as two of the creators of 'modern

[83] Swansea, 30 Oct. 1923; Junior Imperial League, 3 May 1924.
[84] O. Baldwin, *Questing Beast*, p. 9.
[85] H. Maine, *Popular Government* (1885) pp. x, 20–34, 70, 87–8, 97, 106–9, 144–53, 188; J. Roach, 'Liberalism and the Victorian Intelligentsia', *Cambridge Historical Journal* 13 (1957), pp. 58, 80.

Toryism'. As a general statement this has more substance than most Conservative party historians have recognised, and it undoubtedly expressed an aspect of his own experience. Seeley's *Expansion of England* had, Baldwin said, established 'a new conception of Empire' that had become 'the animating spirit of our party'.[86] This conception of Britain and its settler colonies as 'Greater Britain', with its implied case for an imperial federation similar to the United States of America, had three dimensions, all of which would be echoed by Baldwin. It expressed an understanding of national destiny, of Britain as God's instrument and mankind's hope in planting freedom and civilisation across the world. It offered a state doctrine, an external purpose upon which to build a stronger sense of internal cohesion, beyond sectional interests. It was also a response to growing international competition, where a 'world-state' could remain a great power alongside the USA and Russia, and within which trade could continue to flourish and emigration would be the 'remedy for pauperism'.

With Cunningham, Baldwin had a more direct relationship. He was not just the university economic historian, but the college chaplain who presided over the Sunday Essay Society and organised the Trinity College mission. He remained a family friend until his death in 1919, preaching at Wilden, officiating at Baldwin's wedding, and frequently visited by him in Cambridge.[87] His teaching and writings would have been significant to Baldwin in several respects. As a critic of abstract economics, he reinforced a businessman's scepticism towards economic theorists:[88] it is not fanciful to trace something of Baldwin's resistance to Keynes from Cunningham's battles against Keynes's teacher, Marshall. Baldwin's praise for Cunningham in 1927 was for his 'scholarship and erudition' which had 'sapped the foundations of Victorian free trade'. Even in the 1880s Cunningham taught that neither *laissez-faire* nor free trade comprised the absolute truths and benefits assumed by orthodox economists and Liberals. From 1903 he

[86] Cambridge University Conservative Association, 4 March 1927. For Seeley's doctrines, see Wormell, *Seeley*.
[87] A. Baldwin journal, 16 June 1888, 12 Sept. 1892; S. Baldwin to Louisa Baldwin, 18 Sept. 1894, 23 May 1897, 24 July 1912, BF; Cunningham, *Cunningham*, pp. 80–2, 104; and see Jones, *WD* 1.262 (20 Dec. 1923), and *DL* p. 207 (23 May 1936).
[88] See Baldwin's 'Foreword' to the biography of another historical economist, personal friend and, from 1915, colleague on various committees: Ashley, *Ashley*, pp. 8–9, also 151, 155.

became a leading academic supporter of Chamberlain's tariff reform as the economic underpinning for Seeley's 'Greater Britain' – indeed, he was one of the ideologues of Edwardian Conservatism.[89] He argued that economic principles and policy were not dogmatic matters but practical issues of 'national husbandry', which would vary according to economic and moral conditions. Society was not merely a collection of individuals but an organic community, so the state might justifiably intervene to restrain private selfishness for the common good. While economic competition was vital to generate prosperity, it could nevertheless require regulation and was itself creating improved organisation, not least in the form of larger companies[90] (like, he might have said, Baldwins Ltd).

More fundamental were Cunningham's concerns as a clergyman, moralist, disciple of Maurice, admirer of Green, and friend of Toynbee.[91] He emphasised the importance of other aspects of national life than the economic, and of a 'satisfactory' distribution as well as an efficient production of wealth. He argued that the Industrial Revolution – as a process, not as the intention of industrialists – had immiserated and demoralised workers, and that consequently efforts to improve their condition had been, and remained, necessary. Yet while in some senses a collectivist, he attacked those who secularised Maurice's Christian Socialism, and was an impressive critic of state socialism and radical trade unionism. The need for some regulation did not make capitalism, individualism, and inequality any less natural and creative. The true, long-term, interests of employers and workers were identical, and it was through recognition of that truth that socialism and industrial militancy would be most effectively resisted. The means lay in Christian charity and Christian responsibility, particularly the duties of citizenship and work. These were especially incumbent upon the rich, because the extravagance and selfishness of the 'smart set' were among the chief causes of working-class discontent, and because if correctly understood business, property, and

---

[89] Green, *Crisis of Conservatism*, pp. 162–76, 179–83. As a public figure he was important variously as historian, economic commentator, founding Fellow of the British Academy, preacher and religious controversialist, and Archdeacon of Ely.

[90] See the following by Cunningham: *The Growth of English Industry and Commerce* (1882 edn), pp. 6–8, conclusion; *Politics and Economics* (1885), pp. vii–viii, 3–17, 118–26; *The Rise and Decline of the Free Trade Movement* (1904), ch. 7.

[91] Cunningham, *Cunningham*, pp. ix–x, 14, 17, 20–2, 50, 59, 99, 121.

wealth were trusts to be exercised for the good of others: 'the rich
have no right whatever to be idle; they only have the privilege
of choosing the precise way in which they will try to serve the
community'.[92] What Cunningham presented – and probably
helped to impress upon Baldwin – was an economic, moral, and
Christian Conservatism as the positive and truly national alternative to both Liberalism and socialism.

[92] W. Cunningham, *The Causes of Labour Unrest* (1912), p. 28 and *passim*, along with his *The Gospel of Work* (Cambridge, 1902).

CHAPTER 4

Influences: community and service

I

The Baldwins expected to make fortunes, and did so both as industrial entrepreneurs and as provincial and City directors and investors. They also expected to enjoy their wealth, Alfred with his art
and fine wines, Stanley with long winter and summer holidays and
large houses in Worcestershire and fashionable London. Contrary
to biographical tradition, they were not a cheerless family: Wilden
House offered 'bountiful hospitality', jokes, mimicry, and excursions to county cricket and Birmingham pantomimes; Astley Hall
contained 'much laughter & music & dancing',[1] and the London
homes brought visits to art exhibitions, Lords matches, and Gilbert and Sullivan revivals. Yet equally important were a practical
Christian faith, and commitment to a spectrum of public duties.
They believed that work was a religious and social obligation, and
that their firms and investments benefitted not just themselves
and their customers but also their employees and the wider
society. To them capitalism was not inherently an exploitative and
socially divisive system; only selfish and irresponsible individuals
made it seem so. Within the standards set by their income they
disapproved of personal excess and extravagance,[2] and considered
part of their own reward in money and time to be rightly owed to
their workers and to the community in the forms of benefactions
and public service.

These beliefs explain why until 1917 Stanley Baldwin remained
an active businessman rather than becoming a leisured *rentier*.

---

[1] Plowden notes, Baldwin Sussex papers, 1/15/11–13, 1/16/3; P. Burne-Jones to Mrs Drew,
31 Aug. 1917, Mary Gladstone papers, British Library Add. MSS. 46246/254–7; AWB
pp. 65, 67–8; M&B pp. 31–8.
[2] AWB pp. 64–5.

They also explain a distinctive quality of his Conservative party leadership: a defence of property and private enterprise infused with moral and social criticism, even implied sympathy with some Labour party attitudes. Private observations best capture the flavour. He surprised Bonar Law – a less complicated 'business Conservative' – by observing that 'a man who made a million quick ought to be not in the Lords but in gaol'. After the 1929 Labour election victory he made a still clearer distinction between system and individual:

I no more like these very rich men than [Labour] do. These great fortunes are an incidental to the capitalist system, not of its essence. In the making of them I believe that on the whole the lot of the poor is improved, and more widely than if the State took charge of the nation's industries.

The 'great money makers at the beginning of the Industrial Age' were, he later wrote, in 'the Diabolic Succession of Tudor gate-crashers'. He did not regret 'that lack of hardness in the Baldwins that prevented them from becoming millionaires'.[3]

Nor for the Baldwins were duties something imposed and resented, as is too readily assumed by biographers within a different moral environment. Performance of duties was second nature, an inner compulsion to exert oneself and incur sacrifices for purposes which might not bring discernible results or recognition in this world, but nevertheless brought satisfactions as well as inconveniences. As with Alfred Baldwin so with his son, work, wealth, and position were inseparable from an 'ideal of service'. It was entirely characteristic that when Stanley informed his parents in 1892 of his engagement to be married, his hope was that he and his future wife would 'live to be half as good to everybody & as much of a blessing to the community as you'.[4]

These were not empty sentiments, but a way of life. The purpose of the prime minister's 1925 account of the late-Victorian Wilden works – where he knew every worker, where strikes and lock-outs were unknown, and where nobody was ever sacked – will be examined later, but two comments should be made on it as description.[5]

[3] Jones *WD* I.255, 262 (25 Nov., 20 Dec. 1923), II.193 (20 June 1929); Jones *DL* p. 423 (29 Dec. 1938).
[4] Baldwin, *Macdonald Sisters*, p. 190; Baldwin to his mother, 13 April 1892, BF. Cf. M&B pp. 17, 19; Taylor, *Victorian Sisters*, p. 190.
[5] *OE* pp. 42–4.

The first is that it was accurate. Alfred Baldwin treated his employees not as factors of production but as fellow men, and the E. P. & W. Baldwin works and company villages not as economic units but as communities, within which his authority took patriarchal and moral forms. He believed 'that the connection between master and servant should be something beyond one of mere cash and that a master's interest did not cease when he had paid them on Saturday night'. He established good standards of safety, cleanliness, housing and medical provision, and works-supported friendly societies. In the 1880s he was among the first West Midland ironmasters to switch from twelve- to eight-hour shifts. He provided secure and hereditary employment, gave his works managers shares in the firm, addressed his workmen by their Christian names, and assisted necessitous families in money or kind. For him one of the advantages of the enlarged Baldwins Ltd conglomerate was its ability to protect employment when one section of its trade suffered recession. His wife was similarly expected to 'play Lady Bountiful' and provide leadership for the local women and girls. Through works celebrations of family occasions – Louisa's recovery of health, Stanley's birthdays and marriage – the workforce was further identified with the firm. Alfred's main home remained next to Wilden works and his workmen's cottages, and as these grew into a village in the 1880s he built a school and a church, which he decorated with emblems of his family and firm. After obtaining the village's recognition as a separate ecclesiastical parish in 1904, he endowed the clerical living and provided a parsonage. Yet despite this Anglican proselytism – all the family, including Stanley, became Sunday-school teachers – Alfred remained on good terms with his Nonconformist workmen and neighbours.[6] His son continued these relationships. As a young man he played centre-forward in the village football team. He was among the organisers and speakers of the Wilden Works Mutual Improvement Society.[7] When the 1912 coal strike closed Baldwins Ltd's four Midlands works, he paid allowances to their thousand

[6] AWB pp. 25–6, 35–5, 53–4; *DBB* I.116; shareholders' lists, B/WCRO, BLtd; Baldwins Ltd annual meeting, *The Times*, 22 Oct. 1904; A. Baldwin to Louisa, 18 March 1883; Wilden church papers, WCRO 9410; obituaries in B/WCRO 8229/5.
[7] Mutual Improvement Society programmes 1902–4, WCRO 9410/5/xi: Baldwin gave talks on 'England a hundred years ago', and 'The fiscal question'.

workers for six weeks from his own pocket.[8] A local newspaper recorded that the Baldwins 'have never been regarded, as so many employers are nowadays, as exploiters of labour, but on the contrary as large-minded local benefactors, in sympathy with workers and the common interests of the community'.[9]

Stanley Baldwin had cause in the 1920s to present his experience as exceptional, but such industrial paternalism was not in fact unusual in some manufacturing districts during the late nineteenth century; there are striking resemblances between E. P. & W. Baldwin and the 'factory culture' of Lancashire.[10] Although the Baldwins would have considered economic advantage to be a *consequence* rather than the *motive* for such moralised relationships, like these other employers they believed this approach generated increased economic efficiency through good industrial relations. Its success – testified at Baldwins by an absence of disputes and illuminated addresses of gratitude from the workforce – was of manifest importance for the future prime minister as a working example of industrial and social harmony.

Yet the second, equally important, point about Wilden is that it did not constitute the Baldwins' whole experience of industrial relations. As the family firm grew and became a large company, their relationships with workers necessarily became more distant – at Dudley, Cookley, and Stourvale, more so in Monmouthshire, and more again within the Baldwins Ltd conglomerate. Stanley's payment of allowances during the 1912 stoppage was among the last acts of personal paternalism in British heavy industry. In Monmouth and South Wales the workforce was less amenable and trade unions, which had never developed in their original works, were more active. During the 1903–4 depression the Baldwins board temporarily closed its Landore works after the men refused to accept wage reductions.[11] Moreover, in Great Western Railways they participated in a business where employer and trade-union

---

[8] Notice, 30 March 1912, in AWB p. 77, and see *HCDeb* 160, c. 557 (16 Feb. 1923); *OE* pp. 43–4 (6 March 1925).
[9] Cutting *c.*1930, in Stroller, 'Worcestershire villages', vol.I, p. 23, Worcester City Library local studies section.
[10] P. Joyce, *Work, Society and Politics. The Culture of the Factory in Later Victorian England* (Brighton, 1980), esp. chs. 2–5. Both Joyce, pp. 158, 227, and McKibbin, *Ideologies of Class*, p. 8, specify Baldwins as indicative of a widespread pattern.
[11] *Iron and Coal Trades Review*, 6 May 1898 p. 731, 11 Dec. 1903 p. 1725, 8 Jan. 1904 p. 125.

intransigence created unusually difficult industrial relations. Alfred Baldwin took a leading part in the 1907 national railway dispute, while his son experienced the pre-war wave of national strikes at first hand. In these new, larger-scale, circumstances, Alfred favoured conciliation boards bringing together employers and the men directly involved, but disliked trade-union officials as interfering between 'the directors and their employees'.[12] Stanley, as a GWR representative on the new conciliation boards, had more contact with trade unions[13] and took a more positive – and increasingly conventional – attitude towards them. Trade unions had helped raise many workers from 'the position of slaves', and if conducted responsibly could play a valuable part in stabilising industrial relations through 'mutual and collective bargaining'.[14] Far from having been isolated from 'modern' industrial relations, the prime minister had long been exercised by the problem of how to retain industrial peace amid changing economic and social conditions.

II

Like other high-minded and successful businessmen, the Baldwins' philanthropy and service gradually spread out from their own works into local, county, and national life. Following religious custom, Alfred gave at least a tithe of his income to church and charitable causes,[15] and Stanley appears to have followed a similar practice. His wife worked for maternal and children's charities, and their children were taught the duties of their station by delivering food and clothing to the elderly and sick of Astley village. Alfred and Stanley both gave substantial donations to and served as governors or chairmen of Worcestershire infirmaries and schools. Alfred became a prominent lay churchman, active well beyond Worcestershire. Both also participated in local and county civic institutions and administration (table 4). From 1887 to 1892 Stanley served in the Volunteer Force, forming his own artillery

---

[12] A. Baldwin journal, 25 Oct. 1907; Clapham, *Economic History*, III.495.
[13] *Great Western Railway Magazine*, June 1923, p. 247; J. H. Thomas, *My Story* (1937), p. 229; Thomas speech, *The Times*, 1 May 1928.
[14] *HCDeb* 4s.CXC, c. 1436 (22 June 1908); 5s.39, cc. 955–8 (12 June 1912) and 59, cc. 729–32 (5 March 1914).
[15] Plowden notes, Baldwin Sussex papers 1/15/12.

Table 4. *Alfred & Stanley Baldwin: public and institutional positions*

Alfred Baldwin
JP Worcestershire 1879–1908, Staffordshire 1883–1908
Worcestershire County Council, member 1889–97
High Sheriff, Worcestershire 1894
Deputy Lieutenant, Worcestershire 1898–1908

Hartlebury School Board, elected member 1883–?
Bewdley Grammar School, and Hartlebury School, governor

Honorary member of numerous friendly society lodges or courts

Worcestershire Church Schools organisation, president
National Church League, member
Worcester Diocesan Conference, elected member
Canterbury Convocation, House of Laymen, Worcester diocese representative
    1892–1908

Worcestershire Conservative Association, executive committee member, by
    1880
West Worcestershire and Mid Worcestershire Conservative Associations,
    chairman
National Union of Conservative Associations, council member
Midland Union of Conservative Associations, chairman 1893–5
MP West Worcestershire 1892–1908

Stanley Baldwin [in Worcestershire before 1914: see text for later positions]
Areley Kings parish council, member, sometime chairman
Worcestershire County Council, member 1898–1907
JP Worcestershire 1897–1947

Hartlebury School, governor, later chairman of governors
Worcester High School and Malvern College, governor
Kidderminster Infirmary, president (before 1908)

Honorary member of Oddfellows, Foresters and other friendly society lodges
    and courts, from *c*.1888
Stourport Workmen's Club, president 1904

Primrose League, Stourport Habitation, ruling councillor from 1890
Primrose League, secretary of divisional organisation
West Worcestershire Conservative Association, executive committee member
    from 1896
Parliamentary candidate, Kidderminster, 1904–6 (defeated at 1906 general
    election)
MP West Worcestershire 1908–37

battery and becoming a captain.[16] Alfred and Stanley became jus-
tices of the peace – Alfred, unusually, for two counties, indicating
the geographical spread of his businesses – and were elected to
the new county and parish councils created in the 1880s and
1890s. Alfred also reached two of the highest honorific positions
in county government. The many organisational votes of condol-
ence on Alfred's death and representations at his funeral – a great
county occasion – testified to a remarkable range of public involvements, which his son substantially maintained.

Into these activities parliamentary politics fitted less as an
ambition for a 'political career' than as a natural extension of
service, status, and leadership within county society and the business community. From this perspective, becoming a member of
parliament was a crowning achievement – for Alfred 'the highest
honour' he had 'ever looked for' – with satisfactory performance
of constituency and backbench obligations and representation of
commercial interests sufficient in themselves. Parliamentary elections, Stanley Baldwin wrote in December 1910, were 'infernal'
and would be 'unbearable if it wasn't one's rather obvious duty'.[17]
Their parliamentary effort and contact with political leaders lay
chiefly in committee work and interest-group activity – Alfred for
the Iron Trade and Railway Companies Associations, Stanley as a
member of the parliamentary 'railway interest'.[18] Neither said
much in the Commons chamber itself. But to judge Stanley Baldwin's political career before 1914 by the standards of an aspiring
professional politician is inappropriate and misleading. It induces
disparagement of what by other criteria was a successful – and
beneficent – life. An experienced journalist recollected him in
1908 as 'a young man who had already arrived . . . already a success so far as the world goes'.[19] Worse, it misses much that became
important in shaping his political leadership. The modesty of his

[16] AWB p. 55; A. Baldwin journal, 8 Oct. 1888, 17 Jan. 1889.
[17] A. Baldwin journal, 4 July 1892; S. Baldwin to Edith Macdonald, 6 Dec. 1910, BF.
[18] Alfred's correspondents included Joseph Chamberlain, Milner, and Bonar Law, while
Webster – Unionist Attorney-General from 1885, before becoming Lord Chief Justice
(as Lord Alverstone) in 1900 – was a long-standing friend. He himself served on the
Public Accounts, Railway Rates, and numerous other committees. G. Alderman, *The
Railway Interest* (Leicester, 1973) refers to the Baldwins on pp. 148, 184, 194, 319.
Stanley spoke on behalf not just of the GWR but other companies: *HCDeb* 7, cc. 2391–
4 (15 July 1909); 28, cc. 593–4 (13 July 1911); 51, cc. 1481–83 (10 April 1913); 59,
cc. 729–32 (5 March 1914).
[19] Blumenfeld, *All in a Lifetime*, p. 155.

early politics – his relatively late start in Parliament and his detachment from Edwardian 'high politics' – was integral to what later made him so distinctive and effective.

Just as it is important that Stanley Baldwin had family contacts with socialists, so he may have learnt something from similar connections with Liberalism. He married into a Liberal family, and his Liberal brother-in-law, Aurelian Ridsdale, was a fellow MP during his first Parliament. The Baldwin family had been among the leaders of north-Worcestershire Liberalism. Enoch Baldwin, Alfred's cousin and partner in Baldwins, Son & Co., was Liberal MP 1880–5 for the old parliamentary borough of Bewdley and Stourport.[20] Alfred himself had been a Liberal activist during the 1860s and early 1870s. But his Liberalism had a specific character. He was a Palmerstonian, significantly admiring the former prime minister as a great 'Englishman' and feeling himself attached to 'Whig principles';[21] that is to say, his commitments were to 'national values' and constitutional doctrine. He seems never to have warmed to Gladstone.

In 1877 Alfred Baldwin defected to Conservatism. Here he joined the familiar late Victorian drift by businessmen anxious about property rights, but characteristically his own decision was prompted by an issue of religion, constitution and, as he probably considered it, 'nationality': radical pressure for church disestablishment. During the 1880s he warned against the 'infidelity' as well as the 'socialism' of the Liberal party.[22] His political shift – like his earlier conversion to Anglicanism and choice of Harrow and Cambridge for his son's education – might also seem a case of the supposed craving of successful industrialists for acceptance by the social elite. Yet the Baldwins eschewed central features of landed society. Alfred did not move away from the Wilden smoke, and Stanley did not become a gentrified 'man of leisure'; neither participated in squirearchical country sports. While they certainly exemplified the Conservative convergence of industrial and landed wealth, from the moral perspectives of Wilden this seemed an

---

[20] Williamson, 'Doctrinal Politics', p. 187, mistakenly describes Enoch as Stanley's 'uncle'.
[21] *Macdonald Sisters*, pp. 186–7, 191; A. Baldwin journal, 1868–74; A. Baldwin to E. Baldwin, 19 Feb. 1877, B/WCRO 8229/1(iii).
[22] *Berrows*, 21 Nov. 1885. As reasons for his defection he gave disestablishment first, then franchise and land laws, contrasting 'radical ideas' to 'Whig principles': A. Baldwin to E. Baldwin, 19 Feb. 1877, B/WCRO 8229/1(iii).

alliance of equal worlds, with the businessmen having the advantage of representing modernity. When it came to assessing popular opinion Stanley Baldwin in the early 1920s assumed the superior judgement of an industrialist over even the most experienced aristocratic politicians.[23] Nor did the Baldwins experience another purported feature of late-Victorian Conservatism, tension within the new propertied alliance. Alfred Baldwin effortlessly joined the landed aristocrats and baronets on Worcestershire's Conservative executive, and quickly became one of its leading members, as chairman or member of constituency, regional, and national associations. He helped reconstruct the party's county organisation to meet the electoral reforms of the 1880s, and later secured party control of the main county newspapers.[24] His importance in Worcestershire Conservatism was further attested from 1884 as its patrician chiefs offered him candidatures in each of the four county divisions, at a time when these largely remained the prized preserve of landed MPs. He eventually took the safest, West Worcestershire (now incorporating Bewdley and Stourport), at the 1892 general election. There, an obituarist noted, this industrialist had the 'striking achievement' of being regarded by the constituency's farmers as 'a more or less ideal representative'.[25] As with manufacturing and commerce, so with the land: the Baldwins moved freely around different economic and social groups, confirming their assumption and ideal of an essentially unified national community.

For Stanley Baldwin his father's party position did not just give him early political interests and, eventually, an easy route into Parliament – so easy that in his 1908 by-election address he did not state his own opinions but offered himself simply as his father's son. As his father's political lieutenant from 1888, he also obtained experience unusual among top-rank Conservative politicians of the 1920s: prolonged activity in local party organisation,

---

[23] See below p. 207.
[24] Worcestershire Conservative Association minutes, 5 Feb. 1881, 22 Dec. 1883, 4 Feb. 1884, 16 Jan 1892, WCRO 956/1; A. Baldwin journal, various entries 1880–95. For the *Berrows* group of newspapers, see above pp. 79–80. For supposed tensions within the propertied alliance, see e.g. Green, *Crisis of Conservatism*, pp. 15, 87–8, 104–5, 108–9, 117.
[25] Sir R. Temple, and Sir E. Lechmere, to A. Baldwin, 1 April 1884, 15 March 1891, B/WCRO 8494; A. Baldwin to Louisa, 13 May 1891; A. Baldwin journal, 19, 22 March 1890, July–Sept. 1891; *The Birmingham Gazette*, 14 Feb. 1908.

conducted both among voters of distinctly mixed social composition and during two periods of Conservative re-definition in
popular politics – after the 1884 franchise extension, and amid
the early 1900s tariff-reform agitation and Liberal–Labour
revival. West Worcestershire comprised the spa resort of Malvern,
the river ports of Bewdley and Stourport, and a sprawling agricultural area with recently enfranchised rural workers. The neigh-
bouring borough of Kidderminster contained a concentrated
industrial population. West Worcestershire was so securely Conservative that from 1892 to 1935 the two Baldwins were usually
returned unopposed. Yet this did not produce complacency. The
pre-1914 constituency party was renowned regionally as 'a fine
piece of political machinery', which consumed much effort because
its leaders prided themselves on preventing contests which would
divide the community, or failing that to win so convincingly as to
deter future challenges.[26] Kidderminster had a rumbustious local
politics – as Stanley's well-known recollection of his first election
candidature indicates – yet its industrial workers also usually
returned a Conservative, though it contained enough 'radical'
voters to secure his own defeat in 1906.[27] On the one hand Baldwin was familiar with a Conservatism which appealed across social
distinctions, including a working-class Conservatism, but on the
other he retained a Conservative anxiety about 'democracy', stiffened at Cambridge, and he knew from experience that preserving
Conservatism required hard work.[28]

Stanley Baldwin's early politics were therefore no more cloistered than his industrial and commercial involvements. Moreover,
the character of this local politics, and the conceptions he associated with them, were central to his later conduct of national politics. At Harrow he was noted as a 'student' of Disraeli's speeches,[29]
and his earliest political work was with the Primrose League –
the pseudo-Disraelian movement by which provincial Conservative

---

[26] A. Baldwin obituary, *The Worcester Chronicle*, 15 Feb. 1908; West Worcestershire Conservative Association minutes, 25 June 1892, 2 April 1910, 27 May 1911, WCRO 956/
2. There were by-elections after Alfred's death in 1908, and on Stanley's appointment
to the Cabinet in 1921.

[27] *OE* p. 113; GMY pp. 23–4.

[28] It should be added that as businessmen, both were plural voters – casting votes not only
in several Worcestershire constituencies but also in the mining and industrial area of
North Monmouthshire.

[29] Jones, *Lord Baldwin*, p. 4; Jones diary, 17 Sept. 1935.

elites sought contact with the new male voters, and influence over
them through their wives and daughters. In the late 1880s he
co-founded a small rural branch or 'habitation' of the League, and
later the larger Stourport 'Beaconsfield' habitation, which became
a 'great power in the district'. In the 1890s he served as the
League's Worcestershire divisional secretary, and his mother and
wife helped develop a 'Dames' habitation in Kidderminster. By the
1900s West Worcestershire's two habitations had over a thousand
members, supplemented by a Ladies' Conservative Association.[30]
In the interwar period – by which time its *organisational* functions
had been largely superseded by formal Conservative associations –
he continued to attach significance to the League, reviving the
tradition of the party leader becoming its Grand Master and
addressing its annual Grand Habitations.[31]

The Primrose League's importance is well understood, but the
Baldwins were also familiar with two lesser-known instruments of
Conservative popular politics. The National Conservative League
(NCL) was a similar organisation, but designed to achieve closer
communication with working-class life and leisure (it was, for
instance, more associated with public houses). West Worcestershire had ten lodges, including an 'Alfred Baldwin Lodge' at Malvern, with new ones opened by Stanley Baldwin into the 1900s.[32]
More notably, in West Worcestershire the Friendly Societies –
genuine working-class organisations, and the most characteristic
and best supported – in effect became unofficial agencies of the
Conservative party. On becoming the parliamentary candidate in
1892, Alfred Baldwin addressed or was made honorary member
of most Oddfellows, Foresters, Shepherds, and Gardeners
branches in the constituency, attendances which his party agent
treated as political meetings. On his death these branches subscribed to a memorial to him in Wilden churchyard 'in grateful

[30] Baldwin recollections in speeches, 4 April 1930, 7 May, 17 Nov. 1932, 8 Jan., 5 Oct.
1934, 3 May 1935, 1 May 1936; A. Baldwin journal, 1888–92; West Worcestershire
Conservative Association minutes, WCRO 956/5; *The Worcester Chronicle*, 15 Feb. 1908;
M. Pugh, *The Tories and the People 1880–1935* (Oxford, 1985), pp. 116, 236.
[31] Law declined the post in 1912, as in 1938 did Neville Chamberlain – almost with contempt, suggesting it should go to 'a Peer and, if possible, an ornamental Peer': N.
Chamberlain to Baldwin, 17 Jan. 1938, SB 174/18.
[32] *The Worcester Chronicle*, 15 Feb. 1909; A. Baldwin journal, 17 Nov. 1903. There are brief
references to the NCL in J. Robb, *The Primrose League 1883–1906* (New York, 1942), pp.
147–8, and H. Pelling, *Social Geography of British Elections 1885–1910* (1967), p. 193.

recognition of his constant brotherly kindness and practical help'. Stanley Baldwin on succeeding him as MP succeeded also to these honorary memberships, and likewise took much trouble to address each lodge's annual dinners or summer festivals. This was still largely what was meant by 'working the constituency'. As late as 1922 he opened a 'Stanley Baldwin Lodge' of the Royal Antediluvian Order of Buffaloes in Bewdley, in similar fashion to the Oddfellows' earlier formation of 'Alfred Baldwin', 'Louisa Baldwin', and 'Stanley Baldwin' lodges.[33]

In some senses the Primrose and National Conservative Leagues and partisan association with friendly societies were successors of the older politics of patronage and money. While legitimate circumventions of the 1883 Corrupt Practices Act, these easily shaded into the vigorous, but technically illegal, popular traditions of 'treating' – of which the Baldwins were certainly aware, with Stanley's euphemistic description of the 1906 Kidderminster election as 'old-fashioned', and his attempt to become candidate for Worcester after its contest of that year was declared corrupt.[34] Yet it is evident that for the Baldwins the leagues and societies served more fundamental purposes than simple capture of party allegiance: those of social and moral integration, and promotion of self improvement and good citizenship. Given their moral concerns and cultural associations, they took the Primrose League's aim of uniting Disraeli's 'two nations' seriously. Stanley Baldwin's Stourport habitation operated 'on a very democratic basis', with a largely working-class membership and, for all the familiar League entertainments and social events it had the 'fundamental idea of educating all our members in the current politics of the day'.[35] Encouraging friendly societies had been among Maurice's and Kingsley's prescriptions for elevating the labouring population,

[33] A. Baldwin journal, 22 April–28 June 1892; party agent's report and S. Baldwin statement, in West Worcestershire Conservative Association minutes, 25 June 1892, 16 May 1908, WCRO 956/2.
[34] *OE* p. 113; AWB p. 71. For the Corrupt Practices Act as an element in the Primrose League's formation, see Pugh, *Tories and the People*, pp. 36–8. For the Worcester *city* NCL Lodges as agencies of corrupt 'treating', see Report of the Royal Commission on the Worcester Election, *Parliamentary Papers* 1906 xcv.473, pp. 2–3. The Worcester Conservatives preferred Edward Goulding to Baldwin, as an experienced MP backed by the Chamberlains and Tariff Reform League money. J. Amery, *The Life of Joseph Chamberlain*, vol. VI (1969), p. 886, corrects the statement in M&B p. 41 that Chamberlain proposed Baldwin.
[35] At Primrose League Grand Habitation, 1 May 1936.

and it was one in which the Baldwins fully believed. Aside from the company-inspired societies, in the 1880s Louisa Baldwin supported the local Girls' Friendly Society branch and Stanley joined local Oddfellows and Foresters lodges. Alfred and Stanley both treated their honorary lodge memberships as opportunities not just to win votes but to advise and teach the working population. Before the annual dinners or fetes they inspected the lodges' accounts, and their addresses were homilies on sound financial practice and fundamental social and moral values. Stanley typically recommended friendly-society membership as tending 'to make a man a better citizen and a better member of society', because able to 'do good service for himself and the community'. In demonstrating the virtues of self-respect, sobriety, thrift, and fellowship, the societies were 'the greatest schools of men'.[36] In such addresses defence of the economic and social order was linked to conceptions of material and moral progress, and underpinned by an ideal of Christian community made explicit, for example, in Stanley's 1914 address to the inter-denominational Worcester Brotherhood:

They were all members of a Brotherhood, and when they called themselves brothers they were acknowledging the natural Fatherhood of God. They heard a lot about it being an irreligious age, an age of disputes, quarrels and criticisms, but he believed that, over and above all the seething of new ideas ... there never was a time when men were seeking more earnestly to find Christ. Whilst it was a fine thing to belong to a Brotherhood, and to get help from its associations, it was a finer thing to stand erect oneself, and to be one who gave brotherly help to those who needed it. [There was also a] need of sympathy and brotherhood between all classes, [for] rich and poor had much to learn of each other.[37]

It is in these wider terms – as well as those of patriotic sacrifice – that one must understand Alfred Baldwin's payment of the friendly society contributions for all members of the lodges with which he was associated who served in the Boer War, a gesture which he hoped would 'set a national example of generosity'.[38] In this spirit too his son, while accepting the principle of the 1911

National Insurance Act, regretted that it might weaken friendly
societies – replacing a 'moral duty' with a 'state-compelled duty',
and striking 'a blow at the real feeling of thrift and independence
of the nation' and destroying the 'feeling of fellowship and
brotherhood'.[39]

All this constituted a highly didactic approach to popular politics, in which partisan purposes were enveloped within and often
transposed into broader political, social, economic, and moral
teachings – teachings that justified Conservatism yet were conceived as advancing the common good against sectional or class
interests. It was a different outlet for those motives which had led
the youthful Stanley Baldwin to consider ordination and to interest himself in the Trinity College Mission. It was also an experience of politics which together with that as an industrial employer
gave him confidence in his ability to communicate with the labouring population. He always had a sense of 'knowing the Working
Man pretty intimately'.[40]

In terms of Edwardian national politics too, perspectives
informed by Maurice, Disraeli, Chamberlain, and Cunningham
were those which assumed or sought an organic harmony of interests on a Conservative, capitalist, and Christian basis. Baldwin
found good industrial and financial reasons for supporting tariff
reform, but also recommended it as a policy to restore agricultural
prosperity and to improve working-class employment, wages, and
mutual self-help.[41] He attacked Lloyd George's 1909 tax increases
as damaging to business, but also to 'the hundreds of thousands'
of small savers – while declaring himself 'perfectly ready to
shoulder my share of whatever Income Tax [Lloyd George]
deemed desirable', provided the money was 'expended wisely and
for the benefit of the people'.[42] He was one of only twelve Conservative MPs to vote for the second reading of the Liberal Old
Age Pensions Act. His membership of the Anti-Socialist Union was
balanced by that of the Unionist Social Reform Committee, which
by 1914 had generated a distinctively Conservative collectivism.

[39] *Berrows*, 3 June 1911, 31 Aug. 1912, 17 May 1913, 6 June 1914. For concern at cost,
see *HCDeb* 31, cc. 1787–8, 2076–7 (9, 16 Nov. 1911).
[40] Baldwin to Joan Dickinson, 17 Oct. 1916, JD. Cf. 1938 letter in AWB p. 328.
[41] 1906 Kidderminster Election Address, in Hyde, *Baldwin*, p. 35; *Berrows*, 8, 15 Jan. 1910,
8 March 1913.
[42] *Berrows*, 8 Jan. 1910; *HCDeb* 2, cc. 1146–52 (17 March 1909); 5, cc. 442–6 (19 May
1909); 63, c. 2094 (25 June 1914).

Here, as on tariff reform, he was part of a wider party movement
for active if limited state intervention 'to protect the interests of
the community'. The sub-committees on which he served recommended the creation of a new health department, a minimum
wage structure, an agricultural wages board, and a system of compulsory, though firmly 'non-political', industrial arbitration.[43] Still
more significant in retrospect, as political and class tensions intensified from 1909 – over the budget, House of Lords, Ireland, the
Welsh Church, the land campaign, and industrial relations – Baldwin emphasised a conception of 'English' constitutionalism as a
check upon democratic excess, a safeguard of the social order,
and the mainstay of national unity. In language drawn from his
Cambridge years, to be re-used on innumerable interwar
occasions, he declared that 'the important thing that was on its
trial today was . . . Parliamentary government':

Parliamentary government was, perhaps, the most English thing in the
world. It was born in England; it was developed in England; it throve on
English soil; it has been tended by the brains and hands of Englishmen;
and it has been transplanted into the English-speaking countries over
the seas; it had been copied by nearly every civilised country in the world,
and each . . . recognised that it was to England they must look to see
how Parliamentary Government was to be carried out.[44]

III

If Baldwin's entry into national politics was slow and quiet, this
was hardly because he was unconnected or without standing of his
own. Nevertheless, in 1914 he was not an obvious prospect for
high ministerial office. With one motion, a dozen or so short
speeches, and ten questions in the House of Commons in six years,
he was a more articulate MP than his father had been. Yet his
initial refusal to accept the 1912 payment for MPs, his criticism
of 'professional politicians', and his complaint that Parliament
tended 'to take away practically the whole time of a man', confirm

[43] Astor, Ashley, Baldwin *et al.* memorial to Law on agricultural policy, 8 Nov. 1913, Law
     papers 30/4/12; Hills *et al., Industrial Unrest*, pp. iii, 3, 20, 35; Ridley, 'The Unionist Social
     Reform Committee', pp. 396–7, 400–1, 405–8.
[44] *Berrows*, 3 May 1913. Other constituency speeches from 1910 to the outbreak of war
     contained similar themes.

that in attitude and ambition he remained very much a backbench businessman MP.[45]

His position was transformed by the Great War. Most obviously, it created opportunities for his entry into government. More significantly, the War intensified Baldwin's moral attitudes and gave him a desire for a larger political role. He felt admiration and gratitude for the patriotic faith, heroism, and sacrifice of all classes, especially the common people. He experienced personal grief and anxiety, with a nephew and the sons of friends killed in action, and his own eldest son going to the Front in 1918. He was horrified by the human slaughter, yet his belief in a Divine purpose was strengthened. Later he became anxious about the economic costs, increased trade-union militancy, and radicalisation of ex-servicemen. In consequence he placed still more emphasis upon the duties of the rich, the bonds of national community, the need for Conservative idealism and commitment to public service. As he recollected privately in 1938:

It was during the War that I found my soul. There came to me by degrees a changed sense of values, and I began to feel that I might be used for some special work. I didn't know what ... And gradually after much thought it seemed to me that all this bloodshed would be wasted if the world couldn't be made a better place; I felt that the men who had made such sacrifices and in such a spirit were capable of rising to any height, and I began to think out the kind of leadership the country would want when the peace came. The peace came, and by 1919 or 1920 the temper of this country was worse than it had ever been.

It was obvious that the first thing to be done was to pull the country together: to make them realise the brotherhood of the human family.[46]

Such autobiographical references became common motifs in Baldwin's public statements of the 1920s and 1930s, when, as will be seen, they served particular political purposes. Nevertheless, although they tend to foreshorten the timescale, such passages did substantially express his contemporary responses to the War. He had no qualms about supporting 'total war', participat-

---

[45] *Berrows*, 3 June 1911, 8 March 1913, and *The Worcester Daily Times*, 18 May 1914. A persistent undercounting of Baldwin's pre-war speeches originates with Bryant, *Baldwin*, p. 51. Blumenfeld, *R.D.B.'s Diary*, p. 205 (2 Feb. 1908) has a glimpse of the pre-war Baldwin: 'rather shy and not at all politician-like in his manner ... pleasant, cultured, conscientious, but badly dressed man, without much desire to sit in the limelight'.

[46] Baldwin letter 1938, in AWB p. 327, and see pp. 79, 83–90.

ing in backbench agitations for conscription and economic controls. On the outbreak of war he surpassed his father's offer at
the start of the Boer War, undertaking to pay the friendly
society contributions of all volunteer servicemen in Worcester
as well as in his West Worcestershire constituency. Like his
father, he hoped this would set an example for other wealthy
individuals, but he spoke also of the War as an opportunity for
national moral and social renewal:

> The poor in this country might suffer before the war was over, and the
> rich had the chance of their lives to help to carry the poor on their backs
> as far as they could. Possibly, if all classes rose to the fulfilment of their
> duty in this country, this war might yet be one of the greatest blessings
> in disguise ever experienced, in that it might heal many of our internal
> sores, and make us more and more in the years to come live for England
> and for each other, and not for ourselves.[47]

As casualties and costs mounted, so Baldwin increased his own
contributions towards national sacrifice and the creation of an
enduring social cohesion. He funded a convalescent hospital, and
donated substantial sums to other hospitals, the Red Cross, and
other charitable causes.[48] He supported Church of England and
other movements seeking to convert the wartime spirit of co-
operation into a basis for post-war industrial peace.[49] He gave
money to various servicemen's causes, including the 'Comrades of
the Great War' – an ex-servicemen's organisation inspired by the
War Cabinet to counteract suspected radical movements.[50] He
bought large amounts of War Loan.[51] He also began to want ministerial office, and in his frustration – perhaps embarrassment – at
not being offered any full-time war work, he apparently considered
retiring from Parliament and returning to local government.[52]
When appointed to the humblest ministerial post, involving a con-

---

[47] At Foresters' fete, Alfrick, in *Berrows*, 15 Aug. 1914, and see speech for County Relief
Fund, 22 Aug. 1914. *The Birmingham Post*, 23 May 1923, states that his offer eventually
cost him thousands of pounds.
[48] AWB p. 311; Bryant, *Baldwin*, p. 58; *Davidson Memoirs*, pp. 94–5; Roberts, *Baldwin*, pp.
47, 48.
[49] See below, p. 187.
[50] C. Wrigley, *Lloyd George and the Challenge of Labour* (1990), p. 39, for £500 given to the
'Comrades'.
[51] Baldwin to his mother, 11 Feb. 1917, BF, records £50,000 of the latest war loan (around
£1.5 million in modern prices).
[52] This, at least, was his later recollection: see 'Mr Baldwin's Testament', 28 April 1937,
Crathorne papers; at National Union, 24 June 1937; AWB p. 80.

siderable loss of income, he valued it as an opportunity for 'unselfish service'.[53]

These are the contexts for understanding a further action which has been described as 'strange',[54] yet is actually one more, albeit remarkable, indication of the values he had absorbed during his early years and would carry into his political leadership. Baldwin was among those who profited from the war. His Baldwins Ltd shares alone tripled in value, and in 1918 earned not just a high $11\frac{2}{3}$ per cent dividend but also a 25 per cent bonus. Such large and effortless increases in his wealth and income made him uneasy, especially because derived from military production: 'a wicked amount of money which could never have come to me except for the war' – indeed 'blood money'. Before the Armistice he decided to get 'rid of my war profits', beginning with increased charitable donations.[55] But he was disturbed not just in his own conscience, but by what he considered to be a deterioration in the public atmosphere. 'Everybody', he wrote in 1917, 'is out for what they can get during the war and it makes me sick', and he famously described the 1918 intake of new MPs as 'a lot of hard-faced men who look as if they had done very well out of the war'.[56] During the 1919 inflationary boom he feared that 'all classes are in danger of being submerged by a wave of extravagance and materialism', aggravating the national problems of post-war adjustment.

Baldwin's answer to these personal and public anxieties was a larger form of the financial gifts of his father and himself at the outbreak of two wars, this time offered as a thank-offering to mark the conclusion of the peace treaties with Germany in June 1919. After calculating his wealth as £580,000 (around £14 million in modern values), he unburdened himself of his remaining war profits by giving about a fifth – £120,000 (almost £3 million) –

[53] Baldwin to his mother, 11 Feb. 1917, BF, and see Baldwin note, 28 Jan. 1919, in *Davidson Memoirs*, p. 95. His statements on this point are not wholly consistent. In February 1917 he wrote that he had 'never sought' a ministerial place, but a month earlier had written that 'I always wanted a full-time [i.e. war-related] job': AWB p. 81.

[54] M&B p. 72.

[55] Baldwin letter, 2 Oct. 1918, in obituary, *Berrows*, 20 Dec. 1947; O. Baldwin, *Questing Beast*, p. 240. Among his 1918 gifts were £5,000 each to Kidderminster General Hospital and (anonymously) the Worcestershire Prisoner of War Fund.

[56] Baldwin to Joan Dickinson, 28 Nov. 1917, in *Davidson Memoirs*, p. 79; anonymous statement in J. M. Keynes, *The Economic Consequences of the Peace* (1919), in Keynes, *Collected Writings*, II.91, confirmed as Baldwin's statement in *ibid*. XXVII.163 and Jones *WD* I.255 (cf. GMY p. 29n). See, similarly, Baldwin to his mother, 12 Feb. 1919, in AWB p. 82.

towards redemption of War Debt. In a characteristic fusion of moral and patriotic idealism with attempted financial, social, and political stabilisation, he publicised this action half-pseudonymously (as 'F.S.T.', the initials of his ministerial office) in *The Times*, as an example of how the wealthy classes could help revive the 1914 spirit of 'unity and fellowship', reduce the burden of national debt, and relieve pressure for a compulsory capital levy, by seizing 'an opportunity of service' and placing 'love of country before love of money'.[57]

His public appeal produced little response, but in the longer term his private sacrifice had important unintended consequences for Baldwin's politics. When he became prime minister in 1923 his identity as 'F.S.T.' was revealed to the press – not, it seems, by Baldwin himself, but probably by Davidson and Conservative Central Office[58] – with the enduring effect of fixing him in the public mind as an unusually disinterested politician. This was reinforced by the impact upon his personal finances. By 1920 he had given away a total of about £200,000 (over £4 million in 1990s terms).[59] This had unexpectedly damaging effects once the chronic interwar depression began: most of his Baldwin Ltd shares paid no dividends after 1922, and collapsed in value – from 60 shillings per ordinary share in 1918, they were written down to 4 shillings in 1928, and reached a low of 1s. 2d. in 1931 – and his other industrial shares performed nearly as badly.[60] After 1937 his industrial wealth and income were revived by rearmament and a second world war, so that even after gifts to his two sons he still left a substantial sum on his death, around £280,000 (over £5

---

[57] FST letter in *The Times*, 24 June 1919, reprinted in most of the biographies.
[58] The first publication, not quite accurate, was 'Stanley Baldwin. An Appreciation by a Close Personal Friend', in *The Morning Post*, 23 May 1923, later reprinted as a Conservative party pamphlet. Davidson arranged publication of the original 1919 letter, but in *Davidson Memoirs*, p. 94n, he denied responsibility for revealing the author. However, Wickham Steed, who as *The Times* editor in 1919 was another possible source and who published accounts of the incident in a 1925 article and 1930 book on Baldwin, also reported his gift to a Gloucestershire girls' home, which he can only have got from Davidson (see *ibid.*, p. 94).
[59] AWB p. 327; Jones *DL* p. 190.
[60] *Stock Exchange Ten-Year Record of Prices and Dividends* (1926, 1936 edns.); Roberts, *Baldwin*, pp. 43–4. In 1926, after four new share issues between 1915 to 1921, Baldwin had 194,526 ordinary shares and 37,591 5½ per cent preference shares. In Jones *DL* p. 538 (5–7 Jan. 1946) he recalled that the 1928 writing-down cost him £140,000 (around £4 million). For Kenricks (including Baldwin & Sons) shares – which rarely earned a dividend between 1926 and 1941 – see Church, *Kenricks*, pp. 194–5.

million in modern prices).[61] Nevertheless for much of the interwar years his realisable wealth was greatly reduced and his income fell considerably, to a fifth by 1925 and still more later. By his own standards and that of his social position he regarded himself as 'a poor man', able to maintain his expenditure and pay his taxes only by running down his capital and accumulating a bank overdraft. His mother subsidised his 1923 and 1924 election expenses, he sold his London house and came close to selling Astley Hall. His ministerial salary and occupancy of Downing Street houses and Chequers now became financially significant to him. After the 1929 election defeat he only felt able to remain in politics, rather than returning to business, because friends provided financial assistance and lent him a London house.[62] When he approached retirement in 1937 similar arrangements – including offers of directorships – were considered, but became unnecessary after his Cabinet introduced a prime-ministerial pension and his rich son-in-law bought him a (very desirable) London house.[63]

These anxieties indicate a less attractive, discordant, element in Baldwin's character. Compared to the hardships of those suffering long-term unemployment and the means test – the real poor – his difficulties were mild indeed. One can only comment that an unreflective double standard is common among those threatened with declining personal circumstances. Nevertheless, whatever his private worries, his straitened finances produced positive public effects. That his political career involved material sacrifices was important for his sense of purpose, and still more for his reputation. Admission of his reduced capital and income enabled him to express familiarity and fellow-feeling with the effects of the post-war economic depression.[64] Insofar as one can tell he was scrupulous in not allowing his *direct* financial interests to affect his political decisions. But what is more to the point, he did not suffer

---

[61] Summary of estate-duty affidavit, March 1948, BF, gives the gross amount as £338,735; *The Times*, 3 April 1948, has the agreed net total of £280,971.

[62] Jones *WD* I.259, II.138, 192 (7 Dec. 1923, 17 May 1928, 20 June 1929); MacDonald diary, 7 May 1929; Baldwin to his mother, 21 Nov. 1923, 10 March, 12 Oct. 1924, BF; Baldwin to O. Baldwin, 8 June 1929, 24 Aug. 1934, CUL Add. 8795/6, 17; Baldwin to Cory, 21 Feb. 1932, WCRO 9410/5/(ii)5; M&B pp. 260, 529, 589n.

[63] Jones diary, 21 Jan, 18 Feb. 1937; Jones *DL* pp. 314, 330 (15 Feb, 20 April 1937); Baldwin to Joan Davidson, 13 March 1937, JD, and to Dore, 16 June 1937, CUL Add. 8812/224. The house was 69 Eaton Square.

[64] E.g. *HCDeb* 184, c. 1132 (25 May 1925); Manchester, 16 May 1928; Birmingham, 14 Jan. 1931.

even suspicions of such self-interest, suspicions which could have
been politically crippling. This was equally true over industrial
protection (though during the 1923 election it was thought necessary to publish a denial that he retained control over the Baldwins
Ltd management);[65] the 1925 and 1928 agitations for iron and
steel safeguarding (when his decisions went against his private
interests); the 1926 coal lock-out (when a backbench Labour MP
attack on him as a coal-owner backfired, winning him parliamentary sympathy);[66] and over armaments (where his private interest
lay in earlier and larger rearmament). As Conservative party
leader within a new mass democracy, with the Labour party as
principal opponent and industrial relations as a major problem,
there were considerable advantages in the paradox that despite
Baldwin's successful business career, neither in his financial position nor in his moral and political expression could he be presented convincingly as a 'hard-faced' plutocrat, still less as a
'profiteer'.

---

[65] Central Office statement in 'Political Notes', *The Times*, 23 Nov. 1923.
[66] *HCDeb* 197, cc. 1105–12 (29 June 1926); Lane-Fox to Irwin, 4 July 1926, Halifax Indian
papers 17/61.

CHAPTER 5

Purpose and methods

Baldwin's power and success cannot be adequately explained in terms of conventional Cabinet, party-managerial, or parliamentary performance, nor even by precocious use of the new mass media. His form of leadership was unusual – significantly different to that of most contemporaries, and even more to that which has become typical since the 1940s. It was also deliberate in both purpose and method. His own understanding of his main tasks was clear:

You see my job is to try and educate a new democracy in a new world and to try and make them realize their responsibilities in their possession of power, and to keep the eternal verities before them.[1]

On other occasions he described his work as 'preaching'.[2] It will be evident from the last two chapters that this conception of leadership had identifiable sources in his family and education, in aspects of late-Victorian culture and in a specific kind of local politics. These values, ideas, and experiences also shaped further crucial impetuses in his leadership – a particular assessment and a distinctive presentation of the problems of post-war public life.

I

Baldwin's politics were far removed from their subsequent characterisation as 'complacent' or 'escapist'. His Conservatism was acutely contemporary in its concerns, and he expressly contrasted himself to those unable 'to reconcile [them]selves to the age in which we live'. One of the difficulties was, he said, that 'this post-

---

[1] Baldwin to Monica Baldwin, 22 Dec. 1935, BF.
[2] Leeds, 12 March 1925; National Union, 24 June 1937; *Interpreter*, p. 10.

War world is full of pre-War minds'.[3] He himself had no doubt that the world had changed, irrevocably and dangerously. The Great War had not just produced the horror of a million British and Empire dead, millions disabled, and more millions bereaved. It had also created a 'Great Divide' between one age and another. As a Conservative and a businessman, and as someone who had absorbed the cultural anxieties of 1880s Cambridge, he found the 1920s and 1930s a transformed and alarmingly fluid world: 'The times are new and strange and extraordinarily difficult.'[4] This was an insistent theme of his speeches. They had 'left far behind us the age before the war' and entered a 'new era' with 'new movements and new spirits', and 'new problems'.[5] He spoke of changes in old imperial ties, of an unstable, vulnerable peace in Europe, and of disruption in the international and British economies. He spoke also of the extended role of the state, the huge financial burdens on government, of dislocated social relationships, and increased popular expectations. In a great 'breach with the past', familiar arrangements, practices, and disciplines had disappeared: 'the old landmarks had gone, and the buoys which marked the navigation of the dangerous waters had been swept away'.[6]

In a favourite dictum he described how the War had 'vastly accelerated' the pace of change: a half-century or a century of normal social evolution had been compressed into just four years, leaving all nations 'reeling' and 'giddy', and some propelled into revolution.[7] The sufferings and sacrifices of the working classes in particular had stimulated 'new ambitions' and 'a deeper and sterner resolve' to preserve and improve their standards of life, even to create 'a kind of earthly paradise'.[8] Wartime state collectivism had created illusions about the effectiveness of 'dramatic and spectacular' government action – in the peacetime possibilities of political 'short cuts', of curing 'all the ills of the world by

[3] *HCDeb* 276, c. 1134 (29 March 1933).
[4] Manchester, 2 Nov. 1923.
[5] Liverpool, 25 March 1935; National Union, 25 June 1937.
[6] Constitutional Club, 29 Jan. 1925. Cf. Oxford, 8 June 1923; *TTF* pp. 274–8 (30 Jan. 1930).
[7] E.g. Conservative party conference, 7 Oct. 1926; *OI* pp. 91, 115 (1, 3 Aug. 1927); *TTF* p. 278 (20 Jan. 1930); *HCDeb* 276, c. 1134 (29 March 1933); *SOL* p. 32 (26 June 1936); *Interpreter*, p. 88.
[8] Cambridge, 29 Feb. 1924; Aberdeen 2nd meeting, 5 Nov. 1925.

legislation'.[9] From extremes of horror and despair had come rampant demands for change. Yet, Baldwin said, there had been a
terrible reaction when the War was followed by a sharp inflationary boom and then a deep, prolonged, depression. As frustration
of earlier hopes bred disillusionment and anger, the wartime
national unity had dissolved into class tension and industrial conflict. 'The spirit of the age is . . . restless and dissatisfied.'[10]

For Baldwin – particularly the Baldwin who had absorbed
Maine – the difficulties had been magnified by another accelerat-
ing effect of the War: it had brought 'a fully-fledged democracy
before we are ready for it'. The threefold increase in the electorate
had swamped traditional party techniques, by making it 'perfectly
impossible for organisation alone to cope with' the vast numbers
of voters.[11] Worse, it had placed the fate of the nation and Empire
in the hands of 'millions of untrained and inexperienced voters
. . . all alike affected by the restlessness . . . in the atmosphere',
and in their simplicity 'peculiarly liable to be led away . . . by specious appeals'.[12] In a central and much repeated Baldwin notion,
the 'problem of the age' was that 'our people . . . [had attained] a
political status in advance of their cultural status'.[13] Even as he
retired as prime minister in 1937 he said that 'the masses were
not . . . educated' for universal suffrage – 'nor will they be for
another twenty or thirty years. That lag is the danger.'[14]

Baldwin assumed that these conditions had destabilised the
nation. The political agenda had been radically altered, as pre-war
issues were displaced by more fundamental and contentious
economic and social issues. The Liberal party had fragmented,
weakening its ability to lead and moderate the forces of the left.
A more powerful and ambitious trade-union movement and a
genuinely independent working-class politics had emerged. Socialism was now promoted by 'one of the most vigorous and sustained
propaganda[s] . . . that has ever appeared in this country'.[15] 'A
whole army of people' stood ready to believe that 'by a sudden

[9] Plymouth, 25 Oct. 1923; *OI*, pp. 7, 10 (19 June 1926).
[10] Worcester, 31 May 1924.
[11] *HCDeb* 244, c. 810 (4 Nov. 1930); 1912 Club, 20 May 1930.
[12] Constitutional Club, 29 Jan. 1925; Hotel Cecil, 29 June 1923.
[13] Ashridge, 1 July 1929, 1 Dec. 1934; *OI* p. 29 (4 March 1927); Ulster Reform Club, 15
Feb. 1930; Imperial press conference, 25 June 1930.
[14] 'Mr Baldwin's testament', 28 April 1937, Crathorne papers.
[15] Hotel Cecil, 29 June 1923.

transformation' they could for less work and more pay obtain 'conditions of greater comfort than have ever been known'. These postwar shifts intensified the long-held fear of many Conservatives, including Baldwin, that universal suffrage might bring a new politics of class, threatening property and private enterprise, perhaps even parliamentary government. Much more now seemed to be at stake than just the Conservative party's electoral prospects – the economic, social, and political order, and the maintenance of Britain's imperial and international power. The first two post-war elections, in which Conservatives obtained most MPs but only in obviously fluid circumstances and only on low percentages of the national poll, did not assuage these fears.

Baldwin considered the malaise to be very deep. Thanking the Liberal journalist J. A. Spender for a newspaper article on the morning before the outbreak of the next world war, he praised a particular paragraph as 'profoundly true', expressing 'the key to my speeches' since 1922. This passage began: 'In the last twenty years an attack has been made on the moral and religious foundations.'[16] Baldwin located the root of the post-1918 troubles in a crisis of values, expressed in both private and public as an anxious sense of cultural fragility. The War had revealed 'how thin is the crust of civilisation'. For four years men 'climbed to the doors of heaven' but also 'sank to the gates of hell',[17] and appalling legacies remained:

civilisation is but the ice formed in process of ages on the turbulent stream of unbridled human passions, and while this ice seemed to our fathers secure and permanent, it has [now] rotted and cracked . . . and in places the submerged torrent has broken through, leaving fragments in constant collision threatening by their attrition to diminish and ultimately disappear.[18]

The 'mentality of Europe' had shifted, with movements of ideas comparable in force to those of the Reformation and French Revolution.[19] Beliefs and structures which preserved mankind from 'the depth of chaos and anarchy' had been shaken, unleashing

[16] Baldwin to Spender, 4 Sept. 1939, and article, *The Sunday Times*, 3 Sept. 1939, in W. Harris, *J. A. Spender* (1946), pp. 233–4.
[17] *TTF* pp. 274 (20 June 1930); *OE* p. 229 (23 July 1923).
[18] *OE* p. 92 (6 Nov. 1925). Cf. Edinburgh, 24 March 1924; Imperial press conference, 25 June 1930; Primrose League, 3 May 1935.
[19] *SOL* pp. 100–1 (10 April 1937).

savagery, distrust, class hatred, and narrow nationalism. He spoke
often of the loss of a generation of future leaders at all social
levels, disrupting the transmission and renewal of traditional
values,[20] and of how rapid advances in science and technology had
created a confusion of 'mere acceleration with civilisation'.[21]
'Speed' had become a 'god', and material improvement had been
elevated into the greatest or only good.[22] New industrial processes
and mass propaganda had produced the 'terrible danger' that individual character would be destroyed by the development of 'mechanised', mass, minds: 'I dread the mass mind.'[23]

From the destructiveness of the War and its aftermath, Baldwin
drew a warning that progress was not inevitable. Checks, even
retrogression, could come, whether from external or internal
causes. In 1927 he talked privately about 'the ominous signs of an
approaching dark age in which civilisation would again perish'.[24]
His speeches declared that 'another war on the scale of the last
would be the death of our civilization'.[25] Bolshevism – 'a mon-
strosity of the bottomless pit'[26] – and the totalitarian, atheistic,
fascist and communist dictatorships constituted other forms of
civil suicide. No nation could now assume itself immune. As technology 'annihilated space and time in travel', all ideas passed with
'lightning rapidity . . . through the world' and the bad ones could
spread 'through this country as through others'.[27] Even within
Britain, socialism could 'destroy the moral standards of our people' and shatter the delicate economic arrangements that sustained their livelihood.[28]

During the immediate post-war industrial and political troubles
Baldwin wrote that 'we are all dancing on a pie-crust'.[29] Eight

[20] *OE* pp. 63–4 (13 March 1925); *TTF* pp. 305, 322–3 (10 Oct. 1931, 31 Oct. 1935); *SOL* pp. 34, 63 (26 June, 29 July 1936).
[21] *OE* p. 154 (27 Sept. 1923); Stourport, 8 Jan. 1934; Junior Imperial League, 23 March 1935; *SOL* p. 122 (16 April 1937).
[22] *SOL* p. 31 (26 June 1936). Cf. *TTF* pp. 21, 192 (6 March 1934, 13 June 1930); Fripp lecture, 26 Feb. 1932.
[23] *Interpreter*, pp. 62–5; *SOL* pp. 116–17 (13 April 1937).
[24] Henson journal, 21 June 1927.
[25] Primrose League, 3 May 1935. Cf. *OE* p. 106 (8 Jan. 1926); Conservative party confer-ence, 6 Oct. 1933; Wishaw, 20 June 1936; *Interpreter*, pp. 60–1.
[26] Baldwin to Hoare, 1 Nov. 1930, Templewood papers XVIII:3c (36).
[27] Scottish Unionist Conference, 17 Nov. 1933. Cf. Worcester, 14 April 1934; National Labour luncheon, 29 Oct. 1934.
[28] Queen's Hall, 19 Nov. 1923.
[29] Baldwin to his mother, 21 May 1919, BF.

years later he reflected that the General Strike had 'broke[n] up the great deeps', reinforcing his central concern. 'Democracy has arrived at a gallop in England, and I feel all the time that it is a race for life: can we educate them before the crash comes?'[30]

II

These understandings explain Baldwin's view that his main aim should be to make electors 'realise their responsibilities in the possession of power', and keep before them 'the eternal verities'. He dutifully expounded his own party's policies and criticised those of his opponents, but he knew that policy debates alone would have little effect if the political culture became hostile to the very presuppositions of Conservative politics. It was 'not sufficiently realized that what we were at present fighting was not a programme, but an atmosphere, which no amount of promulgation of counter programmes would effect'.[31]

Baldwin nevertheless assumed that this atmosphere could be counteracted. For all his political and cultural pessimism, he still found materials for hope and reconstruction. 'There is so much I hate in this age', he wrote privately in 1933, 'but there is a lot of good, and one must hold to it and have faith' – even though 'it ain't easy'.[32] This was a faith demanded by his religion, but it was drawn also from other aspects of his earlier life: belief in a fundamental popular virtue, 'Whig' understandings of national development, and Worcestershire experiences of a harmonious local community and Conservative working class. These provided some confidence in the supposedly 'true' qualities of the British people, if only they could be saved from political ignorance and delusion. He also offered another, more positive, interpretation of the effects of the War. It had not just generated evil, but been a time 'when the spiritual dominated over the material': when volunteers put country before comfort, when soldiers in the trenches rediscovered a sense 'of the fellowship and the brotherhood of men', when many of the wealthy and educated rededicated their lives to public service, and when the common

[30] Baldwin to Irwin, 26 June 1927 (but unfinished and mislaid, until re-discovered and forwarded in Jan. 1938 (*sic*)), Halifax papers A.4.410.14.2.
[31] Baldwin reported in Irwin to Davidson, 25 Feb. 1930, in *Davidson Memoirs*, p. 306.
[32] Baldwin to Irwin, 8 Sept. 1933, Halifax papers A4.410.14.4.

people displayed much 'devotion, patience and strength'.[33] The example of those years and the sacrifices of the war dead offered – as they had for Baldwin personally – forces of inspiration, constantly renewed through the 1920s and 1930s by innumerable private and public acts of remembrance. So, he declared, the post-war restlessness did not always arise from bad motives; it also expressed a new seriousness and idealism. Many of the electorate were not crassly materialistic: 'a far stronger motive than the desire to lead a more comfortable life' was a desire for escape from 'a starved mental and spiritual existence', and for opportunities to develop their minds.[34] 'There never was a time when there were more people in this country of ours, and especially among the young, determined to make whatever sacrifice is necessary for the advancement of the country's well-being, physical and spiritual.'[35] Britain was an ancient and successful nation which retained respected institutions, rich traditions of public duty, popular initiative and independence, and deep seams of national character and instinct. Even when 'so many old faiths have been shattered, when nothing is taken for granted, and everything is put on the table for examination and for vivisection', it still remained possible to ask the nation 'to stand in the old paths and to show . . . there is nothing that can take the place of honest, hard work, of thrift, of courage, of patience, and of endurance'.[36]

If Baldwin's concerns were contemporary, his form of leadership owed much to late-Victorian models. He frequently invoked Disraeli, most obviously because this served particular strategic purposes (see chapters 6 and 7). But his example may also have suggested a function and style. Like Disraeli and other nineteenth-century politicians, Baldwin understood that politics and government were ultimately a matter of 'discussion, of talk', not just about policies but more importantly about persuading people to accept a particular set of values and enmities.[37] His style was nearly as eccentric as Disraeli's in treating the specifics of policy

---

[33] *The Times*, 13 Dec. 1922; *OE* pp. 61–3, 272–5 (13 March 1925, 19 Dec. 1923); *OI* pp. 92–3 (1 Aug. 1927).
[34] Cambridge, 29 Feb. 1924.
[35] *TTF* p. 315 (10 March 1928).
[36] Aberdeen 2nd meeting, 5 Nov. 1925.
[37] *OE* p. 89 (6 Nov. 1925). Cf. J. Vincent, *Disraeli* (Oxford, 1990), pp. 46, 90. The notion of parliamentary government or democracy as 'government by speaking' or 'explanation' was in truth a Victorian commonplace, to be found from Macaulay to Balfour.

and administration as the work of subordinates, while he concentrated upon the larger matters of interest, opinion, and belief. Baldwin also shared the wider Victorian conception that the duties of responsible political leadership extended far beyond party, to the promotion of shared principles in national life, and even beyond the specifically political. For 'moral values . . . are the foundation of a country's greatness. If moral values flourish in our common life, all will be well with the nation'. It was 'more important to form good habits than to frame good laws'.[38]

Conservative leadership could not be passive or merely responsive; it had to be active and creative. In what Baldwin considered to be a divided and destabilised nation, his aim was to restore solidarity and stability on a Conservative basis. 'The main ambition of my life is to prevent the class war becoming a reality' – or, as he declared publicly soon after becoming prime minister, 'I want to be a healer.'[39] In pursuing this aim, Baldwin adopted the obvious rhetorical strategy of claiming to express the authentic feelings of 'the people'. But this did not mean that he intended anything so self-defeating – indeed, so meaningless – as to interpret or represent 'public opinion', still less the 'spirit of the age'.[40] On the contrary, his purpose was to resist some of the most vigorous opinions and much of the spirit of his time, because these seemed so hostile to Conservatism and to his understanding of national interest. He wanted to prevent socialism from becoming the opinion of the majority, and to check the infiltration of communist and fascist views.

All this required *choices*, choices which had to be re-made as circumstances changed. Even more than his predecessor, Bonar Law, Baldwin thought that in post-war conditions the Conservative party 'on the old lines will have no future in the life of this country'.[41] It had to be re-invented and re-positioned, but this was not an easy task, nor was it obvious how best to proceed. As has always been the case, but was especially so in the uncertainties of the early 1920s, various existing and possible forms of Conserva-

---

[38] *TTF* pp. 46, 87 (14 July 1930, 12 May 1931). Generally, see J. P. Parry, 'The Quest for Leadership in Unionist Politics 1886–1956', *Parliamentary History* 12 (1993), 297–8.
[39] R. Boothby, *I Fight to Live* (1947), p. 36; Edinburgh, 27 July 1923. Cf. *OE* p. 16 (12 Jan. 1925).
[40] See Introduction, p. 9.
[41] Ramsden, *Balfour and Baldwin*, p. 118.

tism were available, and several languages and tones in which to suggest what it meant or might mean. Baldwin had to decide what attitudes to adopt towards competing Conservatisms – whether Austen Chamberlain's dour coalitionism, Birkenhead's brash anti-socialism, the deflationary Conservatism of businessmen and suburban tax-payers, Cecilian aristocratic Conservatism, domestic and imperial die-hardism, Amery's doctrinaire protectionism, or Neville Chamberlain's administrative Conservatism.[42] If he was to dominate his party he needed to distinguish himself from each of these, and project his own particular kind of Conservatism. He also had to choose how to describe economic and social conditions, and the international and political situations. He had to decide what attitudes to adopt towards the Liberal and Labour parties, the trade-union movement, the communists and the fascists: how to characterise them; which of their ideas and symbols to resist, tolerate, or concede; when to do this, and in what ways. Choices had to be made about where to place the Conservative leadership in relation to these various opponents, where best to locate a Conservative 'middle ground', and where to set acceptable outer limits of any Conservative 'consensus'.

For a Conservative seeking stabilisation, the obvious course was to draw together the various natural bodies of resistance to radical change, and to stimulate fresh forms of resistance. In practice this meant capturing substantial parts of the Liberal and quasi-Liberal 'moderate' vote. Whatever Baldwin's personal feelings towards Lloyd George after 1922, the political rationale for hostility towards him was that the Liberal party posed the chief threat to Conservative electoral predominance. Conservative party interests – and Baldwin's own power – demanded the division and defeat of the collective Liberal leadership. Given the 'progressive' antecedents of Liberal politicians and voters, the deeper implication was that their division and capture required not just negative anti-socialism, but indications of constructive and virtuous purpose.

Baldwin thought there was a further and more fundamental imperative, given the enfranchisement of the poor, the envious, the unsophisticated and the innocent, and the emergence of 'evil

<hr>

[42] For the Conservatisms on offer in the early and mid 1920s, see Cowling, *Impact of Labour*, chs. 2–4, 6, 13, 15.

doctrines'. Conservative leadership now demanded 'education'. From the time he first became prime minister, this was a principal theme. 'We have to see that the heart of the nation . . . the key to the Empire . . . is sound, and to do that we must educate and educate and educate.'[43] The Conservative party could no longer be just an organisation for electoral mobilisation and defence of vested interests. It had also to become an agency for mass political 'education', in a larger version of Baldwin's work in the Primrose League habitations, National Conservative League branches, and friendly society lodges of Worcestershire. Not only did the party have to create more Conservative party supporters. It also had a wider task: to influence the politics of the many voters who would never support it. If a dangerous, possibly uncontrollable, polarisation were to be avoided, it had to try and define the nature of acceptable opposition to itself. Non-Conservatives had to be persuaded to act 'responsibly', within the limits of conventional political and industrial behaviour, and not to tolerate socialism, trade-union direct action, or worse. The Labour party itself had to be kept within the pale of the constitution, even at the cost of tolerance towards much of its activity, because its leadership of the political left was preferable to the possible alternatives. This strategy – of accepting, even encouraging, party re-alignments working to Conservative advantage – is plain in Baldwin's private comment after the Liberal setback at the 1924 election:

For some time I felt things were shaping towards the disappearance of the Liberal Party, but I did not think it would come so quickly. The next step must be the elimination of the Communists by Labour. Then we shall have two parties, the Party of the Right and the Party of the Left.[44]

Acceptance of Labour as the second major party did not mean that it was not to be soundly defeated at general elections. For Baldwin the problem here was that the Labour challenge had several dimensions. It did not present itself just as the party of the trade unions, nor only as the party of material advancement for the working population. Its greater appeal was as the party of modern ideals, of democracy, freedom, rights, peace, and the community. How best to counter the Labour threat had been central to Conservative divisions from 1920 to 1924, and Baldwin was not

[43] Primrose League, 2 May 1924.
[44] Jones *WD* I.301 (4 Nov. 1924).

alone in believing that successful resistance could not be mounted just by abuse and obstruction. A belief that the party needed to express its own form of idealism had been prominent in the various strands of Conservative revolt against the Lloyd George Coalition. After the formation of the first Labour government the debate was revived in the Conservative press.[45] Since Baldwin had just lost the 1923 election, few recalled that on becoming party leader he had expressed the same need, and offered his own solutions. But during 1924 and early 1925 his effectiveness in presenting a positive Conservatism became unmistakeable. In this respect too, Baldwin was clear about his task. It was 'to try to breathe new life, new principles, new aspirations and new ideals' into the Conservative party – because 'politics without ideals are no use at all'.[46]

As the educators had to be educated, so Baldwin impressed upon the various Conservative party organisations – National Union, Women's Unionist Association, Junior Imperial League, and Primrose League – the need for party workers to school themselves in economics and civics. He also encouraged the party's training facilities, the Philip Stott College and its later incarnation, the Bonar Law Memorial College at Ashridge.[47] But his chief instrument for 'educating' his party and the electorate – as well as for subverting the Liberal party and consolidating anti-socialist resistance – was his own utterances. For all his use of the new mass media and its capacity to reach huge audiences, Baldwin maintained the late Victorian tradition of addressing extraparliamentary meetings – and he made himself available for more meetings and for a wider range of organisations than any of his predecessors. Elements of his teachings were worked into innumerable parliamentary and platform speeches, implying unusual depths beneath the staple of policy pronouncements, debating points, and tactical statements. They formed the main themes for his speeches to the party's campaigning organisations and impromptu talks to overflow meetings, and received particular emphasis in election broadcasts and party films. More subtly, they

---

[45] Notably *The Times*, 6–18 March 1924, for extensive correspondence and leaders on 'Conservative ideals', with articles by Edward Wood, 'Conservative Beliefs' (14 March), and Lord Salisbury, 'Conservative Policy' (18–19 March).
[46] Dundas Castle, 16 June 1928; Cambridge, 4 March 1927.
[47] *Davidson Memoirs*, pp. 290–2; Ramsden, *Balfour and Baldwin*, pp. 236, 239.

were expressed also in his remarkably large number of addresses to 'non-political' audiences: to civic receptions and chambers of commerce; to professional, artistic, literary, scientific, and sporting associations; to friendly, county, and royal societies; to schools, colleges, and universities; to religious assemblies, and in BBC talks on cultural subjects or marking public occasions.

This emphasis on speeches as political education explains particular aspects of Baldwin's attention to the media – his concern not just to project visual images but to communicate words, his worries about poor speech reports in popular newspapers, and his cultivation of newer media able to reach across party and sectional divides. Before his 1929 election broadcasts he especially enquired what proportion of his listeners was likely to be working class.[48] His speeches and addresses did in fact reach large audiences. They were reported verbatim in the relevant provincial and organisational (educational, denominational, etc.) press, as well as the 'quality' national newspapers. A good many were reprinted as pamphlets. Selections were also published in four volumes which sold well and went into cheap editions. Moreover, his delivery of so many ostensibly 'non-political' addresses to so many different organisations yielded what were in practice significant *political* rewards. Together with the careful selection and avoidance of partisan passages for his collected volumes, they extended his media presentations as a man who touched many aspects of national life, whose authority reached beyond the political to the ethical and cultural, and who was less a party leader than a national spokesman.[49] To an unusual degree he sensed the existence of audiences beyond the ranks of committed party supporters, and had the confidence to appeal to them over the heads of party managers and other politicians – deliberately appearing to 'transcend the bounds of party',[50] and attempting to tap the politics of the unpolitical.

Nevertheless, his breadth of subject matter and his homiletic manner arose from more than just party or personal calculations. They were shaped by his understanding that as the post-war problems lay largely in atmosphere, values, and habits as well as opinions, so he had to administer not only to the mind but to deeper

[48] *Reith Diaries*, p. 102 (13 April 1929).
[49] The prefaces to each volume of his collected addresses are indicative: see esp. *OE* p. vii and *TTF* p. v.
[50] Jones, 'Stanley Baldwin', in *DNB*, p. 50.

springs of conduct: to belief, faith, imagination, not just 'for the health . . . but of the soul of the body politic'.[51] 'You can only drive out of people's hearts the impulses which . . . [are] bad and dangerous for the community by implanting in them something better and something more worth while living for.'[52] Improving upon a famous Disraelian dictum, in 1924 he declared the Conservative aim to be 'sanitation . . . the spiritual sanitation of our people'.[53] Baldwin used not just economic, social, and political argument but also history, literature, art, sport, topography, ethics, and religion to resist what he considered to be the dangerous tendencies of the modern age, and to suggest the superiority of a Conservative culture over socialism and the totalitarian ideologies.

Baldwin's politics, then, operated at several levels. As well as being party leader and prime minister, he was a political teacher and public moralist, even a lay preacher. This explains much of his apparently uneven and idiosyncratic performance, the bewilderment and exasperation of some colleagues and supporters, and the occasional leadership crises. Contrary to the intensifying twentieth-century focus upon programmes, legislation, and administration, Baldwin's deepest concerns were on a different plane and proceeded at a different pace to the ordinary dictates of parliamentary time-table and party need. Consequently he could appear negligent or abstracted, and in routine parliamentary and party speaking become very flat.

Yet he commanded great public respect, and especially when strongly moved he could wield astonishing authority. His real power lay in the roles of teacher and moralist, and in his creation of a public personality able to sustain those roles. In Baldwin's projection of himself as plain, honest, and commonsensical, with an ease and geniality which confounded suspicions of priggishness, he was able to deliver unusually high-minded and seemingly ingenuous messages which few other politicians could have presented without ridicule or offence.[54] He was also able to bring the qualities of teacher and moralist to bear upon the work of party leader and, for much of the time, to shift effortlessly between these functions. Above all Baldwin's power derived from a doctrine which while certainly 'con-

[51] Cambridge, 4 March 1927.
[52] Edinburgh, 27 July 1923.
[53] Unionist party meeting, 12 Feb. 1924.
[54] E.g. *Crawford Papers*, p. 503 (7 March 1925); *Bernays Diaries*, p. 197 (23 May 1935).

servative' was not exclusive to the Conservative party, but had wide foundations in British public life and appealed in some degree to people of all parties and of none. In themselves the things he said were not necessarily – or even usually – new or original. But he would have been much less successful if they had been, because they would have had fewer and narrower resonances. Jones said his appeal was to the 'eternal commonplaces', and if Baldwin himself preferred the phrase 'eternal verities'[55] he was not afraid of describing himself as 'a master of platitudes'. His explanation was that 'a platitude is simply a truth repeated'.[56] A better one would be that popular political culture is largely composed of platitudes. But effective leadership requires ability to select particular platitudes for particular purposes, to deploy those best able to form alliances between disparate interests and beliefs, and to instil them with a freshness that carries conviction. Especially for a Conservative in the new post-1918 conditions, this demanded unusual political talent.[57]

III

The following chapters concentrate upon exposition of Baldwin's doctrine and presentation. The whole range of his public utterances is used, from the obviously 'cultural' and didactic to the most partisan, and the primary – though not sole – perspective is that of Baldwin himself, because only in these terms do his purposes and meanings become clear. The procedure separates out broad themes which in his speeches were interwoven both with each other and with comment on the specific issues of the day. If this seems artificial, it can be said that the procedure has the advantage of identifying consistencies of preoccupation and teaching over long periods; that Baldwin was deliberately persistent in his themes, believing reiteration to be necessary in persuading a new, unsophisticated, electorate;[58] and that it was these themes which most shaped his place in public life.

Another possible objection to this approach requires fuller con-

[55] Jones, 'Baldwin' in *DNB*, p. 50; above p. 143.
[56] *HCDeb* 174, c. 727 (29 May 1924). Cf. *OE* p. 223.
[57] Vincent, *Disraeli*, p. 90: 'Political culture is a question of platitudes, but they must be the right platitudes; and uttering the right platitudes requires genius.'
[58] *Davidson Memoirs*, p. 171; Jones diary, 16 Nov. 1935.

sideration. Baldwin, it is now well known, used speech-writers. He did so to an extent which was new, and which remained unusual among interwar politicians; here again he anticipated a feature of more recent practice. It is a feature which has rarely been examined,[59] but in Baldwin's case it clearly requires investigation because it touches the core of his distinctive form of leadership. How much did he use speech-writers? In what senses were his speeches his own? To what extent were their concerns and messages really his own concerns and his messages? How far can their public effects be regarded as his achievement? Answers to these questions will help with a further, related, problem: how far, and in what senses, did he believe what he said in public?

Baldwin cultivated a relaxed style in public speaking, but this was the product of hard self-discipline. He was not naturally confident on the platform or at the despatch box, and he had to overcome a nervous stumbling and 'gulp' before he achieved his mature fluency – a transformation which one listener thought a 'miracle'.[60] Even so there are descriptions of his distress before even routine speeches, and the strain continued to be shown in his physical fidgets and grimaces while delivering them.[61] After a decade as a highly acclaimed speaker he could still say, simply, 'I hate speaking.'[62] The preparation of these speeches could be as painful as the delivery, 'weighing on my soul like lead'.[63] He wrote formal prose slowly and laboriously, anxiously counting the words as he proceeded[64] and mistrusting the outcome: 'I have never acquired the art of continuous composition: I do an occasional good patch amidst yards of bilge.'[65] Speeches for him were emphatically not the grand literary or intellectual exertions of Disraeli and Salisbury, or even of Balfour and Churchill. He could

[59] For the older practice of leaders composing their own speeches, see A. Chamberlain, *Down the Years* (1935), ch. 20. For an example of modern use of speech-writers, see *The Collected Speeches of Margaret Thatcher*, ed. R. Harris (1997), pp. xiv–xviii.
[60] Lord Reading (on his return in 1926 from five years in India) in A. Deane, *Time Remembered* (1945), pp. 114–15; *Crawford Papers* p. 482 (21 May 1923).
[61] M&B p. 502; AWB pp. 50, 139; Butler memo., 20–21 July 1935, Butler papers G6/57; Blumenfeld, *All in a Lifetime*, p. 158.
[62] Somervell journal, 17 Feb. 1934.
[63] Baldwin to Joan Davidson, 15 April 1930, 1 Oct. 1934, JD.
[64] Jones *WD* II.178, 180, and see e.g. drafts for Edinburgh Rectorial, SB 186/139–45, and Toronto lectures, BF.
[65] Baldwin to Jones, 1 March 1939, Jones papers A6/132.

write excellent short prefaces for other people's books,[66] but however ample the advance notice found it difficult to complete drafts for extended published addresses.[67] Even after his ministerial retirement and when substantially 'plagiarising' his earlier addresses, he needed help with his three Toronto lectures in 1939 and his British Council booklet in 1940.[68] Although he had unique knowledge for the task and collected further materials, he was unable to complete a commission to write the entry on Kipling for the *Dictionary of National Biography*.[69]

These experiences confirmed his view that 'my tongue, not my pen, is my instrument'.[70] Yet the detail, the political or diplomatic delicacy, the variety of subjects, and the sheer frequency of speechmaking demanded by his own conception of leadership were together so great – almost certainly greater than for any previous prime minister – that he did not usually trust in unaided oratorical inspiration. Considerable preparation was necessary, for which he often felt he had insufficient time and ingenuity. 'In the happy pre-war days', he wrote after his first five months as prime minister, 'our Statesmen could lock themselves up for days before a big speech', but 'now you have to prepare at odd moments'.[71] He quickly became dependent upon assistance from others – another aspect of his habit of delegating matters of detail. For non-political addresses, he sought basic ideas, outlines, or passages from qualified acquaintances, for example May Morris on her father, Kathleen Hilton Young on sculptors, Bishop Henson on the prayer book, or Lord Crawford on rural preservationism. His appropriation of striking phrases was not confined to Kipling: the 'manysidedness of truth' came from Lord Shaw of Dunfermline, the Rhine as 'our frontier' from Lady Milner.[72] Hewins, the protectionist economist, provided material on trade and imperialism in 1923

---

[66] Jones *WD* II.11, 13; Jones *DL* p. 369; *Davidson Memoirs*, p. 173. Examples in *OI* pp. 301–4, *TTF* pp. 139–43.
[67] Baldwin to Joan Davidson, 9 Sept. 1924, 15 April 1930, JD; Jones *WD* I.309, 330, II.2, 11.
[68] *Interpreter*, pp. 10–11; Baldwin to Jones, March 1939, Jan.–March 1940, Jones papers A6/132–5, 148–57; Jones *DL* p. 432 (2 April 1939).
[69] Jones *DL* pp. 527–8 (7 Feb. 1945). For collection of material, letters to Baldwin, March–June 1945, in Kipling papers, 1/20–23. Baldwin passed the task on to G. M. Young.
[70] Jones *DL* p. 540 (5–7 Jan. 1946). Cf. 1940 letter in *AWB* p. 325.
[71] *AWB* pp. 122–3.
[72] *The Liverpool Post*, 3 Aug. 1928; P. Donner, *Crusade* (1984), p. 109, but cf. *A. Chamberlain Diary Letters*, p. 266, for a Chamberlain version in 1926.

and 1924.[73] Reith supplied a few passages for broadcasts, notably on the General Strike, and even supplied the closing appeal for Baldwin's 1929 election broadcasts.[74] Dawson helped with some speeches and statements, especially when Baldwin felt beleaguered within his party in 1930–1.[75] Shadow Cabinet or Cabinet colleagues – including, after 1931, non-Conservative members of the National government – supplied drafts on their own areas of ministerial responsibility. On occasion they individually or collectively reviewed or drafted whole speeches.[76] More often preparation was done by party or government officials. Conservative Central Office officials drafted many speeches, particularly during the periods in opposition, for party conferences and for election films. From 1931 they were assisted by the Conservative Research Department, which drafted the 1935 election broadcasts. For political speeches in Scotland, drafts came from the party's Scottish whips.[77] Passages on particular areas of government policy routinely came from officials in the relevant departments.[78] For Baldwin's 1927 Canadian tour, a Dominions Office official both drafted speeches in advance and travelled in his entourage to supply final touches. Stewart helped with Indian speeches, Horace Wilson wrote on industrial relations in the 1920s and foreign policy in the 1930s, and Hankey assisted on imperial defence, disarmament, and later rearmament.[79] Baldwin's private secretaries helped co-ordinate the compilation, and sometimes contributed themselves; for example Patrick Duff's classical education was plundered for his address to the Classical Association.[80]

Above all, there was Tom Jones. He had earlier helped Bonar Law by preliminary discussion and listening to rehearsals, but by

---

[73] Jones *WD* I.252; Hewins, *Apologia of an Imperialist* II.282–3.
[74] *Reith Diaries*, pp. 95, 100, 102–3, 124n10, 184–5, 214–15.
[75] Dawson diary, 31 Jan., 8, 9 Oct. 1930, 3, 5 March, 17 July 1931. The implication in Cowling, *Impact of Hitler*, p. 260, followed in Wiener, *English Culture*, p. 114, that Bryant was among Baldwin's speech writers, derives from a misunderstanding.
[76] E.g. N. Chamberlain to his wife, 15, 22 July 1932, NC 1/26/467–8; Simon diary, 22 May 1935.
[77] Ramsden, 'Baldwin and Film', p. 133; Research Department material in CRD 1/8/1, 1/7/24; and see many drafts in SB 182–204.
[78] E.g. Jones *WD* I.243, 251, II.91; Jones diary, 12 Oct. 1935.
[79] Jones *WD* II.41, 91, 102, 106, 115; Jones *DL* pp. 5 n.2, 330; Roskill, *Hankey* II.427, III.64, 115, 151.
[80] Jones *WD* II.2. Generally, see *ibid.* 91; Fry to Jones, 9 Aug. 1933, Jones papers A6/70; Jones diary, 7 March 1936.

autumn 1923 Baldwin had him writing much of his speeches for
the protectionist election campaign – even though Jones was both
a civil servant and a free trader. While Baldwin was in opposition
during 1924 Jones gave only occasional assistance with literary
addresses, but this was so appreciated that on Baldwin's return as
prime minister Jones became chief advisor for many of his public
statements, whether political speeches or 'non-political' addresses
and occasional writings. He prompted Baldwin with books and articles, and suggested ideas, anecdotes, quotations, or phrases. He
took over Baldwin's incomplete drafts or collected briefs from
others, collating and shaping the various materials into fuller
drafts. Often he did virtually all the work himself, producing complete drafts. Increasingly he took the initiative, to the extent that
in 1925 the Central Office had to dissuade him from writing Baldwin's party conference speech. In 1929 he again drafted many
election speeches. After Baldwin's defeat and after his own retirement from the civil service, his assistance became less regular and
more concentrated on non-party subjects, but it remained substantial and included drafts for some of Baldwin's major addresses and
broadcasts.[81] Unbeknown to Baldwin, when Jones fell ill before
the celebrated address to the Peace Society in October 1935, he
subcontracted the drafting to a civil-service friend, Wilfred Eady.[82]
Jones estimated that about half of *On England* had been written
by himself, and large parts of Baldwin's further three volumes of
collected addresses were his too, along with a third of the Toronto
lectures.[83] Baldwin sometimes admitted to feeling 'an awful fraud'
when delivering Jones's drafts; and when he happened to receive
fees for them, the mutual embarrassment was relieved by agreement to pay the money to Mrs Baldwin's charities.[84] After the
Peace Society address, Baldwin wrote that 'I delivered the speech
with conviction and delight. I almost felt it was my own!'[85]

[81] For just some evidence of Jones's contribution, see Jones *WD* I.238, 243–4, 262, 275, 303, 330, II.4, 61, 179, 277; Jones *DL* pp. 25, 115, 162, 164–5, 414; E. L. Ellis, *T. J. A Life of Thomas Jones* (Cardiff, 1992), pp. 257–9, 296, 316, 324, 374–5, 395. Further evidence is in Jones papers A6, AA4, and SB 182–204.
[82] Jones diary, 1 Nov. 1935; memo, 1 Feb. 1941, Jones papers AA4/58. These correct Ellis, *T. J.*, p. 395.
[83] Jones *WD* II.11 (14 April 1926); Jones *DL* p. 432 (2 April 1939); Jones to Young, 14 April 1948, Jones papers A7/56.
[84] Jones diary, 27 Feb. 1932; Ellis, *T. J.*, p. 296n, and see p. 374 for Baldwin describing himself as 'champion plagiarist'.
[85] Baldwin to Jones, 31 Oct. 1935, Jones papers A6/91.

The evidence of the assistance Baldwin received is so considerable that, as Jones observed, a research student could probably identify the original authors of most of his speeches.[86] In recent and more knowing times the use of speech-writers by politicians has become familiar and unexceptionable. But in Baldwin's time it was so novel, and thought so likely to damage his reputation and the mystique of political leadership, that the public pretence that every word was his own was carefully preserved, even by G. M. Young.[87] Not until 1954 did Jones publicly reveal something of his own contribution, and even then a coyness on the subject long remained.[88] Most of Baldwin's contemporaries made some use of departmental or party drafts, but they still largely composed their own speeches. In 1923 Hankey, despite having written material for Lloyd George and other Coalition ministers, was 'inexpressibly' shocked that Baldwin had speeches written for him. Later, Neville Chamberlain could not think 'how S.B. can bear to read out other people's speeches'.[89] But even Chamberlain and other colleagues did not suspect the extent of his reliance on speech-writers,[90] because they were unaware how many he used. Insofar as some did know that he used speech-writers at all, this may have seemed additional proof of his shortcomings.

Yet despite the assistance Baldwin received, the speeches remained his speeches. Where it mattered, he chose the material and the speech-writers. He knew what he wanted. While he usually found it convenient to take slabs of prose from authoritative or congenial sources, it was certainly not the case, as Amery thought in 1925, that Baldwin accepted 'anything drafted for him'. Amery later discovered this himself, when his proffered drafts on protectionist themes were ignored. Baldwin similarly rejected a Birkenhead draft on the end of the General Strike as 'not in his style'.[91]

---

[86] Jones *WD* II.11.
[87] Jones informed Young that he had drafted some of Baldwin's major speeches, but added that 'I hope and assume you'll say nothing of all this': Jones to Young, 14 April 1948, Jones papers A7/56.
[88] Jones *DL* pp. xxv–xxvi, xxxi, and *passim*. In 1955 Jones said of Baldwin that '*all* his best speeches were his own': Ellis, *T. J.*, p. 296n (my italics). *Davidson Memoirs*, p. 171, claimed that he 'never spoke from a manuscript', qualified on p. 173 to 'not very often'. Even M&B pp. 501–2 understates the position.
[89] Roskill, *Hankey*, II.352 (diary, 9 Dec. 1923); N. Chamberlain to his wife, 22 July 1932, NC 1/26/468.
[90] As is clear from their numerous letters of congratulations on his addresses.
[91] *Amery Diaries*, I.420, and see e.g. I.563–4, II.136–7; Jones *WD* II.56.

Nor could Jones always expect his ideas or drafts to be accepted. By keeping several sources of assistance available, Baldwin could select, add, revise, or find alternatives, until he had something to his own satisfaction. Sensing that the draft General Strike broadcast over which Wilson and Jones had sweated blood lacked a final personal inspiration – 'this tripe' was his description – he showed it to Reith, who produced the famous peroration 'I am a man of peace . . .'.[92] Finding a Hoare draft for a crucial Indian speech in 1931 too diehard, he took it for revision to Dawson.[93] He asked Reith to help amend Jones's draft for the broadcast on the death of King George V, and Jones to re-cast Reith's draft for his last major address as prime minister, to the Empire Rally of Youth.[94]

Draftsmen were chosen because they had ability to express particular purposes or achieve a desired tone. Reith was not just a broadcasting expert, but a Scottish Presbyterian at one time attracted to the Labour party, who was much concerned with elevating popular understanding, evoking 'idealism' among the young, and sustaining Christian values in public life.[95] Jones matched Baldwin's requirements even more closely. Baldwin himself was conscious of how Jones helped broaden his perspective and appeal: 'I am a Tory P.M., surrounded with a Tory Cabinet, moving in Tory circles. You don't let me forget or ignore the whole range of ideas that normally I should never be brought up against if you were not in and out of this room.'[96] This was certainly important, yet their similarities were equally significant: in some sense Jones constituted a left-of-centre version of Baldwin. Aside from his wide official and political knowledge, academic contacts and vast reading, Jones was a Welsh Methodist and – like Baldwin – a near-ordinand influenced by F. D. Maurice's theology. He had Labour sympathies, yet opposed state socialism and industrial conflict. For social improvement he looked to 'civic responsibility' and 'public-spirited voluntary effort'. He helped pioneer wider adult education, believing – again like Baldwin – that there was a 'race

[92] Jones *WD* II.41, *Reith Diaries*, p. 95, both 8 May 1926, and see reproduced verbatim draft opposite p. 272 (M&B p. 412 are mistaken in saying Baldwin simply used notes).
[93] Dawson diary, 3 March 1931.
[94] Jones *DL* pp. 163, 164 (24 Jan. 1935); *Reith Diaries*, pp. 185, 214–15 (21 Jan. 1936, 16 April–18 May 1937); Jones diary, 18 May 1937. The outcomes are in *SOL* pp. 11–20, 156–67.
[95] *Reith Diaries*, pp. 82–3, 99, 100, 124 n.10, 120, 185.
[96] Jones *WD* II.167–8.

between popular education and social catastrophe'. His motto for
the 1920s was 'Reconciliation, Interpretation, Enlightenment and
intellectual integrity to counteract the class war'.[97]
  While Jones or other assistants provided many of the specific
ideas and large quantities of prose, Baldwin usually gave them the
leading themes. They worked to instruction. Sometimes this was
an outline or the outcome of extended discussion, but even if just
a sentence or two he still provided the fundamental point.[98] If at
times he simply read out the resulting draft, he more commonly
added his own material, whether from notes or extempore. Party
speeches and non-party addresses were often patchworks, with sections by others introduced, interspersed, or concluded by his own
passages – and these passages were usually the most significant or
characteristic parts, establishing the tone or moral of the whole.[99]
Recognising this quality, Jones encouraged Baldwin to make major
oratorical initiatives, or on occasion – even momentous ones –
declined to write a full draft but left him to assimilate his briefs
and then to 'trust to the moment for words and phrases'.[100] Baldwin also gave many short impromptu speeches, which again normally expressed his chief and most persistent concerns. On provincial visits, well-prepared political speeches were often followed by
unscripted – but equally fully reported – talks to overflow meetings
or party workers. For example, at Stirling in January 1926 he
began his second speech by describing his main (Jones-drafted)
speech on housing as 'dull', went on to say that sometimes 'the
things one talks about at [smaller] meetings are really the most
important of all', and then spoke vigorously on his favourite theme
of 'democracy'.[101] Non-party addresses could emerge in the same
way. Moved by an occasion in Canada, he discarded a draft by
Kipling in order to express his own feelings. Having struggled with
Duff to write the Classical Association address, he simply spoke

[97] Jones *DL*, p.xxiii; Ellis, *T. J.*, pp. 20–73, 104, 113–14, 151–3, 182–3, 296, 299–303, 307–8.
[98] E.g. Jones *WD* I.306, 309, 312, 325, II.21, 99, 154, 155.
[99] See e.g. drafts for speeches at Plymouth, 25 Oct. 1923; Manchester, 2 Nov. 1923; Albert Hall, 4 Dec. 1924, in SB 182–4; and drafts in Jones papers, A6/5.
[100] Jones *WD* I.326, II.2, 56, 137, 152 (5 Aug. 1925, 8 Jan., 13 May 1926, 17 May, 23 Oct. 1928); Jones *DL* pp. 57, 164 (14 Sept. 1932, 24 Jan. 1936).
[101] *The Glasgow Herald*, 27 Jan. 1926, which like other Scottish papers printed both principal and overflow speeches in full. Jones *WD* II.4 (25 Jan. 1926) records preparation of the first speech.

extempore to the English Association – and obtained equally enthusiastic press notices.[102] Even when assistance was available he produced full addresses or speeches of his own, whether scripts or from notes, including some of the most celebrated: on 'England' in 1924, the March 1925 speeches on industrial peace, on India in November 1929, against the press lords in March 1931, on 'national character' in 1933 and the Canadian dead in 1936, on the Abdication, in New York in 1939.[103] Much that he said in the Commons was improvised from his own basic notes – in contrast to Churchill's elaborate drafts – and he always prepared his own Worcestershire speeches and took great care with election broadcasts. Asquith had early noted 'what good English' Baldwin spoke. Vansittart thought him 'at his best when uninspired by others': when scripted by Jones he was good, 'but not so good as himself'. For his part Jones had no doubt that 'S.B. knows how to write' as well as speak: 'all the best parts' of the Classical Association address were his, and he 'often' improved Jones's drafts.[104]

The essential themes and the tone of Baldwin's speeches and addresses were certainly his own. These were anticipated in his early speeches – those delivered before, during, and immediately after the War – when he certainly did not have draftsmen, and they had firm roots in his education and early experience. These themes and tones were developed extensively during his first five months as prime minister in 1923, as he very deliberately presented himself as a new kind of Conservative leader. These and his later elaborations established a distinctive style and message, one that Jones and his party speech-writers took care to imitate. They wrote not just under direction, but according to pattern. Jones said that 'I only provided him with words to fit the faith which I knew was in him.'[105] Moreover, the 1923–5 speeches,

[102] N. Waterhouse, *Private and Official* (1942), pp. 348–9; *OI* pp. 284–5. See also a significant case in J. D. Jones, *Three Score Years and Ten* (1940), p. 120.
[103] Handwritten drafts survive for 'national character' in Jones papers A6/72; Canadian dead, Crathorne papers; New York, BF; Abdication speech notes are in SB 176. Among numerous indications of his unaided efforts, see Jones *DL* pp. 32, 43, 118, 127, 138, 204, 330, 539–40.
[104] K. Young, *Baldwin*, p. 16; Vansittart, *Mist Procession*, p. 356; Jones *WD* II.2, 11, 13, 39, 167; Ellis, *T. J.*, p. 296n.
[105] Jones diary, 20 May 1937, also 27 Feb. 1932, and see Ellis, *T. J.*, p. 258. Jones's papers contain many transcripts or reports of Baldwin's speeches. This does not necessarily indicate that Jones was their author; they were, rather, essential for reference if Jones was to ensure that his drafts were consistent with those speeches he did not draft.

together with aural and visual impressions in the media, also created that singular political personality which gave credibility to drafts which, read out by anyone else, would have had considerably less impact. So, for instance, while the words heard by the Peace Society in October 1935 were Eady's and Jones's, the effect came from their delivery not simply by a prime minister, but specifically by Baldwin. In these senses, colleagues and commentators were not far wrong when they praised this and other 'ghosted' addresses as supremely Baldwinian.

All this also goes much of the way towards answering the question whether Baldwin believed what he said. Like any other politician his language was highly instrumental. Most of his more specific statements had obvious tactical purposes, as the pressures of circumstance and demands of party or government inexorably placed means and manoeuvre before principle or private belief. Tolerance or agreement, no less than outrage or opposition, could be affected or manufactured, as necessary lubricants in the political struggle. Such statements will not necessarily tell us what Baldwin thought about particular issues, nor anything specific about party or government decision-making. Nevertheless, once their tactical character is understood they may indicate an underlying texture of values. It is equally clear, as the following chapters will show, that Baldwin's more general and persistent themes – his public doctrine – were also manipulative, in seeking to achieve certain strategic aims. Even his public presentation of post-war problems with which this chapter opened were made with an emphasis that reveals a desire beyond the descriptive – to evoke particular reactions among his listeners and readers. Whether this means that these wider themes were as affected as the tactical statements can only be a matter of judgement, though it should be said that an instrumental use of language does not necessarily signify absence of belief: manipulation and principle are not exclusive. But even if his themes were thought to be wholly simulated this would not subvert the principal interpretations offered here, which relate to their *public* purposes and effects.

We have the verdict of one uniquely experienced practitioner, Balfour, whose political memory reached back to the high-Victorian era of Disraelian and Gladstonian oratory. When he had first learned in 1923 that Baldwin 'relied to a very great extent' for assistance with speeches, he had felt confirmed in his initial poor opinion of him: 'a very ordinary sort of person'. By 1929 his opinion had changed. 'No man . . . could achieve what Baldwin had done without putting into it something of his own'; and in having 'always managed to say and do the right thing at the right moment', he had shown himself to be a political 'genius'.[106]

[106] Hankey diary, 30 May 1929.

1. Baldwin in the mid 1920s

2. Wilden House, garden front: the Baldwin family home from 1870

E. P. & W. BALDWIN,

WILDEN IRON WORKS,

NEAR STOURPORT,

MAKERS OF

CHARCOAL and other BEST QUALITIES of SHEET
IRON;
STAMPING SHEETS; CIRCULAR SHEETS;
BLACK PLATES;
THIN IRON, 30 to 40 W.G.;
SHEET IRON PICKLED COLD ROLLED and CLOSE
ANNEALED;
CANADA PLATES;
CHARCOAL and COKE TIN and TERNE PLATES;
BEST CHARCOAL TIN PLATES for DEEP
STAMPING.

All Sheet Iron branded **BALDWIN—WILDEN,** *and marked
with distinguishing quality,*

B.   BB.   BBB.   B Char'l.   EB Char'l.

Tin Plates for
Deep Stamping } *branded* **E. P. & W. B.**
W. H. *Best Charcoal Tin.*

Tin Plates for
general working } ,, **WILDEN** *Charcoal.*
UNICORN *Charcoal Tin.*
ARLEY 👑 *Tin.*

Coke Tin Plates ,, **STOUR** *Coke Tin.*

Tin Plates specially prepared for Gas Meter purposes.

As we find that Sheet Iron is being sold marked with our distinguishing
quality B. BB. &c., we must draw attention to the fact that all our Sheet
Iron has the brand BALDWIN—WILDEN on the *bands of each bundle.*

3. E. P. & W. Baldwin advertisement, 1873

4. The first board of directors of Baldwins Ltd., 1902
Left to right, back: Stanley Baldwin, W. Charles Wright, Roger Beck, Samuel
Dore, Aubrey Butler
front: John Roper Wright, Alfred Baldwin, Isaac Butler

5. Astley Hall, near Stourport-on-Severn: Baldwin's Worcestershire home from 1902

6. With Baldwins Ltd workers in the garden of 10 Downing Street, May 1923

7. *(opposite top)* With Tom Jones and Windham Baldwin, at Astley, 25 November 1923

8, *(opposite bottom)* The 'countryman' at a Worcestershire agricultural show

9. With Neville Chamberlain in Parliament Square, late 1920s

10. A 1929 election poster

11. On campaign, with Mrs Baldwin

12. Before the camera, in the garden of 10 Downing Street

13. The international statesman: opening the London naval conference,
9 December 1935

THE WORCESTERSHIRE LAD

FARMER BULL. "WELL DONE, STANLEY: A LONG DAY AND A RARE STRAIGHT FURROW."

14. On retirement, May 1937; 'farmer' Baldwin thanked for his work in the field of Empire

15. The Baldwin memorial, 1950, beside the B4194 road near Astley village, Worcestershire. The four sides of inscription read: 'Stanley Baldwin 1867 1947/First Earl Baldwin of Bewdley K.G./Three Times Prime Minister/At the Top of This Hill in Astley Hall Lived & Died'

CHAPTER 6

Capitalism and industrial relations

Baldwin's economic and social doctrine emerged from four areas of experience and belief. As a manufacturer he considered industrial capitalism the basis of national wealth. City directorships and Treasury posts reinforced his acceptance of orthodox financial precepts. As a Christian Conservative he prized a stable and harmonious community in which rich and poor respected each other and observed mutual obligations, while as a tariff reformer he assumed that limited forms of state intervention might be desirable. Together these dispositions generated certain policy preferences, yet precluded dogmatic attachments. He read some economics,[1] knew Keynes from the wartime Treasury, and occasionally revealed shrewd economic intuitions.[2] But as an industrialist and pupil of Cunningham he was even more sceptical than most politicians towards economists, and trusted instead the practical, 'common-sense' thinking of the businessman and civil servant.[3] His own experiences gave him no cause to expect serious friction between industrial interests, conventional public finance and his understanding of Conservatism. He did not believe that private enterprise in itself engendered class conflict. Nor did he consider post-war deflation inimical to industry, or protection inconsistent with the gold standard. Nevertheless his various experiences ensured that his economic and social attitudes were not inert, still less reactionary. They meant also that he considered the political

---

[1] See references to economic journals in *HCDeb* 4s.lxiii, c. 2095 (25 June 1914); 5s.170, c. 1985 (10 March 1924).

[2] An unusual comment about the possible benefits of reduced exports (due to distorted terms of trade) in *HCDeb* 169, c. 631 (21 Jan. 1924), bewildered his MPs but impressed economists: see M&B p. 304; P. Hill and R. Keynes (ed.), *Lydia and Maynard* (1989), p. 152. He first made the point (more clearly) at Plymouth, 25 Oct. 1923.

[3] E.g. preface to Ashley, *Ashley*, pp. 8–9; Jones *WD* ii.20 (24 April 1926); *HCDeb* 166, cc. 576–7 (4 July 1923).

difficulty to be less economic fundamentals and policy specifics than a more general socio-economic problem: how to re-stabilise private enterprise, national finance, and social order in the face of a working-class electorate seduced by socialism, and a workforce agitated by 'irresponsible' trade unionism. With economic and class issues now central to politics as never before, and in conditions of heightened social tension, Baldwin had the task – and the opportunity – of creating persuasive Conservative arguments on these matters. He thought himself uniquely qualified to do so.

I

This is not to say that Baldwin's views on economic and social *policies*, as such, were unusual for a front-rank Conservative politician. He made just one policy initiative – the adoption of protection in 1923 – and that was a political failure. Like almost everyone else, he was perplexed by the post-war domestic recession and 1929 world depression. Examination of his handling of these areas of policy nevertheless indicates important characteristics of his political approach.

In one respect he might seem to be a stereotypical interwar Conservative. As a Treasury minister during the post-war transition, he helped create the 'anti-inflationary' financial regime which prevailed until the late 1930s.[4] He had an unpublicised part in the imposition of new expenditure controls from 1919, deflation and debt reduction from 1920, and commitment to a restored gold standard, completed in 1925, as well as the very public and controversial role in the 1923 American debt settlement. Whether he later recognised – as did some industrial leaders – a connection between these decisions and the persistence of industrial stagnation and unemployment is uncertain. Publicly he welcomed the gold standard as 'the coping stone' in the rehabilitation of Britain as an international financial power,[5] but he also presented industrial adjustments to the new exchange levels as 'necessary and salutary' because stable currencies were 'the key to the revival of

---

[4] For the political and ideological aspects of this regime, see McKibbin, *Ideologies of Class*, pp. 265–7.
[5] *HCDeb* 184, cc. 1130, 1134–5 (25 May 1925), claiming a share in 'every one of the steps' in this rehabilitation. In *HCDeb* 110, c. 2972 (14 Nov. 1918), he had given warm support for the Cunliffe Committee report.

trade'.[6] What is obvious is his common ground with the 'anti-waste' protests of middle-class tax-payers, salary-earners, *rentiers*, and businessmen in the Conservative heartlands during the early 1920s. At the Board of Trade and as Chancellor of the Exchequer – when he urged the Cabinet to consider its responsibilities to the tax-payer as analogous to those of a company board to its shareholders[7] – he spoke of price and wage cuts as 'an absolutely necessary precedent' for recovery, and of the 'burden of taxation' as 'crushing our industries'. The government's 'utmost endeavours must be used to lessen the expenditure of the country and to lighten the taxation'.[8]

After he became prime minister, however, he evidently decided that deflation alone was not sufficient to facilitate economic recovery, and that if taken much further might provoke a 'socialist' backlash among the electorate. It is true that the essentials of 'sound finance' were now in place, and that he continued to defend these against purported, and sometimes real, Labour and Liberal assaults. But he effectively called a halt to the more self-interested demands of Conservative backbenchers, constituents, and press. In July 1923 he declared government policy to be 'non-flationist', neither deflationary nor inflationary but aiming to 'do all in our power to keep prices steady'.[9] He also concluded that there was little prospect of further large-scale retrenchment.[10] One effect was a less stringent attitude towards budgetary principles. In the late 1920s he tolerated from Churchill a series of 'window-dressing' expedients to create a nominal budget balance, devices he would earlier have regarded as 'conjuring tricks'.[11]

More significant was an acceptance of what were, by pre-war standards, high levels of social-service expenditure. Another of Baldwin's themes during the 1920s was that Britain had become economically vulnerable because it was 'over-industrialised'. Its eccentrically large urbanised population was dependent both upon

---

[6] Knowsley Park, 25 July 1925; Cardiff, 5 Oct. 1927.

[7] CP150(23), 16 March 1923.

[8] *The Times*, 16 March 1922; *The Sheffield Telegraph*, 8 Nov. 1922; *The Western Mail*, 2 Nov. 1922. These were recurrent themes in his speeches from 1921 to May 1923.

[9] *HCDeb* 166, c. 576 (4 July 1923): a notable statement, winning approval in *Keynes Collected Writings*, XIX.241, 262, 266.

[10] *Amery Diaries* I.344–5 (30 Aug. 1923).

[11] See *The Birmingham Post*, 5 Feb. 1923. For amusement at Churchill's methods, see e.g. *WSC Comp* v/i.984–6.

export markets made less reliable by international competition
and economic nationalism, and upon labour-intensive production
which modern machinery was making redundant. He was explicit
about the possible effects in a Cabinet paper of March 1922:

I feel that we have reached the point or perhaps . . . passed it where we
are able to find continuous employment under satisfactory conditions for
our people. My fear is that we may find even after an expansion of trade
that we shall have with us a pool of unemployed who will quickly degener-
ate into unemployable and become a perpetual danger to the social and
political life of the country.[12]

From this perspective, Baldwin had several leading ideas about
policy. One, despite anxieties about the tax burden, was the
importance of social policies in containing distress and discontent,
and thereby the Labour electoral challenge. The principle of
unemployment insurance had to be preserved, as one of 'the sheet
anchors of the industrial system of this country'.[13] In the late
1920s his government declined to confront the actuarial problems
of the unemployment insurance system, but paid for the larger
numbers of long-term unemployed simply by relaxing its financial
arrangements, and eventually resorting to borrowing. There was
also assistance for those in employment, to provide new evidence
of Conservative goodwill. From late 1923 and more especially in
opposition to the 1924 Labour government, he committed the
party to limited advances in social reform,[14] notably Neville
Chamberlain's housing programme, extension of the pensions
system, and improved maternity and infant care. The derivation
from Baldwin's and several of his colleagues' membership of the
pre-war Unionist Social Reform Committee is manifest, a constructive answer to 'new liberalism' now becoming a positive
response to 'socialism'.

In principle – if not in detail – these social policies were uncon-
tentious between the parties. This was their political purpose, to
demonstrate that the Conservative leadership was attuned to central opinion. They were controversial only among other Conserva-

---

[12] 'Trade Prospects', CP3890, 25 March 1922. For 'over-industrialisation' see also, e.g.
    HCDeb 153, cc. 2417–18 (11 May 1922); Glasgow, 26 July 1923; Plymouth, 25 Oct.
    1923.
[13] *HCDeb* 160, c. 558 (16 Feb. 1923); Aberdeen, 5 Nov. 1925.
[14] E.g. Swansea, 30 Oct. 1923; *HCDeb* 168, c. 489 (15 Nov. 1923); and 1924 speeches
    passim.

tives, especially because of the implications for taxation. Baldwin therefore had to persuade his party to accept what he regarded as the new realities of public finance. It was 'perfectly obvious that ... personal taxes must remain for many years at a high level'.[15] This, it seems, was to be regarded as the necessary price for social and economic stability. Indeed Baldwin appears to have settled upon some notion of a 'social contract', where 'sound finance' (mostly) satisfied the 'middle classes' – and, he supposed, provided the framework for industrial recovery – while enough social expenditure was offered to avoid alienation of the 'working classes'. Faced with particular Conservative criticism in late 1925, his private view was that social-service cuts would be 'a most one-sided policy'. These would seem 'an attack on the working man', and that was 'a fine way of combating Socialism'. It might even provoke assaults on the social order – or as he put it, 'a movement against the monarchy'.[16] His conclusion, stated to the Conservative party conference, was that further large-scale retrenchment could be achieved only by 'sacrifices which would have to be spread widely over all classes of the community'.[17] This, in effect, was the strategy followed by the party leaders when they finally felt compelled to tackle the financial problems of unemployment insurance. Even then they moved with much reluctance, but could count themselves fortunate that the political damage fell mainly upon the second Labour government. During the 1931 financial crisis they embraced MacDonald's principle of 'equal sacrifices' – increases in direct taxation of similar percentage to cuts in social expenditure. In practice, of course, this bore much more heavily on the unemployed worker than on the middle-class tax-payer, but in presentational terms Conservative leaders thought the appearance of 'fairness' extremely important, in preserving social peace and their party's 'democratic' reputation. Nevertheless there were soon business and Conservative party pressures for tax reduction, but these were resisted until the social-service cuts were cancelled too, from 1934.[18]

During the 1920s Baldwin's main economic ideas for dealing

<hr/>

[15] *HCDeb* 170, c. 1984 (10 March 1924).
[16] Jones *WD* I.331 (30 Oct. 1925); Hewins, *Apologia*, II.301 (1 Nov. 1925).
[17] Conservative conference, 8 Oct. 1925. Cf. Aberdeen, 5 Nov. 1925; Conservative conference, 6 Oct. 1927.
[18] Williamson, *National Crisis*, pp. 173–4, 245–7, 301–2, 364–5, 502–3.

with 'over-industrialisation', recession, and unemployment faced considerable obstacles. Assistance to agriculture, in the (illusory) hope of restoring a more 'healthy proportion' between urban and rural workforces, seemed politically unattainable given the large urban electoral majority.[19] As a Chamberlainite he looked particularly to renewed imperial emigration to provide homes for Britain's 'surplus population',[20] and to increased imperial trade and development because the Empire offered 'the only expanding markets in the world in which we have an opportunity of holding our own'.[21] But in this period the Dominions, wishing to preserve their own employment and industries, showed little interest.

At some level Baldwin also wanted protection. As a backbench MP before 1914 he had been a 'whole-hog' tariff reformer,[22] but as a minister after the War he was more sensitive to political complications, because in the face of the Labour challenge so much more seemed to be at stake. Publicly (perhaps echoing Cunningham's teachings) he held that post-war international uncertainties made it impossible to chose an appropriate commercial regime, and 'free trade or a policy of Tariffs was merely a question of expediency, of what was best for a given country at a given time'.[23] Some such position was also demanded by membership of the Coalition government, containing Liberal free traders, as it would later be convenient when trying to draw Liberals into the Conservative party. But his deeper concern was electoral: that new, unsophisticated, working-class and female voters might be still more susceptible than pre-war voters had been to free-trade arguments that tariffs raised the costs of living. When, therefore, he decided in autumn 1923 that a balance of risks favoured an attempt at protection, he gave it a particular political form. As food taxes still seemed 'beyond the pale of practical politics',[24] agriculture would instead receive government subsidies. Industrial tariffs were offered as an employment (rather than a 'business') policy, preserving existing jobs against 'unfair' foreign compe-

[19] Swansea, 30 Oct. 1923.
[20] 'Trade Prospects', CP 3890, 25 March 1922.
[21] Party meeting, 11 Feb. 1924.
[22] For regret at Law's retreat from food taxes, see *Berrows*, 8 March 1913. Cf. Cowling, *Impact of Labour*, p. 277.
[23] *Berrows*, 7 Dec. 1918; similarly, on safeguarding duties, HCDeb 142 c. 1573 (6 June 1921).
[24] *The Yorkshire Post*, 30 Oct. 1922. Cf. Baldwin in N. Chamberlain diary, 25 Oct. 1923.

tition, and offering new employment by forcing the reduction of foreign tariffs. This policy was said to be an undoctrinaire solution to practical problems, but the electoral strategy was no less explicit: it was contrasted to Liberal 'superstitions', yet presented as consistent with principles of labour protection, as embodied in trade unions and social insurance.[25]

When even this presentation failed – not just losing working-class votes, but widening differences between anti-socialists – Baldwin became an arch-gradualist on tariffs, or as he later dignified it 'an eclectic economist'.[26] The agreed shadow cabinet formula of February 1924, that general tariffs would be proposed again only 'upon clear evidence that ... public opinion was disposed to reconsider its judgment',[27] exactly expressed his own attitude, and he required a great deal of persuasion before moving again. The larger cause of Conservative anti-socialism had priority over particular economic policies, however 'right' he and other Conservatives believed them to be. This was most starkly shown where it affected his private interest. Good technical cases for applying safeguarding duties to the ailing iron and steel industry were twice rejected by his Cabinet, in 1925 – when Baldwins Ltd was already in much difficulty – and again in 1928 – the year Baldwins Ltd shares were written down, costing him a substantial part of his personal wealth.

With protection and imperial economic development apparently excluded, Baldwin had little else to offer as policy. This did not make him quite so vacant in ideas as it might seem, given that as a Conservative businessman he never expected that the state itself could – aside from 'sound finance' and tariff reform – have much successful economic effect anyway. This was true even where his government did have policies, as in housing: when in 1925 he first saw 'real slum houses' he was shocked, but not so shocked as to overcome an assumption of 'how impotent one is' to help.[28] It was also shown, rather desperately, in an August 1928 letter to 150,000 employers, asking them to employ displaced miners.[29]

[25] Swansea, 30 Oct. 1923. See also Manchester, 2 Nov. 1923; Queen's Hall, 19 Nov. 1923; Bradford, 29 Nov. 1923.
[26] Jones *DL* p. 50 (29 Aug. 1932). But again a connection with Cunningham's 'historical economics' should be noted.
[27] Party meeting, 11 Feb. 1924.
[28] Baldwin to Joan Davidson, 4 June 1925, in Davidson *Memoirs*, p. 197.
[29] *The Times*, 21 Aug. 1928.

While at the Board of Trade in 1921, he had participated in the
introduction of government employment policies, including public
works, export credits, and loan guarantees.[30] But although these
measures were extended by his 1923 and 1924 governments, he
accepted – indeed faithfully expounded[31] – the 'Treasury view' that
they could have only limited results. Unless carefully rationed,
state-financed employment would be either self-defeating, because
it would re-start inflation, or else nugatory, because it simply
replaced ('crowded-out') privately funded employment. Like most
others in government he considered public-works schemes to be
just temporary relief measures, incapable of creating permanent
work.

Rather, as a Conservative and businessman he expected recovery to come from within private enterprise. Just as the Baldwin
firms had re-shaped their production under market pressures
before the War, so other industries and agriculture should adjust
themselves to the new economic conditions which had
(apparently) stabilised in the mid 1920s. He was not uncritical of
British business. He accepted that some industrialists had '[taken]
things much too easy' in the past, and spoke publicly of 'large
numbers' of 'incompetent' directors and managers who were now
'nothing but parasitical to industry'.[32] He recognised particular
failure in a key area: 'owing to the parochial line upon which electricity has grown up in this country Great Britain is far behind
her competitors in the production of cheaply generated electricity'.[33] The creation of the Central Electricity Generating Board
became a 'keen personal interest', carried through a reluctant
Cabinet.[34] But this instance of state action was strictly defined as
exceptional. The character of the government's other economic
measures in the late 1920s, whether agricultural credits, mer-
chandise marks, labour transference schemes, or de-rating, was

[30] Baldwin to Lloyd George, 12 Oct. 1921, Lloyd George papers F/3/1/14. For Lloyd
George's unemployment discussions (including Baldwin) in Inverness-shire during September 1921, see G. C. Peden, 'The Road to and from Gairloch', *Twentieth Century British
History* 4 (1993), 224–48.
[31] See paragraphs in Plymouth, 25 Oct. 1923, and Leicester, 21 March 1929, quoted in
McKibbin, *Ideologies of Class*, pp. 268–9: both were drafted by the Treasury.
[32] Jones, *WD* II.137, 155 (17 May, 1 Nov. 1928); Glasgow, 22 Nov. 1928. Cf. *OE* p. 35 (5
March 1925).
[33] Conservative conference, 7 Oct. 1926.
[34] Percy, *Some Memories*, p. 135; M&B pp. 393–4.

much more indicative. Their purpose was to assist firms and farmers to achieve their own voluntary re-organisation, or 'rationalisation' as it came to be called. Accordingly, his own task was chiefly that of exhortation, both in private and public. He called upon industry and agriculture to become more efficient by capital reconstruction, amalgamations, new production methods, research, 'scientific management', and improved marketing.[35] He also urged bankers to provide suitable finance and establish 'a close relationship with the industrial world'.[36] Employers could, he said in 1925, raise the efficiency of their industries by 10 per cent.[37] Whatever the existing shortcomings of British business, producers had to show that they themselves could undertake 'rationalisation' if private enterprise was to retain its justification in the face of 'socialism'. Again he had direct private experience, not just in the capital reconstruction of Baldwins Ltd in 1928 but also in the amalgamation of its South Wales steelworks within Guest Keen Baldwins Ltd during 1930.

The world depression from late 1929 mostly confirmed Baldwin's earlier financial and economic opinions. He assumed that renewed emphasis upon 'sound finance' was essential to preserve national credit and capital accumulation, though as already noted the political risks of retrenchment made him slow to call for specific cuts. He wanted the gold standard defended, and his own American debt settlement maintained – in 1932 even declaring that British repudiation of debt 'might bring the world within sight of the end of capitalism'.[38] On the end of these two elements of the financial regime he had helped to establish – the gold standard in 1931, American debt payments in 1933 – there is no adequate record of his opinions, perhaps signifying disappointment or embarrassment. No doubt he thought their collapse the result of intervening international events rather than any fault in the original policies. But like every other Conservative he concluded that the other element of 'sound finance', a strict budget regime, was now still more crucial. He presented the onset of

---

[35] From numerous examples, see Welbeck Abbey, 1 June 1925; Conservative conference, 7 Oct. 1926; Louth, 21 July 1927; Manchester, 16 May 1928; Glasgow, 22 Nov. 1928. For an example of private industrial diplomacy, see Jones *WD* II.174 (5 March 1929).
[36] British Bankers' Association, 30 April 1929.
[37] Welbeck Abbey, 1 June 1925.
[38] M&B p. 690.

cheap money in 1932, economic recovery from 1933, and resumed social legislation from 1935 as demonstrating the effectiveness of this financial rigour; but the period of crisis also created a continuing sense of fragility which became one of his justifications for the perpetuation of the National coalition government.[39]

The collapse of world markets and prices strengthened Baldwin's belief in protection and imperial economic unity. More to the point, although Beaverbrook's 'Empire Free Trade' campaign complicated his responses, the depression created political shifts which overcame his doubts about the electoral appeal of tariffs and brought the Dominions to serious negotiation. He again took care to present tariffs and imperial preference as matters not of dogma but of expediency, but with the Import Duties Act and Ottawa trade agreements he nevertheless felt a Chamberlainite sense of achievement. Free trade was 'dead and buried', and 'they had passed into an entirely new economic system'.[40]

The depression did produce one development in Baldwin's policy opinions. As it undermined earlier efforts at economic reconstruction and intensified radical criticisms of 'capitalism', so he and other Conservative ministers accepted that the state should be more active in trying to improve the performance of private enterprise. From 1932 the National government used import controls, subsidies, and in some cases legislation to put more pressure on farmers to adopt agricultural marketing schemes, and industrialists to undertake further rationalisation. Baldwin now spoke of the need for producers to end 'unrestricted competition' and enter a new era of 'regulated production': a regime where 'protection without' would be matched by 'reorganisation within'.[41] Yet while state intervention was new, these other notions were descended directly from his pre-war experience of trade associations and understanding of American and German industrial success.

In obvious senses, then, Baldwin's views on economic and social

---

[39] E.g. Ilford, 15 March 1932; Sheffield, 25 June 1932; Conservative conference, 6 Oct. 1933; broadcast, 8 June 1935.

[40] Cambridge, 22 July 1933; National Labour luncheon, 6 Nov. 1933. Cf. Jones *DL* p. 25 (28 Jan. 1932).

[41] Sunderland, 2 Dec. 1932; Cambridge, 22 July 1933; Scottish Unionist Association, 17 Nov. 1933. For private interest in re-organisation problems, see Crozier interview, 12 June 1934, Crozier papers. For his belief that domestic protection had assisted 'mass production', Jones *DL* p. 192 (30 April 1936).

policy were affected by assessments of the political situation. This was especially so with protection. Yet he was not merely 'opportunistic', following the lines of least resistance. As might be expected from his own economic position he also had definite opinions and commitments, particularly on 'sound finance'. The most characteristic feature was his attempt to balance this 'sound finance' with social-service expenditure, even in the face of criticism within the Conservative party. Like any other party leader, Baldwin had to juggle the conflicting impulses of private belief, notions of national interest, the demands of his party's supporters, high political manoeuvre, and election strategy. Even so, specific *policies* came from the collective party leadership rather than from Baldwin himself, and could have been as well expounded by any of the alternative interwar Conservative leaders.

II

Baldwin's specific contributions were elsewhere. These derived from a conviction that the economic system would be best defended – and helped towards renewed prosperity – less by policy than by explanation and cultivation of an appropriate spirit. The new electorate required 'education' on the true character of this system, and the new politics of economic and class issues had to be shaped into 'safe' forms. To these tasks he brought a combination of arguments which differed a good deal from those dominant in his party. His was not the rhetoric of a Conservative class warrior, primarily voicing the anxieties of the middle classes and stirring up a wider social fear against parts of the working classes.[42] It was more complex and inventive, and more subtle. It was socially inclusive, with Conservatism identified with or made to seem sympathetic towards the legitimate aspirations of all classes, and as such it presented trade unions, even the Labour party, as having positive places in society. Yet this rhetoric was far from flaccid. It was the more ideologically effective because the anxiety, the negative stereotypes, and the hostility were reserved instead for certain 'working-class' attitudes and types of behaviour.

As Labour became established as the second largest party

[42] See McKibbin, *Ideologies of Class*, ch. 9.

Stanley Baldwin

during 1923 and as a party of government in 1924, Baldwin
displayed much sensitivity towards the power of its primary economic and social myths. Conservatives had to prevent these myths
gaining wider popular credence if private enterprise and 'sound
finance' were to be considered the general interests of all, and not
just the sectional interests of the employing classes. The problem
as he presented it was that before the War the mechanisms of
domestic investment and international trade had functioned 'with
such perfection and absence of friction that few were aware of
[their] existence'.[43] Consequently 'the people to whom we have to
appeal at election time have either lost sight of or have never yet
had a sight of the real processes, and they are only too prone ...
to be ready to accept any explanation that may be put before them
by the ignorant and the glib-tongued'.[44] Now that the War had
'smashed' these processes and created so much distress and suffering, it had to be explained to voters that the industrial and commercial systems were not the result of an 'extra dose of original
sin' among 'capitalists'. Rather they were social and historical
products: the fruits of 'the creative forces of our race' and the
skills of 'our workpeople', activities which had grown 'automatically and empirically' from the 'ever-changing needs of
countries'.[45] The 'capitalism' denounced by socialists as 'the
enemy' of the people or 'the blackest curse that had fallen on
mankind',[46] was in reality a great and beneficent achievement, the
results of which were shared – even, he implied, especially so – by
the working classes. It 'had called millions of people into existence, and ... subdued the forces of Nature ... to minister to their
needs'.[47] It had raised the poorer classes to a 'greater degree of
comfort' than their grandfathers had considered possible. Despite
the post-war depression, it had enabled Britain to maintain even
the workless in 'an unprecedented standard of living': 'no country
in the world's history has been able to do as much as we have for
the unemployed'.[48]

Just as the growth of 'industrialism' had not come from sin, so

[43] *HCDeb* 160, cc. 555–6 (16 Feb. 1923).
[44] Edinburgh, 27 July 1923.
[45] *HCDeb* 160, cc. 555–6 (16 Feb. 1923).
[46] Edinburgh, 27 July 1923; Aberdeen, 5 Nov. 1925.
[47] Leeds, 12 March 1925.
[48] Cardiff, 18 Oct. 1924; Aberdeen, 5 Nov. 1925.

what Baldwin admitted to be its undoubted imperfections – bad working conditions, poverty, slums – had not been caused by 'capitalist' exploitation. These had been unintended, indeed unavoidable, consequences. The nineteenth-century industrial and urban development had been so rapid that no one could have controlled or guided it. Few had even detected the 'seeds that might germinate in time into something unhealthy and dangerous'.[49] Those few had not been Liberals shackled to free trade and *laissez-faire*, nor from a Labour party which had not then existed – even though both parties had 'cultivated [a] fairy tale that they alone are the authors of social reform'.[50] Against this 'fairy tale' Baldwin cast his own myth, in a characteristic appropriation of 'progressive' history. The great humanitarians, reformers and social prophets had been Tories or Conservatives: Wilberforce, Oastler, Sadler, Shaftesbury and, above all, Disraeli.[51]

For all the pre-war propaganda of the Primrose League, the prominence Baldwin gave from his first speech as prime minister to Disraeli – more especially to Disraeli's supposed commitment to 'the welfare of the people'[52] – was a new feature in the rhetoric of Conservative leadership. For many people Disraeli remained an exotic, a political eccentric. A cousin who had known Baldwin well since childhood was surprised at 'his adopting Dizzy as his model ... the furthest I fancy from his modest nature'.[53] But in a new context of socio-economic politics, Disraeli perfectly served Baldwin's purpose by offering a plausible pedigree for Conservative social concern. This was especially so at the moment when the Labour party first entered government, and when Conservatives wished to displace Liberals as the party of moderate antisocialism:

If there is any party in the State which, by its traditions and its history, is entitled to put in the forefront of its work and its programme the

---

[49] *HCDeb* 160, cc. 555–6 (16 Feb. 1923), and see Dundee, 4 June 1925.
[50] Welbeck Abbey, 1 June 1925.
[51] E.g. *HCDeb* 160, cc. 555–6 (16 Feb. 1923); Junior Imperial League, 3 May 1924; Leeds, 12 March 1925; Glasgow, 22 Nov. 1928; Primrose League, 1 May 1931.
[52] Party meeting, 29 May 1923. Cf. Jones *WD* p. 238 (28 May 1923). For the historical reality, see P. Ghosh, 'Style and substance in Disraelian social reform', in Waller (ed.), *Politics and Social Change in Modern Britain*, pp. 59–90. The USRC, predictably, had tried to make something of this supposed Disraelian legacy (Green, *Crisis of Conservatism*, pp. 286–7), but this was unusual.
[53] P. Burne-Jones to Mary Gladstone, 28 May 1923, Mary Gladstone papers 46246/269.

betterment of the conditions of life of the working classes, it is our party. We were fighting the battle of the factory hand long before he had a vote . . . and we were speaking in favour of the combination of working men, long before the Liberals had thought of the subject. It is more than 50 years ago that Disraeli was calling the attention of the country to housing and health questions.[54]

Against the 'misleading and mischievous' socialist doctrines about 'capitalism', Baldwin gave conservative yet democratic descriptions of 'capital'.[55] This supplied the essential 'rain and manure' and 'motive power' of industry, enabling it to grow and provide employment. It was not just the possession of the rich, but like industry and commerce it was a social product – indeed a far more genuine expression of human instincts and community than socialism could be. Capital 'was nothing more and nothing less than the savings of the people', of every class, 'rich and poor alike', made up 'by the coppers as much as by the sovereigns', and including the deposits of working-class institutions: friendly, building and co-operative societies, savings banks and trade unions. It embodied the 'common help of all classes'.[56]

From a conception of capital as truly communal, Baldwin developed further economic arguments for deepening the social basis of Conservative support. First, this conception increased the popular purchase of the 'wisdoms' of sound finance.[57] The working classes were said to have an interest in retrenchment and low taxation as strong as that of the propertied classes, not just because some had now become income-tax-payers, but more as employees and small investors. Whatever its formal incidence, taxation was also communal: it 'has an astonishing way, like water . . . of filtering down and down till it bears on the backs of every class of the people'.[58] Contrary to common assumptions, the real burden of taxation did not fall on the rich: rather, by 'crippling' industry and checking capital accumulation, heavy taxation 'pressed with a crushing weight on the poor', forcing down wages and causing

---

[54] Party meeting, 11 Feb. 1924; and see *HCDeb* 169, c. 633 (21 Jan. 1924).
[55] Welbeck Abbey, 1 June 1925. Although hardly applying this contrast strictly, Baldwin plainly intended to distinguish a term with quasi-Marxist connotations from one with narrower but more fruitful Conservative meanings.
[56] Edinburgh, 27 July 1923; and see Welbeck Abbey, 1 June 1925; Aberdeen, 5 Nov. 1925.
[57] See McKibbin, *Ideologies of Class*, pp. 268–75, 282–3, 293.
[58] *The Birmingham Post*, 5 Feb. 1923.

unemployment. Working-class organisations were also directly affected, with taxation charged on the investments of friendly and building societies, trade unions, and clubs.[59] With the creation of a female electorate, the principles of national finance could also be rooted more firmly in ordinary experience of the home. Every woman was a Chancellor of the Exchequer, and the Chancellor was 'the housewife of the nation'. The 'State is the family writ large'.[60]

Second, Baldwin's presentation of 'capital' helped create an impression of economic permanence. With the growth in working-class savings and investments – 'the enormous increase in the number of financial smallholders', who were 'the greatest asset of the modern state' – socialist denunciations of capitalism were 'in the long run in vain'.[61] The huge sales of War Savings Certificates, with 10,000 new buyers a week in 1925, especially showed that 'the habit of saving small surpluses and investing them . . . has taken root and is firmly established amongst the people'. Their inventor – and we may note, though he did not, his membership of the wartime committee that proposed the scheme – would be among those who did most to destroy 'the gospel of Karl Marx'.[62]

Third, this suggested a rhetoric for increasing stability. During the first Labour government, Baldwin began saying that the Conservative 'weapon' was 'the multiplication of capitalists'.[63] They sought not to 'depress' the people in a 'society of State ownership', but to raise them into 'a society in which, increasingly, the individual may become an owner':[64]

we rejoice over . . . the spread of businesses, of co-operative societies, and of savings certificates among the people. We would like to see every man and woman in this country a capitalist, necessarily, to begin with, in a small way. We would like to see everyone a possessor of something of his own [for this makes him] more careful, more thrifty, more anxious to

[59] *The Yorkshire Post*, 30 Oct. 1922. Cf. Perth, 25 Oct. 1924; North Stoneham Park, 13 June 1931.
[60] Women's Unionist meeting, 12 May 1923; election broadcast, 13 Oct. 1931, from numerous examples.
[61] Welbeck Abbey, 1 June 1925.
[62] Aberdeen, 5 Nov. 1925. Cf. Dundee, 25 Jan. 1929. The 1916 Committee on War Loans for the Small Investor had been chaired by Edwin Montagu.
[63] Welbeck Abbey, 1 June 1925.
[64] *OE* p. 225 (3 May 1924). Cf. Welbeck Abbey, 1 June 1925; Dundee, 25 Jan. 1929.

better himself and to raise his own family ... and through that to give him the impetus which the country needs to send it forward to better things.[65]

The next step was to present Conservative housing policies as part of the same purpose. 'We differ profoundly from the Socialists [in wanting] the people to own their homes.' It was 'impossible to exaggerate the value to the citizen, therefore to the State, of a good home', in promoting self-respect and independence.[66] He even spoke of the possibilities of wider share-ownership, as an alternative to socialist arguments for nationalisation. Workpeople and customers might be allowed easy terms to acquire shares in limited companies, spreading industrial ownership from the few to the many in a process 'blending the owning and the working classes'.[67] In December 1931 he encapsulated this rhetoric by borrowing a pregnant phrase: 'a property-owning democracy'.[68] In these years it had practical meaning only in a great increase in middle-class home ownership – though this had obvious political importance in itself – but it had a broader symbolic significance, in suggesting the party's openness towards new social aspirations.

Baldwin interlocked all this with homilies on individualism, voluntarism, and private enterprise, and their implications for government. But here too he did not simply deploy conventional Conservative arguments. As he accepted much of the state's increased role since the War, and as the party leadership proposed from 1924 to extend it further, so he had to justify a positive function for government, but without concessions towards socialism. In effect he progressively and silently adopted elements of pre-war 'new liberal' language, where state action was legitimated – and de-limited – as support for voluntary effort where it advanced the common good.

His arguments turned as much upon moral conceptions as upon economic efficiency. Socialism was contrary to human nature, 'that sense of the personal independence of the individual human soul

---

[65] Hotel Cecil, 21 May 1924.
[66] Albert Hall, 4 Dec. 1924.
[67] Aberdeen, 5 Nov. 1925. Cf. Cardiff, 20 Oct. 1924; Gravesend, 23 Oct. 1924. The model offered was that said to be developing within American industry.
[68] Aberdeen, 4 Dec. 1931. The phrase was coined by Noel Skelton in *Spectator* articles during May 1923, reprinted as *Constructive Conservatism* in autumn 1924. It was taken up in R. Boothby, J. Loder, H. Macmillan, and O. Stanley, *Industry and the State* (1927), but had no wide currency until used by Eden in 1946.

who meant to make good for his own sake and for the sake of his wife and his children'. Mankind could not be motivated by 'talk of nothing but humanity and society'.[69] It was rather 'the individualist motive [which] has been ... the driving force for progressive races'.[70] While socialists killed independence and initiative by teaching the individual to look to the State, Conservatives aimed to let 'people profit and benefit themselves by the result of their own efforts', because 'only by assisting each individual to stand up and seek to better his own position can we better the position of the whole'.[71]

Yet while further social services might be desirable, it was in the interest of the whole community – the working population itself, as well as tax-payers – for these to be arranged so that self-reliance was not undermined or a benefit dependency created. Government expenditure and social progress were not 'synonymous'. The unemployment insurance system was a necessity, but if allowed to become too large it 'might do the country irreparable harm', while the 'dole' – uncovenanted benefit – risked 'habituating a large proportion of our people to idleness'.[72] Baldwin exemplified a revised Conservative conception of social provision when describing the 1925 pensions scheme: 'state interference in itself is bad, but state help and assistance is necessary to supplement the effort of the individual'.[73] They therefore proposed 'collective contributory insurance', or 'co-operative self-help', which – besides limiting the burden upon tax-payers – preserved self-respect by supporting the incentive to work, and by creating a right tied to a sense of self-denial.[74]

His arguments on industry and agriculture developed in similar fashion. It was a 'complete illusion' to suppose that state control could bring increased production and full employment. To substitute national ownership for 'the great incentive' of profit and gain would destroy that enterprise and competition which alone brought 'efficiency and cheapness'.[75] Yet arguments against state

[69] Edinburgh, 24 March 1924.
[70] Perth, 25 Oct. 1924.
[71] Edinburgh, 24 March 1924; Association of Conservative Clubs, 13 June 1924.
[72] Women's Unionist Organisation, 9 May 1924; Queen's Hall, 15 Oct. 1924.
[73] Welbeck Abbey, 1 June 1925.
[74] Edinburgh, 24 March 1924; also Hotel Cecil, 25 Jan. 1926.
[75] Queen's Hall, 16 Oct. 1924, among many examples. Jones to Lloyd George, 18 March 1919, Lloyd George papers F/23/4/38, reports Baldwin considering coal nationalisation

intervention did not have just an anti-socialist application; the aims of stabilisation and defence of private enterprise also precluded direct Conservative assistance for employers. Politically, successful resistance to socialism required an appearance of even-handedness, to make principled insistence on a limited state seem credible. Economically, even if protection against *unfair* foreign competition became possible, industry and agriculture must not expect the state to cushion them from necessary adjustments to new world market conditions. Above all, moral fundamentals had to be sustained:

One of the great perils of Government interference is that it saps that very self-reliance of our people that has made us what we are ... The control of industry by the State would take away [the] sense of responsibility from the individual, and ultimately would turn the self-reliant man into a shiftless and a useless creature. None but the social enthusiast would carry on his work in those circumstances, and I do not believe that you can ever implant ... that strong sense of social consciousness that would be necessary to keep men up to their social work ... Responsibility must be a matter of the individual ... and I believe we shall best strengthen these motives in him by continuing to teach him that he must, in the first place, rely on himself, that men who conduct businesses must rely on themselves, and that our people as a whole must trust their destiny and rely on themselves.[76]

Baldwin attached great importance to this aspect of his public doctrine. In 1928 he declared that if he had helped 'to get into people's heads that their salvation lies with themselves, I shall not have lived in vain'. For it was 'that creed, burnt into the bones of Englishmen, that made this country what it has been', and it was 'only that creed that will enable us in the future to keep our country at the top and in front'.[77]

Yet such affirmations of economic individualism might have caused difficulties. They could have conflicted with his concern for social cohesion and industrial peace, had he not – as will be seen below – given individualism a particular meaning, and balanced it with other values. His anti-statist language certainly caused him complications in explaining some of his Cabinet's (very limited)

'inevitable'. But amidst exceptional difficulties in achieving government decontrol of the industry this view was even shared by Law, and the view had no wider or later bearings: cf. M&B p. 378.
[76] Edinburgh, 27 July 1923.
[77] Worcester, 7 Jan. 1928.

industrial proposals from 1924, when he had both to distinguish them from Labour policies and to defend them against Conservative criticisms. Here again he appropriated 'new liberal' language under cover of a supposed Conservative inheritance. There was, he said, a distinction between state 'interference' and state 'help'. It was not socialism for the state to work 'in conjunction with the individual' to improve roads and houses, nor was the establishment of a public utility company for electricity an instance of nationalisation.[78] In encouraging co-operation between government and both sides of industry to re-organise production, he tried to re-define the terms of the debate:

> nationalisation and private enterprise … are not simple alternatives. There is an infinite series of intermediate positions between those poles [of] socialism and laissez-faire. Like the North and South Poles in our children's geography books these two poles do not exist. Laissez-faire, pure and undefiled has been dead in the Tory Party … since the days of Disraeli … We must for England's sake shake ourselves free from the shackles of old orthodoxies about capitalism and about labour which have ceased to have any relevance to the world we are now in or the world we are entering.[79]

By the mid 1930s protection, state support for private enterprise, and membership of the National government had completed an important shift. His anti-statist language was replaced by pragmatic yet positive justification of state activity appropriate to what he claimed to be a 'new economic era', but still distinct from socialism. The impact of the Great War and world depression had produced circumstances 'different from any that have existed in the world before', which demanded 'all kinds of things in connection with organising and planning if industries are to survive'. For 'good or evil, the days of non-interference of the Government … are gone': 'laissez-faire' was as dead as the 'slave trade'. Such 'state interference' was 'neither Socialist, nor Liberal, nor Unionist'; it was simply what 'any Government that is really bold enough to tackle these problems' would have to do, 'irrespective of party'.

---

[78] Hotel Cecil, 21 May 1924; Welbeck Abbey, 1 June 1925; Conservative conference, 7 Oct. 1926.

[79] Norwich, 17 July 1926. Baldwin (or his speech-writer) quoted Keynes's recent lecture on 'The End of Laissez-Faire', implying it was a much-belated Liberal recognition of what Conservatives had long known and practised. See also, e.g., *OE* p. 30 (5 March 1925).

The Conservative task nevertheless remained. Whatever 'guardianship Governments may think fit to impose on industry', it would
still be necessary to preserve 'independence of character' and
'individual enterprise and energy', and to ensure that industry
'shall be run in the future as it has been in the past by the men
who know most about it'.[80]

Baldwin accompanied these economic and social arguments
with extensive warnings. These probably expressed his own genuine fears; their effect, nevertheless, was to dramatise and reinforce
his political messages. While he sometimes insisted upon the
'naturalness' and stability of the industrial system, he more often
characterised it as a fragile growth whose unbounded benefits
could easily be lost, with dire consequences. Again his method was
to reveal the unseen and unintended economic 'realities', but here
in the starkest terms. The 'plain fundamental fact' was that as a
heavily populated and highly industrialised island 'we must produce goods and find markets before we can feed ourselves'. Britain's survival and success depended upon a 'delicate mechanism'
of national credit, investment, manufacture, and international
trade, which after the dislocations of the War could not sustain
further shocks or anything 'tampering' with its proper functioning.
'Any economic step which tended to damage the credit and the
industry of our country ... might result in such irreparable
damage that the work of a generation ... could not restore it.'
Anything 'in the way of sudden or radical change is fraught with
immense peril'. He pressed his socio-political point very hard
indeed. Those who would suffer first and most would be the
working men and their families, and not just from a rapid increase
in unemployment: 'every hitch in the production of goods in Great
Britain interferes at once with the reception of food, and is
reflected automatically in the prices that our people pay'. Poverty
would be intensified; the ultimate outcome could be starvation.
Such disasters would certainly result from violent revolution or
communism, and very probably from state socialism – whether by
'government interference' or 'reckless' public expenditure.[81] They
were also, he said, the likely outcomes of industrial conflict.

---

[80] Culzean Castle, 21 July 1934; Liverpool, 25 March 1935. Cf. Glasgow, 30 Nov. 1932;
    Cambridge, 22 July 1933; Leeds and Newcastle, 7, 12 Nov. 1935.
[81] National Unionist Association, 29 June 1923, and Edinburgh, 27 July 1923, to take just
    early instances of much repeated themes: see e.g. 1924 election speeches *passim*, *OI* p.

III

It was to the problem of industrial and social conciliation that Baldwin directed much of his effort during the 1920s. Industrial relations were an area in which he had more knowledge than any other leading Conservative; indeed, experience of employing a large manufacturing workforce was extremely rare amongst leading politicians. Here, Baldwin came to believe, his years at Wilden acquired a national, even providential, significance.[82] In 1925 he declared that the position of trade unions 'touches . . . questions which have interested me during the whole of my working life. I have thought so much about them, and I feel that I have so much to say about them, that my difficulty will be in choosing the little I can possibly say . . . and finding words to express clearly . . . what is in my mind.'[83] This interest was, however, more than just a legacy from his business career. For him, industrial relations were the outstanding domestic problem left by the disruptions of the War and the defects of the Coalition. It was fundamental to the defence and modernisation of the British economic system. It was central also to his conceptions of moral duty in public life and the purpose of Conservative politics: the 'binding together of all classes'.[84]

Industrial relations were the subject of both his first and last House of Commons speeches. In 1917 he participated in a Church of England movement promoting a post-war transformation in relations between 'employer and employed'.[85] As President of the Board of Trade and Chancellor of the Exchequer one of his recurrent themes was that without industrial peace no government could assist commercial or financial recovery. On becoming prime minister, he declared industrial and social cohesion to be among his chief tasks:

I want to see in the next year or two the beginnings of better feeling and unity among all classes of our people. If there are those who want

---

212 (12 June 1926); Douglas Castle, 29 Aug. 1927; *TTF* p. 312 (10 March 1928); Dundee, 25 Jan. 1929.

[82] See p. 278.

[83] *OE* p. 41 (6 March 1925).

[84] *OE* p. 16 (12 Jan. 1925).

[85] Resolution moved by Baldwin at meeting organised by the Church of England Men's Society: *The Times*, 10 March 1917; *Bridgeman Diaries*, pp. 118–19.

to fight the class war we will take up that challenge, and we will beat
them by the hardness of our heads and the largeness of our hearts. I
want to leave this country when my term ends in better heart than she
has been for years. I want to be a healer . . .[86]

Almost all his major speeches during the next four years contained
references to industrial peace. It was, he would say, his 'campaign',
'the teaching [he had tried] to inculcate' or 'the gospel I have
preached'. He persisted despite criticism that he was becoming
platitudinous, and in defiance of considerable counter-pressures
and setbacks. The personal commitment and the elevated tone he
brought to the task are well indicated in his House of Commons
speech announcing the imminent outbreak of the General Strike:

I have worked for two years to the utmost of my ability in one direction.
I have failed so far. Everything that I care for is smashed to bits at this
moment. That does not take away from me either my faith or my courage
. . . Before long the angel of peace, with healing in his wings, will be
among us again, and when he comes let us be there to meet him. I
shall pick up the bits. I shall start again. I may not see what I have
dreamed of in my lifetime, but I know that the seed I have tried to plant
in men's hearts these two years is germinating. I know it is germinating
in the hearts and minds of men, and that it is in that direction, and in
that direction alone, that we shall pass, after much suffering, through
deep waters and through storms, to that better land for which we hope.[87]

In his pursuit of industrial peace he faced strong anti-trade-union
feeling in the Conservative popular press, within his party and, on
occasion, in his Cabinet. Sometimes he did make concessions, or
give way. After 'Red Friday' in July 1925 he found it prudent to
deliver a sterner warning against strike threats than he would
otherwise have wished.[88] In early May 1926 he yielded to Cabinet
pressures to end discussion with Trades Union Congress representatives.[89] He allowed the 1927 Trades Disputes Bill to be shaped
largely by party 'expediency'.[90] More often, especially on the critical early issues during his 1924–9 government, he prevailed. This
was where his personal authority was most evident and where he

---

[86] Edinburgh, 27 July 1923.
[87] *HCDeb* 195, c.73 (3 May 1926).
[88] Jones *WD* I.325–6, 327 (5, 6 Aug. 1925).
[89] *Amery Diaries* I.451 (2 May 1926); *Bridgeman Diaries*, pp. 194–5 (May 1925); Dilks, *N. Chamberlain*, I.464.
[90] N. Chamberlain diary, 16 May 1927. For a sensitive assessment of Baldwin's view, see Percy, *Some Memories*, pp. 136–7.

most influenced policy, in some cases running considerable political risks. In March 1925 he set aside a deeply felt party commitment to legislate against trade-union political funds. In July he took the responsibility for granting the coal subsidy and appointing the Coal Commission. During 1926 he continued negotiations to avoid a General Strike further than most of the Cabinet wished. His ability during 1925 to demonstrate tangible – as well as rhetorical – commitment to industrial peace was of great importance: it enabled him for much of 1926 to occupy a commanding public position, which was crucial to political containment of the industrial relations problem. His method was described by one critic as 'a most curious mixture of the sentimental phrase and the hard act'.[91] It would be more accurate to say that in both word and action he worked by astute modulation of earnest conciliation and ruthless counter-attack.

Despite Baldwin's occasional use of rural or squirearchical imagery, he did not conceal his industrial background. On the contrary, when he first became prime minister newspapers and newsreels were encouraged to emphasise this feature, with workers from Baldwins Ltd brought to Downing Street to be recorded 'congratulating' him for press photographs and newsreels (see plate 6).[92] Even so, this was a calculated, selective, presentation. In a reticence perpetuated in the biographical record, he rarely mentioned his railway boards and never his City office and bank directorship. The projected image was not Baldwin closeted in boardrooms, but Baldwin active at the manufacturing workplace, acquiring the insights and sympathies required for government in a modern industrial society. Sometimes he spoke to industrialists as 'a brother business man', displaying understanding of their difficulties, urging them to modernise, or emphasising a shared practical experience in contrast to Labour or Liberal policies.[93] When announcing his adoption of protection in October 1923 he spoke 'not only as a Prime Minister, but as a man who for years was an employer of labour and who has lived amongst the working

[91] Laski to Holmes, 30 Sept. 1926, in M. Howe (ed.), *Holmes–Laski Letters* (1953), II.881. See Lord Citrine, *Men and Work* (1964), p. 184, for similar bewilderment.
[92] E.g. *The Times*, *The Morning Post*, *The Daily Herald*, 23 May 1923. For newsreel, Ramsden, 'Baldwin and Film', p. 141, and Ramsden film compilation, 'Stanley Baldwin', item 1.
[93] Manchester, 16 May 1928. Cf. Bradford, 29 Nov. 1923; Newcastle, 24 Jan. 1929; Middlesbrough, 19 May 1930; Engineering Employers Association, 14 Jan. 1931.

people' – or, as he put it later, 'the only one of my colleagues who has lived for years under the smoke of factory chimneys' – and so could 'perhaps visualise more than many men in political life what unemployment meant'.[94]

Above all, he established credentials as a particular kind of employer. The Baldwins' firm 'had always been on extraordinarily good terms' with its men, and 'there was no object nearer one's heart than to see that they were all happy and contented and prosperous'.[95] He had, he said, known every workman by name (this became a sketch-writer's cliché) and talked with them as easily about their families and homes as about their work. It was 'a place where strikes and lock-outs were unknown', and where 'nobody ever got the sack'. He also spoke of his personal payment of allowances to his workmen when made unemployed by the 1912 coal strike, and – in pointed emphasis – of how much he had felt the 'monstrous injustice' suffered by blameless men with no interest in the dispute.[96]

Yet Baldwin's evocations of Victorian and Edwardian Wilden did not mean he was a nostalgic reactionary, oblivious or resistant to more recent industrial developments.[97] The exact reverse was true. As a pre-war railway director and still a coal-owner, he knew the industrial effects of the recent growth of national trade unions. As one of the creators and still a principal shareholder of Baldwins Ltd, he understood the development of large multi-divisional, managerial, firms. While his most basic objective in industrial relations was prevention of class conflict and if his particular problem became containment of the coal disputes in 1925–6, he had another major concern – to assist, not to check, industrial change. As already seen, from the mid 1920s he championed the cause of rationalisation – and he believed industrial co-operation, or at least avoidance of worker obstruction and strikes, was crucial to the success of this 'modernisation', of the adaptation to post-war economic conditions.

The purpose of his March 1925 description of the Wilden works

[94] Plymouth, 25 Oct. 1923; *HCDeb* 168, c. 481 (15 Nov. 1923); Glasgow, 28 Nov. 1923 (2nd speech).
[95] Glasgow, 28 Nov. 1923 (2nd speech).
[96] *OE* pp. 42–4 (6 March 1925). See *HCDeb* 160, cc. 557–8 (16 Feb. 1923) and 187, c. 1589 (6 Aug. 1925), also 'The New Prime Minister', *The Times*, 23 May 1923.
[97] Cf. GMY p. 22; Campbell, 'Baldwin', p. 210; Wiener, *English Culture*, pp. 101–2.

could not have been more explicit: it was to dispel outdated public views about industrial organisation, and to draw a contrast with current realities. He doubted if 'all the people in this country realise the inevitable changes that are coming over the industrial system', and so spoke as one who had seen this transformation 'taking place before my own eyes'. He described late-Victorian conditions that were 'already passing' at that time, because he wanted to emphasise the subsequent emergence of a 'new state of industry'.[98] As he declared on numerous occasions, industry was never static but always dynamic, and industrial conditions were now 'absolutely different' from those experienced by their parents.[99] More than this, he claimed that Britain was 'in the midst to-day of an industrial revolution as important as that which occurred a century ago', one which was producing wholly new 'conditions and relations of life'.[100] Small firms and industries were being 'squeezed out', replaced by big limited liability companies and large-scale production. The 'natural accompaniment' of this change was the growth of 'great consolidations of capital' – shareholders and employers' organisations – and 'great consolidations of labour' – national trade unions, labour alliances, and the TUC.[101]

Baldwin drew several conclusions, aimed as much towards reactionary employers and Conservatives as against radical trade unionists and Labour. This transformation was inevitable, and 'must be accepted'. There was 'nothing that could change it'. It was a '*natural* evolution', arising from 'that driving force of necessity in the world that makes people combine together for competition and for the protection they need against that competition'.[102] As with the 'natural' growth of industrialism in the nineteenth century, any unpleasant consequences of these changes were usually the unintended effects of a system rather than instances of malice by employers: 'there was no conscious unfair treatment of these men by the masters'.[103] These effects

[98] *OE* pp. 41–4, 48 (6 March 1925). Cf. *SOL* pp. 106–7 (13 April 1937).
[99] *OE* p. 66 (13 March 1925); Gravesend, 23 Oct. 1924. Cf. Cardiff, 18 Oct. 1924; Welbeck Abbey, 1 June 1925.
[100] Glasgow, 22 Nov. 1928; *OI* p. 8 (19 June 1926).
[101] *OE* pp. 31, 44–5, 66–7 (5, 6, 13 March 1925). Cf. Bradford, 29 Nov. 1923; Gravesend, 23 Oct. 1924; Dundee, 25 Jan. 1929.
[102] *OE* pp. 31, 44 (5, 6 March 1925).
[103] *OE* p. 44 (6 March 1925).

nevertheless posed major challenges for industrial and political leadership: 'one of the gravest problems that all who had the welfare of the country at heart had to devote their minds to, was how were they going to help in the evolution of the industrial system to make it a blessing to the people and not a curse'.[104]

Large-scale organisation could become a blessing in making British industry more efficient and competitive, and so improving the wealth of all; but at present it threatened to be a curse. Replacement of family firms by joint-stock companies broke the 'personal link' between employers and workforce which had earlier 'maintained a community of interest between all classes of the community'.[105] Intensified division of labour and mechanisation produced 'monotonous repetition' which alienated workmen from their work – and 'the adjustment of mankind to the machine is the biggest problem that humanity is up against'.[106] Large consolidations of capital and labour accumulated great power and engendered a 'mass psychology', and tended to become short-sighted and selfish, and 'inhuman, hard' and indifferent towards the individual. Their ideas advanced less rapidly than their strength, and employers associations as much as trade unions used their power to preserve 'uneconomic' forms of production. Both sides became locked in antiquated adversarial attitudes, mutual suspicion, and – re-applying a famous Liberal phrase – the 'methods of barbarism'. The scale and impact of disputes was magnified, so that lock-outs or strikes in one industry affected many others.[107] This, he argued, had already become evident in the pre-war national strikes. But it had been greatly aggravated by the War and the post-war boom and slump, in dislocating industrial relationships and intensifying a politicisation of trade unions.[108] Now, in the delicate conditions of the 1920s, industrial conflict might not just obstruct the rationalisation vital for long-term progress, but even 'sweep back, possibly for years, all chance of returning and reviving prosperity'. It

---

[104] Gravesend, 23 Oct. 1924.
[105] *Ibid.*; cf. *OE* pp. 42–4.
[106] Welbeck Abbey, 1 June 1925; Imperial press gallery, 25 June 1930; cf. *SOL* pp. 107–8 (13 April 1937).
[107] Bradford, 29 Nov. 1923; Gravesend, 23 Oct. 1924; *OE* pp. 44–8 (6 March 1925); *OI* p. 218 (12 June 1926); Conservative conference, 7 Oct. 1926. For use of Campbell-Bannerman's Boer War phrase, Knowsley Park, 25 July 1925.
[108] For a detailed argument, see *HCDeb* 170, cc. 1984–8 (10 March 1924).

might derange national finances, provoke 'class war', and threaten the very stability of the economic system and the state.[109]

Yet while Baldwin emphasised continuing changes and imminent dangers, in a crucial sense he did seek to preserve something from the past – but this was a past which remained very much alive, and was both capable and worthy of being preserved. His appeals for industrial peace can be made to seem naive and vapid, but they were actually neither merely visionary nor delivered into a void. They described practices and ideals familiar to business and trade-union leaders, because he was defending a well-tried industrial relations system dating from the 1890s. Significantly, Baldwin considered the legal foundation of this system to have been a *Conservative*, Disraelian, legacy. He always thought the Balfour government had been culpable – and had contributed to his own 1906 election defeat at Kidderminster – in not restoring this legacy and the party's moral reputation with organised labour, by reversing the House of Lords' decision against the trade unions in the Taff Vale case. His commitment to the system and its crucial obligation of mutuality is manifest in his comment that 'the Conservatives can't talk of class war: they started it'.[110] After the system had been secured by Labour/Liberal legislation, he had personal experience of it on pre-war railway conciliation boards. In the 1920s he knew that its essentials still commanded wide support; and he shared a common hope that it could be elevated from a means to resolve disputes into relationships of positive co-operation.[111] It was because he understood the prevailing character of industrial relations so well that he was 'capable of exceptional powers of class conciliation'.[112] The problem was not that the system itself was under serious challenge: Baldwin knew that most trade-union and TUC leaders were not 'revolutionaries'. It was rather that its operation had come under strain from the post-war economic pressures – which ignited resentments from elements on both sides, trade union and business, Labour and

[109] Election broadcast, 16 Oct. 1924; Cardiff, 18 Oct. 1924; *OE* pp. 31, 34, 38–9 (5 March 1925); Leeds, 12 March 1925.
[110] M&B p. 99. A recurrent theme: see e.g. Jones *WD* II.171 (13 Feb. 1929); Jones *DL* p. 204 (22 May 1936); 1900 Club, 28 June 1932; Primrose League dinner, 17 Nov. 1932.
[111] For this system, see A. Fox, *History and Heritage. The Social Origins of the British Industrial Relations System* (1985), chs. 5–7; McKibbin, *Ideologies of Class*, pp. 27–31, 38–9.
[112] Fox, *History and Heritage*, p. 322, and for a good account of Baldwin's attitudes see pp. 312–16, 320–33.

Conservative. The difficulties were real enough, as the conflict in
the coal industry testified. Nevertheless part of Baldwin's success
arose from his instinct that so well-established a system could best
be defended by presenting it as being under threat.

From the perspective of the established parties and business
leaders, the system worked by 'control through accommodation'.[113]
Its first principle was that the trade-unionised working class
should not in itself be treated as a hostile force, contrasted to all
other social groups or to the 'public interest', as this could be
self-defeating in driving it into more disruptive attitudes. As Baldwin instinctively understood, if Conservatives wanted 'to prevent
the class war becoming a reality' it was best not to act and sound
as if one supposed the class war had already begun, still less to
indulge in needless provocation. He tried hard to impress this
upon Conservative MPs and party activists, most notably by opposing Macquisten's political levy bill on the argument that they
should not 'fire the first shot'[114] – though the argument later backfired, when the General Strike made it impossible for him to resist
a Trades Disputes Bill. Conservative and Liberal leaders had long
believed that trade unions as well as employers' organisations
should be not merely accepted but welcomed, because these were
bodies which stabilised industrial relations by means of voluntary
collective bargaining.[115] There could, Baldwin said, 'be no greater
disaster' than 'anarchy in the trade union world', because it would
be impossible to maintain 'our highly developed system of industry
... unless you had organisations which could speak for and bind
the parties on both sides'.[116] Trade unions, he told Conservative
meetings, were 'necessary' and 'indispensable', because 'you
cannot secure stability and ordered progress unless you have ...
collective bargaining'.[117] He went still further, praising trade
unions as expressions of the working people's self-reliance, initiative, and desire for freedom and social betterment, and providing
a necessary balance against otherwise over-powerful owners and
managers of joint-stock companies.[118]

[113] *Ibid.*, p. 332.
[114] *OE* p. 51 (6 March 1925).
[115] E.g. Bonar Law and Churchill in Fox, *History and Heritage*, pp. 260, 293.
[116] *HCDeb* 195, cc. 1050–1 (13 May 1926). Cf. *OI* pp. 215 (12 June 1926); *SOL* p. 133.
[117] Conservative conference, 7 Oct. 1926; Women's Unionist organisation, 27 May 1927.
[118] *OI* pp. 215, 217–18 (12 June 1926). Cf. Swansea, 30 Oct. 1923, and see pre-war praise
    for the Miners' Federation in *HCDeb* 4s.CXC, cc. 1436–7 (22 June 1908), and support

Another key feature of the system had been that it operated largely independently of the state, enabling industrial relations to be excluded from the sphere of politics. Only in this limited sense was Baldwin 'reactionary', though he considered himself to be doing no more than restoring the integrity of the system. His speeches insistently expressed – and his decisions during 1926 demonstrated – a conviction that government action was not a solution but a large part of the problem. Interventions by the pre-war Liberal Cabinet and especially by the Coalition government had, he said, made existing difficulties much worse. This was one of the indictments against Lloyd George: here 'as in so many other things L.G. has left us a legacy of trouble'.[119] Government inevitably acted with a 'heavier and less skilled hand' than those with close knowledge of the workplace and market, and he went so far as to claim that during the War it had 'broken' the old wages system.[120] Intervention also encouraged employers and trade unions to treat government as an instrument of their own interests. Since the War, he said in 1923, 'the greatest industries in the country had become perfectly incapable of settling their own affairs, and ran in a panic to Downing Street the moment that things looked difficult'. This had to be stopped: if both sides of industry could not solve their own difficulties, 'I say the sooner they put their shutters up the better.'[121] Such dependence on government was the start of a slippery slope towards nationalisation; it undermined self-reliance and enterprise; it created injustices, as essential industries or services could extort advantages denied to weaker sectors; it encouraged trade unions to become more 'political' in their industrial actions. Worse, it destroyed responsibility.

This, Baldwin said, was especially so in coal mining, where there had been so much government interference since 1912 that even he could not avoid some involvement. As he described the problem, both the Mineowners' Association and the Miners' Federation always demanded more than they expected to obtain, and then refused to negotiate seriously with each other – because past

for collective bargaining in *HCDeb* 39, c. 957 (12 June 1912) and 59, cc. 729–30 (5 March 1914).
[119] Jones *WD* II.19 (23 April 1926). Cf. *HCDeb* 195, cc. 58–9 (3 May 1926).
[120] *HCDeb* 170, c. 1985 (10 March 1924).
[121] Edinburgh, 27 July 1923. Cf. Knowsley Park, 27 July 1925.

experience showed that a deadlock would bring government action or money. Every dispute therefore escalated into crisis, each settlement contained the 'germs of future trouble' and both sides became more stubborn, until eventually not even the combined efforts of government and the TUC could reconcile an 'absolutely irresistible force' with 'an absolutely immovable body'.[122] For all his determination to preserve industrial peace, Baldwin was still more determined to break this 'horribly vicious circle' in coal[123] and to prevent it developing in other industries – to the extent of facing a general strike, and the long recession in public support during the further six months of the coal lock-out. These were the product neither of 'indolence' nor 'paralysis',[124] but of a refusal to countenance any settlement requiring further state action in the future. 'My desire . . . is to wean the Coal Industry from the Government, and . . . any agreement must be between owners and men.'[125]

Baldwin's fundamental argument was that government action did not address the real problem: 'no Government on earth can bring about agreement or can end disputes between parties until those parties have at least the will to negotiate, to compromise, to agree to peace'.[126] His aim in the 1920s was to end any expectation that the state alone could solve industrial problems, still less – after the defeat of protection in 1923 – the larger economic difficulties. 'It is little that a Government can do . . . The organisations of employers and men . . . are far more able to work out the solutions of their troubles than the politicians. Let them put the State out of their minds.'[127] It was for this reason that he did not support Cabinet proposals for inclusion of statutory arbitration and conciliation in the 1927 Trades Disputes Bill: collective bargaining worked because it was voluntary, not compulsory. The chief duty of government – and the task he set himself – was

---

[122] *HCDeb* 187, cc. 1581–4, 1589–90 (6 Aug. 1925); 195, cc. 58–60 (3 May 1926); 199, cc. 269–70 (27 Sept. 1926). Baldwin had warned of this problem in its early stages: *HCDeb* 39, cc. 956–7 (12 June 1912).
[123] *HCDeb* 195, c. 59 (3 May 1926).
[124] GMY pp. 120–2; Jones, *Lord Baldwin*, pp. 10–11.
[125] Baldwin to Churchill, 5 Sept. 1926, in *WSC Comp* v/i.774. See also *HCDeb* 195, c. 60 (3 May 1926); F. A. Iremonger, *William Temple* (Oxford, 1948), p. 339; public letter, Oct. 1926, in M&B p. 441.
[126] Knowsley Park, 25 July 1925.
[127] *OE* pp. 34–5 (5 March 1925).

rather to help generate the basic will to negotiate, compromise and agree; to drive the 'militaristic spirit' out of the minds of masters and men, and replace it by a spirit of goodwill towards each other and towards 'their fellow countrymen'.[128]

For this he assumed that arguments and values commensurate with the larger scale of post-war industrial problems would be needed. His answer, most clearly stated while still at the Board of Trade, was to counteract sectional and class interests with the claims of social and national responsibility:

> while we preserve that individualistic self-reliance, which has always been the great attribute of our people, we require to develop more a communal sense which realises that our work is not only for ourselves, for our own shop, for our own industry, but is for our own people and for our own commonwealth of nations . . . The responsibility laid on the trading community . . . is very great . . . [it] is no less than that of feeding and trying to keep in comfort the people of our island . . . We want to realise that and to realise that every check to industry is a check to our own prosperity, that our work is for all and not only for ourselves, and . . . that every deliberate stoppage of production . . . is a deliberate lowering of the standard of life of our people which it should be our duty to preserve and improve.[129]

Feeding the people was, he declared as prime minister, 'the great mission' of masters and men, 'and no higher and finer mission can be found on earth'.[130] Once this shared responsibility was understood, it became incumbent upon both sides to adjust their differences peacefully, and more: to seek mutual understanding and co-operation. 'I hope both sides in industrial life will be slow to assert what they conceive to be their rights and quick to assert what they know in their hearts to be their duties'.[131] Unusually among Conservative politicians but in obvious extension of his own experience and values – 'he believed in every employer being a good employer'[132] – he placed particular onus upon employers. These should consider themselves 'trustees of the whole community' and measure their work not just by the quality and cheapness of their goods, but by 'the quality of the human relationship'

[128] Primrose League, 2 May 1924; Knowsley Park, 25 July 1925; Conservative conference, 8 Oct. 1925.
[129] *HCDeb* 153, cc. 2424–5 (11 May 1922).
[130] Edinburgh, 27 July 1923.
[131] Swansea, 30 Oct. 1923.
[132] Jones in B. Webb diary, 23 June 1923.

established with their workforce in making those goods. 'No management is scientific which forgets the man inside the workman.' Workmen should reciprocate by ceasing to regard 'the masters as monsters incarnate', and by taking 'a more intelligent ... and more sympathetic attitude towards the responsibilities of the employer'.[133] All this could be achieved if obvious steps were taken 'to humanise the system of limited liability'.[134]

The chief requirement was publicity, to dispel the ignorance which fed the 'devils of suspicion and fear'. Employers and managers should disclose the facts of their business to their workmen and trade unions, to help them understand competitive conditions, costs, depreciation, and the rest, and so encourage them to feel greater interest in the well-being of the firm. 'Industrial absolutism' should become a 'thing of the past', because good workers needed 'some other motive than terror of unemployment'.[135] Once adequate information was available, conferences between employers and trade unions could define common aims and agree reciprocal removal of grievances, so that workmen could enjoy sensitive management and greater security, and employers an abandonment of ca'canny and restrictive practices. Baldwin described the main purpose of these talks as industrial 'disarmament' conferences, but he repeatedly expressed a further ideal: that as a shared interest in improved productivity became apparent, they could develop into partnerships for facilitating rationalisation.[136] These were the real cures for Britain's economic and social problems. 'If we could all pull together for twelve months ... [t]his country would not know itself. We would advance from prosperity to prosperity, and fight the worst trade that might come to us, and we should win through.' Or again: 'The standard of life could only be improved by the most perfect co-operation of those who worked with their hands, of those who directed that labour, and of those who supplied the capital.'[137]

Baldwin even suggested that trade unions, instead of squandering their funds in industrial disputes, might purchase company

[133] Bradford, 29 Nov. 1923; Welbeck Abbey, 1 June 1925; Sheffield, 11 Oct. 1928.
[134] *OE* p. 67 (13 March 1925).
[135] Bradford, 29 Nov. 1923.
[136] There are many instances: see e.g. Bradford, 29 Nov. 1923; Junior Imperial League, 3 May 1924; Sheffield, 27 Oct. 1924; *OE* 32–6, 42–3, 67–8 (5, 6, 13 March 1925); Welbeck Abbey, 1 June 1925; Knowsley Park, 25 July 1925; Norwich, 17 July 1926.
[137] Cardiff, 18 Oct. 1924; Association of Conservative Clubs, 13 June 1924.

shares and themselves participate in the control of industry.[138] If this seems naively optimistic, his other proposals recalled the Whitley Council movement which had attracted substantial employer and trade-union support at the end of the War. Before 1926 he could claim that agreements in cotton, steel, and pottery, and consultations in shipbuilding, railways, and chemicals, represented real advances.[139] He expected the defeat of the General Strike to clear the air and create more constructive attitudes,[140] and soon suggested that the 'more enlightened and statesmanlike minds among employers and trade-union leaders' should meet and propose 'some new industrial policy'. Despite the souring effect of the Trades Disputes Bill upon trade-union opinion, his encouragement contributed to the Mond–Turner conference in 1928.[141] But any chance that this might have generated permanent procedures for assisting rationalisation was destroyed by something which no one had predicted – the world depression.

Throughout, Baldwin maintained the traditional position that the state's role was impartially to 'hold the ring' between employers and trade unions – to preserve an attitude, or at least a successful appearance, of even-handedness. Jones's unremarkable comment that Conservative ministers were more at ease with owners' representatives than trade unionists is often quoted.[142] Yet it is also true that trade-union leaders considered Baldwin approachable, fair-minded, trustworthy, and 'very decent indeed'. The TUC President, Pugh, was relaxed about attending secret talks at Chequers.[143] Baldwin did publicly describe the miners' secretary, Cook, as 'hysterical'; but he had already spoken of the 'stupidity' of the mine-owners' representatives.[144] He was careful not to suggest that industrial depression was caused only by wage levels, and to acknowledge the existence of 'defective

---

[138] Cardiff, 18 Oct. 1924; Gravesend, 23 Oct. 1924; Aberdeen, 5 Nov. 1925.

[139] E.g. Bradford, 29 Nov. 1923; Welbeck Abbey, 1 June 1925.

[140] E.g. Kennet, *Self-Portrait*, p. 245 (18 May 1926).

[141] *OI* pp. 224–6 (12 June 1926); and see Conservative conference, 8 Oct. 1926; Douglas Castle, 27 Aug. 1927; Conservative conference, 6 Oct. 1927; Guildhall, 9 Nov. 1927; G. McDonald and H. Gospel, 'The Mond–Turner Talks 1927–33', *Historical Journal* 16 (1973), pp. 810–15, 826; M&B pp. 439–40, 445, 450, 453.

[142] Jones *WD* II.19 (23 April 1926).

[143] Jones *WD* II.22–3, 60 (23, 25 April, 31 May 1926); Citrine, *Men and Work*, pp. 140, 157, 174, 179; GMY, p. 102.

[144] *HCDeb* 200, cc. 2145–6 (8 Dec. 1926); 199, c. 275 (27 Sept. 1926). Cf. Baldwin to Mineowners' Association, late May 1926, in M&B pp. 425–6.

management'. He criticised trade-union obstructiveness, but also that of employers.[145]

Yet obviously enough this 'impartiality' operated only within the parameters of the economic and political assumptions of Baldwin and his Cabinet. The July 1926 Hours Act and Mining Industry Act were both intended to help the whole industry. Yet the first was mandatory upon the miners, while the second was only voluntary for the owners: miners had to work longer, but owners' rights remained sacrosanct. Similarly, Baldwin's ambivalence towards the Trades Disputes Bill related to timing and tactics, rather than its substance. Its primary purpose – to confine trade unions to an industrial, rather than a 'political' role – gave legislative form to a rhetoric about trade-union behaviour which he had developed during the previous three years.

This was the other side of Baldwin's campaign for industrial peace: his accumulation of sufficient political and moral authority to discourage resort to lock-outs and strikes, to denounce sympathetic strikes, and to defeat a general strike. His strategy was so effective because he directed hostility not against trade unions as such, but against certain of their actions and purported intentions; and because his appeals were aimed not just at the two sides of industry, but also towards 'public opinion'. Here a reputation for impartiality, high-mindedness, and conciliation was priceless. It helped Baldwin to speak convincingly on behalf of the 'community' or the 'public', *including* trade unions understood in their 'acceptable' form – and to mobilise this sense of shared public interest against 'unacceptable' trade-union ambitions and activities. If, as he declared, employers and trade unions had great social and national responsibilities, then industrial disputes became 'the most unsocial action that can take place in a civilised country'.[146] He described Conservatives as standing for peace, comradeship, and 'the union of all classes', while defining the working-class consciousness which fed strike action as 'class hatred'.[147] He also tried to make trade-union attitudes seem contradictory and self-

---

[145] *OE* pp. 35, 45–6 (5, 6 March 1925). Cf. Bradford, 30 Nov. 1923; Welbeck Abbey, 1 June 1925. Baldwin was alleged to have told a miners' delegation in July 1925 that the wages of all workers had to be reduced; but the source – Cook – was hostile, and the story was immediately and repeatedly denied.

[146] Edinburgh, 27 July 1923.

[147] E.g. Plymouth, 25 Oct. 1923; Hotel Cecil, 21 May 1924; Association of Conservative Clubs, 13 June 1924; *OE* pp. 66–7 (13 March 1925); *OI* pp. 219–20 (12 June 1926).

interested, and the Conservative government the protector of other working people who were the 'innocent' victims of their actions. A favourite saying was that many in the Labour movement wanted brotherhood with foreigners and peace in international affairs, yet division between their countrymen and war at home.[148] After describing how thousands of women and girls were forced to walk to work during a bus strike he asked 'where was the sympathy on the part of the busmen?' – and answered that 'their sympathy was for themselves'. The national strikes which were supposed to help the working population in reality caused 'suffering and misery to millions', and especially to the poor man, his wife, and his children.[149]

Baldwin's gesture in March 1925 of withholding his government's power to legislate against trade unions was calculated not just as an example of restraint to them, but also to impress the wider public. The grant of the coal subsidy four months later had a similar purpose. Prolonging the effort to secure industrial peace would give more time to educate public opinion, and 'if public opinion is once educated, no Government need fear the result'.[150] By each of these decisions – almost as unexpected and dramatic as those on protection in 1923 – Baldwin reinforced his claim to express the right of the 'community' to protect itself against 'the forces of anarchy'.[151] Privately he wrote that 'buying off the strikes in 1925' had been part of 'the cost of teaching democracy'.[152]

The effects were seen during the General Strike in May 1926. Public support for the government was maintained and the will of TUC leaders was broken by a double-edged strategy. When the Cabinet ended discussions with the TUC representatives, Baldwin preserved a conciliatory tone by blaming the breakdown on 'hotheads' and speaking of his hope that they parted on friendly terms. Later his renewed public appeals for peace, trust, and an avoidance of recrimination did much to ease the TUC's abandonment of the Strike.[153] But between these two phases he struck very hard indeed. He demanded the TUC's unconditional surrender. He

[148] E.g. *OE* pp. 32–3, 228–9 (5 March 1925, 23 July 1923).
[149] Edinburgh, 24 March 1924; Cardiff, 18 Oct. 1924; Knowsley Park, 25 July 1925.
[150] Conservative conference, 8 Oct. 1925.
[151] *HCDeb* 187, cc. 1589, 1592 (6 Aug. 1925).
[152] Baldwin to Irwin, 26 June 1927, Halifax papers A.4.410.14.2.
[153] Jones, *WD* II.33–4 (3 May 1926); official report of Baldwin–TUC meeting, 12 May 1926, in R. Page Arnot, *The General Strike* (1926), pp. 221–3.

spoke of its 'despotic power', its threat of 'civil war' and its attempt to create 'a reign of force', in contrast to the hardships facing 'good citizens' whose livelihood and labour had been put 'at peril'.[154] Here as on other occasions, however, his strongest weapon was that of constitutionalism.

[154] *HCDeb* 195, cc. 71–2, 878 (3, 12 May 1926); statement and broadcast in *The British Gazette* 6, 10 May 1926.

CHAPTER 7

Democracy and public morality

The centrality of economic and class issues after 1918 was a new feature in national politics. Baldwin believed that Conservatives could win the economic and social arguments, but he assumed that success depended upon their being enveloped in a modernised form of an older politics – those of the 'constitution'. Conservatives had always feared that mass democracy might produce a politics of material interests and class conflict, fears which postwar labour unrest and the Labour party's advance seemed to confirm. Yet they themselves could not easily compete with promises of material advantages for the working population, especially after the 1923 defeat of protection. Baldwin was among those Conservatives who thought the party needed to develop an effective non-materialist politics. At its most basic, this was an instinct that 'the social structure could only be preserved by talking about something else' than resistance to working-class demands.[1] But Baldwin understood too that the Labour movement's appeal was not one-dimensional – not merely to material improvement, but to a new democratic public virtue. There seemed to be a still larger problem. Social elites, established institutions, and party leaderships were less respected. How was 'responsible' political authority to be preserved? Could parliamentary democracy be maintained?

If in retrospect Baldwin's warnings seem contrived and exaggerated, this was not how they appeared to much of the political public, with industrial protest and 'direct action' a recurring threat until 1926, with the Labour party an uncertain and volatile force, re-radicalised after the 1931 crisis, and with criticism of parliamentary methods from left and right. Nor, for all his sup-

---

[1] Cowling, *Impact of Hitler*, p. 393; cf. Cowling, *Impact of Labour*, p. 423.

posed insularity, did Baldwin seem alarmist in the contexts of wartime and post-war European revolutions, and dictatorships proliferating across the continent during the 1930s.

Baldwin thought the Labour appeal too powerful and too consonant with post-war popular attitudes to be defeated by negations alone; his whole background and cast of mind led him to believe that a successful positive response was possible. Conservative leadership had to contest Labour claims to a monopoly of democratic conceptions. Yet for this strategy to succeed, it had to take further steps. Successful resistance to 'revolution' from the Labour left required opposition to 'reaction' from the Conservative right – and to any other groups or individuals thought to weaken the best 'democratic' values. It was to these areas that Baldwin directed much of his rhetorical effort. In so doing he established the main feature of his leadership: restoration of the idea that political authority was properly based upon moral authority.

I

It has been seen that Baldwin's attitude towards the new political conditions after 1918 was highly ambivalent.[2] There was fear, which he focused into anxieties about the new electorate: 'democracy' created a 'race for life' which could end in a 'crash'. Yet he also had 'faith', and thought it futile to display resentment towards an irreversible change. 'If he has to work the democratic system, the wise man not only makes the best of it himself, without complaining, but tries to make everybody else feel the same.'[3] This tension between fear and faith was fertile, generating a rhetoric which fused several styles of argument. He expressed 'Whig' beliefs about the appropriate forms of political change, beliefs which had support across all parties. He re-vitalised the language of 'Tory democracy', developed by some Conservatives to imply mutual confidence between their party and the working-class electorate created by Disraeli's 1867 Reform Act. He also revived a traditional language of constitutional defence, sharpened by the arguments Maine and other Unionist intellectuals had directed

---

[2] Above, ch. 5 sections I–II.
[3] *HCDeb* 276, c. 1133 (29 March 1933).

against the 1885 extension of the electorate, with their stress upon the dangers of 'unmoderated democracy'.[4]

After 1918 the Labour party regarded political democracy as all but complete, and looked now to a further stage of economic and social democracy. In contrast Baldwin treated political democracy as a new and live problem: 'democracy is still an aspiration and not a fact'.[5] It remained immature and vulnerable. If it offered opportunities, it also needed effort. It was still the stuff of ideals: 'the most difficult form of government, and therefore the more worthy of our giving our lives to make it a success'.[6] The difficulties of democracy were Baldwin's most insistent theme throughout his leadership and beyond, not just in formal addresses but in countless impromptu talks. Democracy, he declared, 'can rise to great heights; it can also sink to great depths'.[7] A raw and volatile electorate might succumb to impulse, envy, excess, or despair. It might pursue selfish or class interests, or warlike or pacific passions, at the expense of national and imperial interests. It could easily be misled by self-interested or alienated demagogues, intellectuals, and publicists. Any of this might destroy freedom. Again and again he likened democratic government to a point on a knife-edge or the circumference of a wheel, all too liable to topple into tyranny on one side or anarchy on the other.[8] No previous democracy had lasted for long, nor successfully governed an empire. The real problem was not how to 'make the world safe for democracy', but how 'to make democracy safe for the world'.[9] Britain's democracy was therefore still an 'experiment': it remained 'on trial', in its 'testing time'.[10] It followed that 'the great task of this generation . . . is to save democracy, to preserve it, and to inspire it'.[11]

---

[4] For the common view *before* 1918 that Britain was already a 'democracy', because the electorate had a working-class majority, see McKibbin, *Ideologies of Class*, pp. 68–9.

[5] *TTF* p. 40 (14 July 1930).

[6] *OE* p. 220 (3 May 1924). Cf. *ibid.* pp. 149–57 (27 Sept. 1923); *OI* pp. 7–13, 29–36 (19 June 1926, 4 March 1927); *TTF* pp. 20–4, 39–42 (broadcast 6 March 1934, 14 July 1930).

[7] *OE* p. 71 (4 Dec. 1924).

[8] E.g. Rhodes Trust, 18 June 1923; *OE* pp. 149–50, 220 (27 Sept. 1923, 3 May 1924); *OI* pp. 128–9 (6 Aug. 1927). Cf. other similes in Sunderland 2nd meeting, 27 Jan. 1926; broadcast, 13 Oct. 1931; *TTF* pp. 20–1 (broadcast, 6 March 1934).

[9] *TTF* p. 308 (10 March 1928).

[10] *OE* pp. 70, 71 (4 Dec. 1924); *OI* p. 9 (19 June 1926); *TTF* p. 309 (10 March 1928).

[11] *OE* p. 149 (27 Sept. 1923).

Dramatised like this, support for 'democracy' became an extremely effective Conservative position. First, it had positive resonances and a classless appeal. In 1923 it was not obvious that the Conservative party had reconciled itself to the implications of the 1918 enfranchisement, and the Labour and Liberal parties could present it as politically – as well as economically and socially – reactionary. Baldwin transformed the party's image, and reversed the accusations.[12] In persistent, earnest, and eloquent assertions that nurturing freedom and democracy was the Conservative party's 'great ideal',[13] he laid claim to a central area of progressive politics while implying the inadequacy of the self-proclaimed 'progressive' parties to fulfil the task. Second, emphasis on democracy and freedom as fragile growths reinforced the conservative values of stability, 'responsibility', and respect for existing institutions and constitutional constraints. This position – progressive defence, as it were – could be used persuasively to define a narrow ground of acceptable public behaviour, to attack Labour and trade-union deviations from it, and to anathematise 'bolshevism', syndicalism, communism, and, later, fascism. It was also attractive to Liberal anti-socialists or 'constitutionalists'. It even provided a powerful tactical weapon. A common Baldwin technique for containing difficult policy or party problems was to elevate them into 'an acid test of democracy'.

From the moment he became prime minister Baldwin sought to reduce the distance between Conservative leadership and the new mass electorate, to imply that he breathed the democratic atmosphere – even to compete with Labour claims to be the spokesmen of the 'people'. For this he could express genuine aspects of his beliefs and personality, and his sense of distance from 'professional politicians'. He also began with the advantage of his anonymity with the public – the former Coalition leaders' sneers at his 'obscurity' actually helped him – while from October 1923 he had to justify the precipitation of his adoption of protection and calling of a general election. His speeches and newspaper publicity made a virtue of his not being a 'great man', exploiting contrasts with both the Coalitionists' arrogance and Curzon's

---

[12] For a rare grasp of Baldwin's innovations in this respect, see Schwarz, 'Language of Constitutionalism', esp. pp. 1–6, 10.
[13] *OI* p. 32 (4 March 1927).

patrician style to present a model democrat: an 'ordinary man', modest, accessible, reliable, representative, almost 'non-political'. Notwithstanding his privileged education and his wealth, he offered himself as an average man who since childhood had through friendships with working people acquired what no 'exclusively political training' could have provided: 'profound sympathy and affection for the common man' and woman, with those 'carrying on the daily toil of the world'.[14] Even privately he trusted his own instincts against those with far more political experience, telling a sceptical Lord Salisbury that his 'social circumstances made him a better judge of popular opinion' than one 'born in the purple'.[15] This claim to understand the popular mind became a marked feature of Baldwin's public personality. 'I am just one of you', he would say to audiences:

I am just a plain man of the common people. I understand the common people, and I believe that what I am thinking they are thinking. I believe that I am voicing what is in the minds of the dumb millions of this country.[16]

In announcing his conversion to protection in October 1923 he spoke not as a 'clever man' knowing anything of 'political tactics', but as 'a leader of a democratic party' who 'felt the only honest and right thing' to do was to make his views public.[17] In calling a general election a month later, he said 'it would not have been honest to remain in office' without putting the change of policy 'before the country'.[18] After the election defeat his view was that special efforts to exclude the Labour party from government would be counter-productive. It was, he privately explained, far better to be seen to act fairly, according to accepted political convention:

complication rather than help might arise from any symptom of what might be called 'backstairs arrangements' between himself and Liberals. The danger is that we may make it easy and plausible for Labour to say

---

[14] *OE* pp. 15–16, 20–1 (12 Jan. 1925, 7 Nov. 1923). Cf. Commons press gallery, 15 June 1923; Manchester 2nd speech, 2 Nov. 1923.
[15] Salisbury recalling Baldwin's words in October 1923, in Cowling, *Impact of Labour*, p. 415.
[16] Worcester, 24 Nov. 1923. Cf. Manchester 2nd speech, 2 Nov. 1923; *OE* p. 16 (12 Jan. 1925); Cardiff, 15 May 1929.
[17] Plymouth, 25 Oct. 1923.
[18] Reading, 21 Nov. 1923.

we have got our proper chance for turning Baldwin out and getting power, but the Liberals and Tories, being capitalists, are determined to thwart us, and we must stiffen ourselves now into firm alliance against such scheming, and call the country to our aid.[19]

Despite waiting until his government was defeated in the Commons, in public he appeared to accept the electoral verdict with good grace. He promised 'no factious or fractious opposition' and – in contrast to Unionist behaviour after the 1906 election – quickly withdrew the tariff policy in deference, he said, to 'the judgment of the country'.[20]

Baldwin had good personal and party reasons for each of these actions, but his *presentation* had the effect of giving him an impregnable democratic reputation. This had great value during the critical periods of the first Labour government in 1924 and the trade-union challenges of 1925–6. The experience confirmed a remarkable strategic coolness, as when after the 1929 election defeat he calculated the public effects of early resignation. He had asked 'the Democracy to trust him', but 'in the true English spirit he accepts his defeat' and 'the Democracy . . . will take off their hats to him as a good sportsman, who . . . takes his beating like a man'. This would 'count in his favour' at the next election, because the electorate would remember that he had 'played the game'.[21]

Baldwin's rhetorical commitment to political democracy was striking not just in its ubiquity, but also in its ostensible radicalism and non-partisanship. Conservatives traditionally had hierarchical and propertied assumptions about political responsibilities, and these continued to colour the attitudes of many in the party. In contrast Baldwin spoke in Lincoln's terms: 'government of the people by the people'.[22] He even used the language of the Levellers: 'I think the poorest he that is in England hath a life to live as the richest he.'[23] As democracy arose from all the people, so it demanded active citizenship – and he used the democratic word 'citizen' – from all, irrespective of class, status, or party. It could only 'develop and . . . perfect itself . . . and prove itself

---

[19] Archbishop Davidson journal, 12 Dec. 1923.
[20] *HCDeb* 169, c. 117 (15 Jan. 1924); party meeting, 11 Feb. 1924.
[21] Baldwin in Stamfordham memo, 2 June 1929, Royal Archives GV K2223/30, and see M&B p. 527; *HCDeb* 229, c. 63 (2 July 1929).
[22] *OE* p. 70 (4 Dec. 1924). Cf. Aberdeen, 5 Nov. 1925; *SOL* p. 93 (17 March 1937).
[23] *TTF* p. 37 (14 July 1930); *Interpreter*, p. 53.

worthy to survive ... if every man and woman plays his or her part'.[24] Any person who failed to accept their full responsibility prevented democracy from functioning properly,[25] indeed formed 'a weak spot in the body politic that may spread and cause corruption throughout the whole'.[26]

My ideal is that everyone, men and women alike, in all positions of life, and whatever party they attach themselves to, should take political questions ... as seriously as they take any other part of their daily life ...

[I]n so far as each man or woman, whether he be a duke or whether he be a miner, whether he be the driver of a motor car or whether he sweeps the roads, in so far as he fails to do his bit towards making democracy a sweet and clean and good thing ... that democracy is a failure.[27]

The ostensible point was that now the whole people were enfranchised, all should exercise their right so that everyone implicitly registered their support for the existing constitution – and thereby for the responsibilities and compromises inseparable from constitutional action. He was especially emphatic during election campaigns. It was, he said in his first election broadcast, the 'plain and obvious duty' of every elector to record their vote: it would be 'extraordinarily selfish' not to do so.[28]

The summons to the polls was, obviously enough, linked to appeals to vote Conservative. But the connection was not made crudely. An abrupt descent from democratic principle to party interest would have punctured Baldwin's paradoxically 'non-political' persona. It would also have weakened his wider purposes of defending the constitutional structure as a whole, and identifying Conservatism with majority opinion and national aspirations. His speeches therefore made the connection implicitly or negatively. They implied that the ordinary voter, once aroused to 'responsible' citizenship, would naturally resist the extremists of right and left, and most would equally naturally resist Labour or Liberal blandishments. 'Until every man and woman is determined that they will accept responsibility for the government of

[24] Election broadcast, 16 Oct. 1924.
[25] *OI* p. 32 (4 March 1927); Leeds, 22 May 1929; *TTF* p. 20 (schools broadcast, 6 March 1934).
[26] *TTF* p. 310 (10 March 1928).
[27] Stirling overflow meeting, 26 Jan. 1926.
[28] Broadcast, 16 Oct. 1924. Cf. broadcasts, 29 May 1929, 8 Nov. 1935, and most of his speeches in the closing stages of each election campaign.

their country', the 'sane, sober element' would be beaten by the irresponsible 'mass' – those liable to be misled by a demagogue possessed of 'a sufficient gift of tongues to captivate them'.[29] Democracy was government in which 'the will of the minority, however . . . cunningly disguised, is not allowed to triumph over that of the majority'.[30]

Citizenship, then, did not simply involve the responsibility to vote; it also meant exercising that vote 'responsibly'. Parliamentary government would be preserved (and Conservative predominance achieved) by widespread acceptance that democracy was inseparable from particular understandings of democratic responsibility – those which Baldwin's speeches sought to instil. At the time of the 1928 enfranchisement of younger women, he declared that 'a new freedom only means a new duty, for freedom without duty and without obligation is merely licence and anarchy'.[31] Genuine freedom required tolerance, sympathy, dedication, sacrifice – and discipline: all citizens had to practise self-discipline, 'learning to obey, before they rule'.[32] It also required education. 'A democracy cannot function unless it is educated',[33] gaining not just knowledge of public issues, but the ability to distinguish 'truth' from mere 'rhetoric' and statesmen from 'demagogues'.[34] Democracy demanded, in another recurrent phrase, 'eternal vigilance' – between electors and elected, and towards themselves.[35] 'Our governors are responsible to the people. They must be worthy of that trust, and the people must be worthy of good governors. The contract is mutual.'[36]

Each individual had to realise that his or her responsibilities extended far beyond those of self and class. These were responsibilities towards past generations which had struggled for freedom, the war generation which had suffered and died in its cause, and the prosperity and happiness of future generations.[37] There were

---

[29] *OI* p. 32 (4 March 1927).
[30] Aberdeen, 2nd meeting, 5 Nov. 1925.
[31] National Union of Societies for Equal Citizenship, 8 March 1928.
[32] *OI* pp. 12–13 (19 June 1926); *TTF* p. 286 (20 Jan. 1930).
[33] *TTF* p. 304 (10 Oct. 1931). Cf. *OE* pp. 150–3 (27 Sept. 1923).
[34] *OE* pp. 94–7, 152–5, 220–1 (March 1924, 27 Sept. 1923, 3 May 1924).
[35] Rhodes Trust, 16 June 1923; *OE* p. 220 (3 May 1924); Sunderland overflow meeting, 27 Jan. 1926; *TTF* p. 128 (6 Aug. 1927).
[36] *TTF* p. 310 (10 March 1928).
[37] *OE* p. 70 (4 Dec. 1924); *OI* pp. 13, 36, 128–9 (19 June 1926, 4 March, 6 Aug. 1927); *TTF* pp. 310–15 (10 March 1928).

responsibilities towards each other, and towards the community and nations: 'every one of the people . . . must work for the good of the country, and not only for his own good, or democracy will become only a [meaningless] word'.[38] There were also responsibilities to the Empire, to the wider world, to humanity:

Never in the history of the world had there been imposed a task on any democracy such as is imposed upon this . . . When the British people take part in an election . . . they are not only striving for themselves, but they are . . . responsible for hundreds of millions in Asia . . . They are responsible for their own kith and kin across the sea; they are the paramount authority for most of the dark races of Africa; and if we fail in our trust we do not fall alone, but bring down in our collapse a large proportion of the human race.[39]

Indeed, if British democracy failed it would 'shake the fabric of the whole world', because upon it depended the prospects 'for world peace and for world progress'.[40]

Against the supposed dangers from 'democracy' Baldwin therefore cast large responsibilities, intended to act partly as inspiration but more as a constraint. By 1926 he had found a phrase to encapsulate his meaning – an old one, but one which gained new significance during the 1930s: 'ordered freedom', order without despotism, freedom without anarchy.[41] The external form of ordered freedom was the constitutional apparatus of monarchy, law, parliament, local government, party system, and elections. Yet he did not enter into detailed justification of these arrangements. Their qualities were to be assumed and celebrated, not subjected to analysis and opened to controversy. When in 1930–1 a debate about the efficiency of political institutions developed among various members from all the parties – including Churchill as well as Lloyd George and the Webbs – Baldwin acknowledged that there was 'impatience' with democratic government. But even when the debate produced a parliamentary inquiry, he refused to accept its basic terms. Instead he insisted, characteristically, that the problem was a failure not of 'machinery' but simply of 'faith'.[42]

---

[38] Aberdeen, 2nd meeting, 5 Nov. 1925.

[39] Bolton, 28 Oct. 1924.

[40] *TTF* p. 313 (10 March 1928). Cf. broadcast, 16 Oct. 1924; Drury Lane, 18 April 1929; broadcast, 22 April 1929; *TTF* pp. 276–81 (20 Jan. 1930).

[41] *OI* p. 12 (19 June 1926); *TTF* p. 286 (20 Jan. 1930), and many later instances.

[42] *TTF* pp. 40–51 (14 July 1930). See *HCDeb* 244, c. 810 (4 Nov. 1930); evidence, 18 Feb. 1931, in 'Special Report from the Select Committee on Procedure on Public Business',

Baldwin's objective was to maintain and re-invigorate the wide-spread public acceptance of that constitutional faith – a 'principle deep in the hearts of millions of Englishmen who do not belong to our party or any party'.[43] He sought especially to cement the identification of 'democracy' with the 'constitution'. So long as these remained synonymous and so long as Conservative leaders expressed commitment to freedom, the traditional Conservative defence of the constitution would remain as progressive in *appearance* as it was conservative in *practice*. This also meant that despite the creation of a mass electorate, the Conservative party could again be sure that at sensitive moments a cry of 'constitution in danger' would rally great swathes of central, moderate opinion of all classes against its opponents.

II

Observance of constitutional conventions was one guarantee for 'ordered freedom' and Conservative values, but Baldwin was more concerned that these should become an inner belief and habit – just as he wanted private enterprise, self-help, industrial co-operation and social cohesion to remain secure in popular allegiance. For Baldwin these various political, social, and economic values were unified in the ethic of service.

'Service' was the most important word in Baldwin's public vocabulary. It expressed his understanding of Conservative virtue, one superior to Labour and socialist virtue because more natural and closer to social and historical realities. The conception plainly derived from his own family and education, but it had similarities with older aristocratic and gentry conceptions of public duty. Significantly, the Cabinet members Baldwin felt closest to were not fellow businessmen like Neville Chamberlain, but the squirearchical lay churchmen, Bridgeman and Halifax: they 'talk the same language as I do. My other colleagues don't.'[44] His innovation was to fuse traditional landed ideas about mutual duties with high-

Parliamentary Papers 1930–1 (161), VIII.203. For the debate, Williamson, *National Crisis*, pp. 135–7.
[43] Conservative conference, 6 Oct. 1933.
[44] Jones *DL* p. 207 (23 May 1936); cf. *HCDeb* 231, cc. 1305–6 (7 Nov. 1929), for Irwin (i.e. Halifax). For high-minded landed Conservatism see Cowling, *Impact of Labour*, pp. 63, 72–4, 87–90.

minded middle-class efforts to communicate benevolence towards the working classes, and to present the result as a democratic ethic shared by right-thinking men and women of all classes.

As service was Baldwin's personal creed, so it was in terms of service that he understood his own career. Here his sense of being set apart from 'professional politicians' was especially significant. It was important to him that his acceptance of ministerial office required personal financial sacrifices; that in rebelling against the Coalition he had expected his political career to be destroyed, not advanced; and that he became prime minister through no special effort of his own. Privately he was much concerned that those he respected should understand that his unexpected elevations in 1922–3 resulted not from ambition but from his 'single-minded devotion . . . to duty'.[45] This was how he always liked to think of his leadership, as a duty demanding much that went against his personal inclinations: 'I do loathe going back to it all – the publicity, the vulgarity – it's like standing on a dunghill.'[46]

It was also important to him that all this should be recognised publicly as integral to his political character, because his call to service could not have been sustained without personal example. Leadership required evidence of appropriate ethical qualities. He had the considerable advantage of his now much-publicised financial sacrifice and public appeal as 'F.S.T.' in 1919, but even so the appeal was difficult to make without sanctimoniousness. But Baldwin usually succeeded, precisely because he wished to present 'service' as the modest morality of the common man:

I am one of those (of whom there are many here) who when the war broke out were too old for active service, but who were possessed . . . with a consuming desire to do something for our country, and . . . to find where we could most usefully give service . . .

[I accepted office in December 1916 because] I had the opportunity of giving my services to the country without any feeling that it was necessary to be remunerated for them.

There is nothing singular in that. There must have been millions of men who felt as I did. I have never said, or believed, that that service

---

[45] Baldwin in Maclean memo, 25 July 1923, Maclean papers c. 467/52–4. Cf. Stamfordham memo, 22 May 1923, Royal Archives GV K1853/17; Jones *WD* I.243 (30 Sept. 1923); Palmstierna, *Atskilliga Egenheter* extract, Jones papers AA1/27.

[46] Jones *DL* p. 60 (18 Sept. 1932).

which I had the opportunity of rendering was one whit higher or better than any other.[47]

He described himself as a man who disliked the 'limelight', and would be perfectly happy to retire into a quiet country life. Yet he was 'the man on whom the lot has fallen', and he could no more have 'shirked the responsibility' of high office than any other man could.[48]

I am just one of yourselves, who has been called to special work for the country at this time. I never sought the office. I never planned out or schemed my life. I have but one idea, which was an idea I inherited, and it was the idea of service – service to the people of this country. My father lived in that belief all his life, and behind him members of my family . . . It is a tradition; it is in our bones; and we have to do it . . . That service seemed to lead one by way of business and the county council into Parliament, and it has led one through various strange paths to where one is; but the ideal remains the same.[49]

From personal example Baldwin proceeded to public teaching. The onset of mass democracy and the Labour challenge demanded from the powerful and the privileged a stronger and purer dedication to service – a reaffirmation of the cardinal principle that 'unto whomsoever much is given, of him shall much be required'.[50] Rightly conducted – and as Baldwin's valedictions for public figures aimed to demonstrate – politics and government office were not about the pursuit of fame nor 'what you can get', but about 'what you can give and do'.[51] Similarly, to be 'given wealth is to be entrusted with a stewardship': it 'must be used to benefit not only its owner but also the community'.[52] Riches divorced from social responsibility were both a moral evil – as 'a servant, [wealth] had a most useful function to perform, but as a master it meant damnation'[53] – and a political danger: 'that vulgar luxury which flaunts itself in London' formed the 'best propaganda [for] revolutionary

[47] *OE* pp. 61, 62–3 (13 March 1925). Cf. Manchester, 2nd speech, 2 Nov. 1923; Toc H festival, 6 Dec. 1929.
[48] Party meeting, 28 May 1923; Commons press gallery, 15 June 1923; National Unionist Association, 29 June 1923.
[49] *OE* p. 19 (7 Nov. 1923). Cf. party meeting, 28 May 1923, for the premiership being 'unsought and undesired', and *SOL* p. 106 (13 April 1937).
[50] Aberystwyth, 24 Oct. 1928; *TTF* p. 29 (24 May 1929).
[51] *TTF* pp. 308, 312 (10 March 1928). Cf. his advice to a defeated MP in M&B, p. 500.
[52] National Savings Assembly, 20 July 1928; Sheffield, 27 Oct. 1924.
[53] *OE* p. 62 (13 March 1925).

doctrine'.[54] Businessmen in making their fortunes should render service not just by caring for their workforce, but also by helping in local government.[55] Those industries receiving special assistance in the 1930s from import duties had a duty 'to pay back their debt to the State' in the form of help 'to those who are most in need', the unemployed of the depressed areas.[56] His appeal was especially to the young. Public-school children and university students must never suppose that mankind had toiled through countless generations just in order to enable them to enjoy their personal advantages. They must use their education to help others, 'to give back to the less fortunate people of this country and of the world something that you owe for the happiness and for the privileges that have been showered upon all of you'.[57]

Above all there was the example of the war generation – the sacrifices of the dead, wounded, and bereaved. 'I feel very strongly that the only way in which we can pay our debts to that generation ... is to give ourselves to the service of our country and the world.'[58] This was the best 'thank-offering' to the dead. To the tormenting question 'did they die in vain?', the answer was that they would have done so only 'if you and I live in vain'. It was owed to them 'that every one of us resolves afresh today ... that he will devote his life to the service of his country, that he may leave his country such as those who have fallen dreamed they would make it by their deaths'.[59]

Performance of service by political, social, and economic leaders was needed to stimulate a reciprocal performance of service from the 'people'. By 'unselfish service and devotion' they could 'raise the standard of life and the standard of ideals among their fellow men'.[60] This was the antidote to the dangerous tendencies of the age, an ethic to counteract a politics of materialism and class conflict. For Baldwin economic individualism and political freedom

[54] Aberdeen, 5 Nov. 1925 – a passage delivered with 'savage' contempt: AWB p. 139.
[55] Bradford, 29 Nov. 1923; *OE* pp. 64–9 (13 March 1925).
[56] Liverpool, 25 March 1935; *HCDeb* 307, cc. 75–6 (3 Dec. 1935).
[57] Oxford, 15 May 1925. Cf. *OE* pp. 186–7; *OI* pp. 198–205, 210–11 (27 Oct. 1927, 30 March 1926); University College, Aberystwyth, 24 Oct. 1928; *TTF* pp. 285, 304 (20 Jan. 1930, 10 Oct. 1931).
[58] Oxford, 8 June 1923.
[59] Welbeck Abbey, 28 May 1928. Cf. *OE* pp. 64, 272–5 (13 March 1925, 19 Dec. 1923); *OI* pp. 3–6 (3 June 1926).
[60] Primrose League, 2 May 1924.

did not mean selfishness, nor unqualified rights. They meant a self-reliance and a self-respect which generated a sense of respect and a recognition of duties towards others. Like the claims of employers and the privileged, those of workers and the common people were properly subordinate to their responsibilities. A well-adjusted society had no contests over the supposed rights of individuals, least of all those of classes. Quoting Disraeli, Baldwin spoke of the Conservative party wanting:

> to impress on society that there is such a thing as duty . . . we do not pretend that we are any better than others, but that we are anxious to do our duty, and, if so, we think that we have a right to call on others, whether rich or poor, to do theirs. If that principle of duty had not been lost sight of for the last fifty years, you would never have heard of the classes into which England is divided.[61]

In the dangerous post-war world, the language of rights was best avoided altogether. 'Do not talk about our rights; talk about our duties. For if everybody in this country did his duty there could be no question of rights: we should all have them.'[62] Recognition of this truth was fundamental to Britain's post-war condition:

> The assertion of people's rights has never yet provided that people with bread. The performance of their duties, and that alone, can lead to the successful issue of those experiments in government which we have carried further than any other people in this world.[63]

Only in this 'realization of our duties rather than our rights' was there a chance of overcoming the economic difficulties, and sustaining that independence and self-help which would prevent pauperisation and national bankruptcy.[64]

With mutual respect and with duties came that sense of common humanity which united societies and nations. 'Let us never forget . . . we are all members one of another.'[65] From this flowed the essential human qualities of love and brotherhood. 'My own desire, my one desire', Baldwin said in his first broadcast, 'is to get people in this country to pull together, to set up an ideal of

[61] Scarborough, 7 Oct. 1926, slightly misquoting Disraeli in 1844, from W. Monypenny and G. Buckle, *The Life of Benjamin Disraeli*, II (1912), pp. 247–8.
[62] *TTF* pp. 308–9 (10 March 1928).
[63] *OE* p. 71 (4 Dec. 1924).
[64] Constitutional Club, 29 Jan. 1925.
[65] Reading, 21 Nov. 1923. Cf. *OE* p. 226 (3 May 1924); *OI* p. 200 (27 Oct. 1927); *TTF* p. 48 (14 July 1930).

service and the love of brethren in place of that of class war.'
These things were 'at the root of the whole matter'.[66]

Society was not atomistic, the stuff of licence, but nor did it
consist of an anonymous mass, the material for despotism. Service
and brotherhood arose from a sense of the individual: they were
evoked by fellow-feeling towards other individuals in families,
before they spread out to neighbours and beyond. They could not
be generated by abstractions like class or nation, nor imposed by
legislation, nationalisation and state direction.[67] It was upon the
moral quality of its individual members that the lasting progress
of the community or nation depended. By voluntary effort individuals enriched themselves and the community, and in service to
others they dissolved the evils and dangers of materialism. Forti-
fied by religion and music, literature, art, or love of the countryside, such spiritual values would maintain the 'sanity of your own
soul', would 'radiate from you to the masses of the people', and so
would help to make democracy 'fitter and nobler'.[68]

The ethic of service – which would moralise private enterprise
and democracy, while proscribing 'class warfare', socialism, communism, and fascism – constituted a conservative idealism with
much potential for widening support for the Conservative party.
Yet a further advantage of an ethical appeal was that this partisan
objective did not often need to be explicit. Even when addressing
party audiences Baldwin was able to adopt a non-party, 'national',
voice. In a typical arrangement at Birmingham in January 1926,
his main speech consisted largely of an official brief about policy
(mainly electrification), but afterwards he spoke informally on
what was both his personal faith and a classless party strategy:

The real difference amongst men is between those who are prepared to
give more than they get and those who want to get more than they give.
And that difference is found just as much between men whether they
are dukes or [engine] greasers, or anywhere in between ... [T]he kind
of Conservatism ... which I believe in and which can triumph is that
which has for its fundamental policy the policy of service to the country.
And in that sacred service there stand shoulder to shoulder men of every

[66] 16 Oct. 1924. Cf. Bradford, 29 Nov. 1923; Sheffield, 27 Oct. 1924; Constitutional Club,
29 Jan. 1925; *OI* p. 226 (12 June 1926).
[67] Edinburgh, 27 July 1923; *OE* pp. 225–6 (3 May 1924); *TTF* pp. 303, 311–12 (10 Oct.
1931, 10 March 1928).
[68] *OE* pp. 200–1, 264 (7 May 1925, 16 Feb. 1924); *OI* p. 201 (27 Oct. 1927); *SOL* pp.
33–4 (26 June 1936).

class of society ... I believe ... with every fibre of my being [that] ...
the working out of [this] creed can alone bring our country through these
difficult days ... [T]here never was a time when there were more people
in all ranks of society ... who are resolved to do what they can, by their
own service and ... example, to lead their country into those paths of
self-sacrifice, of care for others, in pursuit of peace. And I cannot think
that those forces, properly co-ordinated and welded together, cannot in
the end control the rude forces of disorder, the forces of hate and the
forces of destruction between people and between classes.[69]

For Baldwin, 'service' provided a non-socialist reconciliation
between the individual and the community. It also enabled him to
make the conservative assumption of inequality and the democratic conception of freedom seem compatible. Men and women
were not equal in the common meaning of the word, due to in-
escapable differences in worldly circumstances and abilities; yet
every individual was of inestimable value. 'We are not all equal,
and never shall be; the true postulate of democracy is not equality
but the faith that every man and woman is worth while. Beyond
all the external trappings ... there is a human soul.'[70] In this
deeper meaning of spiritual value, equality did exist: in 'the fundamental right of every human being to be treated as an end in
himself or herself, and not as a tool or a slave'.[71] In a further
sense, all men and women of whatever rank or class could attain
equality by fulfilling their duties:

All my life I believed from my heart the words of Browning. 'All service
ranks the same with God.' It makes very little difference whether a man
is driving a tramcar or sweeping streets or being Prime Minister, if he
only brings to that service everything that is in him and performs it for
the sake of mankind.[72]

III

Baldwin's definition of post-war problems and his appeal to the
values of democratic constitutionalism and 'service' had implications for his attitudes towards Conservative politics, public stan-

[69] Midland Union of Conservative Associations, 2nd speech to young Conservatives, 15 Jan.
1926.
[70] *OI* p. 203 (27 Oct. 1927).
[71] National Union of Societies for Equal Citizenship, 8 March 1928.
[72] *OE* p. 19 (7 Nov. 1923). Cf. p. 63 (13 March 1925). For the Browning quotation, see
ch. 9 n.19.

dards, and treatment of the Labour movement. These in turn had significant, sometimes decisive, effects upon the collective Conservative leadership's strategy and policy. This is not to say that the wider constituency and parliamentary party became shaped in his image, as the revolts from 1929 to 1931 and over India from 1933 to 1935 most plainly show. Other versions of Conservatism were persistent and prominent. Yet the tensions with substantial elements of his party not only emphasise his distinctive approach; they also supplied a particular dynamic in his leadership.

For Baldwin was much concerned that the democratic and ethical values he tried to exemplify should be absorbed by the Conservative party: he wanted to *change* his party. While his doctrine was inseparable from party objectives it also had deeper political purposes, and success here depended not just on his own efforts but on those of his party. Even the party's functions had to be adjusted. The new electors were so numerous and ill-educated and the new Labour opposition was so formidable that party work could not remain largely a matter of mobilising familiar bodies of support with familiar cries. Party organisers had to become also teachers and proselytisers, winning new bodies of support. The party could not 'go on on the old lines', remaining 'too closely identified with vested interests'; it had to be brought 'up to date', and to 'live for the people in the widest sense'.[73] It could neither win elections nor fulfil its 'national' responsibilities if it disregarded the realities and opportunities of post-war politics. So it was not only the 'new electorate' that needed to be 'educated', but his own party too. The task, as he described it in retirement, had been 'to get a reorientation . . . of the Tory party and in Disraeli's words to make it national, i.e. to give it a national rather than a party orientation'.[74]

The most basic requirement was that Conservatives should show themselves to be a 'democratic and democratised Party'.[75] This placed some constraints upon party aims and even required Baldwin himself to suppress some of his preferences – preferences which again show his ambivalence towards 'democracy'. Like most Conservatives, he would have liked to strengthen the House of

[73] *The People*, 18 May 1924: the part of the notorious interview that Baldwin certainly wanted published. Cf. Begbie, *Conservative Mind*, p. 23; Dundas Castle, 16 June 1928.
[74] Baldwin to Pepys-Whiteley, 15 Feb. 1941, CUL Add. 8770.
[75] Sheffield, 27 Oct. 1924.

Lords as a check upon 'socialist' government. Yet he had a larger sense of the risks of appearing to be undemocratic, and of the ineffectiveness of constitutional safeguards which lacked very wide support. For much of the 1920s and 1930s he smothered party pressures for House of Lords 'reform', and he was unhappy even with his own Cabinet's 'reform' proposals in 1927. He thought action would become possible only if – as with trade-union legislation – the Labour movement committed some 'overt act', or if substantial cross-party agreement could be otherwise obtained. But despite occasional hopes, he thought it too divisive even for the National government to attempt.[76] He probably sympathised too with proposals in 1927 to limit the parliamentary franchise by raising the voting age from twenty-one to twenty-five years. Nevertheless, against Churchill and much of the Cabinet his view prevailed that it was just not 'practical politics' to withdraw such a long-established qualification.[77] He did share in a 1928 Cabinet decision to withdraw the local government franchise from poor-law recipients – believed by many Conservatives to result in inflated local expenditure and higher rates – yet in the event the decision was never implemented.[78]

On the other hand Baldwin showed a positive commitment towards equal electoral and civil rights for women. Despite much party and Cabinet opposition – with Churchill again prominent – he understood that once the basic principle of female enfranchisement had been conceded in 1918, an attempt to preserve discrimination against younger women would give Conservatives a reactionary reputation, and that this would be more damaging than any adverse electoral effect from 'flapper votes'. Again the wise course was to make the best of the inevitable. He took the public position that a democracy was 'incomplete and lop-sided' until it represented the 'whole people'.[79] He was also notably

---

[76] Jones *WD* II.62, 103, 105–6 (21 July 1926, 21 June, 1 July 1927); Cabinet Political Committee, 29 Jan. 1934, CAB 27/562; P. Williamson, 'The Labour Party and the House of Lords 1918–1931', *Parliamentary History* 10 (1991), 333–40.

[77] *Amery Diaries*, I.504 (12 April 1927); *Real Old Tory Politics. The Political Diaries of Sir Robert Sanders, Lord Bayford 1910–1935*, ed. John Ramsden (1984), p. 232 (25, 27 April 1927); Women's Unionist Organisation, 27 May 1927.

[78] A. Deacon and E. Briggs, 'Local Democracy and Central Policy: The Issue of Pauper Votes in the 1920s', *Policy and Politics* 2 (1974), 356–7.

[79] Women's Unionist Organisation, 27 May 1927.

welcoming towards the new voters, and attentive towards the party's women's organisation. In contrast to the often patronising attitudes of other leading politicians he did not speak to female audiences largely on 'women's issues', but assumed that their politics were as serious and wide-ranging as those of men.[80]

By a 'democratised' party Baldwin did not mean that the Conservative party's representative bodies should have increased power to determine policy. The leadership's traditional authority was not to be diminished: 'policy . . . is a matter for the leader of the party'.[81] He meant that the party should broaden the social composition of its membership and of its local government and parliamentary candidates. But these statements had a particular context. They were made after the first Labour government took office in 1924, and revived earlier leadership proposals in an explicit response to the Labour party's democratic 'vitality'. He said that Labour had two great institutional strengths. It seemed the only organisation through which able men of the 'lower orders' could rise to the highest public offices.[82] It was also well adapted to modern conditions because its members all paid subscriptions, which both deepened individual commitment and helped finance impecunious candidates.[83] Baldwin urged his party to emulate these arrangements. It should accept that the gifts required for public life were no longer 'the peculiar prerogative of any class and might be found throughout all ranks'.[84] One of his 'ambitions' was, he told the 1924 party conference, that working men 'should take their proper place in the ranks of our party', providing them with a Conservative 'ladder' of public advancement.[85] Constituency associations should increase their fund-raising and subscriptions, in order to end the 'very bad tradition' of selecting only rich candidates who could pay the constituency expenses, rather than the best available men and women. As he later said, he would rather have a shilling apiece from 100,000 individuals than the same amount in £5,000 gifts, because 'our party today rests upon

[80] E.g. Women's Unionist Organisation, 9 May 1924, 27 May 1927, 11 May 1928; National Union for Equal Citizenship, 8 March 1928.
[81] Party meeting, 30 Oct. 1930.
[82] Party meeting, 11 Feb. 1924; Cambridge University Conservatives, 29 Feb. 1924.
[83] Worcester, 31 May 1924.
[84] Association of Conservative and Unionist Clubs, 13 June 1924.
[85] Party conference, 2 Oct. 1924.

a broad democratic foundation. It deserves to be financed by democracy.'[86]

In practice little happened. Baldwin and the Central Office had no control over local associations, and the number of working men selected as parliamentary candidates remained small, never more than a handful. Despite personal unease at the inconsistency with his 'idea of true Tory democracy', he was also unable to end the Central Office's dependence upon the funds and facilities of the rich.[87] Before the 1924 election he thought it important to claim that his party had an increased working-class membership and a 'small band' of working-class candidates.[88] But the realities were too strong, and thereafter this part of his rhetoric fizzled out.

The party could, however, emulate the Labour party and make itself more 'democratic' in other ways. Baldwin was as capable of using crude anti-socialist rhetoric as any other Conservative, but he thought it vital that this should not be the party's only or dominant language. From the beginning of his leadership, he asked Conservatives to cease imagining that the Labour party was an entirely malignant force. He was 'not one of those . . . who believe that the great motive force of Labour is Bolshevism. Bolshevism plays its part, but not the great part.'[89] For many Labour party workers 'socialism' represented an idealism which gave them real belief, faith, and commitment. This was Labour's 'great source of strength': it had men and women 'of a fine and high type' who were well-informed, experienced in propaganda, and patently 'earnest and sincere' in their 'genuine and altruistic' desire to improve the conditions of the people.[90] Consequently, Labour's potential was enormous, because within the new ill-educated mass electorate most voters did not now belong to or have habitual allegiance to any party. Once these voters thought their own interests were secure, many were likely to be attracted by whichever

[86] Worcester, 31 May 1924; Metropolitan Union of Conservative Associations, 25 Jan. 1926. For proposals dating from 1916, see Ramsden, *Balfour and Baldwin*, pp. 252–4.
[87] Hyde, *Baldwin*, p. 295, for comment on the Londonderrys' political entertainment; Jones *WD* II.176–7 (8 March 1929), for embarrassment at fund-raising from millionaires. For the realities of party finance and social composition, Ramsden, *Balfour and Baldwin*, pp. 219–22, 245–9, 253–7.
[88] Conservative conference, 2 Oct. 1924; Sheffield, 27 Oct. 1924.
[89] Party meeting, 12 Feb. 1924.
[90] National Unionist Association, 29 June 1923; Edinburgh, 27 July 1923; party meeting, 11 Feb. 1924. Cf. Cambridge University Conservatives, 29 Feb. 1924; Edinburgh, 24 March 1924.

party appeared most committed to helping the mass of people. So although the Labour party was misguided and tainted by envy, Conservatives had to understand that as a 'spiritual force' claiming to represent the common people it could not be defeated by 'mere abuse' and reaction.[91] It would be beaten only by argument, and by displaying wide social sympathies – by seizing the moral and 'national' high ground.

Baldwin therefore aimed 'to breathe a living force' into his party, to give it 'spiritual ideals', and especially to 'inculcate' these into its younger, rising members. Despite the existence of similar strands of Conservative opinion, he was always conscious of facing 'great difficulties' in persuading the bulk of his party to embrace any form of social idealism.[92] This was a further reason for his invocation of Disraeli. He wanted not just to improve the party's popular presentation, but also to mould the party itself: to supply both reassurance and inspiration by placing himself in a tradition of successful post-parliamentary reform Conservatism. 'It was Disraelian Conservatism . . . with which they could always win, but if they sagged into the old negative habit they never would.'[93] He could even claim a Disraelian precept for extending the female franchise.[94] At party meetings he repeatedly linked the traditional Conservative claim to be the true national party to the realities of the new electorate. No 'purely party programme' could succeed when a much lower proportion of voters had firm party attachments, so while 'holding fast to [party] principles' they had 'to build on them a national policy' which would win the support of 'the armies of those who owe no particular allegiance'. They had to stand for classlessness and 'brotherhood'.[95] Party members had to train themselves as thoroughly, to work as hard, to be still better versed in 'elementary economics', and to show every bit as

[91] Party meeting, 11 Feb. 1924; Cambridge University Conservatives, 29 Feb. 1924; Junior Constitutional Club, 22 May 1924.
[92] *OE* p. 49 (6 March 1925); Dundas Castle, 16 June 1928; Scottish Unionist Association, 29 Nov. 1935.
[93] Conservative conference, 6 Oct. 1933. Cf. party meeting, 28 May 1923; Constitutional Club, 29 Jan. 1925; Conservative conference, 27 Sept. 1928.
[94] National Union of Societies for Equal Citizenship, 8 March 1928. Disraeli had argued in 1848 that if the franchise became a right and was extended to the working classes, there was no logical reason for denying it to women too.
[95] Essex Conservative women, 21 May 1924; Manchester, 26 July 1924; party conferences, 7 Oct. 1926, 6 Oct. 1927.

much sincerity and dedication as Labour party workers.[96] Even in their daily lives they had to exemplify the best democratic values: they had to show themselves to be 'better men' than their opponents.[97] They had to confirm what Baldwin declared in his first widely noticed parliamentary speech, in February 1923: that Conservatives as well as socialists 'dream dreams and hope to see their dreams take practical shape', and were just as committed to the 'betterment' of the people.[98] 'No party that was not saturated with a desire for social service would have the faintest chance of securing the support of the people.'[99]

The effect upon the party's social and economic policies, in the forms of resistance to the more reactionary class instincts of its members and presentation of a constructive Conservatism, has already been indicated. It was what Baldwin wished to demonstrate with protection in 1923, and by his commitment to social reform during 1924. An assessment of *moral* impressions was an important element in his decision-making. The outstanding example was his opposition to the Macquisten Bill in March 1925.[100] His message to his own party was encapsulated at its celebration of the great 1924 anti-socialist election victory, when a different kind of leader might have been complacent or triumphalist:

we have today perhaps the most magnificent opportunity of service to our country that has been given to any party . . . I want to see the spirit of service to the whole nation the birthright of every member of the Unionist party – Unionist in the sense that we stand for the union of those two nations of which Disraeli spoke two generations ago; union among our own people to make one nation of our own people . . . I urge on you all as workers in that great Unionist party to render all the service you can to the common weal in the districts in which you live.[101]

IV

Baldwin's attention to the Conservative party's moral reputation was an aspect of his wider preoccupation with standards in public

---

[96] National Unionist Association, 29 June 1923; party meeting, 11 Feb. 1924; Constitutional Club, 29 Jan. 1925.
[97] Cambridge University Conservatives, 29 Feb. 1924, cf. *OI* p. 13 (19 June 1926).
[98] *HCDeb* 160, c. 559 (16 Feb. 1923). Cf. Edinburgh, 27 July 1923; party meeting, 11 Feb. 1924; Leeds, 12 March 1925; Preston, 30 July 1929.
[99] Junior Constitutional Club, 21 May 1924.
[100] This aspect is caught in Percy, *Some Memories*, p. 90.
[101] *OE* pp. 72–3 (4 Dec. 1924).

life. In his view, if the new democracy was to be 'responsible' it had to have responsible politicians and publicists. If the mass electorate was not to cause damage, it had to be able to identify leaders who could be trusted to pursue the common good. If political conflict was to remain within safe constitutional channels, those controlling the state machinery had to preserve its integrity and ostensible impartiality. The context of political culture had changed in other ways. Traditional elites had lost much of their earlier influence. The 'platform politics' and high-pitched rhetoric which had developed since the 1860s now commanded less popular attention, as other forms of entertainment and leisure became more accessible. The level of political intelligence among voters seemed generally to have fallen. More newspapers were driven by commercial rather than public considerations. Together these pointed towards new political approaches. It has been seen that Baldwin's choice was not to join the prevailing shift towards less 'rational' and more 'sensational' appeals, but on the contrary to attempt to 'educate' the electorate, to raise its political awareness. Beyond that, he thought that leadership must be made to depend not upon class interest or demagogic techniques, but upon a transcendent moral authority expressed at a lower linguistic pitch. It was, he suggested, only by upholding the highest standards that the proper aims of political leaders could be achieved, and the task ultimately eased:

There are those who would empty the conception of the State of all moral qualities ... [S]uch patriotism is not enough. Moral standards ... are the surest way to achieve the fundamental social unity which is postulated by democracy. It would dissolve the abuse of wealth, the empty parade of luxury, the power of the demagogue, and it might even ... curb the sensational press.[102]

One of Baldwin's most striking characteristics was concern with the quality and tone of political language. Sensitised by his literary interests and associations, he was acutely conscious of the power of words and phrases. 'Nations are bound and loosed by them. Three or four simple words can move waves of emotion through the hearts of multitudes like great tides of the sea.'[103] As party leader he felt the pressure of 'guarding every word', knowing his

[102] *OI* pp. 125–6 (6 Aug. 1927).
[103] *OE* p. 78 (6 Nov. 1925).

'every smallest word is liable to burst into flame'.[104] Yet because
the new democracy created the paradox of 'government by discussion' among unsophisticated voters, the dangers from extravagance, distortion, or debasement of language were much
increased. Conservatism might be overwhelmed by inflation of
public expectations, or by disbelief in politicians.

Baldwin resisted this threat in two ways. First, he denounced
'eloquence', 'oratory', 'rhetoric', and 'demagogues'. 'If there is any
class to be regarded with suspicion in a democracy it is the rhetorician – the man who plays on half-educated people with fallacies
which they are incapable of detecting.' As a species of dishonesty,
rhetoric was anti-democratic, indeed 'one of the greatest dangers
of modern civilization'.[105] Second, he attacked the politics of
'promises' – not just as election strategy in 1929, but persistently
from 1924 – as a device to delude voters by 'stunts' or empty
'vote-catching' programmes.

Baldwin was far from devaluing fine speaking or election
pledges *per se*. He was proud of his own ability to speak well, and he
manipulated words (and exercised silence) as much as any other
political leader. His very attacks upon 'rhetoricians' and 'demagogues' are good examples, plainly intended in the 1920s to contrast himself favourably against Lloyd George, MacDonald, and
other opponents. But these also had larger and more interesting
purposes. He aimed to define an appropriate level of language and
expectation for preserving what he considered to be a safe and
stable democracy, and for assisting public receptivity of Conservative 'truths' that could not easily compete for mass popularity –
to resist a destructive politics of high drama and high bargaining.
He wanted it understood that 'the art of statesmanship was a very
different thing from the art of a cinema star'.[106] Responsible politicians were not 'patent medicine vendors', 'wizards', or
'magicians'.[107] It was 'not necessarily the man most fluent of
speech to whom we should entrust the destinies of the country',
because 'to tell the truth needs no art at all'.[108] The public should

---

[104] Lubbock (ed.), *Benson Diary*, p. 303 (2 Feb. 1924).
[105] *OE* pp. 155, 94 (27 Sept. 1923, March 1924), and see pp. 84–92, 93–7 *passim*; *TTF*,
       pp. 35–6 (14 July 1930).
[106] Plymouth party conference, 25 Oct. 1923.
[107] Broadcast, 16 Oct. 1924; Welbeck Abbey, 28 May 1928.
[108] *OE* pp. 97, 94 (March 1924).

feel a 'very wholesome dread' of platform and newspaper rhetoric and the 'depraved appetite' for 'sensations'. They should not be 'misled by phrases', nor believe that 'salvation' lay in words with 'half a dozen syllables'. Instead they should respect 'plain, unadorned statements of cases'.[109]

Baldwin denied any claim to be an orator,[110] and maintained a low-key, simple speaking style. He would say he wanted just to 'talk' with his audiences. At elections he focused the issue not so much upon programmes as upon sincerity and trust. The role of the electorate was not to make decisions which properly belonged to a Cabinet, but 'to judge the character and quality of . . . public men'.[111] The 1924 election was, he claimed – altogether ignoring the Zinoviev letter and 'red scare' – a victory for 'sanity of outlook and sobriety of speech'.[112] He also thought that understatement and frankness were the most effective intonations in coping with the principal opposition: 'his chief asset with Labour was his reputation for plain dealing'.[113] Baldwin's aim was to invert the style and values which had been widely expected from democratic politics – to deflate demagogy and establish a different, safer, demotic idiom. Power, strength, public spirit and truth were to be identified with restraint, humility, moderation, and common sense. 'Spell-binders and fire-eaters' were to be beaten by those able to display 'seriousness' and 'moral goodness'. Public speaking would be valued not for exciting radical demands, but leading 'men to dwell on the thoughts of service to their country and of help to one another'.[114] When in June 1923 Baldwin attributed the 1922 Conservative election victory to Lloyd George's description of Bonar Law as 'honest to the verge of simplicity', he intended to announce a new style of politics.[115]

---

[109] Perth, 25 Oct. 1924; *OE* pp. 60, 96 (16 Feb. 1923, March 1924); Bristol, 25 April 1929. Cf. *TTF* p. 50 (14 July 1930).
[110] E.g. *OE* p. 93 (March 1924); broadcast, 19 Oct. 1924.
[111] Blackpool, 20 May 1929.
[112] Albert Hall, 4 Dec. 1924.
[113] Jones *WD* I.238 (29 May 1923).
[114] Begbie, *Conservative Mine*, p. 27; *OE*, p. vii.
[115] Oxford, 8 June 1923. It should be conceded that this approach began during Law's government – see Cowling, *Impact of Labour*, pp. 241–3 – but Baldwin became the chief exponent.

V

Given Baldwin's moral and political education, this style came naturally to him. Like his father, 'he was too much in earnest' to
attempt to be 'brilliant . . . to dazzle and make a show'.[116] Nevertheless his emphasis upon public morality derived from a further,
more specific, context. Since the Edwardian period and increasingly during the wartime and post-war Coalition governments,
accusations of declining standards in public life and government,
of 'corruption', had been widespread. The arrogance and amorality
of ministers; their shady financial interests; the influence of plutocrats and newspaper proprietors, and the sale of honours: reactions against these real or alleged evils became a palpable political
force, creating a spectrum of moral criticism from diehard Conservatives through independent Liberals to the Labour left.[117]
From October 1922 one of Baldwin's principal objectives was to
establish a Conservative politics which contrasted sharply to these
earlier stains and suspicions. Here motive and focus were provided
by two targets: Lloyd George, and the two 'press lords', Beaverbrook and Rothermere.

Baldwin undoubtedly had some kind of Lloyd George
'obsession', but to be properly understood this has to be qualified
and defined. First, he had a natural interest in such a controversial
predecessor, and Tom Jones – the chief source on this matter –
was best placed as a former member of Lloyd George's entourage
to satisfy his curiosity. The extent of his 'obsession' is magnified
by the accident of our evidence.[118] Second, Lloyd George continued
to pose a real party-political problem. Long after his fall from the
premiership he retained the power to obstruct and embarrass,
even to defeat, the Conservative party, in a manner lost in general-
isations about Liberal party 'collapse' in the early 1920s. Interwar
politics never became fully polarised between Labour and Conservative, and Lloyd George's personal political fund enabled him
to exploit the interstices between the two. At each general election
from 1922 to 1935 the outcome was thought to depend chiefly

---

[116] The Revd D. Robertson, sermon on Alfred Baldwin's death, Feb. 1908, B/WCRO 8229/
7(i).
[117] See esp. G. R. Searle, *Corruption in British Politics 1895–1930* (Oxford, 1987).
[118] Jones *WD* I.243, 244, 255–6 (30 Sept., 20, 25 Nov. 1923), II.179–80, 190, 192 (13
April, 20 June 1929).

upon the choices of Liberal or uncommitted central voters. In 1929 Baldwin attributed his election defeat to the 'spoiling' interventions of so many Lloyd George-financed Liberal candidates. For two periods (1924 and 1929–31) the Liberals held the balance of power in the House of Commons.[119]

Baldwin therefore had strategic reasons for sensitivity towards Lloyd George. These provide one explanation for his long-standing refusal to contemplate co-operation with him, as it would have contradicted the Conservative objective of encouraging Liberal division and decline. The proof lies in his changed attitude after the final Liberal party disintegration in 1931 had reduced these pressures. With the National government in some difficulties from 1933 to mid 1935, he gave serious consideration to an alliance. He 'did not have the same objection to Lloyd George that he used to have, and ... in fact he thought he rather liked him'.[120] In contrast to Neville Chamberlain and non-Conservative ministers, whose opposition to bringing Lloyd George into the Cabinet was decisive, Baldwin did not allow personal enmities to obscure all political calculations.

Nevertheless, Baldwin's more usual hostility went deeper than party strategies. It did so because it became central to his wider purposes. The animus was slow to develop. Indications of his opinions in early 1922 suggest distaste at occasional 'intrigues' within the Coalition government, some distrust of Lloyd George's intentions, and unease about the notorious honours list, but not his later sense of all-pervading 'wickedness'.[121] Perhaps he regarded these as unavoidable blemishes in an imperfect ministerial world, to be endured for the sake of public duty. When he felt depressed he thought not of joining the Conservative dissidents but of retiring from politics completely, even while distrusting his yearning

---

[119] Stamfordham memos; 31 May, 2 June 1929, Royal Archives GV K2223/24, 30; Jones *WD* II.192 (20 June 1929). Probably because Jones remained an admirer of Lloyd George – as well as a Labour sympathiser – he was largely oblivious to the party problem he posed for Baldwin, even in 1929.

[120] *Reith Diaries*, p. 120 (5 Feb. 1935). Cf. A. J. Sylvester, *Life with Lloyd George* (1975), p. 93 (30 March 1933); Jones *DL* pp. 122–3, 139–40, 142, 143–5 (27 Feb., 16 Dec. 1934, 22 Feb., 30 March, 12 May 1935); J. Wrench, *Geoffrey Dawson and Our Times* (1955), p. 322 (6 May 1935).

[121] Baldwin to Joan Davidson, 16 Jan. 1922, in *Davidson Memoirs*, p. 112; Baldwin to his mother, 17 Jan. 1922, BF; *Bayford Diaries*, p. 179 (21 July 1922); Jones *DL* p. 123 (27 Feb. 1934).

for a 'cleaner atmosphere' as a form of 'cowardice'.[122] The events
of autumn 1922, however, persuaded him both that the Coalition
had become a public evil, and that a new start was possible –
what he considered to be a purification of public life, symbolised
in various forms from the reaffirmation of party as the vehicle of
principle, to the restoration of the honours system.[123]

   For Baldwin the overthrow of the Coalition therefore became
a defining moment, with permanent significance. Even after the
General Strike he wrote to a fellow rebel that the overthrow of
the Coalition would remain 'our chief claim to fame', adding – not
altogether jocularly – that considering 'the muck that had to be
shifted' it was an achievement greater than Pride's Purge.[124]
Goaded by the sarcasm of the defeated coalitionists towards
himself and the 1922–3 governments, what he meant by the
'Coalition' and 'Lloyd George' acquired mythic or demonic proportions. In retrospect the Coalition Cabinet seemed like a
'thieves' kitchen', in which 'nobody seemed to have any principles'
and there was 'the most awful cynicism'.[125]

   In reality things were never so clear cut. His own activities and
those of his governments were not – could not be – as 'pure',
truthful, and high-principled as his rhetoric sometimes claimed
them to be. After 1931 he would himself try to dissolve his party's
identity into a coalition. Some honours continued to be bestowed
in dubious, but unpublicised, ways.[126] When party considerations
pressed in 1923–4, he reconciled himself easily enough to admitting some of the leading coalitionists into his Cabinet: Worthing-
ton-Evans, Austen Chamberlain, Churchill, even Birkenhead –
who had been particularly offensive to 'moral opinion' and
unpleasant about Baldwin himself.

   Yet his reprobation of Lloyd George continued – not so much
as the 'dynamic force' he evoked at the Carlton Club meeting,
than as a moral contagion. He 'had a thoroughly bad influence on
everybody with whom he came into contact . . . he looked over a
man's character, detected its weak point, & worked on that'. He

[122] Baldwin to Joan Davidson, 16 Jan. 1922, in *Davidson Memoirs*, p. 112.
[123] For the various ramifications, Searle, *Corruption*, pp. 390–411. For honours, e.g. Baldwin
   to Lady Londonderry, 27 Dec. 1924, Londonderry papers D3099/3/15/14.
[124] Baldwin to Bridgeman, 28 Dec. 1927, Bridgeman papers.
[125] Jones *WD* II.23 (26 April 1926). Cf. Percy, *Some Memories*, pp. 89–90.
[126] Ramsden, *Balfour and Baldwin*, pp. 223–4; D. Marquand, *Ramsay MacDonald* (1977), pp.
   745–6, 747.

would even say that he 'could never feel quite safe with men who had been L.G.'s men': this while he had several of these men as colleagues.[127] Lloyd George was 'a real corrupter of public life',[128] a threat to democratic politics and national interests. He had been a 'dictator' who 'usurped the functions' of other ministers and the Cabinet. His conduct of foreign policy had been 'execrable', destroying the trust of Britain's allies.[129] He was the inveterate conspirator; the arch-rhetorician spinning dishonest slogans; the demagogue peddling 'stunts'. In contrast to Baldwin's financial sacrifices and refusal to sell his pen, he had left office richer than when he entered it and criticised his own country in the American press.[130] He had 'no moral sense at all'.[131]

Lloyd George, it seems clear, fulfilled a particular function in Baldwin's politics. In this moralised conception of public life, Lloyd George – or more accurately a caricatured 'Lloyd George' – supplied necessary elements of contrast, provocation, and justification. The 'press lords' played a similar role.

Baldwin's quarrels with Rothermere and Beaverbrook plainly had much to do with their newspapers' early and persistent criticism of his leadership. Yet the responsibility was not theirs alone: in part they reacted to his evident antipathy towards themselves. At various times Baldwin's colleagues thought there were compelling party reasons for seeking their support, but whenever he could he resisted any concessions towards them.[132] As already noted this was not because he objected in principle to cultivating newspaper controllers, nor to 'press lords' as such. Nor was it just because Beaverbrook and Rothermere competed with him in offering Conservative supporters alternative forms of Conservative policies and strategies, though these disagreements were real enough – whether on imperial protectionism, Indian policy, Rothermere's 1925 descriptions of Conservative social legislation as 'disguised socialism', or on attitudes towards Germany after 1933.

---

[127] Henson journal, 7 Aug. 1926; *Headlam Diaries*, p. 140 (9 Feb. 1928).
[128] Wrench, *Dawson*, p. 219 (17 June 1923). Cf. Palmstierna, *Atskilliga Egenheter*, extract in Jones papers, AA1/27.
[129] Jones *WD* I.243 (30 Sept. 1923); Jones *DL* p. 227 (7 July 1936); typescript of Baldwin–Poincaré conversation, 19 Sept. 1923, SB 108/41–60.
[130] Kennet, *Self-Portrait*, p. 259 (4 Feb. 1928); Hyde, *Baldwin*, p. 284; Jones *WD* II.153 (23 Oct. 1928).
[131] *Bernays Diaries*, p. 246 (3 March 1936). Cf. Jones *WD* II.171 (13 Feb. 1929).
[132] *Davidson Memoirs*, pp. 295–6, 314–34; Williamson, *National Crisis*, pp. 46, 121–2, 126–7, 178–9; Cowling, *Impact of Hitler*, pp. 47–8.

What made them so objectionable was the character of their newspaper ownership. First, they offended Baldwin's views on appropriate public discussion. He had a conception of an 'honourable' press, conducted – even by opponents – with 'honest conviction'[133] and 'high principles', as vital for a healthy mass politics, in helping to 'educate the democracy'.[134] British newspapers taken 'as a whole' were 'the best, the fairest, and the cleanest Press in the world'.[135] In his view Beaverbrook and Rothermere were very different, in directing their newspapers for self-interest, self-promotion, and crude maximisation of circulation. These were 'not newspapers in the ordinary acceptance of the term'.[136] They were a 'gutter press', even 'the Devil's press'.[137] They were mendacious, capricious, and sensational; they pandered to the lowest tastes, and perverted popular opinions and values.[138] They were 'the most obvious peril to democracy'.[139]

Second, Beaverbrook and Rothermere claimed what Baldwin considered to be an improper power. After being flattered with ministerial offices as well as peerages during the War – further counts against Lloyd George – they assumed that their newspapers entitled themselves and their opinions to special consideration in Conservative high politics, irrespective of the conventional channels of party and parliament. Baldwin had much disliked Beaverbrook's appointment as Minister of Information in 1918, and the claims he made on Bonar Law's friendship.[140] He probably knew of Rothermere's attempt to bargain with Law in October 1922,[141] and may himself have received similar demands from both him and Beaverbrook.[142] Baldwin repelled such presumptions by refusing them access to himself and to Downing Street: 'we have got

---

[133] Baldwin to Strachey, 9 May 1924, Strachey papers, and to Sir William Berry, June 1929, in Hartwell, *Camrose*, p. 188; also to the Liberal C. P. Scott, 20 May 1924, 20 Oct. 1926, *Manchester Guardian* archives.

[134] Newspaper Society, 5 May 1925; Queen's Hall, Westminster, 17 March 1931.

[135] Party meeting, 24 June 1930.

[136] Queen's Hall, Westminster, 17 March 1931.

[137] Baldwin to his mother, 8 Aug. 1923, BF; Monica Baldwin note, 1937, in F. Donaldson, *Edward VIII* (1974), p. 258.

[138] Baldwin to Strachey, 9 May 1924, Strachey papers; *Crawford Papers*, pp. 509–10 (22 Dec. 1925); Vansittart, *Mist Procession*, p. 366.

[139] Jones *WD* II.153 (23 Oct. 1928).

[140] Baldwin to A. Chamberlain, 20 Feb. 1918, in Searle, *Corruption*, p. 321, and see A. Chisholm and M. Davie, *Beaverbrook* (1992), p. 167; Jones *WD* I.235 (19 May 1923).

[141] See R. Churchill, *Lord Derby* (1959), p. 457 (diary, 24 Oct. 1922).

[142] *Amery Diaries* I.334 (17 July 1923); Baldwin to Strachey, 9 May 1924, Strachey papers.

this place swabbed out, and I am not going to have it infected again'.[143]

Underpinning all this was much personal dislike. He thought Beaverbrook, like Lloyd George, 'an evil influence', corrupting everyone and everything around him.[144] Both Rothermere's and Beaverbrook's private lives – their material and sexual indulgences – confirmed them in his mind as immoral.[145] The overall effect was that their attacks roused him to an intense moral indignation, reaching beyond defence of his own leadership to preservation of what he considered to be fundamental decencies. An early example was a private comment after his 1923 election defeat:

I will never draw down the blinds until I am a political corpse, but if I become one it will [be] by an honest blow delivered in open fight and not by a syphilitic dagger from a syndicated press.[146]

Baldwin also thought that despite the obvious disadvantages of criticism from the main mass circulation Conservative newspapers, in a larger sense his public reputation for hostility towards the 'press lords' was an asset – and so one well worth sustaining. It was, he said in 1928, 'chiefly because I am regarded as an honest man that I can't go and have any truck with [Beaverbrook and Rothermere]'.[147] The difficulties with them in 1929 to 1931 arose from his determination even in his vulnerability after election defeat to resist Beaverbrook's overtures, and from a remarkably contemptuous rebuttal of *Daily Mail* reports about his acceptance of the Irwin declaration.[148] He hated the subsequent party imperative to appease Beaverbrook, and continued to refuse any dealings with Rothermere. He was shocked at the failure of the Chamberlains and other colleagues to appreciate that by

[143] Vansittart, *Mist Procession*, pp. 366–7. Cf. Begbie, *Conservative Mind*, pp. 18–20; and the notorious *People* interview, 18 May 1924: 'I care not what they say or think. They are both men I would not have in my house.'
[144] *The Diaries of Sir Robert Bruce Lockhart*, ed. K. Young, 2 vols. (1973, 1980), I.108 (29 Sept. 1929); Howard, *Beaverbrook*, pp. 77–8, 115.
[145] Vansittart, *Mist Procession*, p. 367; Henson journal, 25 July 1930.
[146] Baldwin to Carson, 16 Dec. 1923, Carson papers D1507/B/43/9. He had been refining the phrase for some days: Baldwin to his mother, 12 Dec. 1923, BF; *Headlam Diaries*, p. 37 (13 Dec. 1923).
[147] James, *Cazalet*, p. 125 (diary, Sept. 1928).
[148] For shadow cabinet views that he over-reacted, see N. Chamberlain diary, 4 Nov. 1929, and *Amery Diaries* II.53 (7 Nov. 1929).

allowing Beaverbrook to influence party policy – even proposing his admission into the shadow cabinet – they might contain an internal revolt, but only at the cost of damaging its public prestige. He 'rejoice[d]' when Neville Chamberlain's efforts to conciliate 'the lunatics' collapsed.[149]

On two occasions he elevated the dispute into a great issue of constitutional and moral principle. At the Caxton Hall in June 1930 he declared resistance to 'press dictation' to be 'no personal question; it is no party question; it is a national question' – an 'extra-constitutional' attempt of similar proportions to the General Strike. He denounced new Rothermere demands for guarantees on policy and appointments as 'preposterous and insolent'. During the St George's Westminster by-election in March 1931, he declared the issue to be 'whether press or party was to rule'. On both occasions he made Beaverbrook and Rothermere into stereotypical press plutocrats, their minds unbalanced by the 'effect of an enormous fortune rapidly made' – always for Baldwin a source of evil – and their 'souls' poisoned by possession of personal 'engines of propaganda'.[150] A whole system of public values was compressed into the famous sentence at St George's: 'what the proprietorship of these papers is aiming at is power, and power without responsibility – the prerogative of the harlot throughout the ages'.[151]

Although Lloyd George and the 'press lords' posed intermittent electoral or party threats, their chief significance for Baldwin was as moral antitheses and psychological foils which helped define his own public identity and vindicate his leadership. They gave his politics some of their unpleasant edges: hatred, suspicion, self-righteousness – the sense, in 1930, that 'every crook in the country is out for my scalp'.[152] Even so, given considerable cross-party revulsion against the Coalition, Lloyd George, and the pretensions

---

[149] Baldwin to Bridgeman, 9 Aug. 1930, Bridgeman papers.
[150] Party meeting, 24 June 1930; Queen's Hall, Westminster, 17 March 1931.
[151] Queen's Hall, Westminster, 17 March 1931. The traditional account (AWB p. 161) that Kipling supplied Baldwin with these phrases seems accurate: Kipling to Edith Macdonald, 9 July 1930, Kipling papers 11/10, gives an early version, and see Birkenhead, *Kipling*, p. 301. But Kipling probably drew upon a well-known attack on Rothermere's brother, Northcliffe, in A. G. Gardiner, *Prophets, Priests and Kings* (1908), p. 275: 'the type of power without the sense of responsibility – of material success without moral direction'. (I am indebted to Peter Ghosh for this reference.)
[152] Baldwin to Irwin, 16 Oct. 1930, Halifax Indian papers c.152/19/147.

of 'press lords', Baldwin knew that he and his party could draw strength from enmity towards them. In opposing press dictation, he said in June 1930, Conservatives would command the support of 'every decent man and woman in the country' of 'whatever party'.[153]

Yet to consider resistance to Lloyd George – or for that matter Beaverbrook or Rothermere – as Baldwin's chief political aim is to mistake a secondary target for his primary concerns. One has only to reflect upon why he disliked them so much. For him the Coalition government became a public evil because it had damaged respect for Conservative leadership and established government, in ways that disillusioned new voters, repelled moderate opinion and aggravated radical criticism: these were the effects of 'dynamic force'. In magnified forms Lloyd George, Beaverbrook, and Rothermere embodied that delinquency in high places which had to be removed if 'responsible' politics were to be preserved. By contrasting himself to them, Baldwin was better able to impress the chief principles of his leadership upon the Conservative and public mind, and so to accumulate an authority which could consolidate a broad body of resistance to the main political problem in the 1920s and early 1930s – the Labour party.

VI

Baldwin had two broad strategies towards the Labour party, just as he had towards trade unionism. These in turn generated two contrasting public dispositions – 'consensual' and 'partisan' – which created some contemporary and historical puzzlement. Yet these dispositions were not contradictory. They were different methods of achieving the same, obvious, Conservative objective. Baldwin's ability to express the first convincingly yet wield the second with precision was a major reason for his success.

On the one hand Baldwin encouraged the Labour movement's acceptance of existing institutions, conventions and procedures, 'winning [it] for the Constitution'.[154] Competition with a Labour

---

[153] Party meeting, 24 June 1930.
[154] Amery, *Political Life*, III.223 (diary, Nov. 1937).

party at elections and in the House of Commons – through debate and within the checks and limited expectations of party politics – was less damaging and more winnable than confrontation with full-blooded socialism, direct-action trade unionism or 'bolshevism', prepared to use authoritarian and confiscatory powers. For Baldwin these were real dangers. He believed the Labour movement to be a highly unstable coalition, in which the continued predominance of 'gradualist' and parliamentarian elements was by no means inevitable. His fears about the character of its 'extremists' were as lurid as those of most other Conservatives. In late 1924 he still looked for 'the elimination of the Communists by Labour'.[155] He was worried by continued communist influence in trade unions, and by the Independent Labour party's lurch to the left: 'Wheatley and Cook were the men he was afraid of.'[156] While level-headed about TUC aims in 1926, he thought their strike threats encouraged groups of 'revolutionaries'. After 1931 the Labour leadership's proposals for emergency powers and the radicalism of Cripp's Socialist League reactivated these anxieties. In his view, if moderate Labour leaders were to prevail against the 'extremists', and if they and their supporters were not themselves to become dangerously embittered and 'iconoclastic',[157] they must not feel alienated or excluded, unable to attain any of their aspirations within existing political processes. Least of all should Labour be provoked by gratuitous aggression and affronts. Looking back on his career in retirement, he said he had always aimed 'to teach the Labour Members to believe in our English system rather than go hunting in Moscow'.[158]

In this mode Baldwin was restrained, emollient, sympathetic, magnanimous, and inclusive. There was, he would say, no incompatibility of aim and temperament between the best elements of Labour and those of the country at large. He presented the Labour party as consisting very largely of good-hearted, sensible, working men, who had legitimate ideals and 'sane and just views of the

---

[155] Jones *WD* I.301 (4 Nov. 1924). Cf. Stamfordham memo, 7 Oct. 1924, Royal Archives GV K1958/13.
[156] Kennet, *Self-Portrait*, p. 233 (10 March 1925); and see Leeds Town Hall, 12 March 1925.
[157] *Reith Diaries*, p. 217 (28 Nov. 1937).
[158] Baldwin quoted in Crawford to Tweedsmuir, 1 Dec. 1937, Tweedsmuir papers 7214 mf MSS 308. This being the 1930s, he added 'or Rome'.

possibilities of human progress'.[159] On such fundamentals Conservatives had 'no quarrel'.[160] In his 1924 election broadcast, he declared not just that he had 'many friends in the Labour party' but even that he 'could co-operate with many of them'.[161] Certain that personal relationships and House of Commons *camaraderie* could soften political asperities, to him it seemed strategic wisdom – as well as elementary courtesy – for Conservatives to show respect towards working-class MPs denied their own advantages in life. They should avoid wounding displays of social and educational superiority, and be sensitive to differences in pronunciation, language, and codes of behaviour.[162] 'Liberals and Conservatives, Whigs and Tories', each sharing the same *milieu*, had 'always used to abuse each other in the old days with the utmost freedom; but such freedom of abuse would never be understood by the Labour Party ... So don't abuse them; treat them gently.'[163] He impressed these lessons upon new Conservative MPs, and tried (without success) to warn Neville Chamberlain that it was self-defeating for a Conservative minister to give the impression that he regarded the Labour party as 'dirt'.[164] In one valediction to his party in 1937 he said – in a typically inventive gloss on its history – 'never forget that the leaders of the Tory party have always understood and been sympathetic to the working man'.[165] His own claim to be on cordial terms with many working-class Labour MPs, including left-wing 'Clydesiders', had real substance – the product of a social ease and rapport dating from his years in business, continued as an backbench MP, and preserved by his assiduous House of Commons attendance.[166]

In contrast to many other Conservatives in the 1920s he usually treated the Labour party as a conventional political party, with

---

[159] Leeds, 12 March 1925. Cf. Sheffield, 27 Oct. 1924.
[160] Edinburgh, 27 July 1923. Cf. Lowestoft, 17 July 1924; Constitutional Club, 29 Jan. 1925.
[161] 16 Oct. 1924. Cf. Begbie, *Conservative Mind*, pp. 24–5; Cowling, *Impact of Labour*, pp. 406–7.
[162] Cazalet-Keir, *From the Wings*, pp. 103–4; GMY pp. 246–7.
[163] 'Mr Baldwin's testament, 28 April 1937', Crathorne papers.
[164] Earl of Avon, *The Eden Memoirs. Facing the Dictators* (1962), p. 5; Dilks, *N. Chamberlain*, p. 519.
[165] 'Mr Baldwin's testament, 28 April 1937', Crathorne papers.
[166] Above, p. 74. See e.g. Begbie, *Conservative Mind*, p. 28; Grenfell in *Bernays Diaries*, p. 26 (9 Dec. 1932).

every right to consider itself as offering an alternative government. As early as February 1923 he spoke of 'when' the Labour party formed a government, at which time 'we shall all wish them well'.[167] After the 1923 election he privately assisted MacDonald's formation of the first Labour government – though also, it should be noted, strengthening its 'responsible' character – by encouraging two non-Labour peers to join it.[168] He continued to develop cordial personal relations with MacDonald through the 1920s, and briefed him on government business before the 1929 election.[169] After the election, as during 1924, he not only offered 'fair play' to the incoming Labour minority government, but fulfilled the promise by declining to obstruct business, on occasion even saving it from defeat.[170] By this adherence to parliamentary conventions, Baldwin believed that the Labour party would both be attached to the 'constitution' and, through experience of the burdens of government, taught to face 'realities' and abandon socialist dogma. Indeed, he constructed his own 'Whiggish' (and self-justificatory) interpretation of the revolt against the Coalition and his 1923 election defeat, presenting these as steps in a process which advanced Labour's education in political responsibility.[171] After Labour's electoral humiliation in 1931 he took special care to re-build the bridges, observing the customary courtesies and creating new confidences with the new generation of parliamentary Labour leaders.[172]

The willingness of MacDonald and his followers to enter the National government in 1931 plainly owed much to this strategy, though it was an outcome which none could have predicted. Nevertheless an obvious refinement of Baldwin's approach was to try to open divisions within the Labour movement, playing off 'moderates' against the 'extremists'. 'There was', he said, 'a good deal

---

[167] *OE* p. 69 (16 Feb. 1923). Cf. Newcastle, 12 Nov. 1922.
[168] Cowling, *Impact of Labour*, p. 368 (Lord Haldane); Waterhouse, *Private and Official*, pp. 312–13 (Lord Chelmsford).
[169] Jones *WD* II.161, 171, 177 (5 Dec. 1928, 13 Feb., 8 March 1929). During the 1926 industrial disputes, however, he thought MacDonald had been 'thoroughly dishonest': Henson journal, 7 Aug. 1926.
[170] Williamson, *National Crisis*, p. 119. For 1924, Grigg, *Prejudice and Judgment*, pp. 131–2; Cowling, *Impact of Labour*, pp. 381, 409–10.
[171] E.g. Junior Constitutional Club, 21 May 1924; Manchester, 26 July 1924; Constitutional Club, 29 Jan. 1925; Leeds Town Hall, 12 March 1925.
[172] E.g. Baldwin to MacDonald, 28 Feb. 1932, MacDonald papers 30/69/678, for private conversations with Tom Williams. See also Jones *DL* p. 324 (15 March 1937).

more sympathy between Labour and the principles of the Conservative party than between organized Labour and Socialism.'[173] During the 1930s especially, he presented trade unionists and socialist intellectuals as inhabiting different political worlds.[174] Another parting injunction to Conservative MPs was 'never forget to widen the breach between the working man and the intellectual'.[175] After the 1935 election victory, he reflected privately on the possibility of detaching the Co-operative movement from its alliance with Labour: 'they are small investors and proprietors and don't easily swallow Marxism'.[176]

In significant respects, therefore, Baldwin displayed more tolerance towards the Labour movement than had been shown by the Coalition leaders or was usual among his Conservative colleagues. Yet if the broad tone and method were different, this did not make Baldwin any less a Conservative. He only slightly widened the bounds of Labour 'acceptability'. He was as determined as other Conservatives to discredit Labour intentions and actions which transgressed these bounds, and as much concerned in 1923 and 1929 as he was in 1924, 1931, and 1935 to subject the Labour party to decisive election defeats. He implied that the Labour party was never quite what its 'moderate' leaders claimed it to be. However sincere the Labour politicians, however much their ideals might seem to coincide with those of Conservatives, there were still differences in method and specific aim. When in 'consensual' mode, he presented Labour policies and methods as merely misguided, more a cause for sorrow than anger. But during elections and at other times when he thought Conservative interests especially at stake, they were described as dangerous and corrosive of a healthy and democratic community. Now the whole Labour party was said to express not the practical aspirations of working men but the 'tyrannical prescriptions' of 'academic doctrinaires'.[177] During 1924 the real power was said to lie not with the official leaders, but with the 'subterranean' forces of admirers of

[173] Junior Imperial League, 7 May 1932. Earlier examples include Lowestoft, 17 July 1924; Queen's Hall, 15 Oct. 1924; Leeds, 12 March 1925; Cambridge, 4 March 1927.
[174] E.g. Carmunnock, 24 June 1933; Chelsea, 21 Feb. 1935.
[175] 'Mr Baldwin's testament, 28 April 1937', Crathorne papers. Cf. 1922 Committee dinner, 21 May 1936.
[176] Jones diary, 16 Nov. 1935.
[177] Lowestoft, 17 July 1924. Cf. Oxford, 8 June 1923; broadcast, 16 Oct. 1924; Bramham Park, 21 July 1928.

Soviet Russia and 'revolutionary agitators'.[178] The General Strike again showed that 'the nominal leaders do not lead', and were 'unequal to their task'.[179] The reassuring words of *Labour and the Nation* were not to be trusted, because behind MacDonald was Maxton, and behind Maxton was Marx.[180] Until, he said, Labour leaders 'learn to oppose and expose their own extremists they will never secure the suffrages of the people of England'.[181]

In this mode, Baldwin declared that contrary to the Labour party's official professions, as a socialist party driven by extremists it was not at all classless, nor representative of the 'people', nor devoted to service and brotherhood. Here was a major dividend from Baldwin's presentation of a Conservative idealism: a plausible reversal of Labour accusations that Conservatives were the party of materialism and class selfishness. His suggestions to Davidson for a speech to young men give the more elevated version of the contrast he wished to draw:

Feature of post-war politics is that no party without ideals will attract young men, and without young men a party becomes moribund.

What attracted young men to Labour was their apparent eagerness to raise the under-dog.

But in action they are really making life far more difficult for him and, conscious of their inability to effect his improvement, they take refuge in abusing everybody and in preaching class hatred in which every ideal must be consumed as with fire.

Our ideals lead us too to work for the bettering of the human lot, but we know that it comes of the spirit as much as materially, and only in love of humanity can you get that atmosphere and environment of peace in which alone material betterment is possible.[182]

He could express the same point far more bluntly. The 'gospel of hate' and 'class war' which he ascribed in 1923 to communists and Labour 'extremists'[183] was extended during the 1924 Labour government to the whole movement. Conservatives preached 'unity and union and comradeship, while [Labour] preach class war. Between these two gospels there can be no truce.' Labour 'instead of being national and all-embracing', 'was rather a class

---

[178] Lowestoft, 17 July 1924; broadcast, 16 Oct. 1924.
[179] Conservative conference, 7 Oct. 1926.
[180] Royal Albert Hall, 10 May 1929.
[181] Conservative conference, 27 Sept. 1928.
[182] *Davidson Memoirs*, p. 172.
[183] E.g. *OE* p. 59 (16 Feb. 1923); Cambridge, 29 Feb. 1924.

and sectarian party'.[184] The General Strike had been the 'inevitable' product of socialist propaganda.[185] In the 1931 crisis it was not Conservatives who had defended class interests, but 'the Socialist Party' that had stirred up 'open class warfare'.[186]

Baldwin achieved a still more important reversal. By identifying Conservatism with democratic constitutionalism he not only contested the Labour claim to be the true democratic and progressive party. He could also turn 'democracy' and 'progress' into weapons against the Labour party, by exploiting its ambiguous and uneasy relationships with trade unions and socialist radicals. His presentation of the industrial confrontations of 1925–6 as a constitutional issue was deadly, embarrassing Labour parliamentary leaders unable to invent appropriate democratic replies. It was, Baldwin said after Red Friday, 'a very sad climax to the evolution of popular government' that men should 'take a course right against everything for which democracy stands'.[187] A few months later, the constitutional battle-lines were firmly established:

[Conservatives] have always stood ... for the supreme authority of Parliament as representing the will of the majority, for orderly progress, for democratic freedom, and for the utmost liberty consistent with the safety of the State. To-day it is we who hold the lifted torch of democracy while the Labour Party is engaged in snuffing the wick of a lamp that is burning too dimly; ... we are challenged ... by a small minority ... who have made no secret of their desire to undermine the Constitution by revolutionary threat, by industrial war, by the suppression of free speech, and by intimidation. That is the gospel of brute force, and those who preach it are the enemies of democracy and are the true reactionaries.[188]

Once Baldwin translated the General Strike from an industrial dispute into a supposed threat to 'the basis of ordered government' and a 'challenge to Parliament and the road to anarchy and ruin',[189] the TUC leaders themselves grasped that defeat was inevitable. When Baldwin again wanted to hit the Labour

[184] Hotel Cecil, 21 May 1924; Lowestoft, 17 July 1924.
[185] *OI* p. 214 (12 June 1926). Cf. Bewdley, 5 Jan. 1929.
[186] Statement, *The Daily Dispatch*, 27 Oct. 1931. Cf. broadcast, 22 Oct. 1931.
[187] *HCDeb* 187, c. 1591 (6 Aug. 1925).
[188] Conservative party conference, 8 Oct. 1925.
[189] *HCDeb* 195, cc. 71–2 (3 May 1926); statement, *British Gazette*, 6 May 1926; broadcast, 8 May 1926.

movement hard, at the 1931 election, he again described the issue as the maintenance of 'democracy' and 'parliamentary government'.[190] This pattern of alternation between broad 'consensus' and fierce partisanship recurred in the 1930s.

[190] Broadcasts, 13, 22 Oct. 1931. In the second broadcast, he repeated Snowden's accusation that the Labour programme was 'Bolshevism run mad'.

CHAPTER 8

Country and empire

Baldwin expounded not just a politics of public values, but also a politics of place and identity. This aspect of his public doctrine – with its conceptions of 'England' and the 'British' – was prominent and important, but it was not substantive in itself. It was rather a means to provide cultural and imaginative foundations for his system of values, and another method of expressing those values. Nor was this politics parochial or exclusive. While its purposes included resistance to class politics, cosmopolitan ideas, and foreign ideologies, it also communicated a positive message about empire and international influence. It was certainly not a doctrine of 'little England'.

I

Contrary to a common impression, evocations of the English countryside and country life – 'Englishness' defined in rural terms – appeared only rarely in Baldwin's speeches. They were chiefly addressed to specific audiences which expected such things, most famously to the Royal Society of St George, others to the National Trust and county associations, or for introductions to books on 'The English Heritage'. Together these numbered perhaps twenty short passages amidst his several hundred speeches and addresses. Those who read intelligently beyond the first address on 'England' in Baldwin's first volume of collected addresses cannot suppose that English ruralism was among his *major* themes, which were better indicated in the titles of his other three volumes: 'inheritance', 'freedom', and 'service'. Ruralism was not even the main point of the famous 1924 address on the 'sounds, sights and smells' of the English countryside. During the 1930s the subject largely disappeared from his addresses, and is

not to be found in the final expressions of his doctrine, *An
Interpreter of England* and *The Englishman*.

Nevertheless, the countryside and the life of rural villages and
small towns plainly meant much to him. Despite being occu-
pationally an industrialist, urban businessman, and metropolitan
politician, he thought of himself as essentially a countryman and
a provincial. 'Country folk are my own folk', he wrote, 'in London
I am a stranger, in the country at home.' He found it hard to leave
'the enchanted country' to return to the 'prison yard' of Westminster: 'I feel like a sugar beet being dragged out of the soil.'[1] All this
was part of what he wished the public to understand about himself, when on becoming prime minister he was photographed for
the newspapers at Chequers and Astley in the role and attire of a
country squire, and later when he described himself as 'a true son
of the soil', who was 'but a bird of passage' in London, his mind
constantly reverting to the beauties of rural Worcestershire.[2] He
also had a well-known and influential taste for rural fiction. His
praise for Mary Webb at a Royal Literary Fund dinner in 1928
and in reprints of her *Precious Bane* and other novels vastly swelled
her sales,[3] while in the 1930s he similarly recommended the work
of Francis Brett Young.[4]

Yet although he publicly entertained the Old Berkeley Hunt at
Chequers and enjoyed weekend visits to other country houses, he
did not participate in the squirearchical pursuits of hunting, fish-
ing, and shooting: 'the country that I love will still be there when

---

[1] Baldwin to Joan Davidson, 29 Sept. 1920 in *Davidson Memoirs*, p. 112; Baldwin to Bridgeman, 16 Jan. 1931, Bridgeman papers.
[2] *OI* p. 281 (22 Feb. 1927); *TTF* pp. 123–5 (22 Feb. 1929).
[3] Royal Literary Fund, 25 April 1928, and see *The Collected Works of Mary Webb* (1928–9),
for facsimile of Baldwin letter in *Armour Wherein He Trusted* and his introduction (actually
drafted by Jones) to *Precious Bane*. He publicised *Precious Bane* because it happened to be
the first of her novels he read; his favourite was *Golden Arrow*: see Baldwin to Bridgeman,
5 Sept. 1928, Bridgeman papers. Mary Webb's reputation suffered a post-war collapse
which lingers in some commentaries on Baldwin. For an example of recent, more favourable, literary appreciations, see W. J. Keith, *Regions of the Imagination. The Development of
British Rural Fiction* (Toronto, 1988), pp. 129–40.
[4] Worcestershire Association, 21 Feb. 1934. For comment on Baldwin and Young, see
Cannadine, 'Politics, Propaganda and Art', pp. 107–16. Another example of his taste is
A. G. Street: see Jones *DL* p. 33 (5 March 1932). Wiener, *English Culture*, p. 102, gives
Winifred Holtby, *South Riding*, as Baldwin's favourite, but I have found no reference to
her or her book in his public and private statements.

sport is dead'.[5] Nor was his interest that of gentleman farmer, or gardener, or naturalist. He knew something about farming – his father owned a farm at Wilden, which he often visited when young – and 'his' horticultural produce and flowers received prizes at local Worcestershire shows, but he left the supervision of his Astley land and gardens to his wife and staff, and, as his neighbours and friends well understood, his public comments about rearing pigs were intended as jokes.[6] Neville Chamberlain was bemused at how Baldwin was considered a countryman while he himself – a naturalist, angler, and game-shooter – remained known only as a townsman.[7]

Nor did Baldwin's pastoral imagery bear much relation to most of the rural population's economic and social existence. He made no attempt – not even rhetorically – to check the decline of landed estates, a silence with the important effect of helping to detach his party from its aristocratic and gentry roots.[8] He did share a common Conservative view that agricultural labour was healthier, not simply physically but socially and morally, than work in 'dark and denaturalised cities', and he would have liked to assist a 'back to the land' movement and even re-location of factories in semi-rural surroundings (like Wilden).[9] But given the economic and electoral realities, these remained aspirations more than effective influences upon government policies. A similar gap between language and policies existed over the physical fabric of the countryside: his governments' encouragement to road-building, electrification, and suburban house building made him a target of criticism from some rural preservationists.[10]

Baldwin's interests in the countryside took different forms. At the most personal level, these were aesthetic and therapeutic. From early life his letters contain vivid descriptions of rural beauties very like those of the 'sounds, sights and smells' passage.[11] His artistic tastes were influenced by his family connections with

[5] Begbie, *Conservative Mind*, p. 14. See AWB p. 38; also Vansittart, *Mist Procession*, p. 353: 'S. B. was as unthinkable at bloodsports as he would have been near caviare or baccarat.'
[6] Jones, *Lord Baldwin*, p. 7; GMY p. 25; AWB pp. 69–70.
[7] Cazalet-Keir, *From the Wings*, p. 95.
[8] P. Mandler, *The Fall and Rise of the Stately Home* (1997), pp. 227–8, 241.
[9] Begbie, *Conservative Mind*, p. 20.
[10] Mandler, *Fall and Rise*, p. 241.
[11] Baldwin to Davidson, and Joan Davidson, 31 Aug. 1920, 1 March 1921, JD.

Morris, and thereby with the 'Arts and Crafts' movement. His main recreation and psychological restorative were long country walks.[12] In the larger and public sense, his identification with and praise of rural and small-town life had cultural and social sources and meanings. These in turn had subtle but strong political implications, which – plainly enough, when 70 per cent of the British people lived in cities or towns – had less to do with rural areas themselves than with the urban, suburban, and industrial populations.

This is not to say that Baldwin's ruralism was bogus or crudely calculated. It was instinctive, part of what he and many others of his class and time had absorbed from late-Victorian wealthy, educated, provincial, and Conservative culture – a 'gentry ideal' that comprised not merely ownership of a country estate or manor house, but more a code of values and responsibilities. Nor is it properly understood if it is considered simply as nostalgia, still less as 'escapism' or 'anti-industrialism'. While Baldwin's ruralism and other evocations of the nation and national life will not survive detailed assessment for their descriptive accuracy, that is because their purposes were not sociological or historical, but cultural and ethical. As he understood it, the problem was 'how to keep the urban Englishman true to the rural type', to what he conceived to be the people's 'true nature'.[13] Of course his evocations were idealisations, but this was precisely because their intention was symbolic and exemplary – concerned not to dwell upon unfortunate features in the past and present, but to emphasise their positive aspects and to stimulate the best and most constructive energies for the future.

Ruralism had its most basic aspect in helping to suggest a certain type of political leadership. The expressed preference by public men for the privacy and peace of country life had a familiar pedigree reaching back to classical models. It signified lack of personal ambition, hatred of the merely factional, and devotion to public service – exactly the distance from professional, career,

[12] E.g. M&B p. 41. 'Specimen Day', 1927, Mackenzie King papers, memorandum C41777, records an habitual hour-long walk before breakfast, presumably in London parks. He was often accompanied by close friends, such as Joan Davidson and Lord Hanworth. There were further walks out of London at weekends, and at Aix-les-Bains he walked the hills while his wife took spa baths.
[13] Begbie, *Conservative Mind*, pp. 20, 21.

politics that Baldwin wished to project for himself. The terminology of 'country' had further resonances in the sense of 'provincial', again implying contrast with metropolitan vanities and contact with the ordinary life of most people. More particularly ruralism provided a counterpoise to Baldwin's actual economic status, and its potential political connotations. We have seen that in the early stages of his leadership he himself, as well as the newspapers, stressed his experience as a large-scale industrialist – but also his wish to be considered a special kind of industrialist. From several perspectives it was important for him to avoid any impression that he might harbour class-warrior, pro-industrial 'trust' and anti-trade-union instincts – as a paternalistic employer with benevolent intentions; as a new leader of a party with a traditional rural-based elite, anxious to preserve social peace; and as a Conservative hoping to win Liberal sympathies and to conciliate Labour opinion. To modify a hostile journalist's observations, he needed 'to exorcise the street-corner suspicion' that he might be an 'Anglo-Saxon counterpart of the stern figures of Krupp and Thyssen and Stinnes'.[14]

Baldwin offered various forms of reassurance, from speeches exuding goodwill and invoking the Disraelian myth, to the implied sensitivities of his associations with the worlds of art and literature. Another was to distance himself from post-war industrial strife and hard-faced employers by emphasising a rural, squirearchical persona. Probably only part-consciously, he played upon nineteenth-century Conservative and Liberal conceptions that country society provided a model for a well-ordered and contented urban and industrial society, one presided over by a disinterested and dutiful governing class which the people could and should trust.[15] In practice, all this was probably most reassuring to the rural, public service and professional core of Conservatism, and to high-minded Liberals. Yet labour leaders and urban and mining workers too can have had no doubt that Baldwin was an unusual kind of Conservative businessman.

More important, Baldwin assumed that rural themes supplied some of the spiritual and imaginative material which might help

[14] P. Guedalla, *A Gallery* (1924), pp. 124–5.
[15] See also Begbie, *Conservative Mind*, p. 25, for Baldwin's claimed sympathy for the 'continuance of the feeling which existed in old times between the squire and the villager'.

248 *Stanley Baldwin*

soothe away the sores of class politics and industrial conflict. Contrary to many readings, he did not pretend that Britain was still a rural society. He knew and said – even amidst his most celebratory passages – that much of what he cherished was no longer 'the childish inheritance of the majority of the people'. It constituted a 'vanished England', or at least one which was 'being urbanised fast'.[16] Nevertheless he thought that the countryside and rural life remained a reality to the urban population, in the sense of surviving as inherited memory, cultural tradition, and continuing ideal – as their 'spiritual home'. At the very least, he said, it was manifested in the desire of working people to cultivate even a tiny bit of garden or allotment, to visit parks and have flowers in their homes, or in men seeking out rural streams to fish.[17]

For Baldwin, the cultural and social significance of what he considered to be a 'very deep and profound instinct' was that it preserved a body of fundamental communal values. As he said to a National Trust meeting:

We have become largely an urban folk, but there lies deep down in the hearts even of those who have toiled in our cities for two or three generations, an ineradicable love of country things and country beauty . . .; and to them, as much as and even more than to ourselves, the country represents the eternal values and the eternal traditions from which we must never allow ourselves to be separated.[18]

Baldwin assumed the continued potency of pastoral values long entrenched in English culture – values which had a family presence not just from Morris but also in Kipling's Sussex stories and poems. In this tradition the countryside and rural life symbolised all sorts of good things – stability, continuity, tranquillity, harmony, perspective, imagination, and honesty – set against the transience, turbulence, tensions, clamour, pretences, divisions, shallowness, and materialism of urban life.[19] So in private Baldwin

[16] *OE* pp. 6, 7 (on 'England', 6 May 1924); *TTF* pp. 139, 141 (24 Feb. 1927); *SOL* pp. 30–1 (26 June 1936); *Englishman*, p. 31. Cf. Campbell, 'Baldwin', p. 210; Cannadine, 'Two Worcestershire Lads', pp. 104–7; Jenkins, *Baldwin*, pp. 31–2.
[17] *OE* pp. 8, 129 (6 May 1924, 19 May 1925); *OI* p. 305 (24 Feb. 1927); *TTF* p. 116 (6 July 1928); *Englishman*, p. 31. Begbie, *Conservative Mind*, p. 20; *Davidson Memoirs*, p. 105.
[18] *TTF* p. 120 (10 Feb. 1931). This helps elucidate his 1924 'sounds, sights and smells' passage, though its meaning should have been clear enough from the preceding and succeeding pages: see *OE* pp. 6, 7–8.
[19] See e.g. R. Williams, *The Country and the City* (1973); A. Howkins, 'The Discovery of Rural England', in R. Colls and P. Dodd (eds.), *Englishness. Politics and Culture 1880–1920* (1986), pp. 62–84; Wiener, *English Culture* (for the examples more than the conclusions).

could write of letting 'the peace of the country soak into my bones' or of how it 'would take a great deal of urbanization to destroy our simplicity', and declare that 'life in the country makes you see things whole'.[20] Such feelings, again with obvious connections to Morris – and again irrespective of his own government's policies – led him to appeal for the preservation of the countryside and its wildlife, of ancient towns and buildings, vernacular styles and traditional craftsmanship.[21]

Yet although Baldwin disliked some aspects of contemporary urban and industrial society, his love of the countryside and use of pastoral imagery did not – as in some, but not all, versions of the tradition – constitute a rejection of modernity or yearning for permanent escape from the metropolis. For that would have contradicted Baldwin's most deeply felt commitments: his personal and public creed of duty and service. Certainly the rural was a 'sanctuary', offering 'comfort' and 'solace', but the very purpose of this 'tranquillising healing power' was to assist the discharge of urban duties.[22] The countryside provided the spiritual re-charge that restored proportion, improving the ability to succeed in industrial, commercial, or public work. This was true even when the rural existed only as recollection amidst urban duties: 'memories of the long peace of the countryside' were a 'viaticum' which the 'wise man takes about with him'.[23]

The rural was above all a means of suggesting that there were ancestral voices, immemorial values, 'old-fashioned virtues', and a common inheritance that bound the nation together. It provided an imagery which reinforced a larger theme: his insistence upon the importance of place and historic roots. The most powerful sources of personal and collective identities were not the modern, divisive, calls of class, but the supposedly 'natural' allegiances to locality and community. What made the 'sounds, sights, and

[20] Baldwin to Joan Davidson, 12 Aug. 1925, in *Davidson Memoirs*, p. 197; Baldwin to Bridgeman, 28 Dec. 1927, Bridgeman papers; Baldwin in July 1935, in R. A. Butler, *The Art of the Possible* (1971), p. 30.
[21] *OE* p. 129 (19 May 1925); Royal Society of Arts, 26 Jan. 1927; *TTF* pp. 113–18, 120–2 (6 July 1928, 10 Jan. 1931).
[22] *OE* pp. 128–9 (19 May 1925); *TTF* p. 121 (10 Jan. 1931); *OI* p. 81 (30 July 1927). Cf. *OE* p. 10 (8 Aug. 1925); *TTF* p. 124 (26 Feb. 1929); *SOL* pp. 125–6 (27 April 1937).
[23] *TTF* p. 323 (31 Oct. 1935). For Baldwin finding relief from political anxieties in 'countryside reminiscence', see e.g. *Headlam Diaries*, p. 117 (27 April 1927); *Crawford Papers*, p. 558 (19 Feb. 1935).

smells' of England so significant was that they implanted this 'love of home'.[24] According to Baldwin 'every Englishman keeps in his heart that corner of the country in which he was bred, or in which, if he be unfortunate enough to be bred in a town, his parents or his grandparents were bred'.[25] He himself became fascinated with his family's history, collecting materials for a family pedigree and searching out the countryside and buildings of the ancestral Baldwin domain, Corvedale in Shropshire.[26]

Nevertheless Baldwin's appeal to place and roots was far from restricted to English – still less to 'southern' English – pastoralism. His self-projection as a rural squire gradually faded, probably because he felt his public persona had become sufficiently well established on wider grounds. Or he may have been discouraged by his wife, who lacked his cultural instincts and eventually told him he should abandon his 'pose as a simple country squire' because 'it had never deceived me and by now probably deceived very few others'.[27] Whatever the reason, it did not change his essential style and purposes. As he had always done, he continued to speak with similar lyricism about Scotland, Wales, and Northern Ireland as he did about England. Each region, it seemed, had equally evocative 'sounds, sights and smells' of its own. Indeed as Conservatives became the dominant party in Scotland, he delivered many speeches there on Scottish themes, sometimes invoking his Macdonald ancestors as evidence of shared sympathies.[28] Again, he spoke with no less warmth about the big cities, ports, and industrial areas, whether Manchester, Liverpool, Plymouth, Bradford, Leeds, Newcastle, Belfast, Swansea, Cardiff, Glasgow, or Edinburgh.[29] He praised the special features of each region or city – their occupations and products, civic buildings, institutions

[24] *OE* p. 8 (6 May 1924).
[25] *TTF* p. 152 (23 April 1932). Cf. pp. 136–7 (8 Nov. 1933); *Englishman*, p. 31.
[26] W. Byford-Jones, *Corvedale. The Earl Baldwin Country* (Shrewsbury, 1938), pp. 48–9, 57; *Crawford Papers*, p. 558 (19 Feb. 1935); Jones *DL*, pp. 154, 160, 268 (18 Sept. 1935, 7 Jan., 18 Sept. 1936). For research, see Baldwin to Constance Marshall (née Baldwin), 1927–34, B/WCRO 8229/12(ii). The official 1935 pedigree, commissioned from the College of Arms, is in B/WCRO 8229/15.
[27] James, *Cazalet*, p. 223 (diary, Jan. 1940).
[28] To take examples just from the collected addresses: *OE* pp. 237–43, 249–52; *OI* pp. 37–40, 44–53; *TTF* pp. 189–93, 194–6.
[29] E.g. *OE* pp. 253–8; Swansea, 30 Oct. 1923; Manchester, 2 Nov. 1923; Bradford, 29 Nov. 1923; Cardiff, 18 Oct. 1924; Leeds, 12 March 1925; Edinburgh Merchant Company, 3 Nov. 1927; Liverpool, 25 March 1935.

and traditions, history and famous inhabitants – appealing always to local and regional pride and the sense of community. As he made abundantly clear, his favourite authors were *not* Mary Webb or other English ruralists but Sir Walter Scott and that most urban of novelists – 'one of the greatest creative geniuses of all time' – Charles Dickens.[30] Nor were rural authors the only modern writers he publicly commended. Another was that Bradford exponent of an urban 'realism', J. B. Priestley.[31]

Baldwin's Englishness, Worcestershire loyalty, and ruralism were prominent because they constituted his own imaginative sense of identity, and provided an example of local allegiance for others. But his purpose, the evocation of national unity, required public admiration for many other forms of *British* identity – though also silence on the divisive forces of Irish nationalism and Irish Catholicism: this was manifestly a rhetoric facilitated by the 1921 partition of Ireland. If Baldwin shared the conventional tendency to say England when he meant Britain, and if he occasionally laboured the confusion,[32] he nevertheless spoke frequently of Britain and the British. Nor was he so foolish and self-defeating as to think of Conservatives as just the English national party. It was not only in his Scottish, Ulster and Welsh speeches that he continued to speak of the *Unionist* party.

Baldwin's appeal was to 'the intense local attachment', to 'the charm and spell and genius of place', to 'the boundary stones of our spiritual estate', as the natural foundation of national values: to the 'lesser loyalties which are the nursing mothers of larger loyalties'.[33] He sometimes echoed Kipling: 'it may be true that we were given all the world to love, but our affections are small, and so they have one place that they love over all'.[34] But the implications were always political. The best and safest allegiances were those rooted in family, home, and locality, before radiating out 'in ever-widening circles' to town or county, country and nation, to the Empire and only then to the brotherhood of all men.[35] They

[30] *OE* p. 5; *OI* pp. 239–40, 286–7, 291; *TTF* pp. 155–72; Dickens Fellowship dinner, 7 Feb. 1930.
[31] *TTF* p. 13. See Baldwin to Priestley, 12 March 1934, 23 July 1938, Priestley papers, for cordial personal exchanges.
[32] *OE* p. 1; *TTF* p. 139.
[33] *OI* p. 81; *TTF*, p. 322.
[34] *TTF* p. 332 (31 Oct. 1935), paraphrasing the beginning of Kipling's 'Sussex' (1902).
[35] Perth, 25 Oct. 1924; *TTF* pp. 311–12, 322–3 (10 March 1928, 31 Oct. 1935); *SOL* p. 144 (12 May 1937).

emphatically did not begin with abstract notions of humanity: 'No
nation of Mrs Jellabys will ever prosper.'[36] Nor were they found in
international ideas, and they altogether by-passed conceptions of
class. To a Welsh audience he declared:

> We cannot without damage to our soul's health destroy the roots which
> bind us to the land and language of our birth. The love of country is a
> deep and universal instinct, freighted with ancient memories and subtle
> associations. Men who deny their national spiritual heritage in exchange
> for a vague and watery cosmopolitanism become less than men; they
> starve and dwarf their personalities; they turn into a sort of political
> eunuch.[37]

II

For Baldwin, then, home and love of home were to be understood
as the proper sources of collective identities and of mental and
spiritual qualities. Together these formed what in his various celebrations of England or rural life was always his main subject: the
'national character'. The 1930s equivalent of his 1924 address on
'England' – with exactly the same themes but with history replacing the countryside as invocation – was a BBC broadcast with the
explicit theme of 'National Character'.[38] This conception had a
long pedigree in popular as well as elite culture, with 'John Bull'
as a familiar emblem. It had been formalised in several strands of
Victorian thought and literature, and received new stimulation
from Great War patriotism and post-war anxieties about internal
and external threats. Baldwin's contribution as prime minister
was to confer special status upon one version of it, and as Conservative leader to give it a more concentrated and effective political slant. He portrayed this 'national character' not just by rural
imagery, but more extensively through the gamut of literature,
history, art, science, sport, anecdote, and autobiography, as well
as in valedictions and dedications. He also reconciled particularity
with nationality by asserting that while each locality, county, or
region of the United Kingdom generated its own distinctive virtues, these all contributed to 'the rich variety of our national
inheritance', or the 'common stock that makes up the character

---

[36] Primrose League, 1 May 1931; Cf. *TTF* p. 312 (10 March 1928).
[37] *OI* p. 51 (1 March 1927).
[38] Compare *TTF* pp. 12–14 (25 Sept. 1933) with *OE* pp. 2–5, 8–9.

of the British race'.[39] In this sense 'Englishness' was not exclusive, but both absorbent and penetrative – fertilised by, and fertilising, the best qualities of the Scots, the Welsh, and (some of) the Irish. Even Celtic nationalisms were to be understood as consistent with British unionism.[40]

In Baldwin's version of the national character this unity in diversity was a vital feature, and not simply in its regional forms. As his collected addresses clearly show, his model Englishmen and Britons were not just squires, farmers, and rural labourers. They were also seafarers, soldiers, artists, teachers, sportsmen, scientists, merchants, engineers, industrialists, inventors, patriotic workers, voluntary society members, clergymen, philanthropists, and public servants. For he described the English and the British as 'a people of individuals', possessing 'diversified individuality' – a variety which, as Dickens, Mary Webb, and Priestley variously showed, flourished as much among the common people as among the propertied and educated. They were independent, realistic, truthful, and honourable, with a deep love of freedom. They were resourceful, with the 'knack of producing geniuses'. They had an innate sense of decency, justice, and fair play, and 'profound respect for law and order'. While naturally peaceable, once roused they became 'great fighters', persistent and ruthless. They were 'made for a time of crisis', were 'serene in difficulties', and faced challenges with calmness and cheerfulness: 'we grumble . . . but we never worry'. They were a 'people distinguished . . . above all things by an abiding sense of duty'. They were 'the kindest people in the world', displaying 'profound sympathy for the under-dog' and 'a brotherly and a neighbourly feeling' through all classes. The 'hard and grim individuality of the national character' was thereby tempered by a 'spirit of co-operation' and 'habit of working to common principles'.[41]

That post-war British life in practice displayed large divergences from these qualities was exactly Baldwin's point. In the new economic, social, and political conditions everything now

---

[39] *OI* pp. 55, 38.
[40] E.g. for Scots: *OI* pp. 37–40; *TTF* pp. 191–2; Glasgow, 22 Nov. 1928; for Welsh: *OI* pp. 48–9, 51–2; St David's Day message, *The Western Mail*, 28 Feb. 1925; for Irish: Belfast, 14 Feb. 1930.
[41] *OE* pp. 2–5, 8–9, 40, 72; *TTF* pp. 12–14; *Interpreter* pp. 18–24; *Englishman, passim* – just some of the many examples.

depended upon the attitudes and mood of 'the common people': upon how they regarded themselves, or how they could be persuaded to regard themselves, and upon what they expected from their political leaders. Baldwin often spoke of his 'trust in the people', of their natural common sense, moderation, tolerance, their general wholesomeness:

I have that ineradicable belief and faith in our people which sustains me through good times and evil, and it is because of this that I have every confidence that, whatever troubles may come to this country ... the native strength and virtue of our people will overcome everything.[42]

At some deep level this confidence was genuine. Nevertheless such public reiteration testified to his fear that the 'native strengths and virtues' were in danger of being replaced by something unpleasant. These statements therefore had not a passive but an active purpose: to challenge and inspire 'the people' to resist selfish and destructive temptations, and act upon what were widely imputed to be their finer instincts. Baldwin portrayed what he conceived to be the true and better national self, one to which he really believed 'the people' aspired, but also one which epitomised and would preserve what he wanted to impress upon public thinking – self-reliance, social cohesion, service, ordered freedom.

According to Baldwin, it 'was never the Englishman's way' to look to the government in every difficulty: whether in economic or social affairs 'he always asked to be left alone, to conduct his own work as he thought best in his own way'. This independence and initiative, 'burnt into the bones of Englishmen', had 'made this country what it has been, and it is only that creed that will enable us in the future to keep our country at the top and in front'.[43] The British were naturally a pioneering, mercantile, and industrial nation, with a great aptitude for mechanical invention.[44] All 'the best movements and the best things in our country from the beginning of its history' had come not from government compulsion but from voluntary effort. These included the characteristic popular

[42] *OE* p. 16 (12 Jan. 1925), and e.g. Worcester, 24 Nov. 1923; *OE* p. 62 (13 March 1925); *TTF*, p. 247 (21 March 1928); election broadcast, 22 April 1929; Baldwin in Begbie, *Conservative Mind*, pp. 20–1.

[43] Louth, 21 July 1927; Worcester, 7 Jan. 1928. See Edinburgh, 25 July 1923; Bramham Park, 21 July 1928.

[44] *OE* pp. 143–4 (20 March 1924). Cf. Plymouth, 25 Oct. 1923; Leeds, 12 March 1925; *OI* pp. 14–26 (16 Feb. 1927).

institutions: trade unions and co-operative societies, like friendly societies, building societies, and the adult education movement, had 'sprung from the ranks of the people' and 'developed outside the State'.[45] These movements had provided the people with experience of brotherhood and co-operation, helping to bind together

the mass of our folks, in the industrial areas, in the big towns, in the small towns, in the villages, in the remote countryside ... [All were] linked together by common hopes and by common needs, and as I believe by readiness to give service to one another and to their country.[46]

These movements had also instructed the common people in citizenship and democratic principles – not that they needed much instruction. For 'the innermost core of the British Constitution' was carried in 'our hearts', parliamentary government was 'flesh of our flesh and bone of our bone', and freedom was the 'air we breathe'.[47]

These various qualities were not just inherent in the national character. Baldwin also asserted that they were peculiar to Britain and the English-speaking nations. The claim was buttressed by deployments of the still almost universally accepted 'Whig' version of the national past, and owed much to his own undergraduate reading of Stubbs and Maine. 'No nation in history has combined in the same degree political liberty, economic enterprise, and Imperial responsibility.'[48] Britain was the 'birthplace' of popular combinations, 'the home of constitutional liberty and political freedom'.[49] In the modern world democracy was a 'thing of British origin and British development'.[50] An island situation, a blending of the best features of the Saxon, Celtic, Norse, and Norman races, the ancient democracy of the village community and a distinctive Reformation had together generated a unique history of self-

[45] *OI* pp. 215–18 (12 June 1926). Cf. *OE* pp. 148–9, 263–4 (27 Sept. 1923, 18 Feb. 1924); National Savings Association, 20 July 1928; Abbey Road Building Society, 25 Feb. 1933; *TTF* p. 13 (25 Sept. 1933); Independent Order of Oddfellows, 23 May 1934; *Interpreter*, pp. 48–9; *Englishman*, pp. 22–7.
[46] National Savings Assembly, 9 June 1933.
[47] *OI* p. 223 (12 June 1926); *TTF* pp. 5, 17 (4 July 1935, 6 March 1934). Cf. *OE* p. 153 (29 Sept. 1923); parliamentary press gallery, 29 March 1935; Halstead, 20 July 1935; *Interpreter*, pp. 9, 46–7, 48–9.
[48] Welbeck Abbey, 28 May 1928.
[49] *OI* p. 215 (12 June 1926); Bolton, 28 Oct. 1924.
[50] Widnes, 28 May 1929.

government and evolutionary progress, of underlying 'rock-like stability', of struggle yet reconciliation, of a 'precious heritage' and 'birthright' which imposed a 'sacred trusteeship'.[51] The nation's one modern experience of civil war and dictatorship had been unnatural, brief, and conclusive: it had only reinforced the national attachment to cohesion and liberty.[52] This past and these qualities showed that the British people had nothing to learn from Russia, Germany, Italy, or any other country, for they had enjoyed freedom and representative government centuries before those ideas were even understood elsewhere.[53]

Here was the main purpose of Baldwin's evocations of 'England', 'Scotland', 'Wales', 'Ulster', and the British national character; this was where these conceptions became resistant, and acquired a political cutting edge. Native individualism and voluntarism were incompatible with bureaucratic control, with state collectivism, with uniformity and the mass mind: 'we do not want masses. We want Englishmen.'[54] The Englishman would not 'mould himself into any common mould', and nationalisation was 'contrary to the instincts and the traditions of our people'.[55] In its socialist aims the Labour party even contradicted its own origins and nature, seeking to crush the very qualities of independence which had created and still sustained it. Native realism, common sense, local attachments, and love of home made the British impervious to the abstract theories and cosmopolitan sympathies of deracinated socialist 'intellectuals' or 'intelligentsia' – 'a very ugly word for a very ugly thing'.[56] Mary Webb was to be regarded as a far more representative figure than Beatrice Webb. Above all, native tolerance, brotherliness, love of freedom, and constitutionalism gave immunity to class conflict, revolution, and dictatorship.[57]

---

[51] *OI* p. 12 (19 June 1926); Welbeck Abbey, 28 May 1928. Cf. *OE* pp. 39–40 (5 March 1925); *TTF*, pp. 3–5, 7–12 (4 July 1935, 25 Sept. 1933); Youth Conference on Democracy, 3 Feb. 1939; *Interpreter*, pp. 12–17, 35–6, 50–1; *Englishman*, pp. 11–12. The Maine and Stubbs-derived belief in the significance of the village community is clear in his choice of an A. L. Smith quotation in *OE* pp. 39–40, *TTF* pp. 11–12; *Interpreter*, pp. 47–8.
[52] *TTF* pp. 17–18 (6 March 1934); National Labour *News-Letter*, July 1933; Worcestershire Association, 21 Feb. 1934; *Interpreter*, p. 52; *Englishman*, pp. 15–16.
[53] E.g. Cardiff, 18 Oct. 1924; *OI* pp. 220–1 (12 June 1926); Conservative conference, 6 Oct. 1933; *TTF* pp. 17–24 (6 March 1934).
[54] Begbie, *Conservative Mind*, p. 21, and see *OE* pp. 5–6 (6 May 1924).
[55] *TTF* p. 13 (25 Sept. 1933); Conservative conference, 7 Oct. 1926.
[56] *OI* pp. 123–4, 295 (6 Aug., 28 Oct. 1927).
[57] E.g. *OE* pp. 59, 274 (16 Feb., 19 Dec. 1923); *OI* p. 11 (19 June 1926); *TTF* p. 5 (3 July 1935).

In a more imaginative and eloquent version of a common Conservative device, Baldwin so defined Englishness and Britishness that it became easy to stigmatise undesired loyalties, ideas, and conduct as 'unEnglish' or 'foreign'. The crucial, operative, passage in his 1924 address on 'England' was not that on country 'sounds, sights and smells'. It was rather the passage which declared that 'the Englishman is all right as long as he is content to be what God made him, an Englishman, but gets into trouble when he tries to be something else'.[58] What this meant in overtly political terms was:

This country of ours has been the birthplace and the home of some of the greatest movements that have yet arisen for human freedom and human progress, and the strength of our race is not yet exhausted. We have confused ourselves in Great Britain of recent years by a curious diffidence and by a fear of relying upon ourselves. The result has been that many of those who have been eager for the progress of our country have only succeeded in befogging themselves and their fellow countrymen by filling their bellies with the east wind of German Socialism and Russian Communism and French Syndicalism. Rather should they have looked deep into the hearts of their own people, relying on that common sense and political sense that has never failed our race, from which sufficient sustenance could be drawn to bring this country once more through all her troubles.[59]

'Class hatred' – Baldwin's term for working-class consciousness as well as for communism – was always presented by him as a 'foreign' import. So, from 1933, was fascism. Otherwise, his contrast between 'English' and 'unEnglish' shifted according to what he wanted to say about the Labour party and trade unions. Sometimes he meant that it was just the extremists of the far left who peddled 'poisonous dogmas of foreign manufacture'.[60] Sometimes he affected encouragement to Labour moderates: 'I want to see our British Labour movement free from alien and foreign heresy. I want to see it pursued and developed on English lines, led by English men.'[61] At other times he implied that the Labour movement was infected with 'foreign' doctrines – that socialism itself was unEnglish, so much so that it could not even describe itself in

---

[58] *OE* p. 2. See *OI* p. 38 (7 June 1926), for virtually the same form of words applied to the Scotsman, and *TTF* p. 14 (25 Sept. 1933).
[59] *OE* pp. 153–4 (27 Sept. 1923).
[60] Bradford, 29 Nov. 1923; Conservative conference, 8 Oct. 1925.
[61] *OI* p. 224 (12 June 1926). Cf. pp. 30–1 (4 March 1927); Southend, 20 Oct. 1924.

the purity of English monosyllables but had to resort to foreign polysyllables.[62] During the 1924 election he described much Labour propaganda as a 'poisonous alien imported plant, which, if allowed to spread, will choke the life of this country'.[63] The election result was a victory for the 'English sanity of outlook'.[64] The trade-union troubles of 1925–6 were largely inspired by a 'foreign source', yet the 'common sense and the good temper of the people' had saved the nation during the General Strike. Even many of the strikers had, as *British* workmen, been 'uneasy in their minds and their consciences'.[65] After the August 1931 crisis, he said that the Labour ex-ministers had in 'running away' from government responsibilities forgotten 'they were Englishmen and only remembered that they were Socialists'. The 1931 National government election victory became another triumph for the 'British character'.[66]

However indirectly, then, Baldwin's various portrayals of 'England' or Britain were a form of anti-socialism and anti-communism, and later also anti-fascism: a means of adding patriotic, symbolic, and emotional force to his moral, economic, social, and political teachings. Where they did not equate the national character wholly with Conservatism – Baldwin's 'national party' – and later with the National government, they allowed legitimacy only to the most conservative manifestations of the Labour movement. By presenting himself as an archetypal 'Englishman' or 'a plain man of the common people' – something he did so successfully that cartoonists took to depicting him with, or as, 'John Bull' (plate 14) – Baldwin intended to personify the national decencies and to imply a union of hearts which transcended differences in station and excluded class conflict, and which encouraged the people to trust himself and other 'responsible' national leaders. But while all this was an obvious form of stabilisation, it was not on that account reactionary. His appeal to the past was selective and constructive. It was to spiritual roots, tradition and continuity where these would preserve Conservative

---

[62] Perth, 25 Oct. 1924; and see *OE* p. 60 (16 Feb. 1923).
[63] Broadcast, 16 Oct. 1924.
[64] Albert Hall, 4 Dec. 1924.
[65] *OI* pp. 213, 218–20, 222–3 (12 June 1926); Conservative conference, 7 Oct. 1926; Albert Hall, 10 May 1929.
[66] Liverpool, 21 Oct. 1931; Aberdeen, 4 Dec. 1931.

conceptions of moral responsibilities, hierarchy, constitutional processes, property rights, private enterprise, and national cohesion. It was not to obsolescent technologies, agrarian stagnation, inefficient industrial structures, or outmoded aristocatic attitudes. Despite the rural and historical symbolism, the 'national character' and the national inheritance were in Baldwin's hands those of the capitalist individualist, the company moderniser, the collective bargainer, the social voluntarist, the public servant, the active citizen and democratic constitutionalist. They were also those of the imperialist.

III

Baldwin had little *direct* experience of the Empire and imperial policy-making. At the Board of Trade he supported emigration to relieve unemployment, and faced Lancashire cotton industry complaints about Indian tariffs. His apparent interest in becoming Secretary of State for India in March 1922 – just like his refusal of Dominion governorships in 1920 – indicated only a desire for domestic political promotion.[67] On becoming prime minister he privately admitted to knowing 'little of the Dominions'.[68] He might have said that he knew still less about India.

Nevertheless, the Empire had been a significant presence in his life, and it became integral to his political imagination and public doctrine. Dominion markets had been vital to the Baldwin companies after the imposition of the McKinley tariff, and as already noted he visited customers in Canada in 1890. He and his father had imperial investments, and during 1916 he took Canadian railway directorships in the belief that 'it may be of use for one's business to be in close touch with what is going on in Canada'.[69] In the Kiplings and his Macdonald uncle – secretary of the Wesleyan Methodist overseas missions – he had family examples of 'the white man's burden' in the non-white Empire. His undergraduate contact with Seeley and *The Expansion of England* remained mani-

---

[67] Cowling, *Impact of Labour*, pp. 162–3, 202, for possible promotion on Montagu's resignation; Baldwin to Davidson, 27 May 1920, in *Davidson Memoirs*, p. 95, for Law suggesting the governor-generalships of South Africa and Australia.
[68] Dawson memo, 17 June 1923, Dawson papers 70/16–23.
[69] Baldwin to his mother, Ladyday 1916, BF.

fest in his mature speeches. His father had joined the Royal Colonial Institute in the 1880s, and made closer relations with the 'colonies' (Dominions) part of his election platform in the 1890s.[70] He himself became a Chamberlainite tariff reformer and admirer of Milner.[71] During a Cabinet discussion on India in the early 1930s he went so far as to say that 'as a Conservative his fundamental creed was the preservation of the Empire'.[72]

After he became party leader, the Empire evoked special exertions from him. In 1927 he became the first serving prime minister to visit an overseas Dominion, travelling across Canada to deliver twenty-six speeches from the Atlantic ports to the western provinces. He also chose to lead the British delegation at the first overseas Imperial Conference, at Ottawa in 1932. He spoke often on imperial themes, and these featured prominently in his collected addresses. He gave prime-ministerial endorsement to imperial propaganda bodies, including the 'Empire Day' movement.[73] Aided by an increased frequency of imperial gatherings and the beginning of imperial radio broadcasts, by 1937 he was regarded in the Dominions as well as Britain as the foremost *imperial* statesman of his time. His main valedictory speeches were on Empire themes or for Empire audiences, and a last cartoon had John Bull thanking 'farmer' Baldwin for his work for 'Empire' (plate 14). During his retirement he planned to visit some of the Dominions.[74] Although ill-health intervened, and he declined invitations from Dominion governments involving renewed official work,[75] in April 1939 he again visited Canada to lecture, broadcast, and meet political and newspaper leaders. In his Imperial Relations Trust, established in 1937, he recruited members of the

---

[70] E.g. Alfred Baldwin speech, *The Worcester Herald*, 20 July 1895.

[71] *OE* pp. 181–90; Westminster Abbey, 26 March 1930.

[72] Cabinet 16(33), 10 March 1933.

[73] See *OE* pp. 213–18; *OI* pp. 67–71; *TTF* pp. 25–9. One of his last acts as prime minister was to help launch the Empire Youth Movement: *SOL* pp. 156–67. For these movements, see J. M. MacKenzie, *Propaganda and Empire. The Manipulation of British Public Opinion 1880–1960* (Manchester, 1984), pp. 231–40.

[74] Jones *DL* p. 206 (23 May 1936); Jones diary, 21 Jan. 1937; *Reith Diaries*, p. 214 (16 April 1937).

[75] H. Blair Neatby, *Mackenzie King* (Toronto, 1976), III.244, for proposed chairmanship of Royal Commission on Canadian Dominion and Province relations; *The Times*, 9 Aug. 1937, for invitation to Australian sesquicentennial celebrations.

official and labour establishments to improve mutual knowledge and contacts among the peoples of the Dominions.[76]

While Baldwin often used the terminology of a unitary 'Empire' and 'imperialism', the words also had three more specific meanings, each with different connotations: the voluntary association of 'white' settler Dominions, the Indian Empire or, less commonly, the dependent colonies. While some Conservatives, notably Curzon and Churchill, stressed 'Empire' as focused upon India, for Baldwin it primarily meant the white Dominions – Seeley's 'Greater Britain' and Chamberlain's chief area for 'imperial unity'. As a Chamberlainite, he also came from that body of Conservative opinion which, contrary to much hard experience, believed that 'Greater Britain' imperialism could be made a popular cause with the British electorate. Baldwin's contributions were to adjust Conservative presentations of Empire to post-war conditions, and when India was forced upon his political attention, to handle it rhetorically not as a distinct issue, but to assimilate it to conceptions about the 'white' Empire.

This did not mean that Baldwin was preparing an end to Empire. In his speeches there was never any question of imperial disintegration or decline, except as a disaster to be avoided. 'The Empire ... one and indivisible' was 'our greatest heritage' and something 'infinitely precious', the 'master hope' not just of Britain but of all the Empire's members.[77] He even offered a confident riposte to Joseph's Chamberlain's famous 1902 image of the weight of Britain's imperial responsibilities: 'if the Titan has known moments of weariness, if our burdens are heavy, our shoulders are yet broad, and they have long been fitted to bear the vast orb of our fate'.[78] 'My deepest conviction', he declared in 1930, 'is that this Empire has got to hold together', while in a 1935 broadcast on India he followed Churchill in declaring that 'the greatest days of the Empire still lay ahead'.[79] The political pressures for such public assertions are plain, and in private he was not so con-

[76] See above p. 57. For the Trust's work see Jones *DL* p. 336 (3 May 1937), and MacKenzie, *Propaganda and Empire*, pp. 85, 137–8.
[77] Primrose League, 2 May 1924; *OE* p. 216 (24 May 1925).
[78] *TTF* p. 25 (imperial broadcast, 24 May 1929). Chamberlain had said that 'The weary Titan staggers under the too vast orb of its fate.'
[79] Imperial Press Conference, 25 June 1930; broadcast, 5 Feb. 1935.

fident. But even though pursued by presentational re-definitions and policy adjustments, his efforts to strengthen imperial sentiments and loyalties are equally clear. As such, they were in accordance with interwar government intentions.[80]

In their broadest aspects, Baldwin's pronouncements on Empire had three dimensions. The first, already mentioned in chapter 7, was to reinforce his aim of domestic stabilisation, and consolidate support for his party. Emphasising 'tremendous' responsibilities for the whole Empire – 'kith and kin' in the Dominions, countless millions in India, and 'backward and primitive' colonial races – was one of Baldwin's devices for impressing upon 'British democracy' the need to support 'stable government and wise statesmanship', and, by obvious implication, to distrust the Labour party.[81] Since the 1880s identification with Empire had been a familiar Conservative strategy for trying to strengthen social solidarity and to attach popular patriotism to the party. Indeed fulfilment of imperial responsibilities, long deployed to suggest the Conservative elite's special fitness to govern,[82] became democratised as Baldwin presented it as a task demanding 'the conscious enthusiasm and participation of our people of all ranks and of all classes'.[83]

The second dimension was to persuade ignorant, self-interested, or idealistic voters to support the continuance of Empire. He presented this as a major problem, repeatedly declaring that no previous democracy had successfully governed an empire: 'Can the British democracy do what has never been done before? Can it preserve an Empire?'[84] Post-war popular aspirations or prejudices might prove resistant to some of the domestic repercussions of Empire, notably the costs of imperial defence and imperial tariffs. Intensified democratic and 'humanitarian' opinion might object to continuing autocratic rule and military action in some territories.

---

[80] For a good rebuttal of 'retreat from Empire' interpretations, see J. Darwin, 'Imperialism in Decline? Tendencies in British Imperial Policy between the Wars', *Historical Journal* 23 (1980), 657–79.

[81] See pre-election broadcasts, 16 Oct. 1924, 22 April 1929, and p. 211 above.

[82] Green, *Crisis of Conservatism*, pp. 16–18, 59–77, 194–206; Fox, *History and Heritage*, pp. 239–46.

[83] *OI* p. 69 (Empire Day broadcast 1927). See *OE* pp. 216, 222 (Empire Day 1925, 4 Dec. 1924).

[84] Junior Imperial League, 2 May 1924. *OE* pp. 219–23; *OI* pp. 13, 29; *TTF* pp. 274–82, are just a few of numerous further examples.

With the Labour party's advance, radical criticisms of the Empire as an instrument of exploitation and oppression might be more widely accepted.

The third dimension was to help convince the Dominions and India that their best future lay within the Empire. Once again Baldwin was acutely conscious of the impact of the Great War. Here, as in other respects, 'a century of evolution' had been 'compressed into half a decade',[85] creating new conditions and new relationships with potentially damaging consequences. The Dominions' contribution to the war effort had led to British ratification of their autonomous status, in the 1926 Balfour Declaration and 1931 Statute of Westminster. The wartime stimulus to Indian nationalism had produced the 1917 Montagu commitment to allowing increased native participation in Indian government. Privately Baldwin did not welcome these changes. In 1933 he commented wryly that 'some curious things had been done in relation to the white parts of the Empire by such Imperialists as the late Lord Balfour and Mr Amery'. In 1935 he admitted he was not really happy 'with the way things were going' in India, but 'it was the lesser of two evils'.[86] Nevertheless, as with the onset of mass democracy at home, he thought it pointless to show resentment towards irreversible changes and far better to develop constructive forms of conservation.

Baldwin understood these aspects of the imperial problem in his usual manner, as matters partly for policy but mostly for persuasion. As the Empire's formal constitutional bonds loosened, it became still more necessary to emphasise shared interests and values, encouraging its various peoples to 'visualise the Empire as ... one eternal and indestructible unit'.[87] His aims were therefore to 'educate our democracy as to what our Empire stands for', and 'to instil through the people in this country and the Dominions belief in ourselves and in our future, that faith in our heritage which alone can bind us together in the years to come and alone enable us to progress'.[88]

Conscious that in post-war conditions pre-war forms of imperial-

[85] *TTF* p. 278 (20 Jan. 1930); *HCDeb* 260, c. 343 (24 Nov. 1931).
[86] Cabinet 16(33), 10 March 1933; *Reith Diaries*, p. 120 (5 Feb. 1935). See also his private 'diehard' reaction on Ireland, in Jones *WD* III.233 (29 July 1924).
[87] Conservative conference, 21 Nov. 1929; see Oxford, 9 June 1923.
[88] Primrose League, 2 May 1924; Liverpool, 28 April 1931, and see *OE* pp. 216–18.

ist assertiveness would offend domestic, Dominion, and Indian sensitivities, Baldwin emphatically distanced his party from what he called 'rather sinister' and 'militaristic' meanings of imperialism.[89] Instead he endorsed alternative Conservative definitions, characteristically drawing upon strains of imperial idealism shared across party boundaries, more particularly with Liberal imperialists. Empire was not about jingoism, 'flag-wagging', and 'painting the map red', nor about exploitation, 'selfishness in public policy', and 'riding roughshod over the world'.[90] Imperialism had 'been emptied of any aggressive meaning which it may once have had, for it has been redeemed and ennobled by the sacrifices of the Great War'.[91] Baldwin's empire was rather a new kind of empire – which he contrasted to those of Rome, Germany, Austria, Russia, and France – because it was a natural expression and extension of the various facets of the British national character. It had been created not by conquering armies but by the 'bone and sinew of our people', people of all classes.[92] With the British characteristics of courage, initiative, enterprise, and love of adventure, some had pursued the mercantile spirit in India and Africa, while love of freedom, good homes, and country life led others to the open spaces of the Dominions.[93] In these senses the British were naturally an 'imperial race', and there was nothing paradoxical in saying that rural England had helped to generate an overseas Empire.[94] This empire was not one of mere material interest and subjugation, because the British had carried with them their unique traditions, values, and ideals. It was an empire presented chiefly in ethical and spiritual terms: an empire of service, duty, justice, good government, and the evolution of freedom in brotherhood.[95] The British Empire was so different from all other empires that 'we must give the word Empire a new meaning, or use instead the title of Commonwealth of British Nations'.[96]

[89] *OE* pp. 185, 222 (15 May 1925, 3 May 1924).
[90] *OE* pp. 71, 185 (4 Dec. 1924, 15 May 1925); *OI* p. 68 (Empire Day broadcast 1927), and see Oxford, 8 June 1923; Primrose League, 2 May 1924.
[91] Manchester, 2 Nov. 1923.
[92] *OE* pp. 222, 214 (3 May 1924, Empire Day 1925); *OI* pp. 67–8, 136 (Empire Day, 6 Aug. 1926).
[93] *OE* pp. 8, 213–14, 222.
[94] *OE* p. 8 (6 May 1924).
[95] *OE* pp. 72, 214, 222 (4 Dec. 1924, Empire Day 1925); *OI* pp. 136–7 (6 Aug. 1927).
[96] *OE* p. 214 (Empire Day 1925); see *OI* p. 68 (Empire Day broadcast 1927).

As the dependent colonies were not an issue in British political debate Baldwin, like other leading politicians, rarely spoke of them. When he did, his theme was the ethic of service. He declared one of the new, British, meanings of imperialism to be that of trusteeship: helping 'people who belong to a backward civilisation, wisely to raise them in the scale of civilisation'.[97] Provision of peace, justice, development, and education to 'a great heritage of many races, many languages and religions' had evoked a British 'record for hard, unselfish, disinterested work ... never ... surpassed by any Imperial Power'. So long as the British people discharged their solemn trust to 'humanity' in this spirit, 'we need seek no other title to Empire'.[98]

India would not have featured much more prominently or imaginatively in his speeches, had it not become a divisive issue within Conservative politics from 1929 to 1935. Not only was India secondary in his own conception of Empire, but he also assumed that the issue commanded little popular appeal. In this sense, the Indian controversy was for him a distraction from the party's essential purposes. Even so, he committed himself to Indian constitutional reform, in defiance of considerable Conservative opposition. Because he judged it to be as fundamental to the character of British politics and his own party as it was for Britain's relations with India, it generated some of his most notable speeches – not just for their immediate political success but also for their developments in Conservative doctrine.

Some of Baldwin's earlier statements on India had a die-hard tinge. British rule alone preserved India from 'bloody anarchy', and the Conservative party would 'firmly resist any attempt to bring about any form of separation'.[99] Privately 'he sometimes almost wished England could leave [India] for twenty years', in order to teach the 'baboo politicians' a lesson in the indispensability of the British presence.[100] Yet well before 1929 he also spoke of Britain's 'stupendous task' of guiding 'our Indian fellow sub-

[97] *OE* p. 186 (15 May 1925); and see *TTF* p. 281.
[98] *OE* pp. 185–6 (15 May 1925); *TTF* pp. 28–9, 281 (imperial broadcast, Empire Day 1929, 20 Jan. 1930).
[99] *The Manchester Guardian*, 11 Feb. 1922; Primrose League, 2 May 1924, and see e.g. Manchester, 26 July 1924.
[100] *Reith Diaries*, p. 100 (21 Feb. 1929).

jects' towards 'self-government within the Empire', even 'in the fullness of time' to 'equal partnership with the Dominions'.[101] The Simon Commission's purpose was to advance the process of making 'the people of India . . . active partners in the control of their own lives and destinies'.[102]

Within conventional official views, these statements were not inconsistent. The crucial idea was British and Indian *partnership*, achieved *within* the Empire and on British terms. Baldwin understood Irwin's proposed offer of 'Dominion status' in these terms, yet was impressed by its advance upon existing policies as a means of coping with Indian nationalism. When informed of it while still prime minister, he was unusually enthusiastic – 'thoroughly interested' and 'extraordinarily receptive'.[103] But he also anticipated that many Conservatives would dislike it as too advanced, and after his 1929 election defeat he feared that it might be caught up in Conservative attacks on the Labour government. With Irwin's plans still secret, he tried to smooth the path by elevating Indian policy into a national question, high above party conflicts. It was, he said in July 1929, and as he repeated on later occasions, 'the most difficult question of all before us', requiring the efforts of 'a united Parliament' and 'self control on both sides'.[104] His formal assent to the Irwin Declaration in September 1929, taken without prior consultation with his colleagues, was presented by his critics as casual and naive, and when faced by a hostile shadow cabinet he resorted to claiming to have been misled about the Simon Commission's attitude. Yet his decision was taken with deliberation, following discussions with Irwin, and he knew it involved a 'considerable personal risk'.[105] A better interpretation is that it was as calculated an attempt to pre-empt party obstruction as his actions over protection had been in 1923. He did not repudiate Irwin's main principle, defending the promise of

---

[101] Primrose League, 2 May 1924; *OI* p. 71 (Empire Day broadcast 1927).
[102] Guildhall, 9 Nov. 1927.
[103] Dawson to Irwin, telegram and letter, both 8 April 1929, Halifax Indian papers 18/ 241, 243.
[104] *HCDeb* 229, c. 63 (2 July 1929). Examples of later re-statements are *HCDeb* 231, cc. 1308, 1312 (7 Nov. 1929); 247, c. 748 (26 Jan. 1931); 249, cc. 1424, 1426 (12 March 1931); 260, c. 1407 (3 Dec. 1931).
[105] Baldwin to Joan Davidson, 7 Oct. 1929, JD; to MacDonald, 21 Sept. 1929, MacDonald papers 344, and to Snowden, 28 Oct. 1929, SB 103/124–7. For the circumstances and controversy, see Moore, *Crisis of Indian Unity*, pp. 63–94.

'Dominion status' in the Commons even as his front-bench colleagues threatened to rebel and force his resignation. He then obtained Labour Cabinet assistance, in the form of public reassurances, to pacify his own followers. Although the episode made him temporarily feel 'the hopelessness of trying to liberalise the Tory party',[106] he continued to work in tacit alliance with the Labour Cabinet against much of his own party, despite colleagues who remained sceptical, wavered (like Hoare in early 1931), or (like Churchill and Salisbury) eventually led the Conservative revolt. His decision not to head the Conservative delegation at the Round Table Conference was taken in order to assist the reform process, because it left him freer to defend his leadership and because by obliging Lloyd George, as a fellow party leader, to keep out of the conference too, it reduced the risk of the negotiations being wrecked by party manoeuvres.[107] Even under the National government, with formal alliances established with Liberal and Labour supporters of Indian reform, with the contingent of diehard Conservative MPs proportionately smaller, and as wider Conservative support was rallied, his commitment remained decisive. It is unlikely that any other Conservative leader would have made Indian reform an issue of confidence in himself, as Baldwin did repeatedly over five years.

Irwin's strategy appealed to Baldwin as a bold stroke of practical idealism, combining expediency with principle and faith. This was as true for British politics as for Indian government, and Baldwin's handling of the issue had similarities with his reactions towards the new British electorate and the Labour party. Within Britain, Indian constitutional reform would reconcile the arrival of parliamentary democracy with the maintenance of imperial administration. The Indian question was, he said in July 1929, 'the supreme, the acid, and ultimate test of how fit we are for ... democratic conditions'[108] – meaning on the one hand Labour readiness to countenance imperial government, and on the other Con-

---

[106] Baldwin in Lytton to Irwin, 20 Nov. 1929, Halifax Indian papers 18/309. *HCDeb* 231, cc. 1311–12 (7 Nov. 1929), for continued support for Irwin; Baldwin in Henson journal, 9 Nov. 1929, for possible resignation; MacDonald diary, 10 Nov. 1929, and Baldwin–MacDonald published correspondence, 11 Nov. 1929, for Cabinet assistance.

[107] Schuster, and Baldwin, to Irwin, 9 and 16 Oct. 1930, Halifax Indian papers 19/143a, 147.

[108] *HCDeb* 229, c. 63 (2 July 1929).

servative recognition of the inevitability and advantages of reform. By insisting upon the 'national', non-party, status of Indian policy, he aimed not simply to contain Conservative criticism but to preserve the domestic base for imperial stability. He repeatedly invoked what for Conservatives was a particularly doleful lesson, and one which played a large part in his private attitude towards the issue. Ireland had, he said, been lost because it became a matter of party warfare. Government policy had alternated between firmness and concession, allowing the problem to fester and become so embittered that ultimately – as he himself encountered it in the Coalition Cabinet – the choice lay between two evils, war or surrender.[109] As on domestic issues the task was to educate, to 'liberalise', the Conservative party, to make it understand that in post-war conditions Conservative success demanded willing acceptance of change, in order to make change safe and beneficial. 'A party must be progressive to live', and for a 'progressive party' Indian reform was the only possible course: any other could lead 'to the destruction of the party'.[110] So although Conservative opinions on India ranged from those of 'Imperialists of the Second Jubilee to young advanced Democrats' who supported Irwin, Baldwin chose not the short-term, prudential route of compromise between these two extremes but the long hard road of leading the party towards the 'advanced' perspective.[111] He knew the personal motivations in Churchill's opposition on India – preserving his own prominence amidst Conservative protectionism and then his exclusion from the National government[112] – and persistently sought to deflate him by references to his earlier support, as a Liberal minister, for imperial reform.[113] But Churchill's greatest offence was that in regressing to his youthful experience of India, becoming 'once more the subaltern of Hussars of '96', he

[109] *HCDeb* 247, cc. 746–7 (26 Jan. 1931), and 276, cc. 1137–8 (29 March 1933); Worcester, 29 April 1933; National Union Central Council, 4 Dec. 1934, and see Baldwin interview in Crozier, *Off the Record*, p. 26 (12 June 1934).
[110] *HCDeb* 260, c. 1401 (3 Dec. 1931); and see 276, c. 1140 (29 March 1933).
[111] Jones *DL* p. 5 (11 March 1931).
[112] Interview, 12 June 1934, Crozier papers, even clearer than in the printed version, Crozier, *Off the Record*, p. 25, where Baldwin's recollection is more accurate than A. J. P. Taylor's footnote: see Williamson, *National Crisis*, pp. 124–5, 180–4, 474–5.
[113] Lord Lloyd memo, 4 March 1931, Lloyd papers 19/5; *HCDeb* 249, cc. 1423–4 (12 March 1931) and 276, cc. 1136–7 (29 March 1933); broadcast, 5 Feb. 1935.

also wanted the whole 'Tory party to go back to pre-war'.[114] The diehards claimed to be realists and called the reformers sentimentalists, but the reverse was the case. The diehards were deluded by a reactionary sentimentalism, and it was the reformers who were the realists.[115]

Within India the reality was that 'the unchanging East had changed'.[116] In a metaphor later borrowed by Macmillan to still greater public effect, Baldwin declared that 'there is a wind of nationalism and freedom running round the world and running as strongly in Asia ... as in any part of the world'.[117] In private he made the point more prosaically: 'rightly or wrongly we have done with the old India; there's a new one afoot and we must make the best of it'.[118] In the face of the Indian Congress party's demand for an independent unitary state outside the Empire, the Conservative reformers' strategy was to recruit support from the Indian Princes and Muslim and moderate politicians in a federal state which, while extensively self-governed, would long remain under ultimate British stewardship – Irwin's 'Dominion status with safeguards' – and always within the Empire. Baldwin himself spoke of Congress as unrepresentative extremists, of 'loyal' moderates, of the Princes providing 'stability', and of guarantees being secured for vital British interests. This, he said, was a properly Conservative policy, in contrast both to the provocation of diehard immovability and to the socialist desire to hand India over to Gandhi.[119] The strategy can be made to seem cynical. But most Conservative reformers thought they were granting a remarkable degree of self-government – the maximum consistent with the character and diversity of the Indian population, and with British responsibilities as well as interests. They believed peaceful, just, and representative all-India self-government was possible only

---

[114] Baldwin to Davidson, 13 Nov. 1930, in *Davidson Memoirs*, p. 355.
[115] *HCDeb* 249, c. 1418 (12 March 1931), and 276, cc. 1132–5, 1138–9 (29 March 1933); Baldwin interview, 12 June 1934, Crozier papers.
[116] *HCDeb* 249, c. 1425 (12 March 1931); and see 276, c. 1135 (29 March 1933).
[117] National Union Central Council, 4 Dec. 1934, as given in *The Times*; H. Macmillan, *Winds of Change* (1966), p. 318, has 'blowing' instead of 'running'.
[118] Jones *DL* p. 29 (27 Feb. 1932).
[119] E.g. Newton Abbot, 6 March 1931; Malvern, 18 June 1931; *HCDeb* 276, cc. 1139–40 (29 March 1933); Albert Hall, 12 May 1933. See Crozier, *Off the Record*, pp. 26–7 (12 June 1934), and Irwin in *Bayford Diaries*, p. 249 (31 July 1933), for the proposed Indian federal parliament being 'a very Tory Assembly'.

under British trusteeship. To them, accordingly, preserving the essentials of the British presence in India was less self-interested than morally justified.[120]

The assumption or hope was that alliances contrived by constitutional arrangements would in time develop into a willing imperial partnership, based not just on material ties but on shared beliefs. Baldwin's public emphasis was always upon the latter – and he deprecated resort to racial prejudice in the intra-party debate, indeed his first major Indian speech contained an extraordinary invocation of a shared ancestry of Europeans and Indians in 'the great Aryan race'.[121] From long centuries of torpor a 'new India' had arisen, made 'dynamic' because for a hundred years the British had educated Indians in Western political theories and British democratic principles. As Britons above all should know, once the ideas of freedom, self-government, and national unity had been implanted they could never be suppressed. Any attempt to do so would be contrary to Britain's past work in India and to its national traditions, and could only be counter-productive.[122] 'You cannot reverse the engines without breaking the machine.'[123] The federal proposals 'might save India to the Empire, but if they were not introduced we should certainly lose it'.[124] On the other hand, as he said privately, a great deal might be gained by 'keep[ing] faith with the Indians'.[125] Those Britons who had educated Indians in British ideas had done so in order to bring 'our various races together by a sympathetic understanding of political principles'. By acting upon those principles Britain would maintain its moral authority, and Indians would continue to look to it for guidance as the best model of, and most experienced teacher in, parliamentary government.[126] This would encourage and strengthen a co-operation and friendship which was the best and only lasting

---

[120] Moore, *Crisis of Indian Unity*, and Bridge, *Holding India to the Empire*, stress the calculated defence of British interests, but for the context of belief see C. Bridge, 'Conservatism and Indian Reform', *Journal of Imperial and Commonwealth History* 4 (1976), 176–93.

[121] *HCDeb* 231, cc. 1307–8 (7 Nov. 1929). For his fighting the spirit which employed such terms as 'negrophiles', see *HCDeb* 249, c. 1425 (12 March 1931).

[122] *HCDeb* 260, cc. 1402–3 (3 Dec. 1931); 276, c. 1136 (29 March 1933); Manchester, 29 June 1933; National Union Central Council, 4 Dec. 1934; broadcast, 5 Feb. 1935.

[123] *HCDeb* 249, cc. 1425–6 (12 March 1931).

[124] Cabinet 16(33), 10 March 1933. See *HCDeb* 276, c. 1133 (29 March 1933); Worcester, 29 April 1933.

[125] Jones *DL*, p. 29 (27 Feb. 1932).

[126] *HCDeb* 260, c. 1402 (12 Dec. 1931); broadcast, 5 Feb. 1935.

security for Britain's material interests. A trade boycott, he told a Lancashire audience worried about its cotton exports, could not be stopped by the bayonet; as the Indian legislature's acceptance of the Ottawa Conference agreements demonstrated, the best economic safeguard was goodwill.[127] Greater freedom, wider enfranchisement, more participation in government would 'cement the bond' between Britain and India, leading to 'real union'.[128] The British Raj would remain until its work was complete, but a time would come when it would cease to be necessary because a self-governing India would be a loyal member of the British Commonwealth.[129]

Perhaps from private belief but certainly as public conviction, by 1933 Baldwin had absorbed India into the common interpretation of the development of the Empire of British settlement. In this view changed relationships were understood not as discontinuities, but in terms of the national genius for adaptation and political evolution. In an extended or transplanted 'Whiggism' – the imperial counterpart of the accepted account of the domestic emergence of democratic constitutionalism – change represented the continuous growth of a living organism towards superior and more lasting forms. He expounded his own version of this most fully when broadcasting on Indian policy in February 1935:

Now, is our Empire one that rises and falls, as other Empires have fallen? Or do we genuinely believe that we have found a way of keeping our Empire young and vigorous and of preserving it from decay? I think we do. We believe surely that by teaching our Dependencies to govern themselves, by making them as they learn the lesson responsible for their own affairs, we shall preserve their loyalty and ensure their co-operation and their unity with us. An Empire fertilised by self-government grows into a Commonwealth of Nations ... The Empires of the past which have perished had not discovered this secret ...

We have learnt from experience that we shall preserve our Empire if we succeed in giving the units the right amount of liberty in the right way in the right time. There is no other way of preserving it.[130]

In an obvious sense such statements were rationalisations or apo-

[127] Manchester, 29 June 1933. See also Albert Hall, 12 May 1933; broadcast, 5 Feb. 1935; *HCDeb* 297, cc. 1717–18 (11 Feb. 1935).
[128] *HCDeb* 276, c. 1140 (29 March 1933).
[129] Worcester, 29 April 1933; *HCDeb* 297, cc. 1721–2 (11 Feb. 1935).
[130] Broadcast, 5 Feb. 1935.

logias for unavoidable withdrawal from direct rule, but it is more striking that they did not admit any weakening of the imperial connection. As Baldwin said, it was indeed the case that although the 'old-fashioned, hard-shelled Conservative' had predicted disaster from grants of responsible government to Canada and South Africa, these Dominions had remained within the Empire and in 1914 joined Britain in a European war.[131] 'Commonwealth' may have been a new meaning for 'Empire', but Baldwin treated the two terms as synonymous: 'Commonwealth' was the form of a *preserved* and even strengthened Empire. The remarkable change in his and other Conservative reformers' public position on India was not a retreat from Empire. It was, rather, the acceptance – however far in the future – of a multi-racial Commonwealth.

V

However, when Baldwin spoke of Empire he most often meant the self-governing Dominions – as the areas of British emigration, the most capable of attracting interest across all classes, just as they appealed to his own sense of idealism. As a Seeleyite and Chamberlainite, he had spoken before the War as an imperial federationist, hoping that 'we might yet build up, out of the scattered Empire, one great homogeneous country', with efficient constitutional machinery for bringing together 'councillors from the Empire'.[132] During the 1920s he continued to speak of a unified Empire – 'one home and one people' with 'one citizenship' – as among the 'most cherished ideals' of Conservatives.[133] Their 'dream' was of a United Empire like the United States, drawn together by radio and improved water and air transport, within which people could move themselves, their homes, and their businesses as naturally as they did between New York and California, or from Bristol to Newcastle.[134] The fact that the Dominions had attained greater autonomy meant only that there was a 'duty of statesmanship . . . to see that the bonds [of] Empire became

---

[131] Manchester, 29 June 1933, and for contrast to American colonies, broadcast 5 Feb. 1935.

[132] *Berrows*, 1 Jan. 1910, 4 May 1913.

[133] *OE* pp. 71, 222–3 (4 Dec., 3 May 1924); and see e.g. Oxford, 8 June 1923; Manchester, 2 Nov. 1923.

[134] *OE* pp. 213, 222–3 (4 Dec. 1924, Empire Day 1925); *OI* pp. 68–9 (Empire Day broadcast 1927); *HCDeb* 245, c. 1544 (27 Nov. 1930).

stronger and stronger'.[135] His speaking tour of Canada the year
after the General Strike and Balfour Declaration was intended to
counteract the spread of American influence, and 'evil propaganda' claiming that 'Great Britain is a decadent country' and
that the Dominions were 'tying themselves to a corpse'.[136] The
Ottawa Conference in 1932 had, he thought, come 'just in time'
to keep the Dominions together economically, but now provided
material supports for renewed unity in the future.[137]

In Baldwin's version of Chamberlainism, economic objectives
played their usual large part. In a more competitive and national-
istic world, Empire was 'essential to our life', providing the industrialised and crowded homeland with food, markets, and space for
emigration. If the Empire broke up, Britain would 'perish'.[138] He
did not delude himself that the Dominions would remain dependent producers of food and raw material. Dominion autonomy had
complicated attempts to achieve imperial tariff reform, while
Canada was 'destined to become one of the main manufacturing
countries in the world'. But he claimed that Dominion industrialis-
ation would strengthen the Empire's status as an economic bloc,
and increase the demand for British workers. The modern form
of Empire economic unity was a negotiated co-ordination and
rationalisation of imperial production.[139]

Especially before 1932, however, imperial economic policies
were controversial within Britain and a source of friction with the
Dominions. Material interests alone could not sustain imperial
consciousness, nor did Baldwin wish them to be regarded as the
only or strongest unifying forces. 'We need something more profound than profit-making.'[140] Glossing over the existence of French
Canadians, Afrikaners, and Irish republicans, he often presented

---

[135] United Club, 3 Nov. 1932, and see e.g. *TTF* pp. 198–200 (15 Aug. 1932).

[136] *OI* pp. 173–4 (27 Aug. 1927). The chief reason for his visit was to accompany the Prince
of Wales to celebrations of the Canadian federation's diamond jubilee; but see also
Baldwin to Irwin, 15 Sept. 1927, Halifax Indian papers 17/253f; Hyde, *Baldwin*, p. 284.

[137] Baldwin to Lothian, 4 Sept. 1932, Lothian papers 261/39; Jones *DL* p. 50 (29 Aug.
1932). See Conservative conference, 7 Oct. 1932; United Club dinner, 3 Nov. 1932.

[138] Primrose League, 2 May 1924; Bolton, 28 Oct. 1924; Conservative conference, 21 Nov.
1929.

[139] E.g. Coliseum, 5 Feb. 1930; Ulster Reform Club, 15 Feb. 1930; *HCDeb* 236, cc. 1545–
6 (13 March 1930). For an Australian appreciation of his 'entirely modern' outlook
towards the Dominions, see Menzies, *Afternoon Light*, p. 99.

[140] *Interpreter*, p. 31, and see *OE* p. 72 (4 Dec. 1924); *TTF* pp. 201–2 (15 Aug. 1932); *SOL*
p. 151 (24 May 1937).

the Empire as an empire of the 'British' race, bound together by kinship, a common culture, and inherited memories. Just as urban dwellers retained attachments to their ancestral rural homes, so the English-speaking peoples in the Dominions cherished a love of their 'Mother Country':

> they never lost that golden thread of the spirit which drew their thoughts back to the land of their birth. Even their children, and their children's children, to whom Great Britain was no more than a name, a vision, spoke of it always as Home.

These ties were 'light as air, but strong as links of iron'.[141] Significantly, Baldwin's favourite Kipling story, 'An Habitation Enforced', invoked a transatlantic, transgenerational, and life-enhancing instinct for roots. Because the Dominions shared with Britain 'a common tradition which transcends all local loyalties and binds us as one people', they formed a 'family of nations'.[142] As the only remaining constitutional link between them was the monarchy, this had to be presented as a powerful symbol of unity and focus of loyalty. King George V was a 'father' of all 'his people' across the Empire, all 'members of his wider family'. In an imperial broadcast on the King's death, Baldwin made a point of revealing that in his last hours he had asked 'How is the Empire?'[143]

Yet for all his emphasis upon economic benefits and British kinship, Baldwin's greater appeal was to an Empire 'compacted of the great spiritual elements – freedom and law, fellowship and loyalty, honour and toleration'.[144] It had grown 'because of the spirit of freedom which ran in its veins. Liberty is its life-blood', and self-government and parliamentary institutions were its natural political forms.[145] Here as elsewhere in his doctrine, paradoxes disappeared or, rather, reappeared as strengths. Just as true freedom was not licence, so self-government was not separation.

---

[141] *OE* p. 214 (Empire Day, 1925). For Baldwin echoing 'An Habitation Enforced' to suggest the potency of the British 'home' even for Americans, see *TTF* pp. 153–4 (23 April 1932).

[142] *OI* p. 136 (6 Aug. 1927); *OE* p. 215 (Empire Day 1925).

[143] *SOL*, pp. 11, 17 (21 Jan. 1936). See *OI* p. 72 (30 July 1927); *TTF* pp. 25, 309 (Empire Day 1929, 10 March 1928).

[144] *OI* p. 137 (6 Aug. 1927).

[145] Liverpool, 28 April 1931; *OI* pp. 131, 136–7 (6 Aug. 1927); *TTF* p. 281 (20 Jan. 1930); *SOL*, p. 151 (24 May 1937); *Interpreter*, pp. 24, 31–3.

Separatist desires in the Dominions arose from a sense of subordi-
nation, but with their achievement of equal status with Britain
their grievances would dissolve and closer co-operation become
natural. 'It is the active power of the principle of liberty . . . which
really unites us and forms the cement of the British Empire.'[146]
Not only had freedom been reconciled with unity; so had diversity.
Just as England, Scotland, Wales, and Ulster remained themselves
while being also British, so each Dominion – absorbing such non-
British elements as the French Canadians – formed its own identity and 'soul' without weakening its imperial attachment.[147] The
great proof had been the 'instant, spontaneous and whole-hearted'
Dominion support for Britain in the Great War.[148] It was in these
senses that Baldwin transcended his earlier ideas of a British
racial federation after 1929, to accommodate India in a vision of
a multi-racial Commonwealth.

There were, he said, yet further reasons for commitment to
Empire. The imperialism which did not involve jingoism,
oppression or exploitation constituted an Empire of service, not
just among its own peoples but for all peoples. The British Empire
was a 'great force for good' in the world:

It stands in the sweep of every wind, by the wash of every sea, a witness
to that which the spirit of confidence and brotherhood can accomplish in
the world. It is a spiritual inheritance which we hold in trust not only for
its members, but for all the nations that surround it.[149]

The Empire–Commonwealth formed a stable unit in the chaotic
post-war world, and an example of how free nations could resolve
their differences by negotiation, and flourish by co-operation. As
he repeatedly declared, the Commonwealth was 'an achieved
example of a League of Nations' – the 'principal pillar' and 'great
instrument' of peace in the world.[150] Indeed, because the Empire's
very purpose was to spread the ideas of freedom, justice, truth,

[146] *OI* p. 79 (Quebec, 30 July 1927). See e.g. *TTF* pp. 26–7 (Empire Day broadcast 1929);
Worcester, 29 April 1933.
[147] *OI* pp. 78–9 (Quebec, 30 July 1927); *TTF* p. 202 (Ottawa, 15 Aug. 1932).
[148] *OE* p. 215 (Empire Day 1925).
[149] *OI* p. 71 (Empire Day broadcast 1927).
[150] *TTF* p. 202 (15 Aug. 1932); Conservative conference, 21 Nov. 1929; *OE* p. 233 (23
July 1924). See also Imperial Conferences, 1 Oct. 1923, 19 Oct. 1926; *OI* p. 137; *TTF*
pp. 27, 278; *SOL* p. 121; *Interpreter*, pp. 34–5.

service, and 'what is noblest in human achievement' to the remotest corners of the earth, its continued unity was fundamental to the welfare of mankind.[151]

To me the greatest value of the Commonwealth of Nations ... is not necessarily an area in which to make money, but it is space in the world for the spreading of and the increase of our own race because I believe our own race to be the best in the world, and I believe that the progress of the world, morally and spiritually as well as economically, is bound up in the spread of our people with their ideas and with their ideals ... that is why we regard these Empire or Commonwealth questions as far the most important that exist today.[152]

Shortly after he first became prime minister, Baldwin said that 'it may yet some day be possible for peoples in so distracted a Continent as Europe to feel there may be something for them to learn from the development, from the union, and from the ideals of our great Empire'.[153] In 1932 he spoke privately of the Ottawa Conference as 'one more attempt to keep the sane forces of the world together'.[154] In these respects, from 1933 he increasingly thought that the Empire's time had come.

---

[151] *OE* pp. 185–6, 234 (15 May 1925, 23 July 1923); *TTF*, p. 26 (imperial broadcast, Empire Day 1929); and see Hotel Cecil, 20 June 1924; *Interpreter*, p. 31.
[152] *HCDeb* 174, cc. 2161–2 (18 June 1924), and see *OE* p. 72 (4 Dec. 1924).
[153] *OE* p. 234 (23 July 1923).
[154] Jones *DL* p. 43 (3 July 1932).

CHAPTER 9

Soul and providence

Baldwin's themes of individual freedom, mutual service, social cohesion, and a new imperialism could be understood in secular terms alone, as qualities emanating simply from 'national character' and the national past. He himself maintained that these qualities had a more fundamental origin and significance. Here private faith and public profession came closest, and provided much of his inner sense of purpose. This being so, he also deployed religion in a political – and sometimes partisan – manner. Baldwin extended a common Victorian conception that an appropriate form of Christianity could promote social responsibility and national integration, while sensing the party possibilities in a post-war subsidence of denominational conflict and growth of new moral anxieties.

I

A perceptive reviewer observed that Baldwin was 'profoundly religious in a way in which it is given to few men to understand the meaning of religion'. This was not an intellectualised religion but a 'very simple, very deep' faith.[1] Insofar as it was expressed in words other than those of the Bible and Book of Common Prayer, like many others he found these not in theological works but in Robert Browning's poetry – in the faith of *A Death in the Desert*, refreshed by seasonal re-readings of *Christmas Eve* and *Easter Day*.[2]

[1] Anonymous review of AWB, in *The Times Literary Supplement*, 10 Feb. 1956; Davidson, 'Stanley Baldwin', *Cambridge Review*, 24 Jan. 1948.
[2] Jones *DL* p. 539 (5–7 Jan. 1946: an example of positive influence from Butler of Harrow); GMY p. 206; AWB p. 109. For the 'cult' of Browning as a religious teacher among both Anglicans and Nonconformists up until the mid 1920s, see A. Wilkinson, *Dissent or Conform? War, Peace and the English Churches 1900–1945* (1986), pp. 13–17.

He had real belief in Divine judgement, in resurrection and the afterlife, and in the efficacy of prayer.[3] His faith in a providential order and in Divine guidance was particularly strong.[4] He accepted the reality of sin and need for repentance, but also the power of righteousness and Christian love to assist in the ultimate redemption of the world.[5] In its emphasis upon individual conscience, duty, and moral values it was also a profoundly Protestant faith. Jones thought 'his conscience was more active than his intellect'.[6]

That Baldwin's political beliefs were somehow connected to his religious faith is not in itself remarkable. What was unusual in the 1920s and 1930s was his public enunciation of a religious conception of politics, and the particular character he gave to this Christian politics. This was a more important and persistent feature than his 'ruralism', although it too must not be overstated. It was less extensive than that of many Victorian politicians, since in a more secularised yet also – after the horror of the Great War – bereaved and spiritually stricken society, restraint was necessary to avoid incongruity, embarrassment, or offence.[7] Nevertheless it was sufficiently prominent to be recognised as one of his most distinctive characteristics.

Baldwin's readiness to speak out in such terms was encouraged by his unexpected appointment as prime minister, which intensified his wartime sense of being 'called' for special work. Contemporary statements confirm his recollection in retirement:

I could see the hand of God in it, and I recognised that my peculiar life had been a preparation for the very work that lay before me. The problem was to get at the soul of the working people. I found that those long, quiet years at Wilden had given me a knowledge of them that few men in politics had. The lines of my policy grew clear, and I *knew* that I had been chosen as God's instrument for the work of the healing of the nation.[8]

---

[3] Baldwin to Edith Macdonald, 6 Dec. 1910, and to his mother 6 Feb. 1916, 11 Feb. 1917, 6 June 1918, 12 Feb. 1923, BF; to Halifax, 25 Dec. 1938, 23 July 1940, Halifax papers A4.410.14.10–11; AWB p. 328.

[4] AWB p. 81; Jones diary, 20 May 1937; Baldwin to Halifax, 23 July 1940, in GMY p. 250; Cazalet-Keir, *From the Wings*, p. 106.

[5] AWB p. 90; speech in *Kidderminster Shuttle*, 19 Feb. 1921; *OE* p. 211 (13 March 1925).

[6] Jones *DL* p. xxx, and see W. Steed, 'Stanley Baldwin', *Review of Reviews*, May–June 1925, p. 409.

[7] See e.g. Leeds, 13 March 1925, replying to newspaper sneers that he was a 'revivalist'.

[8] 1938 letter in AWB p. 328 (original italics). Compare Baldwin speech, 7 Nov. 1923 (*OE* pp. 19, 20–1), and Mrs Baldwin's observation that his appointment indicated 'the guidance of a Divine Hand', in *Daily News*, 23 May 1923. See also Begbie, *Conservative Mind*,

No less than Churchill in May 1940, Baldwin felt himself to be 'walking with destiny' – though in him both the conviction and its manifestations were more properly Christian.[9] He and his wife began each morning at Downing Street or Chequers kneeling together in prayer, to 'commend our day to Him' in the faith that they were working for 'the country and for God's sake'.[10] A statesman, he seemed to think, was 'a politician who tries to do the Will of God'.[11] As his career lengthened, as successes mounted and as new tasks emerged, he felt 'increasing faith'. In 1936 he spoke 'quite simply but intensely of his belief that God could still make some use of him'.[12]

These beliefs generated that strong sense of duty and faith, the 'mystical compulsion', which sustained Baldwin in what he considered to be the 'rather sordid', contingent, and so inevitably frustrating activity of politics – in which 'one can't expect to see any result of one's work'.[13] 'We can only go on by knowing that the courses of the World are in the Hand of God, & that so long as we are serving righteousness, we are doing his Will.'[14] While his politics had obvious hereditary and social origins, in both their Conservatism and their idealism they had equally plain connections with this form of providentialism. It brought a devout tone to many of his public pronouncements – especially evident in his speeches on industrial peace during March 1925 – and it contributed to his remarkable resilience in the face of defeats and criticism, as during the party rebellions and newspaper attacks of 1930–1, when 'the Lord ... delivered [Rothermere] into my hands'.[15] Both these qualities were manifest in the striking determination and earnestness of his first six months as prime

pp. 18, 22–4; Baldwin in 1925 in Palmstierna, *Atskilliga Egenheter*, in Jones papers AA1/27.

[9] The famous sentence in Churchill, *Second World War*, 1.601, reads: 'I felt as if I was walking with destiny, and that all my past life had been but a preparation for this hour and for this trial.' See P. Addison, 'Destiny, History and Providence: The Religion of Winston Churchill', in Bentley (ed.), *Public and Private Doctrine*, pp. 236–50.

[10] Mrs Baldwin reported in March 1925, in Jones *DL* p. xxxiv: Jones thought this 'perhaps the truest clue' to Baldwin's personality.

[11] Begbie, *Conservative Mind*, p. 30.

[12] 1938 letter in AWB p. 328; Jones *DL* p. 206 (23 May 1936).

[13] Begbie, *Conservative Mind*, pp. 14, 18; Baldwin to Irwin, 8 Sept. 1933, Halifax papers A4.410.14.4.

[14] Baldwin agreeing with Bishop Henson, in Henson journal, 21 June 1927; cf. public statement below.

[15] Baldwin in the 1940s, in GMY p. 152.

minister, and in their protectionist climax – a mood captured in a private comment (with its characteristic Worcestershire colloquialism) after the 1923 election defeat: 'everyone who tries in politics to do the thing he believes in simply and honestly is sure to come a smeller. The martyrs did. Christ did.' At the end of his ministerial career he found spiritual contentment in a sense that he had fulfilled that most difficult injunction: 'Thy will be done.'[16]

Nevertheless, except when dealing with Lloyd George and the press lords, Baldwin's inner strength did not become dogmatic self-certainty and self-righteousness. Nor was he priggish: his sense of humour was 'a little earthy', and his attitude towards Edward VIII's *private* relationship with Mrs Simpson was surprisingly indulgent.[17] The nature of his belief in Divine Providence was significant, not just for his personal values but for his public doctrine. It was low-keyed, and 'democratic' in its implications – providing the foundation of that moral egalitarianism noted earlier. As the best informed of his early pen-portraitists observed, he thought a man 'however commonplace' could be used by, and might co-operate with, 'the divine energy', provided 'he sincerely desires selflessly to serve his fellow men, and earnestly seeks his strength from the sole source of spiritual power'.[18] 'All service ranks the same with God.'[19] Because all forms of service collectively contributed to the Divine purpose, these generated faith and hope even amidst the great problems of the post-war world:

if I did not believe that our work – . . . the work of all of us who hold the same faith and ideal, whether in politics or in civic work, wherever it may be – if I did not believe that that work was done in the faith and the hope that at some day, it may be a million years hence, the Kingdom of God would spread over the whole world, I could have no hope, I could do no work, and I would give my office over this morning to anyone who would take it.[20]

His own sense of co-operation with Providence was matched by a feeling of humility at being 'chosen' for the work of national lead-

[16] Jones *WD* I.259 (7 Dec. 1923); AWB pp. 326, 328.
[17] *Ibid.* p. 192 (and for an example, K. Young, *Baldwin*, p. 80); below, p. 326.
[18] Begbie, *Conservative Mind*, pp. 13–14.
[19] *OE* p. 19. From Browning, 'Pippa Passes' (1841): 'All service ranks the same with God / With God whose puppets, best and worst / Are we: there is no first and last.'
[20] *TTF* pp. 92–3 (2 May 1928), also Congregation Union Assembly, 8 May 1929.

ership, by a sense of the imperfections and complexities of life, and by an anxious and 'incessant search for God's will'. Although he believed that 'in my public life I have been increasingly led', he also felt 'increasingly dependent' on prayer.[21] When in 1933 he wrote morosely to that eminent Christian layman, Halifax, that 'I thought once I might have accomplished something: I have accomplished nothing', his standard was less any temporal judgement than that *sub specie aeternitatis*. Another Christian Conservative colleague counted him among 'the holy and humble of heart'.[22]

This devout yet modest faith was an obvious feature of the public as well as the private man. One example was his much-remarked response to a journalist when he first entered Downing Street as prime minister: 'I need your prayers more than your congratulations.'[23] Another was his account, when characterising the spiritual conflict within human nature, of his own daily struggle and his many failures to fulfil the confirmation vow to renounce 'the world, the flesh and the devil'. In 1932 he spoke of how in the work of government he often felt 'a still small voice that challenges all my efforts, searches out my motives, questions the meaning of everything that I do, and forces me to stand, as it were, in the full glare of the white light of eternity'.[24]

Christian spirituality surfaced even in Baldwin's ordinary round of party and prime-ministerial speeches. By post-war standards his political language was rich in the phraseology and cadences of the New Testament, Book of Common Prayer, and *Pilgrim's Progress*. These inspired some of his most evocative phrases: his February 1923 appeal to 'faith, hope, love and work'; his 'prayer' during the Macquisten Bill debate for 'peace in our time, O Lord', and his broadcast message on the outbreak of the General Strike that 'peace on earth comes to men of goodwill'. Many observers noted

---

[21] 1938 letter in AWB p. 328, and see p. 326, and Jones *WD* I.252 (24 Oct. 1923).
[22] Baldwin to Irwin, 8 Sept. 1933, Halifax papers A4.410.14.4; Percy, *Some Memories*, p. 193.
[23] *The Evening Standard*, 22 May 1923, and see Baldwin to his mother, 22 May 1923, in M&B p. 169. The statement was recalled many times over the next few years, most significantly among free churchmen. There is an instructive contrast in Conservative prime ministerial styles: in the same circumstances in 1979 Mrs Thatcher did not ask for help from the prayers of others, but herself recited a prayer to the assembled journalists, photographers, and television cameramen.
[24] League of Nations Union, 26 Oct. 1928; *TTF* p. 197 (15 Aug. 1932).

a religious force in some of his speeches: 'you can almost see the spiritual effort with which his big thoughts are dragged up from the depths of his soul in a kind of agony'.[25]

So unmistakeable were such testimonies to Christian faith that from 1924 Baldwin received numerous invitations to address or assist religious organisations. Conscious that there was some risk in mixing religion and politics, he was initially uncertain whether as prime minister he should address specifically denominational meetings.[26] But he soon welcomed these invitations as opportunities to reassert the Christian basis of British life, and to suggest a public religion which would reinforce his conception of post-war needs. The significance he attached to these pronouncements was emphasised by the re-publication of many of them in his volumes of collected addresses.

The values he most wanted to preserve were, he said, Christian in origin, and could be sustained only by continued Christian belief. More specifically these were Protestant values, as – in a further silence licenced by Irish partition – his public doctrine ignored the existence of Roman Catholics. For all its ancient Greek antecedents, the real 'seed-bed of modern democracy' had been the Protestant emphasis upon the individual soul and 'the assembling together of the brethren in the church congregation'.[27] The lasting basis and guarantee of political freedom remained spiritual freedom: the belief that each individual and each nation was directly responsible to God for their actions on earth. The 'real democratic feeling of valuing a man for what he is' depended not upon the delusion of secular equality, but upon recognition of this democracy of human souls.[28] Social and economic self-reliance were corollaries of each individual's responsibility for his own eternal salvation.[29]

Yet, Baldwin said, this uniquely Christian conception of the individual as an independent moral agent did not imply selfishness, for it was inseparable from love and duty towards other individuals. In language derived from F. D. Maurice, he spoke of the

[25] Hogg (later 1st Lord Hailsham) in Begbie, *Conservative Mind*, p. 114.
[26] Jones, *Three Score Years and Ten*, pp. 119–20.
[27] *TTF* p. 38 (14 July 1930); and see e.g. *SOL* p. 166 (18 May 1937); *Interpreter*, pp. 49–50, 53–4.
[28] Rhodes Trust dinner, Oxford, 16 June 1923; and see Nonconformist Unionist League, 8 April 1924; *TTF* pp. 101–2 (30 Jan. 1929); *Interpreter*, pp. 23–4; *Englishman*, p. 22.
[29] Edinburgh, 27 July 1923. Cf. Begbie, *Conservative Mind*, p. 26.

'Fatherhood of God' necessarily including the 'brotherhood of man'.[30] From the responsibility of all men towards their Maker flowed the duties of service and maintenance of social cohesion. In performance of these duties man fulfilled his true nature: human personality 'was best realised in fellowship with our brother men in service. Man's unlimited duty to his fellow-men was the very basis, the cornerstone and foundation of the Kingdom of Heaven'.[31] Conversely, aside from its temporal benefits the merit of social duty was that it constituted a form of 'religious education', teaching that salvation was to be found in love and brotherhood rather than in selfish isolation.[32] 'I believe', he said during the 1924 election campaign, 'that love can cast out hate, and that brotherhood can cast out enmity. And it is brotherhood we want, and it is brotherhood to which I call the nation at this election.'[33]

II

For Baldwin, then, politics – particularly post-war politics – ultimately had a religious basis and form. It consisted of a struggle between rival 'faiths' or 'gospels', in which party workers were 'missionaries' or 'apostles'. As a near-ordinand he described a political career, properly understood, as 'really a kind of ministry'. Politicians like priests ultimately achieved their purposes by reaching beyond all 'external trappings' and ministering to 'the human soul'.[34] It was not by the reform of institutions but by the reform of motives that real, permanent improvement would be achieved. 'We work', he told a Conservative meeting, 'to try to make the soul of this new democracy worthy of the enormous trust that has been given to it', and to try to build foundations with 'enough human energy, enough human faith and enough human love' to benefit future, 'happier generations'.[35]

Baldwin instinctively thought in such terms, but his instinct was sharpened by a religious interpretation of the world since 1914.

[30] *SOL* p. 166 (broadcast, 18 May 1937); Youth Conference on Democracy, 3 Feb. 1939.
[31] *OE* p. 226 (3 May 1924); City Temple, 8 May 1929.
[32] *OI* p. 200 (27 Oct. 1927).
[33] Sheffield, 27 Oct. 1924.
[34] *OE* p. 197 (Wesleyan Methodist dinner, 11 Feb. 1926); *OI* p. 203 (27 Oct. 1927).
[35] *OI* p. 36, also p. 34 (4 March 1927). See 1938 letter in AWB p. 328, for getting 'at the soul of the working man'.

The Great War had intensified the struggle between the 'forces of good and evil'.[36] It had been a 'great sin' committed by the leading nations, which mankind was paying for in the troubles of the post-war world.[37] The War had unleashed the 'manifest forces of Satan', spreading spiritual destitution, erecting 'false gods' and kindling the 'gospel of hate'.[38] There were the personal evils of despair, or irresponsible pleasure-seeking as psychological instinct was exalted over moral virtue.[39] In 1932 he made a notable attack upon what he called the 'modern movement' – that of left-wing, secular, intellectuals – with its ridicule of so-called 'bourgeois culture' in the name of 'happiness empty of moral content'.[40] There was also the public evil of class bitterness. Worst of all was a materialistic or mechanical view of life.

So many of our troubles . . . seem to me to arise from the growing materialism of the age . . . The higher qualities have sometimes given way to the lower – the spiritual to the material. Yet materialism means slavery – slavery of the mind to the things of the body; and slavery in the end means destruction.[41]

Politically it was just a few short steps from this to the 'mass mind', and then down the slippery slope to worship of the state and tolerance of brute force, and on to the terrible 'heresies' of communism and fascism, crushing freedom and personality and threatening not merely democracy but civilisation itself.[42]

Against these 'forces of darkness' there needed to be a 'general advance and assault'.[43] In this struggle a right-minded and effective politics had to be a Christian politics, defending and stimulating the springs of individuality, spirituality, and morality. 'The thing that had lain nearest to his heart', Baldwin declared in retirement,

[36] *HCDeb* 211, c. 2633 (prayer-book debate, 15 Dec. 1927); Toc H festival, 6 Dec. 1929; Westminster Abbey, 10 Nov. 1938.
[37] *SOL* p. 162 (18 May 1937); cf. Manchester, 2 Nov. 1923; *TTF* p. 275 (20 Jan. 1930); AWB p. 90.
[38] *OE* p. 196 (11 Feb. 1926); Baldwin used the last phrase in numerous speeches.
[39] Manchester, 2 Nov. 1923; *OE* p. 196 (11 Feb. 1926); *TTF* pp. 83–4 (12 May 1931).
[40] Fripp lecture, 'Happiness and Success', 26 Feb. 1932.
[41] *SOL* pp. 122–3 (16 April 1937). Cf. *OE* p. 154 (27 Sept. 1923); *TTF* p. 192 (13 June 1930).
[42] National Free Church Council, 8 April 1935; *SOL* pp. 101–2, 116–17 (10, 13 April 1937).
[43] *HCDeb* 211, c. 2636 (prayer-book debate, 15 Dec. 1927).

had been the welfare of our people, and, more than that, what he might call the soul of the people . . . In these days, amid the incalculable effects that had resulted from the War . . . at a time when . . . mankind tended more and more to be mechanized, regimented and drilled – at that time above all others statesmen should never lose sight of . . . the essential dignity of the human, individual soul.[44]

Still more obviously, the churches and associated movements had a renewed and urgent contribution to make to public life. Responsible politicians would encourage and assist this work, conscious that the character and progress of a people was moulded much less by politicians than by religious leaders.[45] Far from Christianity having 'done its work in the world', that work had 'hardly just begun'.[46] There was 'nothing the country needs so much' as another religious revival, a 'new revelation', another St Francis or John Wesley.[47] And the materials were available. The 'very manifestation' of satanic forces was 'calling other forces into the field'; 'mystery of mysteries, they all saw good coming out of evil' as new spiritual impulses emerged.[48] 'The struggle against materialism in the hearts of our people is one of the greatest struggles of this age', but it was also an age in which there had never been 'more people struggling . . . to live to the highest ideals', nor 'more widespread longing in the heart and mind for what was good'.[49]

What Baldwin wished the churches and Christian politicians to promote was a version of the Victorian broad-church ambition – a Protestant but non-sectarian national faith and public morality (again disregarding Roman Catholics, and the sectarian politics of Northern Ireland). 'There are', he declared in 1929, 'many forms of spiritual endeavour in the world. There are diversities of gifts. God fulfils himself in many ways, and His love is far wider than our minds.'[50] When in 1927 he spoke of his 'dread' at the association of religion with politics,[51] he meant only that he

[44] Guildhall, 5 Nov. 1937.
[45] *OE* pp. 198–9, 206–11 (7 May, 12 March 1925); *OI* p. 56 (23 June 1927); *TTF* pp. 104–5 (30 Jan. 1929).
[46] *OE* p. 210 (12 March 1925).
[47] *OE* p. 195 (11 Feb. 1926); Toc H festival, 6 Dec. 1929. Cf. Percy, *Some Memories*, p. 204. For a similar pre-war comment, see *HCDeb* 55, c. 281 (8 July 1913).
[48] *OE* p. 196 (11 Feb. 1926); Toc H festival, 6 Dec. 1929, and see Primrose League, 2 May 1924.
[49] *TTF* p. 192 (13 June 1930); *OE* p. 209 (12 March 1925); Toc H festival, 6 Dec. 1929.
[50] *TTF* p. 110 (10 April 1929).
[51] *HCDeb* 211, c. 2637 (prayer-book debate, 15 Dec. 1927).

wanted no revival of the conflict between the established and Nonconformist churches which had still shaped party politics in the Edwardian period. As an Anglican who thought of England, Wales, and Scotland as spiritual communities, he continued to support the principle of church establishment. But he also appealed to Nonconformists to consider their pressure for disestablishment and disendowment as diversions from their essential tasks, and likely to produce spiritual loss on all sides.[52] Within the Church of England he was, like his father, self-consciously independent of any church party, describing himself as a 'Churchman in little more than name'.[53] From this perspective, he declared the Church of England's glory to be a comprehensiveness which enabled it to draw strength from the equally valuable traditions of Evangelicalism and Anglo-Catholicism. On the great issue of Prayer Book revision in 1927–8 his concern lay not with the liturgical details, but with what would 'best serve the religious life of the nation' and most advance not just the Church's own unity but also its co-operation with other churches.[54] He welcomed the post-war reduction in interdenominational tension and the movements towards church reunion in England and Scotland as acknowledgements of the need for Christian unity against the 'common foe'. 'To-day and for the future all men of religious spirit, whatever they may call themselves, must cling together to hold fast what they have, lest the whole be swept away.'[55]

Baldwin was as conscious of his Nonconformist ancestry as he was of his Anglican membership, and sought to represent and encourage this new spirit of Christian alliance in ways which for a Conservative leader were often novel. He interpreted his party's traditional commitment to the maintenance of religion in the 'widest sense'.[56] He became a president of Toc H (the interdenominational movement for ex-servicemen), and a vice-president of both the Society for the Propagation of the Gospel and the British and Foreign Bible Society. He also reached well beyond

[52] *HCDeb* 211, c. 2633 (15 Dec. 1927), and 218, c. 1313 (14 June 1928).
[53] Baldwin to Lady Bridgeman, 24 Oct. 1932, Bridgeman papers. See A. Baldwin to Louisa, 14 Oct. 1865, B/WCRO 8229/6(ii): 'no party in the church would own me'.
[54] *HCDeb* 211, cc. 2632–7, and 218, cc. 1312–20 (prayer-book debates, 15 Dec. 1927, 14 June 1928).
[55] *TTF*, p. 100 (30 Jan. 1929); Nonconformist Unionist League, 8 April 1924; and see Church of Scotland and United Free Church general assemblies, 7 June 1926.
[56] Primrose League, 3 May 1935.

the Conservative party's traditional Church of England base to support and celebrate organisations, individuals and values which as recently as 1914 many of its members had regarded as hostile to Conservatism. He addressed more free church gatherings than he did those of the established churches, including, in 1925 and 1935, the National Free Church Council – once the powerhouse of Nonconformist support for the Liberal party. He helped fund-raising campaigns by the Congregationalist and Baptist Unions.[57] He claimed great pride in, and large debts of principle and personality to, his Quaker and Methodist forebears. The 'independent and sturdy individualism' of Nonconformists which Conservatives had long feared or hated as a threat to authority, became in his addresses a major contribution to national life.[58] With ecumenical even-handedness he praised the work of the Wesleys, Whitefield, Spurgeon, Clifford, Booth, even (in a rare gesture towards English Catholicism) Newman and Manning. To the assembled Free Church leaders he spoke of the contemporary Anglican social thought of Henson and Temple, characteristically presenting their contrasting views as really 'two sides of the same thing'. Among Methodists he linked Wesleyanism with Tractarianism as the Oxford movements of successive centuries.[59] The style and purpose of this syncretism is well illustrated by a passage from a political speech in the Nonconformist heartland of Cornwall:

[The] dualism of the Church and the chapel taken together has been the most potent influence in the life of our country. The one fostering, perhaps, more than the other the respect for authority and tradition and the sense of historical continuity; the other laying its main emphasis on the individual obedience to the eternal law.

They ... had both been, and are, and will be great social forces with great political consequences. Both at their best penetrate life with serious purpose, and are in constant war with that spirit of secularism which finds its paradise in idleness and frivolity, with which no country can ever prosper.[60]

---

[57] Jones, *Three Score Years and Ten*, pp. 119–20 (May 1925); *TTF* p. 100 (30 Jan. 1929).
[58] *OE* pp. 269–70 (8 April 1924); *TTF* pp. 101–2 (30 Jan. 1929).
[59] *OE* pp. 198–9, 206–9 (7 May, 12 March 1925); *TTF* pp. 38, 94, 107 (14 July 1930, 1 Nov. 1928, 10 April 1929). That Baldwin was entering territory unfamiliar to Conservatives is indicated by his originally praising Clifford as the chief architect of the Baptist Union. In the reprinted version this was corrected to J. H. Shakespeare: compare report in *The Times*, 31 Jan. 1929, with *TTF* p. 101.
[60] Tregrehan, 23 June 1927.

The public faith which Baldwin wished to promote was the religion of the common man. The Christianity he commended was not one of institutional complications, ecclesiastical subtleties, or ascetic rejection of the world. It was 'a way of life and not an organisation', for 'numbers in a church and the riches of that church are as dust and ashes besides the daily life of unselfish devotion to the service of the brethren'.[61] It was the religion absorbed from the vernacular Bible and popular hymns, which through a 'reasoned balance between inward conviction and outward expression' became woven into the texture of everyday life.[62] It was a simple and 'practical religion', concerned less with sacred acts as such than with secular acts undertaken from a spiritual motive,[63] and accepting the world 'openly and joyously as a moral world where spirit and sense mingle inextricably, where passions are not to be escaped but tamed, where work, pleasure and wealth will find their proper place if subordinated to moral ends'.[64]

On occasion Baldwin described this religion through the example of the Wesleyanism of his parents' original persuasion, but it was also the incarnational Christianity of Maurice and Kingsley adopted by his father. It celebrated the 'spark of the Divine which exists in every human soul', and assumed the natural innocence, decency, and dignity of the ordinary man and woman.[65] It understood also that the wisdom which began with fear of the Lord and with forsaking evil was greater than the knowledge of the highly educated and the cleverness of the intellectual.

This was the deepest source of Baldwin's distaste for the 'intelligentsia'. He certainly did not devalue intelligence and learning in themselves. As a governor of several schools and chancellor, rector, or honorand of numerous universities, he spoke frequently of the importance of education, scholarship and intellectual freedom. To these, however, he linked 'piety' or 'wisdom' as equally

---

[61] *TTF* pp. 96, 99 (1 Nov. 1928).

[62] *TTF* pp. 90–1, 97 (quotation), 79 (2 May, 1 Nov. 1928, 12 May 1931); *OI* p. 80 (30 July 1927).

[63] *TTF* pp. 97, 80–1 (1 Nov. 1928, 12 May 1931).

[64] Fripp lecture, 26 Feb. 1932.

[65] *OE*, p. 201 (7 May 1925). Baldwin's few specific commendations of the Revised Prayer Book concerned its shift from an Old Testament to a New Testament spirit, notably the alteration of the phrase 'all men are conceived and born in sin' to 'all men are from their birth prone to sin': *HCDeb* 218, c. 1317 (14 June 1928).

important qualities.[66] The intelligence and education he attacked were rather those taking the common but debased forms of 'pride of intellect' and 'surfeit of mere knowledge'. These bred arrogance, presumptuousness, irreverence, 'crystalline hardness of soul', even sin.[67] They produced the intellectual – more especially the socialist intellectual – whose 'god was his intellect', who preached the 'worship of material things', and who would impose the 'terrorism' of putting his theory before people and of elevating the mass above the individual.[68]

These kinds of intelligence obstructed knowledge of human nature and appreciation of the 'innate decency of wisdom'. Worst of all they obscured the truth that goodness, understanding, and wisdom were democratic and found often, perhaps most often, among the humble and uneducated.[69] Doctrinaire socialist intellectuals deserved the greatest contempt, because they affected an exclusive sympathy for the working people and claimed a special loyalty from them – both of which were belied by their own dogmatism and by the large working-class support for the Conservative party. They were 'usurpers in the affections of the working-classes'.[70] Baldwin delighted in examples of moral vigour and common sense among ordinary men and women, and of how the supposedly illiterate were literate in their simple goodness and wisdom. The Worcestershire salutation, 'May God, good-will and good neighbourliness be your company', was a favourite.[71]

These qualities and this religious vision were the sources of Baldwin's belief in 'practical idealism', the elevated status and trust he gave to 'commonsense', and his love for and identification with the common people. They were also a further source of his acceptance of the burden of political service. Christian love, he wrote privately after the 1923 election defeat, was what

[66] University College, Aberystwyth, 24 Oct. 1928; *TTF* pp. 294–5, 302–3 (10 May 1930, 10 Oct. 1931).
[67] University College, Aberystwyth, 24 Oct. 1928; *HCDeb* 236, cc. 1538–9 (13 March 1930); *TTF* pp. 294–5 (10 May 1930); M&B p. 208.
[68] National Free Church Council, 8 April 1935; Baldwin in Butler memo, July 1935, Butler papers G6/57; Begbie, *Conservative Mind*, p. 24.
[69] University College, Aberystwyth, 24 Oct. 1928; *OE* p. 20 (7 Nov. 1923); *OI* pp. 124, 288 (6 Aug., 28 Oct. 1927).
[70] Begbie, *Conservative Mind*, p. 24.
[71] Baldwin to his mother, 25 Dec. 1911, BF; Jones *WD* II.21 (25 April 1926); *OI* pp. 283, 295–6 (22 Feb., 28 Oct. 1927).

alone makes it possible to carry on in public life . . . The longing to help the bewildered multitude of common folk is the only motive power to make me face the hundred and one things I loathe so much. And the longing to help only comes from love and pity.[72]

III

Baldwin spoke of the churches having a role in encouraging and provoking politicians to maintain the highest ideals in the conduct of government. This did not, however, mean that he considered religious leaders had special insight and authority on particular political issues, nor that they should 'take sides' on party questions. From his perspective, their advice should be detached, morally wise, non-partisan.[73] In practice, he assumed that this precluded criticism of fundamental Conservative positions, with the effect that he resented what he considered to be clerical 'interference'. The Archbishop of Canterbury's leadership of an Anglican–Free Church attempt to fulfil a non-partisan role during the General Strike – to create middle ground between the TUC and government – was discouraged. In contrast, the Roman Catholic Archbishop of Westminster was thanked for his outright condemnation of the Strike – a striking, but private, breach of Baldwin's natural Protestant loyalties.[74] Baldwin was much annoyed by the subsequent attempt by Temple and a group of fellow bishops and Free Church ministers to arbitrate in the coal dispute, stingingly comparing them to 'the Federation of British Industries . . . trying to bring about a reunion of the Particular Baptists with the Anglo-Catholics'.[75] This was not just because their intervention wrecked a chance of a settlement, but also because he thought it displayed blindness towards the danger from 'the latent atheist bolsheviks, like Cook'. It nearly cost Temple ecclesiastical promotion, though in 1929 Baldwin relented and offered him the Archbishopric of York with his customary courtesies.[76] Later, as

---

[72] Baldwin to Mrs Davidson, 24 Dec. 1923, in *Davidson Memoirs*, p. 193.

[73] *OE* pp. 208, 210 (12 March 1925).

[74] *Reith Diaries* p. 94 (7 May 1926); S. Mews, 'The Churches', in M. Morris, *The General Strike* (1976), pp. 326–7, 333.

[75] Norwich, 17 July 1926, and see Baldwin to Bishop Kempthorne, *The Times*, 19 July 1926. For the rebuke (with precise phrases mis-remembered) continuing to rankle, see W. Temple, *Christianity and Social Order* (1940; 1942 edn), p. 9.

[76] Jones *WD* II.63 (21 July 1926); Baldwin to Irwin, 15 Sept. 1927, Halifax Indian papers 17/253f; Iremonger, *Temple*, p. 359.

will be seen, he was similarly critical of Free Church ministers who joined in agitations on foreign policy during 1935.

Baldwin looked to the churches not to comment on policy but to assist 'responsible' political leaders in stimulating the spiritual life and self-reliance of individuals, and in regenerating the moral life of the nation.[77] He also expected them to teach 'that real Christian brotherhood ... which does not recognise class'.[78] In the age of the French and Industrial Revolutions, Wesleyan Methodism was supposed to have 'stood between England and the monstrous upheavals on the Continent', to have 'arrested social cleavage by uniting all grades of society in the bonds of a common religious ideal', and to have generated a commitment to public service and in time produced 'the best types of labour and co-operative leaders'.[79] As in the past, so in the present: the modern contribution of the churches to public life was to help preserve the country's ideals and moral cohesion in the face of the post-war secularism and materialism which were the roots of modern political 'heresies'. Above all, by preaching the ideal of the Kingdom of Heaven the churches helped to dispel the disease of despair and to sustain the faith which enabled individuals to perform their work and duties, and without which 'as a people we shall go down and perish for lack of vision'.[80]

Baldwin did not identify Christianity with Conservatism, and was far from denying the presence of good Christians in other parties and in none. But he did mean that while Christians might disagree over large areas of policy, consistency required all of them to unite in upholding the fundamentals of ordered freedom and individual responsibility, together with their corollary – acceptance of economic and social inequalities, however moderated. He also meant that on the whole Conservatism, as re-spiritualised under his leadership, was the political creed most firmly based upon and most consistent with Christian values, and was therefore the appropriate rallying point for the great majority of the nation in the face of new threats to those values. More precisely, from the moment when, during the first Labour government, Baldwin spoke to the Nonconformist Unionist

[77] *OE* pp. 206–9 (12 March 1925); *TTF* pp. 85–7 (12 May 1931).
[78] Church of Scotland General Assembly, 7 June 1926.
[79] *TTF* p. 95 (1 Nov. 1928); *OI* p. 57 (23 June 1927); *Englishman*, pp. 26–7.
[80] *OE* p. 211 (12 March 1925); also Conservative conference, 25 Oct. 1923.

League,[81] there was a recurrent appeal to religious Liberals – all
the more effective because left implicit when he addressed Free
Church meetings – to join with Conservatives against a 'socialism'
which, whatever its expressed higher ideals, was assumed to be
materialistic and divisive in practice, and against the frankly anti-
Christian doctrines of communism and fascism.

Nor did Baldwin identify Christianity with 'Britishness'. Nevertheless, he expressed a common British belief that Protestantism
had in some special sense 'made' the nation, and the English
Reformation conviction – still, in semi-secularised forms, central
to national ideology – that the Lord had peculiarly favoured the
English and charged them with special tasks. Two things had, he
said, done most to form the national character and the national
community. First, the Scottish and especially the English Refor-
mations had broken the divine right not just of the Pope but also –
in time – of kings.[82] Secondly, the special power of the English
Bible had 'penetrated the life and thought of our people in the
seventeenth century and transformed their daily experience, . . .
shaped [their] lives and coloured [their] traditions', so that 'consciousness of human weakness and dependence on God stamped
itself on the English character'.[83] From these foundations had
come the twin pillars of national greatness and social cohesion:
not merely ordered freedom, but an imperative conscience. 'Deep
down in every British heart, irrespective of party, lies a profound
sense of what we believe to be right . . . it is one of the most potent
forces in our lives'.[84] The 'lay religion' of the English people was
'Conduct and Duty'.[85]

The 'English secret', he declared, was acceptance of the Christian doctrine of the 'essential dignity of the individual human
soul'. This explained the nation's historic success, and the British
Empire's continuing existence.[86] To a providentialist such gifts –
British exceptionalism, political stability, evolutionary progress,
and large global responsibilities – were evidence of immanent
meaning and transcendent duties. Baldwin like Halifax and many

[81] 6 April 1924.
[82] Youth Conference on Democracy, 3 Feb. 1939; *Interpreter*, pp. 49–50, 53–5.
[83] *TTF* p. 90 (2 May 1928); *Interpreter*, pp. 19–20. See also Rhodes Trust dinner, 16 June
1923; *TTF* p. 148; *Englishman*, pp. 14–15, 17.
[84] *HCDeb* 167, c. 1820 (2 Aug. 1923).
[85] *Englishman*, p. 17; and see *OE* p. 72; *TTF* pp. 81–2, 85; *Interpreter*, pp. 20–1, 23–4.
[86] *SOL* pp. 164–6 (18 May 1937).

other leading Conservatives and Liberals was a 'Christian imperialist', in the sense of assuming that the Empire had a profound significance. 'The history of mankind', he declared, 'was not a purposeless history. It was a manifestation of the Divine purpose.' They were therefore 'bound to think of [the British Empire] less as a human achievement than as an instrument of Divine Providence for the promotion of the progress of mankind'.[87] Although Baldwin supported Bible and missionary societies, like other Conservatives he probably thought that within the dependent Empire the providential task was fulfilled less in direct efforts to convert 'the heathen', than in a practical witness to Christian civilisation provided by the service and trusteeship of British colonial administrators.[88] In the world more generally, he believed that both the past and the present revealed a still more fundamental mission. Britain was 'ready once more to lead the way of the world as she was destined to do from the beginning of time, and to show other peoples . . . what real political freedom is'.[89]

---

[87] Congregational Overseas Dominions meeting, 8 May 1929; *TTF* p. 26 (imperial broadcast, Empire Day, 1929).

[88] Congregational Overseas Dominion meeting, 8 May 1929, and see *OE* pp. 185–90; *TTF* pp. 82, 103–4, 285–6.

[89] *OE* p. 154 (23 Sept. 1923).

CHAPTER 10

Armaments and anti-totalitarianism

While Baldwin had a strong sense of British identity and interests and was suspicious of internationalism, this did not mean he had an insular mind, still less – as was asserted in the 1940s and 1950s – that he was inattentive towards international problems and 'did not like foreigners of any kind'.[1] His engagement with foreign and defence issues differed little from his treatment of domestic and imperial issues. He participated in a collective decision-making process; when major difficulties arose he thought hard about the fundamentals; and he was imaginative in seeking public consent to government objectives. As the international crisis developed from 1933 he was sensitive not just to the diplomatic and military threats, but also – unusually so – to the ideological and moral challenges. These threats and challenges had profound domestic implications, which he believed could be contained only by creating an even stronger consciousness of 'national unity' than that which had been mobilised against the socialist and trade-union threats of the 1920s.

I

Baldwin's presentations of 'Englishness' – constructed for particular political and moral purposes – should not obscure the realities of his personal experience and his ministerial objectives, nor even his wider public positions. He was not among Kipling's patriots 'who only England know'. Before 1914 he had travelled to North America and around central Europe on business, and spent several

---

[1] GMY pp. 61, 62–3, is typical nonsense, but the quotation from Jones *DL* p.xxxiii is more remarkable, as he certainly knew better. Perhaps by the early 1950s it was too easy to remember Baldwin's more off-hand comments, and misunderstand his misgivings about Jones's attempts to arrange a meeting between him and Hitler.

weeks each winter and summer in Switzerland, Italy, Germany, or France. For all his attachment to rural Worcestershire, he preferred after 1921 to resume his earlier habit of long summer holidays in France, normally at Aix-les-Bains. In private he was every bit as lyrical about the Swiss Alps or French hills as he was about the English countryside.[2] He was fluent in French and well acquainted with French literature.[3] He understood some German, had a conventional love for German classical music, and on his 1898 tour visited the Reichstag and tried to appreciate Wagner.[4] His interests in the ancient classics and in history gave further dimensions to a conception of Britain as part of European culture and politics.[5]

In his public teachings patriotism was a vital quality, but one he distinguished from what he called the 'curse' of chauvinism. Nations should be themselves and resist any foreign ideas likely to corrode their essence, yet they should also respect and benefit from the best features of other nations. Love of one's own country should not be perverted into hatred of other countries. 'No nation can live unto itself alone and flourish. No nation has achieved anything worth while except with the help of others. You love your own country best and serve humanity most not when you despise the achievements of other nations, but when you accept them and fuse them with your own national genius and personality.'[6] Baldwin certainly spoke of Britain as having a unique history, a superior national character, the best political institutions, and a providential mission. But he spoke also of how it had been shaped by early invasions of continental races and by modern relations with continental states.[7]

'Let us never forget this', Baldwin said in June 1923, 'that while we are Englishmen, Scotsmen, Welshmen, Irishmen, we are at the

---

[2] E.g. Baldwin to his mother, 20 May 1912, and to W. Baldwin, 22 Sept. 1922, BF; AWB pp. 113–14, 128–9.

[3] For literature, Carrington, *Kipling*, p. 552; Butler memo, 20–21 July 1935, Butler papers G6/57.

[4] Family papers show that he took German lessons in the late 1880s and 1890s, but by the 1930s he did not trust himself to speak it with German representatives: *DGFP* series C, VI.759–60. He took the precaution of using an interpreter when he met Poincaré in 1923. M&B pp. 33–4 add an ability to read some Russian.

[5] E.g. *OE* pp. 99–118 (8 Jan. 1926).

[6] *OI* pp. 48–9, 51–2 (1 March 1927); cf. *TTF* pp. 14, 282–3 (25 Sept. 1935, 20 Jan. 1930).

[7] *TTF* pp. 7–11 (25 Sept. 1933); cf. *OE* pp. 102–8 (8 Jan. 1926); *Interpreter*, pp. 11–17.

same time Europeans.'[8] One Cabinet colleague thought him 'much less insular-minded' than Sir Edward Grey, and reported him saying in the early 1920s that his ideal in foreign policy was to be a 'good European'.[9] He knew that, even if isolation had ever been desirable or practicable, another effect of the Great War had been the economic and physical destruction of that isolation. In the 1920s British economic recovery – and therefore social and political stability – depended upon reconstruction in continental Europe. More basically still, he was acutely conscious that 'our island story is told'. For 'with the advent of the aeroplane we ceased to be an island. Whether we like it or not, we are indissolubly bound to Europe'.[10] Despite, or correctly understood, because of, Britain's vast extra-European interests and commitments, it had to be a diplomatic force on the continent – 'to act, in the words of Disraeli, as "a moderating and mediatorial Power" in the Councils of Europe'.[11] In the face of rearming continental states after 1933, he attacked isolationist ideas as 'crude', 'childish', 'a most dangerous heresy'.[12] During the run up to the 1935 election his answer to isolationist imperialists in his own party was that 'the maintenance of the Empire' depended upon 'the maintenance of [the] heart of the Empire in Europe'.[13] Against isolationists of the left and centre he argued that if Britain were to stand wholly alone in Europe, it would have to turn itself into an 'armed camp' and 'give up all hope of . . . social progress'.[14] Britain simply could not afford 'to refuse to play our part in the continent in which the hand of God has placed us'.[15] He had already defined the strategic implications in July 1934:

since the day of the air, the old frontiers are gone. When you think of the defence of England you no longer think of the chalk cliffs of Dover: you think of the Rhine. That is where our frontier lies.[16]

None of this meant that Baldwin thought he should initiate or

[8] Oxford, 8 June 1923.
[9] Percy, *Some Memories*, p. 133.
[10] *OE* p. 235 (23 July 1923). Cf. *ibid.* p. 24 (5 March 1925).
[11] Imperial Conference, 1 Oct. 1923.
[12] Conservative conferences, 6 Oct. 1933, 4 Oct. 1935.
[13] Conservative conference, 4 Oct. 1935.
[14] Wolverhampton, 28 Oct. 1935; *TTF* pp. 325–8 (31 Oct. 1935).
[15] Conservative conference, 4 Oct. 1935.
[16] *HCDeb* 292, c. 2339 (30 July 1934).

conduct foreign policy himself. As chairman or senior member of the Cabinet, the Committee of Imperial Defence and their various disarmament and defence sub-committees, he presided over the collective supervision of the Foreign Office and armed services departments. By 1933 no minister had more experience at the highest levels of the foreign and defence policy machinery, nor – given his wartime 'spy committee' work – with the intelligence services. From meetings with officials, defence experts, and publicists, and from official and social contacts with foreign ambassadors and diplomatic intermediaries,[17] he was better informed than he often seemed to be. He would confer with British Embassy staff in Paris and with French ministers on his way to or from his holidays in Aix-les-Bains,[18] where he received visits from ministers and officials attending League of Nations conferences at Geneva.[19] Nor did he doubt his ability, when he thought it appropriate, to take a leading part in international diplomacy. During his first four months as prime minister in 1923 his main ambitions were European, to resolve the Ruhr crisis and achieve Franco-German reconciliation – work which contributed towards the Dawes Conference in 1924. After Anglo-American relations crumbled in the hands of Austen Chamberlain and Bridgeman in 1927–8, he intended, if successful at the next election, to visit Washington and take naval disarmament into his own hands[20] – exactly as MacDonald was to do after the Conservative defeat. He also became engaged when he could not feel full confidence in foreign secretaries. In 1923 he re-drafted some of Curzon's major diplomatic statements, and dealt directly with the French president.[21] From 1932 to 1935 he was among the senior ministers who helped an indecisive Simon make up his mind.[22] Throughout the whole period, where he felt clear commitments his opinion was decisive –

---

[17] E.g. Baldwin to Joan Davidson, 15 April 1928, 13 March 1937, JD; Jones *DL* pp. 152–3, 289 (1 June 1935, 25 Nov. 1936); *DGFP* series C, I.165–6, VI.759–60 (15 March 1933, 13 May 1937), and see M&B 344–5, 735, 749, 779.

[18] E.g. *Davidson Memoirs*, p. 198 (14 Sept. 1925); Baldwin to Joan Davidson, 19 Sept. 1928, JD; Jones *DL* p. 115 (14 Sept. 1933); *DBFP* 2s., V.612 (22 Sept. 1933).

[19] E.g. A. Chamberlain to Baldwin, 12 Sept. 1927, SB 129/13–16; Baldwin to Joan Davidson, 8 Sept. 1934, JD.

[20] Jones *WD* II.155, 156, 161 (1, 12 Nov., 5 Dec. 1928).

[21] *Amery Diaries* I.334 (12, 19 July 1923); M&B pp. 187–90, 193–201.

[22] Jones diary, 17 Nov. 1934; A. *Chamberlain Diary Letters*, pp. 445, 480 (3 July 1933, 6 April 1935).

whether on the Locarno pact in 1925 or the Anglo-German naval
treaty in 1935.

Nevertheless Baldwin was untouched and untempted by
illusions about the grandeur of foreign policy. After his meeting
with Poincaré in September 1923 had shown that international
tensions would not yield to his style of personal goodwill,[23] he was
confirmed in his view that diplomacy was a murky and treacherous
activity demanding specialist knowledge and intuitive grasp. As in
domestic policy-making, his supposed aloofness was not disregard
of duty but deliberate choice. He did not lack cogent views of his
own on the main foreign and armaments issues, but he judged
that – under general Cabinet scrutiny – the detailed proposals and
the negotiations were best left to the responsible ministers and
officials. This would also avoid the kind of damage to British policy
caused, as he believed, by Lloyd George's prime-ministerial med-
dling.[24] So he 'never professed to be an expert in foreign affairs'[25]
but gave his trust and support successively to Austen Chamberlain, Hoare, and Eden. With these, his contribution towards policy-
making was one 'much more of general reflection than of specific
suggestion'.[26] Given other pressures, he did not pretend to a particular interest during periods when nothing of special importance
was happening, especially after the Dawes Conference and
Locarno Pact seemed to have fulfilled his 1923 desire to 'settle
Europe'.[27] Foreign secretaries and officials fascinated with their
craft could be exasperated by such detachment, and even mistake
it for general disinterest. At the end of his ministerial career,
cursed with hindsight about the continued deterioration in European relations, he did come to regret that he had not asserted
himself more in foreign affairs.[28] Nonetheless when on 20 May
1936 Baldwin told Eden he wanted better relations with Hitler
and to Eden's question of 'how?', replied 'I have no idea, that is
your job', this expressed an intelligible view of the different func-

[23] His trust in sincerity and frankness is even clearer in the original French typescript, 19
Sept. 1923, SB 108/41–60, than his official version in *DBFP* 1s., xxi.529–34.
[24] E.g. Cecil memo., 30 March 1926, Cecil papers 51080.
[25] 1936 comment in M&B p. 806. Cf. AWB p. 317.
[26] Simon diary, 19 Feb. 1938. Cf. A. *Chamberlain Diary Letters*, pp. 264, 456–7; Viscount
Templewood, *Nine Troubled Years* (1954), p. 167; The Earl of Avon, *The Eden Memoirs.
Facing the Dictators* (1962) (cited hereafter as *Facing the Dictators*), p. 298.
[27] E.g. Vansittart, *Mist Procession*, pp. 347, 351, 359.
[28] R. Boothby, *Recollections of a Rebel* (1978), p. 126; AWB p. 317.

tions of prime minister and foreign secretary. Yet he was also prevaricating, because in reality he was extremely interested in a new possibility – a secret invitation to meet Hitler which, unbeknown to Eden, Tom Jones had brought from Germany earlier that morning.[29]

II

In understanding that isolation from Europe was impossible, Baldwin did not conclude that Britain should be ready to fight on the continent, nor that it should enter into alliance commitments with other states. Among the most striking features of his public statements were his cataclysmic prophecies about the effects of another European war. These served obvious political purposes after 1933 – simultaneously establishing credentials with peace opinion, soothing isolationists, justifying rearmament as a deterrence, and answering advocates of military alliances. Their sources nevertheless ran much deeper than mere political expediency. His own horror at the slaughter and moral degeneration of the Great War and his anxieties about its social and political consequences were projected into a dread of any future war, the more so because of his revulsion against further developments in military technology. The effect – a profound attachment to peace – dominated his responses to the foreign crises of the 1930s, and created considerable tensions in both his policy attitudes and his public statements.

Again and again during the 1920s and 1930s he said that as the Great War had shaken civilisation, so a second great war would 'be the end of civilisation'.[30] Between 1914 and 1918 the instincts of the primeval savage had erupted through the thin surface of modern human nature. Even the most decent societies were brutalised. The British public had been shocked by German poison-gas attacks and bombing raids on cities, yet it soon tolerated and even demanded their use by British forces.[31] The modern

---

[29] Avon, *Facing the Dictators*, p. 374 (diary, 20 May 1936); Jones *DL* pp. 202, 205–9, 218 (20, 22–3 May, 8 June 1936).

[30] E.g. *OE* pp. 106, 229–30; Aberdeen, 5 Nov. 1925; *HCDeb* 270, c. 638 (10 Nov. 1932); Conservative conference, 6 Oct. 1933; Primrose League, 3 May 1935; Wishaw, 20 June 1936.

[31] *OE* pp. 227–30 (23 July 1923); League of Nations Union, 26 Oct. 1928; *HCDeb* 270, cc. 631, 634–5 (10 Nov. 1932).

interdependence of nations and the mobility and range of modern
weapons had now made war between great powers almost impossible to localise: 'if that fire is ever lighted again on the Continent
no man can tell where the heather will stop burning'.[32] The
increased 'prostitution of science to the service of barbarism'
meant there could be 'no limited liability' in a new, still more
terrible sense. Now 'every man, woman and child' had become
vulnerable.[33] In May 1935 he told the House of Commons that
while studying air-raid precautions he had

been made almost physically sick to think that I and my friends and the
statesmen in every country in Europe, 2,000 years after our Lord was
crucified, should be spending our time thinking how we can get the
mangled bodies of children to the hospitals and how we can keep the
poison gas from going down the throats of the people.[34]

Another war, he said later, would cause 'misery compared with
which the misery of the last War was happiness'. Across Europe
peoples would 'revolt against all their leaders', and the continent
would be reduced to a 'state of barbarous anarchy from end to
end'.[35]

On the diplomacy for avoiding catastrophe, Baldwin's views
were a version of those distilled collectively in Cabinet: to contain
the German threat by a combination of conciliation and checks. It
was accepted that Germany had real grievances, even, Baldwin
came to think, that the 'Versailles peace was iniquitous'.[36] But
treaty revisions should be by agreement among the European
powers, and be dependent upon further agreements: both regional
pacts of mutual guarantee – as in the Locarno pact, and its proposed extensions – and multilateral disarmament or, later, bi-
lateral arms limitation, as in the Anglo-German naval agreement
and proposed air conventions. Like other ministers he thought
part of the problem was the attitude of the French: the excessive
price they demanded for their own security, their pact with Soviet
Russia in 1935, and their efforts to drag Britain into alliance sys-

[32] Wishaw, 20 June 1936. Cf. *TTF* p. 326 (31 Oct. 1935); *SOL* pp. 41–2 (2 July 1936).
[33] National Free Church Council, 8 April 1935; Worcester, 18 April 1936. Cf. election
broadcast, 25 Oct. 1935; Women's Unionist conference, 14 May 1936.
[34] *HCDeb* 302, cc. 372–3 (22 May 1935).
[35] Wishaw, 20 June 1936; Guildhall, 9 Nov. 1936. Cf. *Interpreter*, p. 113.
[36] Jones *DL* p. 227 (7 July 1936).

tems that would divide Europe into two hostile camps – a cause, it was generally believed, of the Great War. He was also resistant to those in the Foreign Office he thought 'obsessed' by a belief that Germany was inevitably hostile.[37] His own primary sense in 1934–5 was that 'no one knows what the new Germany means – whether she means peace or war'.[38] It followed that the appropriate strategy was to prepare for all possibilities. Baldwin knew the Nazi regime was unpleasant – he received, and asked for, numerous reports on German conditions – and would be hard to keep to its pledges.[39] Rearmament and close diplomatic relations with France and other Western powers were necessary precautions. But he also thought Hitler might want peace, and so was determined to keep 'the door open for Germany to enter into any possible collective system of security'.[40]

Towards Hitler, he was conscious of the difficulty in knowing 'what goes on in that strange man's mind'.[41] Initially the main danger seemed to be that he was ignorant and inexperienced in foreign affairs, so Baldwin was 'very anxious indeed' that personal contact should be established with him.[42] In the winter of 1933–4, as again during May 1936, he seriously considered unofficial invitations to visit him. But each time he eventually consulted the foreign secretary, and accepted Simon's and then Eden's advice not to pursue them. During the first period the doubt arose precisely from the naivety of German proposals, during the second because it seemed one could 'not believe a word they say'.[43] On both occasions it was probably also thought that such a high-level meeting might strengthen Hitler's position, while arousing suspicion from the French and other friendly governments (though Baldwin possibly intended a private meeting after his

---

[37] Jones diary, 27 Feb. 1934, referring to Vansittart and Tyrrell.
[38] Crozier, *Off the Record*, p. 27 (12 June 1934). Cf. Jones *DL* p. 129 (28 April 1934); Jones diary, 18 Sept. 1935.
[39] Jones diary, 21 April, 5 Aug. 1935. See SB 120–3 for reports, some requested by Baldwin.
[40] Jones diary, 27 Feb. 1934, 21 April 1935. Cf. Crozier, *Off the Record*, p. 27 (12 June 1934).
[41] Address to Conservative defence deputation (hereafter 'Conservative deputation'), 29 July 1936, *WSC Comp* v/iii.290.
[42] Baldwin in Cabinet committee, 15 Dec. 1933, 5 Feb. 1934, in M&B pp. 750, 751.
[43] Conservative deputation, 29 July 1936, *WSC Comp* v/iii.291. For 1933–4, E. Tennant, *True Account* (1957), pp. 164–72; Davidson memos, Jan, 11 Feb. 1934, JCCD 205. For 1936, Jones *DL* pp. 194–210, 214–15, 218, 224 (May–June 1936).

retirement[44]). Instead, he encouraged the visits to Berlin by Eden in February 1934 and Simon and Eden in March 1935. After the German re-occupation of the Rhineland in March 1936 he thought that if the French could be stopped from 'letting loose another Great War', Hitler might now consider himself satisfied and accept a general settlement.[45] If not, if there was to be war, his hope was that Hitler would do as he had written in *Mein Kampf* and direct his ambitions towards Eastern Europe.[46]

If for Baldwin one purpose of British diplomacy was to preserve a general European peace, his more basic aim – given the horrors of modern warfare – was to keep Britain clear of any war that did not threaten its own strategic frontiers. His public statements that war could not be localised did not mean that he thought Britain should automatically join a war on the other side of the continent. Nor should Britain be dragged into a Mediterranean war, nor – despite German and Italian as well as Russian breaches of non-intervention agreements – should it allow the Spanish civil war to 'set the whole of Western Europe on fire',[47] the more so because Italy and Spain were distractions from the greatest threat to itself. His private view was that British interests demanded ultimate support only for the Low Countries and France. Only if Hitler went 'stark mad' and chose to attack in the West should Britain 'have to try and get everybody against' the Germans and 'have the whole of Europe in the war again'. Otherwise, Baldwin was 'not going to get this country into a war with anybody for the League of Nations or anybody else or for anything else'.[48] After the proximity of war over Czechoslovakia finally led a British prime minister to meet Hitler, Baldwin publicly praised Chamberlain's visits and the Munich pact because if there 'were a 95 per cent. chance of war . . . I would hold to the 5 per cent. till I died'.[49]

[44] Blomberg memo, 13 May 1937, *DGFP* series C, VI.759–60, reports Baldwin as volunteering this suggestion with some keenness. The report is hard to assess. No other source indicates such a desire, and these may simply have been placatory words. But it might have been a real ambition, delayed by his post-retirement exhaustion and then made to seem unnecessary by Halifax's meeting with Hitler in November 1937.
[45] Baldwin in Cabinet 18(36), 11 March 1936.
[46] Conservative deputation, 29 July 1936, *WSC Comp* v/iii.290, 291. Cf. Hinchingbroke note, Oct. 1938, in M&B p. 1047.
[47] *HCDeb* 316, cc. 151–2 (29 Oct. 1936).
[48] Conservative deputation, 29 July 1936, *WSC Comp* v/iii.289, 290–1. Cf. Cabinet committee, 17 May 1934, in M&B p. 768; Jones *DL* pp. 191, 206 (30 April, 23 May 1936).
[49] *HLDeb* 110, c. 1392 (4 Oct. 1938). Cf. Baldwin to N. Chamberlain, 15, 26, 30 Sept. 1938, NC 13/11/618–20, for support and congratulations.

Like most leading Conservatives, Baldwin had always been ambivalent towards the League of Nations. The League Covenant, disarmament, and collective security were ideals which Britain should play a part in turning into practice. They also served British interests by underpinning the international *status quo*. But because not all the major powers were members, the League could not yet deliver universal disarmament nor complete security. Accordingly, Britain would best sustain its unusual global responsibilities for peace by safeguarding imperial defence and pursuing more limited regional agreements. Given the great public faith in the League of Nations, this attitude meant that a tightrope had to be walked between displaying a commitment towards it, yet restraining innocent enthusiasm and excessive expectations.[50] Here the League of Nations Union – the all-party focus for British public support of disarmament and the League – had a particular capacity to irritate and embarrass. Whenever possible Baldwin avoided addressing its meetings, because he felt difficulty in 'steer[ing] between the Scylla of cursing them and the Charybdis of mush and poppycock'.[51]

The difficulties raised by the League became more acute as the international order faced greater challenges. As chairman of the Cabinet Far Eastern committee during the Japanese attack on Shanghai in early 1932, Baldwin became convinced that with the USA and Russia outside the League and so under no obligation to assist collective security, 'sanctions are a mistake' and could not be enforced against a 'first-class power'. League enthusiasts failed to grasp that without full co-operation from all other states, enforcement of economic sanctions would require a naval blockade. This would risk escalation into war, as either the original aggressor retaliated or else non-League trading nations resisted. The risk would fall largely upon Britain as the greatest naval power, yet it lacked the resources to act as the League's chief armed agent as well as fulfilling its own strategic commitments.[52] By early 1933 Baldwin could not 'make up his mind whether the League has helped or hindered peace'.[53]

---

[50] E.g. *OE* pp. 230–4 (23 July 1923); Primrose League, 2 May 1924; League of Nations Union, 26 Oct. 1928; three-party disarmament meeting, 11 July 1931.
[51] Baldwin to A. Chamberlain, 17 Feb. 1933, AC 40/5/13. SB 133 contains numerous refusals of invitations.
[52] M&B pp. 727–9.
[53] Jones *DL* p. 93 (19 Feb. 1933).

He thought the Americans were the main 'devils of the piece'.[54] Here his views were still more ambivalent. He understood that in international affairs Britain had become ultimately dependent upon the United States. In public he celebrated Anglo-American friendship, and spoke of his deep thankfulness when American troops arrived in 1917.[55] During the phase of war-debt settlements and reparations' revisions in the mid 1920s, when Britain needed American financial goodwill, he evoked the 'common ideals' of the 'English-speaking peoples' – the American share in English freedoms – as the basis for the 'salvation' of the world.[56] Yet this sense of dependence also generated private irritation at what he considered to be the United States's shortcomings in fulfilling its international obligations – and, more importantly, strengthened his sense of the dangers of Britain's position in the 1930s. His real feelings in 1917 had been distaste at celebrations of 'the entry of an ally nearly three years too late'.[57] He thought Europe's post-war troubles were 'to a very great extent due to the withdrawal of America' from its promises to guarantee the peace.[58] The Far Eastern crisis in 1932 confirmed that it was 'completely useless in international matters'; Americans offered 'nothing . . . but words, big words, but only words'.[59] Nevertheless, unlike Chamberlain he assumed they always had to be taken into account. Given also the threat from Japan – its ability, as he put it, to 'knock us out in the Pacific and land in Australia'[60] – and the Japanese and German departures from the League of Nations during 1933, American unhelpfulness greatly increased the risks of practical action to support the League. During Cabinet discussions on French security in 1934 Baldwin took it as 'generally accepted that sanctions meant war', and insisted that they could not be contemplated without American participation.[61]

Only reluctantly during 1935, as Germany became still more

[54] Jones *DL* p. 57 (14 Sept. 1932).
[55] E.g. *OE* pp. 259–60 (25 April 1925).
[56] E.g. *The Times*, 1 March 1923; Rhodes Trust, 16 June 1923.
[57] Baldwin to his mother, 20 April 1917, 6 April 1918, BF.
[58] *The Political Diaries of C. P. Scott 1911–1928*, ed. T. Wilson (1970), p. 445 (26 Oct. 1923). Cf. Jones *DL* p. 191 (30 April 1936).
[59] Baldwin to Cecil, 12 March 1933, Cecil papers 51080; Jones *DL* p. 30 (27 Feb. 1932). Cf. Jones diary, 27 Feb. 1934; and 'anti-America' in James, *Cazalet*, p. 179 (13 Feb. 1936).
[60] Jones diary, 27 Feb. 1932.
[61] Cabinet committees, 28 March, 1, 17 May 1934, in M&B pp. 754, 767, 768.

menacing and as Italian aggression in Abyssinia threatened to wreck the League completely, did Baldwin allow himself to be persuaded by Hoare and Eden and by hopes of American co-operation that collective security and economic sanctions had to be tried. Even then he accepted a risk of war only on a Cabinet understanding that Britain must not fight Italy alone and that Anglo-French efforts to achieve a settlement should continue. The public objective was an 'honourable' cessation of the Abyssinian war, agreeable to the combatants and the League.[62] The Hoare–Laval crisis in December 1935, followed six months later by the Abyssinian defeat and the British abandonment of sanctions, exposed just how precarious this attempt to balance between conflicting hopes and fears had been. However, the larger source of those policy débâcles lay in the manner in which the League of Nations was drawn into the politics of rearmament.

III

For Baldwin, the vital armaments issue was that of air forces. Sharing prevailing British military and political opinion, he spoke of aerial explosive, incendiary, and gas bombardment as first-strike weapons, aimed at civilians, capable of delivering a decisive 'knock-out blow', and – before radar detection of aircraft – impossible to stop once an attack was launched. Bomber aircraft had removed the protection of the English Channel. They were also the principal cause of the fear which de-stabilised continental European relations.[63] He felt so strongly on the matter that he 'wished every aeroplane could be destroyed, and never another built'.[64] In 1932 he not only proposed international abolition of air forces in Cabinet. He was also prepared to suspend his suspicion of international assemblies, giving some thought to presenting the plan himself to the Disarmament Conference.[65]

In the event, the internal and diplomatic objections were too

---

[62] Cabinets 43, 47, 50(35), 24 Sept., 16 Oct., 2 Dec. 1935; N. Chamberlain diary, 29 Nov. 1935; *HCDeb* 307, cc. 65–6 (3 Dec. 1935).

[63] E.g. *HCDeb* 270, cc. 631–8 (10 Nov. 1932); 286, c. 2076 (8 March 1934); 302, cc. 371–2 (22 May 1935).

[64] Jones *WD* II.155 (1 Nov. 1928). Cf. *HCDeb* 270, c. 635 (10 Nov. 1932); Junior Imperial League, 23 March 1935.

[65] Cabinets 26–7, 30–1(32), 4, 11 May, 1, 7 June 1932; Bialer, *Shadow of the Bomber*, ch. 1; Roskill, *Hankey* III.63 (13 Nov. 1932).

great for him to persist. Characteristically, Baldwin considered the objections, especially the argument that it would be circumvented by conversion of civilian aircraft to military use, to be at root psychological and ethical matters. It was at this level that he thought he could best contribute. In his view the problems were that mankind never renounced its inventions, and more particularly that younger men had an unthinking enthusiasm for flying. Nevertheless some way had to be found to 'Christianise' the use of aircraft.[66] For this reason his House of Commons speech on aerial warfare in November 1932 – 'the bomber will always get through' – was deliberately dramatic. He wished to shock the consciences of wide British and continental audiences, in the hope of provoking a moral upsurge, especially among the young – a tide of opinion which might make international control of civil aviation possible, as the precondition of aerial disarmament.[67]

The hope was always extremely optimistic, and over the next year it shrivelled in the face of still harsher realities. After Germany left the Disarmament Conference in October 1933, the fears which had produced Baldwin's focus upon international aerial *dis*armament switched to concentration upon British aerial *re*armament. His determination to avoid war now developed into a leading role in defence and rearmament policies, as his aim became 'peace at almost any price, but at the same time to be ready that no man might attack them'.[68] In a July 1934 Cabinet committee he said that 'at all costs we must put ourselves in a position to make it extremely difficult for Germany to attack us suddenly'.[69]

In speaking with 'appalling frankness' in November 1936, Baldwin's retrospective account of 1933–4 was distorted by the intervening years of international deterioration, enlarged arms programmes and Churchillian criticisms – and by misjudged rhetorical ambition. He deliberately understated the earlier phase of rearmament, and superfluously yet damagingly entered into hypo-

[66] Cabinet 26(32), 4 May 1932; Primrose League, 23 March 1935.
[67] *HCDeb* 270, cc. 632–8 (10 Nov. 1932). For gestation, Jones *DL* pp. 57, 64 (14, 27 Sept. 1932); Roskill, *Hankey* III.63–4 (13 Nov. 1932).
[68] Glasgow overflow meeting, 18 Nov. 1936. He became acting chairman of the ministerial committee assessing the first Defence Requirements Committee report, May–July 1934, and chairman of the Defence Policy and Requirements Committee from March 1935 and of the Committee on Foreign Policy and Defence from January 1936.
[69] Bialer, *Shadow of the Bomber*, p. 51. Cf. Crozier, *Off the Record*, p. 27 (12 June 1934).

thetical reflections about why a programme of 1936 proportions had not been introduced and an election mandate not sought in 1934 – at a time when no one, not even Churchill, had considered either of these to be at issue.[70] In fact during 1934 itself, German intentions were uncertain; any military threat was estimated to be four or five years away, and serious arms limitation negotiation still seemed possible. In these circumstances Neville Chamberlain's arguments for beginning with an expansion of the Royal Air Force rather than the army and navy were compelling, and these conformed to Baldwin's and the Cabinet's strategic assumptions and diplomatic ambitions. In any armed confrontation with Germany, it seemed obvious that France would provide continental land defence and that Britain's main defence force would be the RAF. A large capacity for air defence and counter-attack would deter an attempted 'knock-out blow' and help bring Hitler to negotiations on treaty revision and arms limitation, thereby removing the need for wholesale rearmament. Given those views, the lower financial cost of an air deterrence mattered a great deal at a time when continued recovery from economic depression and financial crisis still seemed essential for internal stability and international strength. Expanding the RAF was also regarded as the most important and expedient form of rearmament in terms of domestic opinion, by allaying what Baldwin described as the 'semi-panic' fears of the public about their vulnerability to bomber attacks.[71]

Even so the Cabinet and its advisors anticipated considerable criticism, which they feared could mount into a crippling political opposition and perhaps even non-cooperation from the labour movement. Baldwin himself thought that on peace and armaments much of the electorate was as unsophisticated or utopian, and potentially as volatile and disruptive, as he had earlier believed it to be on economic and social matters. Consequently as the Disarmament Conference began to break down during 1933 the by-election setbacks fell into a pattern he and other ministers had expected, a pattern to which – as remained apparent in his

---

[70] *HCDeb* 317, cc. 1144–5 (12 Nov. 1936).
[71] Cabinet committee, 2 July 1934, in Bialer, *Shadow of the Bomber*, p. 51. There were some differences between Baldwin and Chamberlain, with Baldwin initially wanting more rearmament and more attention to Far Eastern defence: M&B p. 771. For the agreed rationale, see Gibbs, *Rearmament Policy*, pp. 105–7, 110, 533–9, 809.

November 1936 speech – he was highly sensitive. In one sense the position seemed still more brittle than in the mid 1920s. The attachment to disarmament and peace was strong not only among labour leaders and the working classes, but also in the moral and religious opinion of the middle classes; and it was mobilised not just by the Labour party, but by the Liberal opposition and the non-party League of Nations Union. The 'national unity' and Conservative predominance secured in the exceptional circumstances of the 1931 financial crisis might be broken as the peace issue helped the Labour party recover and trade unions regain popular esteem, and especially if it caused the National government to lose many of the Liberal, moderate, and 'floating' voters. From November 1933 Conservative party analyses of by-election results indicated that all this was happening on a substantial scale, threatening at the next election to leave the government with at best a small majority.[72] Not only did national defence seem at risk; major economic, social, and political threats to Conservatism might again be unleashed.

Here was a new form of the problem which had preoccupied Baldwin since 1922: could 'democracy' face the unpleasant realities of government? As the Cabinet's chief advisors stated, a 'moral disarmament' had occurred which, in changed conditions and 'as a result of persistent and almost unopposed propaganda', had fallen below the point of 'national safety'. Rearmament required an extension of the task which Baldwin had made his own: 'education' of the public.[73] The responsibility and the obstacles now seemed greater, demanding the utmost care. A disarmament and peace consensus, ingrained in the new electorate since 1918, had to be converted to an acceptance of a rearmament which – given widespread belief in Grey's dictum, that 'great armaments' led to war – could easily be misrepresented as government willingness to go to war. Some Labour propaganda was reported to be declaring that Conservatives 'want war. Your husbands and sons will be cannon fodder.'[74] Cabinet members themselves had troubled con-

---

[72] Brooke memos 30 Nov. 1933, Nov. 1934, 25 July 1935, CRD 1/7/16; Gower to Baldwin, 1 Aug. 1935, SB 47/103–8.

[73] Report of the Defence Requirements Committee, para. 162, CP 64(34), 5 March 1934. Cf. service ministers in Cabinet 18(34), 30 April 1934.

[74] Ball to Lloyd, and Ball memo, 13, 22 Nov. 1934, CRD 1/8/1, used by Baldwin at Glasgow, 23 Nov. 1934.

sciences.[75] All wished to avoid provoking the German government into an even greater arms race. Baldwin was conscious that his speeches were now scrutinised in Paris and Berlin, and could have effects upon the diplomatic atmosphere.[76] There was the further complication of having to reply to domestic criticism from opposite directions, for disarmament and greater rearmament, for collective security and isolationism. Beyond this, the difficulty as Baldwin understood it was 'to scare' the people into understanding the international dangers, yet 'not scare them into fits'.[77] Consequently at various times there were things which he felt he could not safely say – about Germany or Italy or France, about strategic contingencies, about deficiencies in British defences but also the scale of Cabinet plans to repair them. He later recalled that 'one made a speech with one's mind full of facts which one could not disclose'.[78] He and the Cabinet did not neglect rearmament; they proceeded with what they considered to be adequate programmes, and increased them as assessments of the threat changed. But they understandably 'handled it gingerly', exercising extreme care with their own and their officials' public phraseology.[79]

During the first phase of rearmament debates from March 1934 to June 1935 Baldwin used several techniques. He argued that the government and its Labour, Liberal, and League of Nations Union critics were agreed on ends – peace and ultimate disarmament – and differed only on means, narrowing the differences to safer dimensions. He implied that opponents of rearmament had reduced national defence and the 'sacred subject' of peace to party objectives.[80] On defence issues which were not yet pressing and which diplomatic effort might still make unnecessary – especially a possible expeditionary force to help defend the Low Countries – he thought the public should be 'educated' gradually, by suggestion and selective silences: 'the less that was said about other matters [than RAF expansion] the better'.[81] On the immediate issue,

[75] Halifax to Baldwin and reply, 19 July 1934, SB 1/108–9.
[76] E.g. Tyrrell (Paris) to Baldwin, 19 Oct. 1933, SB 121/59–62; Warner (Foreign Office) to Fry, 10 Aug. 1936, SB 124/60.
[77] Conservative deputation, 29 July 1936, *WSC Comp* v/iii.287–9.
[78] Mrs Burge note of conversation with Baldwin, 24 April 1940, BF.
[79] Vansittart, *Mist Procession*, pp. 444–5. See Fisher to Baldwin, 26 Feb. 1935, SB 1/80a–c, for the Cabinet toning down the draft of the 1935 Defence White Paper.
[80] E.g. Glasgow, 23 Nov. 1934; Chelsea, 21 Feb. 1935.
[81] Cabinet 26(34), 27 June 1934. Cf. Cabinet committee, 11 June 1934, in M&B pp. 770–1.

however, he confronted the peace oppositions with the need in a
democracy to have the courage 'to tell the truth' to the people.[82]
On the truth of German rearmament, he said that the danger of
a knock-out blow – and so all cause for civilian 'panic'[83] – would
be removed by ensuring that Britain would not 'be in a position
inferior to any country within striking distance of our shores'.[84]
Towards the League of Nations, the truths which he began re-
defining during 1934 were that collective security demanded not
disarmament but a capacity for armed enforcement, because sanctions involved the possibility of war.[85] Rearmament was to be
strictly proportionate to these two needs: to 'repair gaps' in
Britain's defences, and to fulfil collective obligations to resist
aggression. It could not be mistaken for participation in an arms
race.

From late 1935 one of Baldwin's themes was that in contrast
to dictatorships able to prepare and threaten war at will, 'one of
the weaknesses of a democracy ... is that until it is right up
against [a crisis] it will never face the truth'. Because its assent
and commitment waited upon harsh realities that would compel
it to think and learn, 'a democracy is always two years behind a
dictator'.[86] While plainly offered to excuse the relative military
unpreparedness exposed by unexpectedly rapid German rearmament and by the Abyssinian crisis, these statements accurately
recorded great shifts in opposition and public attitudes towards
support for rearmament. What they glossed over were the Cabinet's own painful education in Hitler's and Mussolini's readiness
to defy existing levels of deterrence, and the effort that Baldwin
had put into assisting 'democracy' to absorb 'the truth' as the
German and Italian threats deepened the political difficulty.

During 1935 the approaching statutory expiry of the Parliament elected in October 1931 dictated that, in contrast to 1933–

[82] *HCDeb* 292, c. 2339 (30 July 1934). Cf. *ibid.* 289, c. 2140 (18 May 1934); 299, cc. 46 (11 March 1935).
[83] *HCDeb* 289, cc. 2140–1 (18 May 1934); 292, cc. 2331–2 (30 July 1934); 295, c. 877 (28 Nov. 1934).
[84] *HCDeb* 286, cc. 2076–8 (8 March 1934), and often repeated: e.g. Conservative conference, 4 Oct. 1935.
[85] *HCDeb* 289, c. 2139 (18 May 1934); 292, cc. 2328–9 (30 July 1934); Glasgow, 23 Nov. 1934.
[86] *HCDeb* 305, c. 152 (23 Oct. 1935); 317, c. 1144 (12 Nov. 1936). See e.g. *HCDeb* 309, cc. 1829–30 (9 March 1936); Worcester, 18 April 1936; Conservative deputation, 29 July 1936, *WSC Comp* v/iii.287, 288.

4, the problem really did become that of obtaining an election mandate to allow a free hand on rearmament – now to be accelerated, widened and increased not just for air deterrence but, if all other efforts failed, for possible all-out war. The Abyssinian crisis had particularly impressed upon Baldwin how insufficient British armaments were to meet the changed scale and nature of the armed threats. The navy, he said privately, was a 'collection of old junk'. The 'truth' he thought the public should now be told was that 'if we are to count at Geneva or anywhere else in a world which harbours Germany, Italy and Japan, we must be strong'.[87] But to the Labour and Liberal oppositions had now been added the complications of the Peace Ballot, giving increased salience to the League of Nations Union and apparent opportunities for Lloyd George's Council of Action. In these circumstances, Baldwin made still greater – but also more complicated – use of the League of Nations, until its real importance became less a consideration in foreign policy than an instrument in domestic politics.

The Abyssinian crisis, while dangerous in itself, was neither the chief threat nor an issue on which the Cabinet wanted armed conflict. Its electoral significance was that it enabled public positions about collective security and resistance to Italian aggression to be used to secure acceptance of increased rearmament for self-defence against Germany. Given Baldwin's ambivalence about the League itself, the effect was that his electoral stance had several layers. He re-affirmed commitment to the League, now described as 'the keystone of British policy'. There would be 'no isolated action' in the Abyssinian dispute; there was 'no spirit of national antagonism' towards Italy. He emphasised still more that collective security required adequate armaments, because there were 'risks of peace' – those of peace-keeping – as well as risks of war. The League Covenant might have to be maintained 'by force of arms'. He spoke extensively about the League having been 'crippled' by the non-membership or departure of great powers and about collective security being 'incomplete'. Further rearmament, it was implied, was necessary because the League and collective security might fail. The government did not want 'huge forces', only 'modernisation', especially of the Royal Navy.[88]

---

[87] Jones diary, 17–18 Sept. 1935.
[88] These themes were developed from March 1935, and became intertwined during the election campaign; see esp. Conservative conference, 4 Oct. 1935; Worcester 19 Oct.

Much in this was ambiguous, and attempted to have every side of the argument. Baldwin's language became not so much careful as cunning; as he said in other contexts, 'truth' was many-sided. In terms of its intended audience – peace opinion – the pledge of 'no great armaments'[89] was accurate in that the government did not wish to provoke an arms race; but it understated the scale of armaments that the government now thought essential. To League supporters 'no isolated action' sounded like support for collective security, but it also meant that Britain would avoid the risk of fighting Italy alone. As his expressions of support for League action made far more impression than his reservations about its effectiveness – largely because he could not reveal the Cabinet's well-founded doubts about French support – serious misunderstandings arose over the Cabinet's Abyssinian policy. But Baldwin thought he had gone as far as was yet safe in turning popular idealism towards recognition of unpopular realities, and in his view he achieved the vital purpose which justified the dissimulation – a large election victory which could without serious challenge be treated as a mandate for doing whatever seemed necessary for national defence.[90]

After the election Baldwin endeavoured to present the subsequent embarrassments of the Hoare–Laval crisis, the Rhineland crisis, and the abandonment of sanctions against Italy as further proofs to 'democracy' that peace and security demanded 'increased armaments at hand and ready'.[91] What tempted him into his public 'frankness' in November 1936 was not simply self-justification against Churchill and other Conservative critics. There was, first, belief that the government's new defence, administrative, and industrial preparations – the main theme of his speech – were rapidly restoring the margin of national safety. Second, there was relief at the decline in popular 'pacificism' and at the conversion of the Liberal and Labour parties to rearmament. Third, as with 'the bomber always gets through', he meant

1935; *HCDeb* 305, cc. 151–3 (23 Oct. 1935); election broadcast, 25 Oct. 1935; Wolverhampton, 28 Oct. 1935; *TTF* pp. 328–39 (31 Oct. 1935).

[89] *TTF* p. 339 (31 Oct. 1935); election film, report in *The Times*, 31 Oct. 1935.

[90] E.g. Worcester, 18 April 1936; 14 May 1936; Coltness House, 20 June 1936; *SOL* p. 42 (2 July 1936).

[91] *HCDeb* 309, cc. 1829–30 (9 March 1936). Cf. League of Nations Union deputation, [13 Dec. 1935], Murray papers; Jones *DL* p. 160 (7 Jan. 1936); Coltness House, 20 June 1936; *SOL* pp. 40–2 (2 July 1936).

to shock in order to inspire. His frankness was 'appalling'. He understated the earlier rearmament for a rhetorical purpose: to declare that 'our democratic people' were slow and reluctant to appreciate the perils they faced – the better to assert that once convinced they became indefatigable. 'They may come a little late, but my word, they come with certainty when they do come; they come with a unity not imposed from the top, not imposed by force, but a unity that nothing can break.'[92] The argument he wished to make – one absolutely vital to establish in public belief during the late 1930s – was that

when a democracy has decided on its course there is no reason on earth why it should not be every whit as efficient, working by conviction and free will, as any dictatorship working under pressure and compulsion . . . In switching right round and changing course it has no less determination, it has no less capacity, and it has no less staying power.[93]

IV

Arguments about air parity, collective security, and the League of Nations were only Baldwin's more specific strategies. His main technique for steeling 'democracy' for rearmament was related to his wider understanding and teachings about the international and national problems. Ruminating on holiday at Aix-les-Bains in September 1933, he was struck by a sense of derangement and foreboding:

I have come to the conclusion the world is stark mad. I have no idea what is the matter with it but it's all wrong and at times I am sick to death of being an asylum attendant.
I think we are the sanest but the disease is spreading.[94]

This was not merely gloom at the deteriorating prospects for disarmament: he had diagnosed something more fundamental and still more ominous. Earlier than most other British politicians, he grasped that Hitler's Germany shared many features with Stalin's Russia as well as Mussolini's Italy, and identified all three as manifestations of a single, rampant, malignancy – what he usually

[92] *HCDeb* 317, c. 1144–5 (12 Nov. 1936).
[93] Glasgow, 18 Nov. 1936, elucidating what he had meant six days earlier.
[94] Baldwin to Jones, 14 Sept. 1933, in Jones *DL* p. 115.

called 'dictatorship', but also learned to describe as 'totalitarian' government.[95]

This perception and its implications became both the principal feature of Baldwin's public doctrine, and his most favoured political instrument. It came so easily to mind and struck him so forcibly because much of what he had said in the 1920s now became prophetic. The spread of totalitarianism seemed to fulfil his warnings about the vulnerability of freedom and democracy in the face of destructive forces unleashed by the Great War, and more specifically about the dangers to British constitutionalism from imported foreign ideas. Since 1930 he had occasionally spoken of 'popular government' losing 'ground in many countries'.[96] But from 1933 he insistently expressed a sense that 'ordered liberty' was everywhere in retreat or under siege. The world had 'largely lost faith in democracy', and dictatorships had become 'a vogue'.[97]

Hitler's accession was the most obvious demonstration, but so strong was Baldwin's sense of international infection that his holiday despondency in 1933 and his most anxious public comments during the following winter were prompted by developments elsewhere. 'Strangest of all, the United States of America . . . has given powers to her President . . . as great as any dictator has . . . in Berlin or Rome or in Moscow.'[98] Although Roosevelt's New Deal legislation did not fulfil his worst fears, in 1935 he still described the USA as 'struggling and making every kind of experiment'.[99] Then again, after earlier speaking of Britain and France as the 'only two great countries in the world that had a democratic constitution', he now added the 'instability' of French governments as a 'source of anxiety'.[100] Amid proliferating dictatorships and faltering democracies, Baldwin's leading images became those of a Britain still firm yet increasingly alone and in danger of being overwhelmed. It was 'almost the only country . . .

[95] In *HCDeb* 299, c. 53 (11 March 1935), he spoke of 'what I believe are called authoritarian countries – I believe that is the right expression'. Soon afterwards he began using 'totalitarian': National Free Church Council, 8 April 1935. Cf. *SOL* pp. 115, 140; *Interpreter*, p. 45.
[96] E.g. *TTF* pp. 40, 42 (14 July 1930).
[97] Worcester, 29 April 1933; National Labour *News-Letter*, July 1933.
[98] Edinburgh, 17 Nov. 1933. Cf. Jones *DL* p. 115; Stourport, 8 Jan. 1934.
[99] Himley Hall, 8 June 1935.
[100] Stourport, 8 Jan. 1934; Himley Hall, 8 June 1935.

steering the ship of popular government in safety through stormy waters'.[101] It was 'the last stronghold of freedom, standing like a rock in a tide that is threatening to submerge the world' – the 'one rock of stability in a world of shifting sands'.[102]

As Baldwin described the totalitarian regimes – Russia, Italy, Germany, and their imitators across Europe – their most disturbing feature was that all existed by the eradication of individuality. They perverted education and modern communications into 'machinery for mass impression and mass consciousness', with the object of creating a single 'mass mind'.[103] They ruled by force and regimentation, 'dealing with human nature' as if 'dealing with mechanics', and so establishing 'slavery'.[104] Soon 'from the Rhine to the Pacific there will be a people running into millions who have been trained to be either Bolshevik robots or Nazi robots'. This was a crisis of the most profound nature: 'the great danger that faces humanity today is the danger of the loss of freedom'.[105] The Spanish civil war revealed a further danger, 'the most dangerous thing in this world to-day': both communism and fascism had produced 'large bodies of men who are prepared to fight and to die for an abstract creed', to create fanatical wars of mutual destruction.[106]

If Baldwin had difficulty understanding the ultimate sources of this 'madness', he nevertheless presented an interpretation of its more immediate secular causes. Dictatorship was the extreme outcome of that post-war confusion of material acceleration with human realities about which he had long warned – the product of impatience, aggravated by the effects of the world depression.[107] Its virulence was assisted by a new press and radio which 'annihilated' distance, time, and frontiers.[108] 'Ideas are on the wing today', and 'ideas may be a greater peril to democracy than the sword'.[109]

---

[101] Worcester, 29 April 1933.
[102] *TTF* p. 23 (broadcast 6 March 1934); Osmaston Manor, 16 June 1934. Cf. National Labour luncheon, 6 Nov. 1933; Ashridge, 1 Dec. 1934; Himley Hall, 8 June 1935.
[103] *SOL*, pp. 101–2 (10 April 1937). Cf. Stourport, 8 Jan. 1934.
[104] Worcester, 14 April 1934, also Osmaston Manor, 16 June 1934; *TTF* pp. 23–4 (broadcast, 6 March 1934).
[105] Ashridge, 1 Dec. 1934. Cf. *Interpreter*, pp. 107–8.
[106] *HCDeb* 316, c. 150 (29 Oct. 1936). Cf. Guildhall, 9 Nov. 1936.
[107] E.g. Edinburgh, 17 Nov. 1933; Stourport, 8 Jan. 1934; *TTF* p. 21 (broadcast, 6 March 1934).
[108] Edinburgh, 17 Nov. 1933; Worcester, 14 April 1934.
[109] *Interpreter*, p. 61; New York, 16 Aug. 1939. Cf. press gallery dinner, 29 March 1935.

'No country is immune, and the example of one country may be followed swiftly by a country half-way across the world.'[110] Britain itself was not necessarily secure, again because of the tendency towards a 'mass', 'mechanical' mind created by the mass media and by modern organisation; here too there was criticism of parliamentary institutions and a spread of communist and fascist ideas.[111] As the ideological battle sharpened in the later 1930s, he became particularly worried about the influence of the Left Book Club and an infiltration of 'Red' propaganda into newspapers, reviews, and the BBC.[112] As Chancellor of Cambridge University and with many other contacts in the educational world, he almost certainly had some inkling that Marxist ideas had become fashionable among the young.

Baldwin also warned that dictatorship had spread rapidly because its two forms were dynamically connected. Communism and fascism had much in common, but in other respects they were opposites which developed by reaction against each other. He had no doubt which had started the process. Fascism was bred by communism, and in that sense alone it was more comprehensible and less objectionable. In Italy and Germany dictatorships of the right had arisen from fear of revolution and dictatorship from the left, and fascist parties were likely to grow elsewhere only if communism or other extreme forms of socialism became a threat. The original 'energising force' for totalitarianism came from Russia.[113]

This certainly did not mean that Baldwin had fascist sympathies. To him fascism and Nazism were only marginally less horrible than communism. But it did reinforce his conviction that communism was the most corrosive of civilised values, and so in any balance of evils the one which should be most strongly resisted. This added an ideological edge to his private opinions on foreign policy. There were good diplomatic, strategic, and especially humane reasons (preventing another 'great war') for

[110] Edinburgh, 17 Nov. 1933.
[111] E.g. Stourport, 8 Jan. 1934; National Labour luncheon, 29 Oct. 1934; Junior Imperial League, 23 March 1935; *HCDeb* 316, c.151 (29 Oct. 1936); *SOL* pp. 101–2 (10 April 1937).
[112] Baldwin, Davidson, and Bryant correspondence, May 1937, July and Nov. 1938, June 1939, JCCD 230, 232, 262.
[113] *Interpreter*, pp. 37, 65–7. Cf. Carmunnock, 24 June 1933; Worcester, 14 April 1934; Conservative conference, 4 Oct. 1935; *HCDeb* 313, c. 1238 (10 June 1936); Glasgow, 18 Nov. 1936.

disliking the Franco-Soviet pact and avoiding conflict over the Rhineland, but he offered the further consideration that a Franco-Soviet victory over Germany 'would probably only result in Germany going Bolshevik'.[114] There were similarly good pragmatic reasons for keeping out of the Spanish civil war, but he also told Eden that 'on no account . . . must he bring us in to fight on the side of the Russians'.[115] Again, as Britain's vital interests did not obviously include being drawn by France into an Eastern European war, he would have been content to see 'the Bolshies and the Nazis' left to fight each other.[116] When arguing the cause of Anglo-German peace with German representatives, he was not above suggesting an anti-communist solidarity between the two countries.[117]

Baldwin's anti-totalitarianism went deeper than ordinary party and government concerns. It became his keynote in a series of valedictory addresses on leaving office in 1937, and it was the subject on which he made extensive plans for renewed work in retirement. This was the purpose of his National Book Association, and his involvement in the Association for Education in Citizenship. It produced attempts with Davidson to find a multimillionaire to endow a large expansion of 'political education'.[118] It was also the reason why at the age of seventy-one he twice crossed the Atlantic to lecture and broadcast in Canada and the United States.

Nevertheless as a party leader and senior minister in the mid 1930s he also directed anti-totalitarianism towards particular political objectives. At first partisanship predominated. From 1933, as the 'national crisis' of 1931 receded, he offered anti-totalitarianism as the new, imperative, justification for continuation of the National coalition. Just as democracy was breaking down or under threat elsewhere, 'if you have a weak or feeble Government, if the sane parties are split in this country, you may

---

[114] Cabinet 18(36), 11 March 1936.

[115] Jones *DL* p. 231 (27 July 1936).

[116] Conservative deputation, 29 July 1936, *WSC Comp* v/iii.291. Cf. K. Young, *Baldwin*, p. 129, and for a similar view reported about Spain, J. Edwards, *The British Government and the Spanish Civil War* (1979), p. 38.

[117] *DGFP* series C, vi.759–60 (13 May 1937).

[118] Davidson to Sir W. Cox, 25 Oct. 1938, and to Lord Greenwood, 16 Nov. 1938, JCCD 258. The aim was a trust fund of between a half and one million pounds. Both Nuffield and Ellerman were approached: for the latter see Roskill, *Hankey* iii.327–49.

see a slide here . . . to some form of Bolshevism or Fascism'.[119] It was 'as essential now to continue the National Government as it was two years ago', in order to maintain 'steady progress' towards prosperity without 'any constitutional upheaval or recourse to . . . dictatorship'.[120] Well into 1934 he said that at the next general election the great issue would be whether the country was to stand 'four-square against any attempt to lessen, minimise or break its ancient faith and its ancient liberty',[121] and this remained a secondary or subliminal theme right up to the 1935 election.[122]

When Baldwin first took up that theme one purpose had been to help contain Conservative India critics, by warning of dire possibilities if their rebellion wrecked the National government. But it became especially directed against what he described as 'a marked change of method and mentality' in the Labour movement, due to the influence of the Socialist League of Cripps, Attlee, Laski, and Cole. The 'gospel of gradualism' was, he said, being replaced by a dangerous socialist extremism. Its proposals for emergency powers to modify the constitution and impose state economic controls constituted a 'doctrine of revolutionary dictatorship', seeking 'despotic power'.[123] It was 'closely allied to Bolshevism', yet also 'a proletarian Hitlerism'.[124] Following his double strategy of the 1920s he sometimes said that such 'extremism' was inherent in the very character of the Labour movement, repeating the pattern revealed in 1931 by the TUC's attempts to 'dictate' to the Cabinet.[125] The choice was between 'the constructive policy of the National government and the destructive policy of the Socialist Party'.[126] At other times he expressed confidence in the common sense and patriotism of most Labour party supporters, and urged them to preserve their 'free-minded' and constitutional traditions against the delusions of alienated 'so-called'

[119] Worcester, 29 April 1933.
[120] Carmunnock, 24 June 1933; broadcast, 12 Oct. 1933.
[121] Preston, 14 Feb. 1934. Cf. Worcester, 14 April 1934; Women's Unionist conference, 11 May 1934.
[122] E.g. Himley Hall, 8 June 1935; Liverpool overflow meeting, 4 Nov. 1935; broadcast, 8 Nov. 1935.
[123] Article, 'The New Tyranny: A Dictatorship of the Left', National Labour *News-Letter*, July 1933. Cf. Carmunnock, 24 June 1933; Stourport, 8 Jan. 1934; Ashridge, 1 Dec. 1934.
[124] Carmunnock, 24 June 1933; Conservative conference, 6 Oct. 1933.
[125] National Labour *News-Letter*, July 1933.
[126] New Year message, *The Times*, 28 Dec. 1934. Cf. broadcast, 12 Oct. 1933.

intellectuals.[127] Usually he asserted that the main danger from the Socialist League was that it could provoke a rapid growth in Mosley's British Union of Fascists (BUF), and so precipitate British politics into a continental-style battle of ideological extremes.[128] These public statements certainly overstated his private assessment of the Cripps and Mosley movements – though in 1934–5 he did collect information on BUF membership and finance – but they did not exaggerate his fears of what might develop if constitutionalism were not stoutly defended.[129] What is most striking is the ruthlessness of his counter-attack against the Labour opposition as it sought to recover from its 1931 defeat, seeking not simply to rebut its policy proposals but to discredit it as subversive of British liberties.

However, as the international situation deteriorated and as rearmament became the main political problem, Baldwin began putting anti-totalitarianism to more fundamental, and less partisan, uses. When in early 1934 Tom Jones the official suggested that the country should be made to realise 'that we seem to be shaping for another war', Baldwin the politician replied: 'I would not put it that way. I would say that we are the only defenders left of liberty in a world of Fascists.'[130] Two years later, speaking confidentially to Conservative privy councillors, he said that this was how he had best prepared the nation. 'I have often spoken of the danger to democracy from dictators which I think is the one line whereby you can get people to sit up in this country.' He admitted his reticence, as necessary in warning a nervous public without causing panic: he had 'not dotted the i's and crossed the t's'. But by speaking insistently about democracy and dictatorship he believed he had greatly eased the acceptance of rearmament.[131]

He had done this most often by simple juxtaposition, with speeches on foreign policy and defence containing or ending with passages on liberty or the constitution: 'I would like before I sit

---

[127] Carmunnock, 24 June 1933; Chelsea, 21 Feb. 1935.
[128] Carmunnock, 24 June 1933; Worcester, 14 April 1934; Osmaston Manor, 16 June 1934.
[129] K. Young, *Baldwin*, pp. 109–10; Hutchinson (Home Office)–Fry letters, Jan.–Feb. 1935, SB 9/343–6. But see Jones *DL* p. 130 (12 June 1934), for lack of anxiety about Mosley. His one extended attack on the BUF came after the violent Olympia meeting: Osmaston Manor, 16 June 1934.
[130] Jones *DL* pp. 123–4 (27 Feb. 1934).
[131] Conservative deputation, 29 July 1936, in *WSC Comp* v/iii.289.

down to say a few words about freedom.' He spoke also of the
unpredictable and aggressive character of dictatorships: unre-
strained by public opinion, with populations at their instant command; able to prepare secretly and act swiftly and unexpectedly;
directing attention from domestic problems and strengthening
internal unity by stoking an aggressive patriotism and external
ambitions.[132] He aimed especially to puncture the basic delusion
of peace opinion – whether in the Labour and Liberal oppositions
or the League of Nations Union – that dictatorships might respond
to the same sentiments as democracies. The main 'truth' which
the people needed to be told was that 'we are too apt in this
country to believe that all the peoples of the world are animated
by the ideals which animate us. That is not true at the moment.'[133]
The dictatorships regarded the League of Nations not as an instrument of moral reformation but as 'a pawn in the struggle for
national power and domination'. They put 'power' before peace,
before the brotherhood of man, above 'everything'.[134] He was particularly plain with the Free Church ministers and Anglican clergymen, the 'Men of God', who were so active in the various League
and peace movements: there was no longer a Christian public opinion in Europe to which Britain could appeal, and as he told some
privately, a stiff letter to Hitler might produce not a stiff reply
but 'a bomb on your breakfast tables'.[135] When he evoked a sense
of armed threat in public, it was in terms of the challenge to the
higher ideals. Far from the world being safe for democracy, 'the
world has never been an unsafer place for democracy'.[136]

To-day there were vast areas of the earth's surface, and vast populations,
where the people were being drilled into a belief which was the very
antithesis of everything we stood for. That might some day be dangerous
. . .
   We knew that our ideals, that our civilisation, were worth preserving,
and if these were going to be preserved they must be defended in such
a way that there could be no country, there could be no tyranny, that

---

[132] E.g. National Labour luncheon, 29 Oct. 1934; *HCDeb* 295, cc. 872–5 (28 Nov. 1934);
299, cc. 53–4 (11 March 1935); 302, c. 366 (22 May 1935); Conservative conference,
4 Oct. 1935.
[133] *HCDeb* 292, c. 2339 (30 July 1934).
[134] National Free Church Council, 8 April 1935.
[135] W. R. Matthews, *Memoirs and Meanings* (1969), p. 205. Cf. National Free Church Council, 8 April 1935; Jones diary, 18 Sept., 12 Oct. 1935.
[136] *HCDeb* 299, c. 58 (11 March 1935); National Free Church Council, 8 April 1935.

would not think twice and thrice before they attempted to force their views on our free people.[137]

All this was embedded in a widening and deepening of Baldwin's objectives and strategies. More than other leading Conservatives – certainly more than Neville Chamberlain, and earlier than Churchill – he decided that foreign threats and rearmament demanded renewed efforts to generate the strongest possible feelings of national cohesion: to reduce political divisions, dissolve class feelings, and ensure co-operation from the labour force.

The clearest indication was his changed attitude towards the Labour movement. During 1935 he returned to a more emollient position – not, as he saw it, capitulating to Labour opinion, but emphasising areas of agreement and trying to draw the Labour party into accepting Cabinet foreign and defence policies as truly 'national'. After having spent two years casting doubt on its commitment to constitutionalism, in May of that year he surprised and moved Labour MPs with a tribute to their dedication in helping to 'keep the flag of Parliamentary government flying in the world'. 'I know that they, as I do, stand in their heart of hearts for our Constitution and for our free Parliament.'[138] After the TUC had in September acknowledged that League sanctions against Italy could mean war, he invited Citrine to Chequers to encourage him to accept the need for increased defence preparations.[139] After Citrine and Bevin had helped to defeat Cripps, to remove the party's pacifist leaders, and to commit it to possible military action against Italy, he claimed the Labour movement as supporters of the Cabinet's foreign policy and – this at the Conservative party conference – reverted to celebrating trade unionism as 'an integral part of the country's life', as a 'great stabilizing influence' preventing industrial chaos, and as 'a bulwark of popular liberty' against communism and fascism.[140]

Even if an obvious intention was to deflate Labour opposition before the general election, Baldwin's manner of doing so indicates a wider significance. During the election campaign he delivered the usual ritual criticisms, but eschewed the rhetorical

---

[137] Glasgow, 23 Nov. 1934.
[138] *HCDeb* 302, c. 371 (22 May 1935). See Attlee's reply, c. 373, and Jones *DL* p. 149 for Lansbury reported as 'in tears'.
[139] Citrine, *Men and Work*, pp. 352–4 (14 Sept. 1935); AWB pp. 344–5.
[140] 4 Oct. 1935.

exaggerations made during the 1924 and 1931 elections. During
1936 he extended his public appeal to an underlying consensus,
and in Cabinet discussions 'attached the utmost importance' to
developing trade union 'goodwill', as this was 'absolutely vital' to
implementation of the defence programme. 'With that co-
operation this country in five years time would fear no one.'[141] To
a deputation of Churchill and other Conservative defence critics,
he suggested that they might confer with leaders of the Labour
movement to help create cross-party agreement on rearmament.[142] Some of his valedictory addresses aroused comment for
concentrating more on conciliation of Labour than upon foreign
and defence policies,[143] but Baldwin would have said this missed
the elementary truth that Labour co-operation had become essential for success with the policy objectives. His parting advice to
Conservative and National MPs was 'never do anything to increase
the sense of bitterness between parties in Parliament. Never go
out of your way to irritate or anger the Labour party. Remember
that one day we may need them.'[144]

Among Baldwin's objectives in retirement was 'to keep in touch
with Labour',[145] as part of a broader ambition for putting the
status of elder statesman and his own personal prestige to good
use. 'I can spend my remaining days in guiding the nation through
non-political channels towards the greater unity which, while I was
Prime Minister, I gradually brought to pass after the purge of the
General Strike.'[146] A characteristic idea was to host private dinners
at which the new King and Labour party leaders – as His Majesty's
Opposition and potential ministers – could become acquainted.[147]
His concerns were manifested more substantially during his temporary re-engagement with parliamentary politics from March
1938 to March 1939. He took Eden's resignation as foreign sec-

---

[141] Cabinet 11(36), 26 Feb. 1936; and see appeal to trade-union opinion when introducing
the 1936 Defence White Paper, *HCDeb* 309, cc. 1828–9 (9 March 1936).

[142] 29 July, and see 23 Nov. 1936, in *WSC Comp* v/iii.290, 425–6.

[143] Esp. Jones in *DL* pp. 381, 382 (2, 14 Dec. 1937), *Lord Baldwin*, p. 20, and 'Baldwin' in
DNB, p. 50, and as the probable source for GMY p. 247.

[144] *The Political Diary of Hugh Dalton*, ed. B. Pimlott (1986), p. 205 (16 June 1937). Cf. 'Mr
Baldwin's Testament, 28 April 1937', Crathorne papers; *Reith Diaries*, p. 217 (28 Nov.
1937).

[145] *Reith Diaries* p. 214 (16 April 1937).

[146] Reported in Davidson to Cox, 25 Oct. 1938, JCCD 258.

[147] Jones *DL* pp. 303, 330 (11 Jan., 20 April 1937). At least one such dinner was held: *The
Times*, 8 Dec. 1938. M&B p. 1047n suggests there were others.

retary to mean that Neville Chamberlain was destroying what he now considered to be his 'life's work' of giving politics an overall 'national' rather than narrowly 'party' character. Chamberlain's combative prime-ministerial style, contradicting his own parting advice to government supporters, would only create 'an impression that the govt. is swinging to extreme right' and cost it 'the shifting vote' he had captured in 1935. By provoking Labour MPs to reciprocate in a return to 'the Party dogfight', it would become impossible to preserve 'a national foreign policy'.[148] During the Munich debate in the House of Lords he spoke of the crisis as having swept away 'every barrier of class', and created 'that same spirit of brotherhood that I remember in August 1914'. He called for restored party co-operation: 'there is nothing more important ... than that [on defence issues] there should be no difference of Party, and that Liberals and Labour and the Government should all work together'.[149] Over the next five months he made private efforts to promote Eden's idea of a reconstructed 'government of national unity' including Labour representatives, but could make no impression upon Chamberlain.[150] Even so, he continued into early 1940 to be consulted by trade-union and Labour leaders – even Cripps – who wanted such a reconstruction.[151]

Baldwin's efforts to advance 'political education' had a similar cross-party intention, even where the organisations had indirect Conservative party or government backing. The National Book Association was planned chiefly to counteract the Left Book Club, but it also sought to supersede the Right Book Club: its purpose was *national*. Baldwin became president on condition that its appeal should be 'upon the widest possible grounds', embracing 'everyone ... from the Right to the Left' who agreed that the chief ideological enemy was communism and that 'all who stand for democracy and constitutional evolution should stand together' – though under its editor, Bryant, it moved to the right and attracted accusations of fascist sympathies, contributing to

---

[148] *Harvey Diplomatic Diaries*, pp. 115, 126 (12 March, 13 April 1938); Baldwin to Davidson, 11 April 1938, in M&B p. 1043.

[149] *HLDebs* 110, c. 1393 (4 Oct. 1938).

[150] *Harvey Diplomatic Diaries*, pp. 211, 213, 249, 256 (10, 13 Oct. 1938, 29 Jan., 22 Feb. 1939); Jones *DL* pp. 418–19 (30 Oct. 1938).

[151] Cripps to Baldwin, 13 June 1939, SB 174/153; Cripps diary, 19 June 1939, in *WSC Comp* v/iii.1525; Bevin and Citrine in Baldwin to Davidson, 18 Jan. 1940, JD.

Baldwin's resignation in July 1939.[152] Both the Association for Education in Citizenship, founded by a Liberal, and the British Association for International Understanding, which was Conservative-inspired, included representatives of all three parties as vice-presidents and speakers.[153]

Increasingly from 1933, Baldwin aimed to stimulate a more unified and focused national opinion. He thought of dictatorship or totalitarianism as the product of 'ideology', meant pejoratively as the reverse of the humane and pragmatic traditions of British politics. The task was to resist 'ideology'. Nevertheless, what he himself sought to develop was itself an ideology – a democratic doctrine which in its own way would be as compelling and unyielding as those of the dictatorships. He assumed that national strength, in the forms of internal stability and an agreed military deterrence, depended upon the erection of strong ideological and moral defences; and that these would become more effective the more they were based not upon the negative qualities of fear but upon positive values. As expanded rearmament brought heavier financial and industrial demands, and especially as war became more possible, he spoke of the need for a motive able to

unite the people . . . to make the sacrifices necessary for their own preservation, to have such a faith in the eternal value of what they stand for that they become immune to subversive attempts from left or right and can prove their capacity to defend themselves if need arises by force of arms.[154]

Democracy, he would say, was too easily taken for granted: 'we sometimes noticed it no more than the air we breathe'. But mere 'lip-service' was no longer enough.[155] The strength of dictatorships lay in a unity, commitment, efficiency, and rapidity of action which a democracy – by its nature as a free and individualistic society – could not easily emulate. Nevertheless Britain now had to do this

---

[152] Davidson–Bryant correspondence, May, June 1937; Baldwin to Davidson, 24 July 1939, JCCD 230, 262. The NBA committee included Conservative party officials. For Bryant, see A. Roberts, *Eminent Churchillians* (1994), pp. 292–300.

[153] For the AEC, see E. D. Simon *et al.*, *Constructive Democracy* (1938). For BAIU origins, N. Chamberlain to Baldwin, 7 Dec. 1938, enclosing memos from Ball of the Conservative Research Department, SB 174/19–21.

[154] *Interpreter*, p. 68. Cf. Junior Imperial League, 23 March 1935; Glasgow, 18 Nov. 1936; *SOL* p. 102 (10 April 1937).

[155] *Interpreter*, pp. 46–7. Cf. *TTF* p. 17 (broadcast, 6 March 1934); Women's Unionist conference, 11 May 1934; Ashridge, 1 Dec. 1934, etc.

if it were to survive.[156] The 'people of an ancient democracy' had
to show 'by their cohesion and purpose and will' that they were
'no whit inferior to those of any dictatorship'.[157] Yet, as Baldwin
tried to persuade his audiences to believe, the cause of a democracy's apparent difficulties was also the source of its ultimate
superiority. Persuasion and consent might take longer than command and compulsion, but the effect was far greater. The democratic ideal of the 'moralised solidarity of the group' was stronger
than the totalitarian ideal of 'the mechanised solidarity of the
herd'.[158]

In shaping this anti-totalitarian ideology, Baldwin developed
and re-directed many of the themes and images he had used
against socialism and trade unionism in the 1920s. Broadcasting
on 'National Character' shortly after his summer 1933 reflections
on the world's madness, he spoke of it as 'a good thing at a time
like this, to take stock ... of our national characteristics ... and
generally to investigate ... how [they are] fitted to help us in
the struggle that lies before us'. The qualities of the British, he
concluded, 'were never more needed in the world'. 'Our people
are fitted to pass through whatever trials may be before us, and
to emerge – if they are true to their own best traditions – a greater
people in the future than they have been in the past.'[159] A few
days later he revived the issue of 'the maintenance of the Constitution' – a product 'as native to our country and to our people as
oak or ash or thorn', that had guaranteed their freedom and made
them great.[160] Repeated many times and in various forms through
the rest of the decade, the messages were insistent. As the bene-
ficiaries of a long and unique history of ordered freedom and
public service, the British should consider themselves resistant to
'those two alien plants' of 'Communism and Fascism'. For the
British to think of resorting to dictatorship would be 'an act of
consummate cowardice, an act of surrender', and worse; if they
lost their freedom and democratic government 'the soul of the

---

[156] E.g. Stourport, 8 Jan. 1934; election broadcast, 8 Nov. 1935; Glasgow, 18 Nov. 1936;
New York, 16 Aug. 1939.
[157] Conservative conference, 4 Oct. 1935.
[158] *Interpreter*, pp. 108–9. Cf. Glasgow, 18 Nov. 1936; New York, 16 Aug. 1939. We have
seen (p. 313) that this was the intended message of his 'appalling frankness'.
[159] *TTF* pp. 7, 14 (25 Sept. 1933), and see e.g. *Interpreter*, pp. 9–31, and *Englishman, passim*.
[160] Conservative conference, 6 Oct. 1933. The imagery of 'oak, ash and thorn' came from
Kipling, *Puck of Pook's Hill* and *Rewards and Fairies*.

nation will die', and 'life would not be worth living'. So they must
not indulge in petty or fractious criticisms of Parliament but do
their utmost to uphold their 'priceless heritage' of freedom and
stable representative government. They should preserve and
renew their traditions of service and active citizenship, and value
the Empire as an example to the world of how freedom brought
loyalty, tolerance, co-operation, and peace.[161] And as war seemed
more likely after Munich, further increasing the desirability of
social cohesion and moral commitment, he went further – like
Eden, Churchill, and other prominent Conservatives accepting a
need for further rhetorical gestures towards labour opinion.
Democracies had to become 'in the eyes of their citizens more and
more worth living and dying for', by striving with 'more insistence
and passion than ever before to make real the twin ideals of social
justice and individual freedom' and to develop between privilege
and class hatred 'a middle way' of 'political equality and economic
opportunity'.[162]

                                   V

This context of intensified constitutional and ideological concern
helps to explain the overwrought atmosphere of the royal Abdication, with its extraordinary sense of national and imperial crisis.
Edward VIII's personal sexual morality was not the issue. Baldwin
would have tolerated the King's relationship with Mrs Simpson if
she had remained, in his phrase, 'a respectable whore', a secret
consolation for the public burdens and restrictions on a monarch's
life.[163] Rather, the issue was the maintenance of the public values
which it had become the monarchy's chief function to express and
uphold. This function, not any personal qualities of successive
kings, explains the peculiar hyperbole of conventional public references to the monarchy. Baldwin himself had spoken of the Crown
as the essential symbol – above party, reaching across classes – of
national allegiance, continuity, cohesion, and stability, and of its
increased importance since the 1926 Balfour Declaration as the

---

[161] Accessible examples of the style, found in passages in most of his speeches from late
     1933, are *TTF* pp. 3–6, 18–24; *SOL* pp. 100–4, 118–23; *Interpreter, passim.*
[162] *Interpreter*, pp. 111–12.
[163] See P. Ziegler, *King Edward VIII* (1990), pp. 248, 293. Cf. *Reith Diaries*, p. 196 (16 April
     1937).

only remaining constitutional link between Britain and the Dominions. 'If in any cataclysm the Crown vanished, the Empire would vanish with it.'[164] During 1935 and 1936 – with vast audiences primed successively by the Royal Jubilee, George V's death, and an imminent coronation – he, along with many other public figures, drew out a special contemporary significance of these functions. While its direct power had diminished, 'the influence of the Crown, ... the necessity of the Crown, has become a thing of paramount importance', because events elsewhere had shown 'the enormous value of that steadfast, continuous, traditional, non-political head'. The monarchy was the 'greatest bulwark of a free democracy against dictatorship and tyranny'.[165] Baldwin maintained that this was especially so because, paradoxically, in a democratic age George V's embodiment of the best national qualities had increased its 'great moral power'. By his 'character' and 'complete dedication to duty' he had won the respect, reverence, and love of the people everywhere in the Empire. 'Service' had been his 'guiding principle'. He had 'rigorously trained [his will] to place the public interest first and last', and 'through [his] example men had led better lives in the accomplishment of their daily duties ... at home and to their country'.[166] This was monarchy cast in a 'Baldwinite' role.

The new King's offence was not so much against the prevailing marriage code in itself – nor did it lie in his purported political views.[167] The offence lay in the implications of his attachment to Mrs Simpson for the broader public morality and the constitutional integrity which were now perceived – especially by Baldwin – as underpinning the nation's unity and strength. It threatened to destroy respect for the Crown as a symbol of selfless duty, especially when a sacrifice of personal happiness would be measured against the war dead's sacrifices for 'King and Country'.[168] It could set the King's will against those of the other

---

[164] *OI* p. 72 (30 July 1927); *TTF* p. 309 (10 March 1928).

[165] Primrose League, 3 May 1935, 1 May 1936; and see *Interpreter*, pp. 41–2.

[166] *SOL*, pp. 11, 18–19 (imperial broadcast on the King's death, 21 Jan. 1936); *HCDeb* 308, cc. 12–13 (23 Jan. 1936).

[167] Nowhere does Baldwin mention any complaint about the King's supposed sympathies for the Welsh poor or for Germany.

[168] The comparison, and the shock it produced, was common among the many hundreds of letters Baldwin received from the general public during and after the Abdication crisis, in SB volumes 143–50.

institutions of state and church, and re-open delicate issues of imperial relations. It raised doubts at home and abroad – potentially corrosive and demoralising in the long term, however far-fetched they currently seemed – about Britain's strength and stability. The danger of national and imperial division were among Baldwin's chief reasons for raising the issue with the King.[169] After the issue became public he thought it relevant to inform the Cabinet that a Labour MP had asked 'are we going to have a fascist monarchy?'[170] He may have been aware that when a 'King's party' seemed to be emerging, even some Cabinet ministers momentarily supposed that 'a *coup d'état* was not impossible', with an election on the issue of the King's marriage leading to an attempt 'to upset the Parliamentary system altogether'.[171]

Once the King had declared his determination to marry Mrs Simpson even if he had to abdicate to do so, Baldwin was adamant that abdication was the only course and the sooner the better – prepared if necessary to offer the government's resignation, and armed with carefully gathered support from the Labour and Liberal leaders, TUC secretary, and Australian and Canadian government representatives. For him the alternative possibility of a morganatic marriage, with its obvious taint of something devious and unworthy, would have been hardly less subversive of public standards than that of Mrs Simpson becoming Queen: 'Is this the sort of thing I've stood for in public life?'[172] He became progressively appalled at the King's lack not just of a sense of responsibility to the nation and Empire, but also of what he considered to be any moral or religious sense.[173] The prospect of a 'King's party', and the support for the King and publicity given to Mrs Simpson from those whose judgement he most distrusted or whose values he most despised – Churchill, Lloyd George, Mosley, Beaverbrook, Rothermere and his son and, in North America, the Hearst

[169] Mrs Baldwin memo, 17 Nov. 1937, BF; *SOL* p. 72 (abdication speech, 10 Dec. 1936).
[170] Cooper, 'Abdication Diary' (27 Nov. 1937), Cooper papers 2/16/13. Cf. P. Ziegler, *King Edward VIII* (1990), p. 304.
[171] Cooper, Stanley, Morrison, Hore-Belisha, and Brown conversation, 4 Dec. 1936, in 'Abdication Diary', Cooper papers 2/16/20. Cf. MacDonald diary, 4 Dec. 1936.
[172] Jones *DL* p. 288 (25 Nov. 1936).
[173] Mrs Baldwin memos, 17 Nov., 9 Dec. 1936, BF; Monica Baldwin's report, in Donaldson, *Edward VIII*, p. 302.

press[174] – confirmed his sense of the dangers, and his determination to re-affirm the national decencies with a new king.

Baldwin's House of Commons speech on the Abdication is celebrated for its account of the personal drama of his dealings with Edward VIII, but his real themes lay in the sub-text: national and imperial unity, constitutionalism, the 'guarantee ... against many evils that have affected and afflicted other countries', 'moral force', the guardianship of democracy and freedom.[175] In his 1937 coronation broadcast he presented a monarchy with its symbolic power – or 'Baldwinite' function – not simply restored but intensified by George VI's 'sacrifice' in accepting the burden of an unexpected duty:

Let us dedicate ourselves ... to the service of our fellows, a service in widening circles, service to the home, service to our neighbourhood, to our county, our province, to our country, to the Empire, and to the world. No mere service of our lips, service of our lives, as we know will be the service of our King and Queen.[176]

VI

For Baldwin, what resistance to totalitarianism demanded most of all was a strengthening of the nation's and Empire's grasp of spiritual fundamentals. It was here that not just his public teachings but also, it appears, his personal faith underwent the most development. They did so because he interpreted totalitarianism as an atheistic assault upon Christianity. For some years he had spoken of communist Russia as an example of 'what happened to countries when national morality failed'. Attacks on 'revealed religion' had created the conditions 'for that diabolical hate without which Communist triumph and supremacy could not be achieved'.[177] During 1934 he came to see Nazi interference with German churches and persecution of pastors as a new outbreak

---

[174] Baldwin believed that Mrs Simpson had some deal with the Hearst press: Nancy Dugdale diary, 26, 27 Nov. 1936, Crathorne papers.

[175] *SOL* pp. 70, 72, 78–80, 83 (25 Dec. 1936).

[176] *SOL* p. 144 (imperial broadcast, 12 May 1937); and see pp. 141–2 (5 May 1937) for using the example of the new King when appealing for conciliation in a coal-mining dispute.

[177] Primrose League, 5 May 1933. Cf. Douglas Castle, 27 Aug. 1927; Coliseum, 5 Feb. 1930; Primrose League, 4 April 1930.

of this 'awful heresy', similarly celebrating the 'mass mind' and 'idolatrous conception of the State'.[178] As Christianity stood for the sanctity of human personality and the ideals of liberty and brotherhood, so 'if freedom has to be abolished and room to be made for the slave State, Christianity must go because slavery and Christianity cannot live together'.[179] The great question had therefore become 'whether the civilization of Europe . . . was to be a Christian civilization or a pagan civilization'.[180] Another formulation of his sense of elemental spiritual conflict was an image of modern Europe regressing to something very like the old wars of religion.[181]

In August 1939 Baldwin declared that when speaking for democracy,

> I would always stress the spiritual rather than the political foundations . . . It is a recognition of the dignity of man and of his individuality, and that [this] dignity and individuality are his as a child of God [which] is the unbridgeable gulf between democracy and the isms that . . . for the time being control so large a part of Europe.

Spiritual effort, he had said four months earlier, had to be emphasised also if in organising for rearmament and possible war, democracies were not themselves to follow dictatorships in succumbing to the effects of mass methods.[182] From the mid 1930s Baldwin had indeed made religious liberty and spiritual values a larger part of his public teachings, sustained by his own sense of being 'increasingly led' and by friends who thought the 'world requires not only a statesman but also a good man who does not hesitate to speak in plain terms of Christianity'.[183] Most indicative was his extension of the supposed Disraelian precepts for Conservatism. During the 1920s he had frequently recited the conventional trilogy of constitution, Empire, and welfare of the people. From 1933 he added religion; in 1935 he gave this the most emphasis; in 1936 he placed it first. There must, he said with

[178] Ashridge, 1 Dec. 1934; message to BAIU, *The Times*, 30 March 1939. Cf. *SOL* pp. 164–5 (18 May 1937).
[179] Ashridge, 1 Dec. 1934. Cf. Primrose League, 3 May 1935.
[180] National Free Church Council, 8 April 1935.
[181] *HCDeb* 316, c. 150 (29 Oct. 1936). Cf. Jones *DL* p. 124 (27 Feb. 1934).
[182] New York, 16 Aug. 1939; *Interpreter*, p. 106.
[183] Tyrrell to Baldwin, 21 May 1935, SB 123/198–9. Cf. *Reith Diaries*, p. 120 (17 Jan. 1935).

ecumenical flourish in May 1935, 'in this country ... not be one inch of ground that shall ever be ceded to those who fight the battle against whatever we may mean by religion'. Religious freedom guaranteed political freedom.[184]

Less obvious but equally indicative was Baldwin's interest in the Oxford Group, Frank Buchman's Christian revivalist movement which gained a remarkably large British following during the 1930s. Like other leading politicians Baldwin resisted its efforts to obtain his public endorsement, because some of its methods provoked controversy and because it tended to use the names of prominent figures for its own purposes.[185] But he was aware of its activities through family members, the Davidsons, Halifax, Salisbury, and other friends and, 'profoundly' interested by their reports, in December 1936 he invited Buchman to explain his work to him at Chequers.[186] Like numerous MPs and peers of all parties, he was attracted not simply by the Group's success in turning many young people towards Christian commitment, but by a hope that its spiritual energy and international activity might help to check the spread of communist and fascist ideas. This, paralleling Baldwin's own objectives, was emphasised by the Group renaming itself 'Moral Re-Armament' in May 1938. Although at Chequers Baldwin demurred to Buchman's appeal that he should become 'the authoritative voice for the spiritual rebirth of the Empire',[187] the Group's activities may have been among the influences that stimulated him to give a marked Christian tone to his last speeches as prime minister, including a call to the Empire to provide 'spiritual leadership'. Seeking in April 1939 to impress North American audiences with the depth of British resolve to resist totalitarianism, he spoke in Buchmanite terms of a 'spiritual rearmament' proceeding alongside the 'material rearmament'. There was a 'searching of heart ... going on amongst our people', a re-examination and return to the 'fundamentals of their faith'.[188]

---

[184] Primrose League, 5 May 1933, 3 May 1935, 1 May 1936.
[185] For attempted recruitment, Baker, Buchman, and Bardsley letters to Davidson, 1936–7, JCCD 226, 229, 233. For dislike of methods, G. Lean, *Frank Buchman* (1985), p. 255; Baldwin to Davidson, 20 Aug. 1941, JCCD 283.
[186] Baldwin reply noted on Salisbury to Baldwin, 19 Oct. 1936, SB 171/272; Lean, *Buchman*, pp. 249–50, 254–5.
[187] *Ibid.* p. 255.
[188] *SOL* p. 120 (imperial broadcast, 16 April 1937); *Interpreter*, p. 106.

As much as Churchill in 1940, Baldwin from the mid 1930s spoke of Britain and the Empire having a mission to save mankind from the triumph of tyranny. 'We are a tremendous obstacle to [the] slave State spreading further west.'[189] More than any other country 'we are today the guardians and the trustees for democracy [and] ordered freedom'.[190] He did not, however, mean that Britain should lead an armed crusade against the dictatorships. In his understanding, Divine Providence operated in inscrutable ways; the emergence of new evils might be part of the plan; in a complicated world many choices were not between good and evil, but between greater and lesser evils. Even in the face of the appalling regimes of Hitler and Mussolini – 'madmen', 'lunatics'[191] – he long thought war to be the greater evil. This dread of war and his sense of British interests exceeded and constrained his anti-totalitarianism. Moral and ideological resistance must assist deterrence and defence, not provoke military attack. 'The day is long past', he declared during the Abyssinian crisis, 'when this country would seek by arms or any other method to overthrow the form of government existing in another country.'[192] Wanting reduced international tension, he sometimes even denied that he was criticising the German, Italian, or Russian regimes: these were a matter for their own peoples to determine.[193] Right up to August 1939 he spoke of Western democracies and totalitarian states being able to co-exist.[194] His most urgent meaning of 'spiritual leadership' was shown during the Czechoslovakian crisis, when in his one participation in a Buchmanite initiative he headed a group of former ministers, military leaders, and other public figures in an open letter. This, written by Salisbury, declared that 'the real need of the day is . . . moral and spiritual rearmament'.

God's Living Spirit calls each nation, like each individual, to its highest destiny, and breaks down the barriers of fear and greed, of suspicion and hatred. This same Spirit can transcend conflicting political systems, can reconcile freedom and order, can rekindle true patriotism, can unite all

[189] Ashridge, 1 Dec. 1934.
[190] Himley Hall, 8 June 1935. Cf. *TTF* p. 23 (broadcast, 6 March 1934); *SOL*, pp. 59–60, 120–3 (14 July 1936, imperial broadcast, 16 April 1937).
[191] E.g. Jones *DL* p. 191 (30 April 1936); Avon, *Facing the Dictators*, p. 445.
[192] Worcester, 19 Oct. 1935.
[193] E.g. *HCDeb* 295, cc. 872–3 (28 Nov. 1934); Conservative conference, 4 Oct. 1935; *SOL* p. 101 (10 April 1937).
[194] *Interpreter*, pp. 67, 118; Worcester, 20 May 1939; New York, 16 Aug. 1939.

citizens in the service of nations, and all nations in the service of mankind. 'Thy Will be done on earth' is not a prayer for guidance, but a call to action. For His Will is our Peace.[195]

After the Munich settlement he declared in his last parliamentary speech – as impressive as any during the previous fifteen years – that in the preservation of peace the world's prayers had been answered, as if the 'finger of God' had 'ratified again His Covenant with the children of men'.[196]

Baldwin's evocation of Britain's responsibility towards the rest of mankind and, implicitly, towards God, had three aspects. It invested anti-totalitarian values, 'national government', rearmament, defence preparations, and imperial cohesion with a surpassing importance which could arouse faith and commitment. The British people should feel they were performing 'that great function which is ours to-day – while saving ourselves to save the world at large'.[197] Second, it expressed a belief that the British Empire offered inspiration and hope to the oppressed peoples of continental Europe. He did not suppose that the Buchmanite open letter could have any effect on the September 1938 crisis, but considered it important as 'a voice from England to like-minded people in every country'.[198] His recurring image was that of a light, a flame, or a 'torch of freedom', to be kept alive 'until other nations come to see our ways'.[199]

There is no country . . . where there are not somewhere lovers of freedom who look to this country to carry the torch and keep it burning bright until such time as they may again be able to light their extinguished torches at our flame. We owe it not only to our own people but to the world to preserve our soul for that.[200]

Third, he wanted to intimate that if in the last resort Britain were driven into war, this would unquestionably be a 'just war'[201] – a

---

[195] *The Times*, 10 Sept. 1938. For drafting, Salisbury to Baldwin, 4 Aug. 1938, SB 174/79; Baldwin to Mrs Davidson, 9 Sept. 1938, JD. Other signatories included Amulree, Clarendon, Kennet, Lytton, Sankey, Stanmore, Field Marshals Birdwood and Milne, Admiral Lord Cork and Orrery, and Air Marshal Lord Trenchard.
[196] *HLDeb* 110, c. 1394 (4 Oct. 1938).
[197] Primrose League, 3 May 1935. Cf. *SOL* p. 151 (12 May 1937).
[198] Baldwin to Joan Davidson, 9 Sept. 1938, JD.
[199] *TTF* pp. 5–6 (4 July 1935). Cf. p. 23 (broadcast, 6 March 1934); Conservative conference, 4 Oct. 1935.
[200] Ashridge, 1 Dec. 1934.
[201] *HCDeb* 289, c. 2140 (18 May 1934).

war not for selfish national interests but for the defence of freedom and Christian civilisation, and therefore one in which Britain would call upon the support of all other democratic nations. 'It may well be', he said as early as December 1934, 'if the world proceeds as it is proceeding now, that the day may come when those who have still preserved their freedom will have to stand together lest freedom perish from the earth.'[202] After the Munich crisis he tried to have 'faith that the prayers of millions will prevail' and that peace would be preserved. Nevertheless with a deepened perception of 'spiritual wickedness in high places',[203] he used his remaining influence to help prepare the public mind for the possibility of war.

If war came there could, he declared, be 'but one result', because armed with the cause of 'the liberty of the human spirit' the nation would fight 'with a unanimity of all classes and all ranks that has never been seen in any war that has yet taken place'. For all his earlier scepticism about the Americans, he knew that Britain would need their assistance in war and his two North American visits were intended to help recall the United States as well as Canada to an English-speaking and democratic solidarity.[204] Despite his earlier opposition to Eastern European commitments, he expressed 'perfect agreement' with the Cabinet guarantees from March 1939 to Poland, Greece, and Romania as a 'thoroughly British policy' of resisting attempts to dominate Europe – in the hallowed tradition, even in some sense the providential purpose, of resistance to Philip of Spain, Louis XIV, Napoleon, and the Kaiser.[205] When Dunkirk and the fall of France left Britain to fight alone, like other British Christians he found solace and strength in a sense of Britain as the particular instrument of God's plan.[206]

In May 1937 he attached much importance to his last major address and broadcast as prime minister. Here he proclaimed 'his faith', encapsulating his most fundamental teaching:

[202] Ashridge, 1 Dec. 1934.
[203] Baldwin to Halifax, Christmas Day 1938, Halifax papers A4.410.14.10.
[204] Baldwin to Davidson, 23 Jan. 1939, JD; interview and address in New York, 13, 16 Aug. 1939.
[205] *Interpreter*, pp. 117–18. Cf. Worcester, 30 Jan., 20 May 1939; Jones *DL* pp. 424–5 (20 Jan. 1939).
[206] Baldwin to Halifax, 23 July 1940, in M&B pp. 1058–9. See, similarly, Cazalet-Keir, *From the Wings*, p. 106.

The torch I would hand to you, and ask you to pass from hand to hand along the pathways of the Empire, is a Christian truth re-kindled anew in each ardent generation. Use men as ends and never merely as means; and live for the brotherhood of man, which implies the Fatherhood of God. The brotherhood of man to-day is often denied and derided and called foolishness, but it is, in fact, one of the foolish things of the world which God has chosen to confound the wise, and the world is confounded by it daily.

We may evade it, we may deny it; but we shall find no rest for our souls, nor will the world until we acknowledge it as the ultimate wisdom. That is a message I have tried to deliver as Prime Minister in a hundred speeches.[207]

---

[207] *SOL* pp. 166–7 (18 May 1937). The actual words were supplied by Jones: see Jones diary, 18 May 1937. But they expressed a shared belief drawn ultimately from F. D. Maurice, and Baldwin delivered them with particular conviction and force: Jones diary, 20 May 1937; Amery, *Political Life* III.222.

Conclusion

How, then, are Baldwin's remarkable contemporary reputation and long ascendancy to be explained? What contributions did he make to Conservative politics and national life?

It has been argued that adequate answers are not to be found in the more familiar aspects of political leadership, those of policy-maker, executive, tactician, manager. This is not to say that he was cocooned from everyday politics and government. Like every leading politician he was subjected to the shifting pressures of events and party conflict, and engaged in the interminable policy debates and tactical manoeuvres through which those pressures are handled. All these affected the presentation of his basic messages. Nevertheless, the sources of Baldwin's power and significance lay elsewhere: in certain extraneous and exceptional qualities that he brought to the particularity of political practice. These consisted of a style of leadership which could create a commanding impression of detachment, and a public doctrine which harnessed 'national values' to Conservative causes.

I

Describing one of his last addresses, Middlemas and Barnes commented that 'the Anglican Church had lost a great preacher and a great moralist when Baldwin renounced a vocation at Cambridge fifty years before'.[1] It might be added that the church's loss had been the Conservative party's gain. Not only did Baldwin himself understand his function in this light; it was in these or similar ways that many contemporaries, conscious of witnessing something unusual, attempted to understand his leadership. A. G.

[1] M&B p. 1050.

Gardiner, the veteran Liberal journalist, wrote that 'he has none of the attributes so common to the politician'; rather 'he belongs to the pulpit ... and raises grave issues in the spirit of the preacher rather than of the statesman'.[2] Others likened him to a 'revivalist' or 'prophet',[3] or noted his 'brooding aloofnesses'.[4] Summarising his contribution in 1937, Neville Chamberlain described him as 'a combination of poet, philosopher, sage and statesman'.[5]

Those exasperated by other aspects of Baldwin's leadership often found themselves impressed by his speeches and addresses.[6] Later generations used to different styles of public speaking might be sceptical about his more earnest and general flights. Yet while 'an irreverent PPS' can be found joking that as Baldwin spoke 'the sign of a cross appeared above his head',[7] such criticisms were surprisingly rare among contemporaries. His effect was all the greater because far from being a solemn, stiff figure he seemed modest and affable, as ready with light banter as high seriousness, and because his force of delivery came not from conventional oratorical techniques but from what contemporaries described as 'character', 'sincerity', or 'simplicity' in the sense of straightforwardness. With these qualities he could hold audiences 'in the hollow of his hand'.[8] He could, Chamberlain wrote in 1935, 'raise us above ourselves and express what we would like to believe we had thought'.[9] For another Conservative ten years earlier, he had 'that rarest and finest of all the qualities of a leader – the power of liberating and calling in aid the deeper moral motives that lie in the hearts of men'.[10]

Such moments of moral authority go some way towards explaining his success. The famous example is that of the Macquisten political levy bill in early 1925. In Cabinet his 'simple homely

[2] A. G. Gardiner, *Certain People of Importance* (1926), pp. 10, 6.
[3] E.g. *The People*, 7 Dec. 1924; *The Daily Express*, 7 March 1925; *The British Weekly*, 12 March 1925.
[4] Crawford to Tweedsmuir, 1 Dec. 1937, Tweedsmuir papers Acc. 7214 mf MSS.308; Cf. Jones, 'Stanley Baldwin', *DNB*, p. 50; Menzies, *Afternoon Light*, p. 98.
[5] *HCDeb* 324, c. 686 (31 May 1937).
[6] E.g. *A. Chamberlain Diary Letters*, p. 397 (19 Dec. 1931).
[7] *Bernays Diaries*, p. 197 (23 May 1935). *The Daily Express* meant to be critical when commenting on his 'revivalism' in early 1925 – see his reply at Leeds, 12 March – and for another hostile view, see Bracken in AWB p. 168.
[8] Masterman, *Masterman*, p. 355.
[9] N. Chamberlain to Baldwin, 2 Nov. 1935, SB 170/52–3.
[10] 'Figures of the Session', by 'a Back-bench Conservative', *The Times*, 12 Aug. 1925.

eloquence' prevailed where Birkenhead's formidable skills as a
legal advocate had failed.[11] In the Commons he reduced some
listeners to tears, and after a stunned silence there was applause
as 'Party feeling was sunk in something bigger and the House was
at one.'[12] Churchill, a student of great parliamentary occasions,
'had no idea he could show such power . . . The whole Conservative
party turned round and obeyed without one single mutineer . . . I
cease to be astonished at anything.'[13] Baldwin made other political
speeches with comparable effects, but his main impact came less
from such set-pieces than from his stream of addresses and
impromptu passages, in what Lord Salisbury called an 'immense
work in raising public sentiment and public conviction'.[14] A contemporary biographer, Wickham Steed, caught the peculiarity of
his leadership, even if he understated Baldwin's influence in Cabinet: 'Deduct his social and political "sermons" from his record as
a public man, and his performance will look meagre. Expunge the
poetic and ethical elements from his best speeches, and the resi-
due seems small.'[15]

Nevertheless, Baldwin's power did not derive just from his form
of utterance; it came much more from what he said. Here again
changed attitudes have obscured his impact. To those unsympathetic to his purposes or insensitive to the context, his themes
have seemed banal or empty. This was sometimes true of his contemporary opponents, whether Lloyd George, Churchillians, Beaverbrook, Keynes, the Labour left, or the die-hard right. It became
especially so in the reaction against interwar values after 1940, a
reaction which has continued to colour many later accounts. If his
appeal is to be understood, it is necessary to reach beyond the
usual sources for historians of party and policy to a consideration
of contemporary political culture.

Baldwin's anxieties were shared by almost all Conservatives in
the 1920s: that the emergence of independent working-class politics in a context of a 'new electorate' might condemn their party
to a permanent minority, and its causes to effective extinction.[16]

---

[11] *Amery Diaries* I.398 (27 Feb. 1925). Cf. *A. Chamberlain Diary Letters*, p. 274 (1 March
   1925).
[12] Masterman, *Masterman*, p. 355; Lady B. Balfour to Lytton, 11 March 1925, BF.
[13] *WSC Comp* v/i.424 (8 March 1925).
[14] *The Yorkshire Post*, 5 April 1927.
[15] Steed, *Baldwin*, p. 141.
[16] See e.g. Jarvis, 'British Conservatism and class politics', pp. 64–5, 69–73.

Many Liberals as well as Conservatives feared that the effects of the Great War had shaken the fabric of British society. The task, it was widely thought, was not to get 'back to normality', because 'normality' had been forever destroyed. The task was new: that of stabilisation in transformed economic, social and political conditions. Baldwin's response, like that of some Conservatives after the previous extensions of the electorate in 1867 and 1885 – but by no means the reaction of all Conservatives either on those occasions or now in the 1920s – was to adopt an inclusive attitude towards the new voters. Consequently, although he assumed a low level of political intelligence and deliberately spoke in simple terms, and while he certainly used images and catch-phrases, his rhetorical appeal was not just 'non-rational', as some historians have characterised Conservative rhetoric.[17] It contained much reasoned argument, because his purpose was didactic: to raise the level of political awareness, if plainly in a particular – Conservative – form. Then again, much of what he said was in some obvious sense conventional. But it was precisely this quality which provides a further explanation of his commanding public position. For his purposes required the identification and deployment of unifying public themes, reaching across social and political distinctions. These were to be found in the shared cultural sub-stratum underlying party differences.

Ruralism is a good example, not because it was one of Baldwin's major themes but because his 1924 remarks on the English countryside became so celebrated and have continued to define images of him – even, it has been suggested, acquiring a life of their own as the *'ur-text'* for innumerable later evocations of 'Deep England'.[18] These effects are explicable only in terms of a wide cultural attachment to rural imagery. It can be found not just among other Conservatives, but among Liberals – Grey, Fisher, G. M. Trevelyan, Keynes – and among such Labour politicians as Lansbury and MacDonald, who in 1925 published rural descriptions as lyrical as any from Baldwin.[19] Much ruralism was actually

---

[17] McKibbin, *Ideologies of Class*, pp. 96–8; Matthew, 'Rhetoric and Politics', pp. 50–6.

[18] P. Wright, *On Living in an Old Country* (1985), pp. 82–7. Baldwin's own satisfaction with the passage lay less in its content than its quality as spoken prose: Jones *WD* II.11, 13 (14 March 1926).

[19] See examples in Wiener, *English Culture*, ch. 6; Wright, *Old Country*, pp. 76–84; D. Cannadine, *G. M. Trevelyan* (1992), ch. 4. MacDonald's book was *Wanderings and Excursions*. R. Skidelsky, *John Maynard Keynes* II (1992), pp. 216, 526, reports that Keynes succumbed

an *urban* phenomenon, and its appeal was spreading among all classes of the more mobile interwar urban population, as shown variously by increased domestic tourism and country 'rambling', the layout of new middle-class suburbs, and an outpouring of popular books on country and village themes. As its wide appeal suggests, none of this was necessarily anti-industrial or anti-modern, any more than the medievalism of the industrial leaders of Victorian Manchester or Bradford had been.[20] It has been better described as 'conservative modernity', an imaginative aid easing the transitions and tensions within urban society.[21]

A similar range of reference existed for Baldwin's more prominent themes. Conceptions of a British (and English, Scottish, and Welsh) 'national character' and its supposed constituents were familiar in a literary and political culture whose contemporary portraitists included the Conservative publicist Bryant, the Liberal political scientist Barker, and the socialist moralist Orwell. Dalton's *Practical Socialism for Britain* opened with a description of national characteristics which could be mistaken for that of Baldwin.[22] Even Baldwin's 'anti-intellectualism' connected with widely held notions of British national identity.[23] While economic issues were manifestly contentious, the qualities of self-reliance and voluntary association were as prized in their own way within the Labour movement as they were among Conservatives and Liberals. So too – despite obvious practical differences – was industrial co-operation; and it has been written that in Baldwin's hands 'the application of the traditional strategy of rule to industrial relations was brought to something approaching an art form'.[24] After the Great War imperialism became a larger presence in

to the 'romanticism of the soil', and unlike Baldwin really did take to breeding pigs. See also a later Marxist reminiscence, which reads very like Baldwin's passage: Williams, *The Country and the City*, pp. 3–5.

[20] See C. Dellheim, *The Face of the Past. The Preservation of the Medieval Inheritance in Victorian England* (Cambridge, 1982).

[21] Mandler, *Fall and Rise of the Stately Home*, pp. 225–8, 275. See also A. Potts, '"Constable Country" between the wars', in R. Samuel (ed.), *Patriotism*, 3 vols. (1989), III. 160–86; P. Mandler, 'Against "Englishness": English Culture and the Limits to Rural Nostalgia, 1850–1940', *Transactions of the Royal Historical Society*, 6s.vii (1997), 155–75.

[22] A. Bryant, *The National Character* (1934); E. Barker, *The National Character* (1927); G. Orwell, *The Lion and the Unicorn* (1941); H. Dalton, *Practical Socialism for Britain* (1935), pp. 4–5.

[23] T. W. Heyck, 'Myths and Meanings of Intellectuals in Twentieth-century British National Identity', *Journal of British Studies* 37 (1998), 192–221.

[24] Fox, *History and Heritage*, p. 280.

ordinary British life than ever before, in much less controversial forms than in its Edwardian manifestations.[25] Despite declining church attendance, there was no marked secularisation until after 1945. Christian belief, or at least a diffusive Christian sensibility and respect for moral virtue defined in broadly Christian terms, remained considerable, and had ceased to be divisive in party-political terms.[26] Numerous strands of thought – Christian, Idealist, Fabian, New Liberal, Tory, imperialist – had together placed promotion of national cohesion and an ethic of service among the highest public values, however different their specific proposals for achieving them. Constitutionalism remained a pervasive assumption, underpinned by a 'Whig' historical vision long entrenched as the consensual national interpretation of the British past. Nevertheless, post-war conditions re-opened doubts across the political spectrum about the capacity of 'the people' to sustain 'democratic' responsibilities, generating concern about the character of mass culture and especially about the printed media and the cinema – concern perhaps best expressed in the significance attached to the BBC as a counter-weight.[27] Linked to these anxieties were issues of political morality which had aroused cross-party attention since the Edwardian period, and especially under the Coalition government.

Baldwin's 'commonplaces' therefore had resonances which were both deep and contemporary. He himself supposed that his power lay in a special ability to understand and articulate the views of the 'common man': 'I give expression, in some unaccountable way, to what the English people think. For some reason that appeals to me and gives me strength.'[28] Political leaders need to believe in their own representativeness, and one of Baldwin's strengths was that many others shared this assessment of himself. In these respects, the claim was significant. Yet in any literal sense it was untrue. Not only did it falsely assume a uniformity in public attitudes; it also overstated his powers of insight and ignored evidence

---

[25] See MacKenzie, *Propaganda and Empire*.
[26] The membership for all Christian churches reached its numerical peak in 1927: R. Currie, A. Gilbert, and L. Horsley, *Churches and Churchgoers* (Oxford, 1977), pp. 25–31. For the limited character of secularisation, see e.g. H. McLeod, *Religion and Society in England 1850–1914* (1996); D. Hempton, *Religion and Political Culture in Britain and Ireland* (Cambridge, 1996).
[27] E.g. D. L. LeMahieu, *A Culture for Democracy* (Oxford, 1988).
[28] May 1925, in Palmstierna, *Atskilliga Egenheter*, extract in Jones papers AA1/27.

to the contrary. In October 1923 it was not Baldwin the 'average man', but Salisbury the man 'born to the purple' who better assessed popular opinion towards protection.[29] Once he reached high office Baldwin's contact with ordinary men and women was as slight as that of other leading politicians, and even these contacts could be misleading: enthusiastic crowds during his 1929 election tour deceived him into thinking his party would win.[30] His misjudgement of 'public' feeling was still greater in the first phase of the Hoare–Laval crisis. Plainly enough, even at his most ascendant he commanded the support of at best a majority of 'the people'.

The claim that he _interpreted_ public opinion is also misleading because it obscures his real activity, that of shaping it. He implied this himself in another description of his work, that of 'education'. His special faculty was not passive, but active. It consisted, first, of imprinting on the 'public mind' an unusually attractive identity for himself, and one giving him a great political asset: an impregnable reputation for rectitude. Second, if the materials he drew upon were often conventional, what he did with these materials was exceptional. He was able to invoke certain ideas and values held by otherwise different parts of the community, to give what were often minority opinions an appearance of wider representativeness, and in these ways help to win assent or acquiescence to what he and his party or government wanted. Garvin's _Observer_ provides an example of many newspaper descriptions of the effect:

He evokes the family feeling among Englishmen with a sureness of touch that controversial routine seems incapable of blunting. No Prime Minister has spoken more intimately to the spirit that animates our ordinary life, or been in a truer sense the Public Orator. The secret lies in his understanding of the treasures that most unite and most enrich us – tradition, natural beauty, and social good will.[31]

Baldwin could create such impressions because his family and early life had given him unusually eclectic opinions, sympathies, and personas – industrialist, paternalist employer, countryman, bookman, 'common man', 'broad church' Christian – together with

---

[29] See above, p. 207.
[30] Baldwin to Joan Davidson, 20 May 1929, in _Davidson Memoirs_, p. 303; Jones, _WD_ II.186, 190, 191 (1, 20 June 1929).
[31] _Observer_, 30 Oct. 1927.

a literary skill in using simple words to potent effect. Add the contributions of Tom Jones and other speech-writers, and his public personality became almost a coalition in itself. Add again his non-party addresses, radio broadcasts, and 'preaching', and it can be understood how he could appear to transcend 'politics' and acquire a sort of second, parallel, existence – where his party leadership fell away and he somehow moved outside or above partisan politics. This was a formidable source of strength, enabling him to speak from an ostensibly 'disinterested' position, over the heads of other (divisive) politicians. At times even his Labour and Liberal opponents were drawn into responding to him 'irrespective of party'. At his most effective he could seem to be 'the authentic spokesman of the nation', even 'the incarnation of the national will'.[32]

Yet his touch was not always successful, and it inevitably became less sure the more policy and tactical particulars were at issue. His self-consciously 'non-political' persona itself had potential weaknesses. It caused problems with the more partisan members of his own party, and gave him a dangerous sense that he did not need to sustain an appearance of hard application to 'political' business. On occasion his purpose was so elevated or his attempted rhetorical effect so ambitious that he caused bewilderment. His audience was deeply moved by his November 1932 speech on air disarmament, but hardly anyone grasped his meaning: some even got the reverse of what he meant.[33] His 'appalling frankness' falls into the same category of misapprehension. His gift for words could be too effective, producing phrases with awkward afterlives: 'the bomber will always get through', 'telling the truth to the people', 'lips unsealed'. Because he considered the main problems to lie in the condition of hearts and minds, he could be content with an acclaimed speech where others expected executive action. Sometimes his very persuasiveness created misleading impressions. It was not inconsistent to appeal for industrial peace in 1925–6 while wanting to de-politicise industrial relations; nevertheless, his refusal to impose a government settlement on the coal industry and his acquiescence in the Trades Disputes Bill

---

[32] *The Times*, 28 May 1937; Salter, *Security*, pp. 194–5; Jones, 'Stanley Baldwin', in *DNB* p. 49.
[33] *Headlam Diaries*, pp. 250–1 (10 Nov. 1932); *A. Chamberlain Diary Letters*, pp. 419–20 (12 Nov. 1932); *Amery Diaries* II.287 (12 Nov. 1932); *Bernays Diaries*, p. 14 (11 Nov. 1932).

seemed to many non-Conservatives a kind of betrayal. Considered as electoral strategy, his presentation of rearmament and the Abyssinian problem at the 1935 election was technically brilliant; but once the realities of government diplomacy intruded, the public shock was more damaging than it might otherwise have been.

Yet what he was chiefly thought to represent was so respected that his 'non-political' reputation came to his rescue, giving him a remarkable capacity for recovery. As has been well stated, his 'mistakes were apt to be attributed to probity and his successes regarded as a due reward for virtue. He tended to receive from the public and even from many of his opponents the benefit of the doubt.'[34] His excruciating apology over the Hoare–Laval pact was for almost all his listeners less a spectacle enjoyed than an embarrassment shared. When Attlee as Labour leader questioned Baldwin's personal honour, he instantly lost the House and destroyed any chance of an opposition success.[35]

Baldwin's 'non-political' persona also magnified his ability to achieve political objectives. While he appealed to 'national values', promoted 'consensus', and exuded goodwill, his politics were certainly not hollow or dilute. He had beliefs and purposes of his own, even a sense of personal mission. He put particular interpretations of 'national values' to partisan uses, and the consensus he sought was a Conservative consensus. His goodwill was selective; the function of a preacher or moralist is to judge and admonish. Like all successful politicians, he emphasised contrasts – with 'bolshevism', 'socialism' or fascism, for example – in creative ways. He chose enemies from whom he could draw strength, most obviously Lloyd George, Beaverbrook, and Rothermere. He juggled individuals for public effect and to preserve his own position. In these respects, as the number and eminence of his defeated opponents testifies, he was 'a tough operator' of 'high accomplishment'.[36]

One diarist thought that 'History may make him out a great man, half Machiavelli, half Milton', while another commentator

---

[34] D. Southgate, 'Baldwin 1923–1932', in Southgate (ed.), *The Conservative Leadership 1832–1932* (1974), p. 198.
[35] Attlee and A. Chamberlain in *HCDeb* 307, cc. 2028–9, 2040 (19 Dec. 1935); Simon diary, 19 Dec. 1935; B. Baxter, *Westminster Watchtower* (1938), pp. 15–17.
[36] Cowling, *Impact of Hitler*, p. 261.

offered a still more acute juxtaposition: a 'Methody Machiavelli'.[37]
The force lies with the 'Milton' and the 'Methody': these – words
and moralism, more than conspiracy or party management –
enabled him to be a 'Machiavelli'. He would try to foreclose legitimate areas of debate by transposing them into fundamental
issues, an 'acid test of democracy' or suchlike. We have seen class
consciousness presented as 'class hatred', the TUC as challenging
the constitution, socialism as 'proletarian Hitlerism'. Yet here too
his public personality and the character of his appeal worked to
remarkable effect. His attacks on the press lords and Lloyd George
stuck, as they were meant to. But his attacks on other Liberal
leaders and on the Labour party and the TUC rarely left permanent bitterness, and did not prevent him from regaining his 'non-
political' status. Here were further rare sources of strength: the
good opinion of opponents, and their willingness to accept the
elevated position he set for himself.

II

It has been seen that Baldwin thought the Labour movement
needed to be treated with some sensitivity: it had to be beaten but
not alienated. Accordingly, 'though merciless to the Labour party
electorally he was conciliatory to Labour politically'[38] – indeed
exceptional among Conservatives in the consideration he often
expressed not just towards the party but the trade unions too. He
was exceptional also in the attitudes he evoked among their leading members.

This must not be overstated. Irreducible differences remained
and the rhetorical conflict was unabated; at these levels, he faced
persistent Labour criticism and occasional abuse. Many refused to
be taken in by him. Even the most friendly could sometimes doubt
his competence and be sceptical of his intentions. Nevertheless
Labour admiration for him remains striking. This was not just the
result of his personal cordiality, but a response to his public doctrine and strategic decisions. He did not speak of workers merely
as factors of production nor as an underclass, but as fellow men

[37] *Channon Diaries*, p. 143 (30 Jan. 1938); Sidney Dark (editor, *The Church Times*) quoted in
C. Brooks, *Devil's Decade* (1949), p. 73.
[38] I. Gilmour, *The Body Politic* (1969), pp. 69–70.

and women. He did not treat the Labour party and trade unions as 'enemies within' but as legitimate – even, he appeared to say, admirable – parts of the political and industrial systems. His public generosity towards the Labour leadership as it first entered government in 1924 and his conciliatory gestures towards the trade unions in 1925 made a large impression. In certain respects he spoke their language and seemed to share their ideals: fairness, co-operation, 'brotherhood', 'service', 'democracy'. Laski, the Labour intellectual, imagined that it was just 'tradition rather than fundamentals that has placed you among the forces of the right'.[39] Among Labour MPs, we are told, he had 'not an enemy' and was 'trusted by all'.[40] MacDonald thought he had turned 'Disraelianism . . . from a sham . . . into an honest sentiment of pleasing odour'.[41] Even after 1931, Henderson 'enthusiastically' named him as the non-Labour leader he most admired and could best work with. Lansbury declared in the Commons that 'when I listen to [Baldwin] at any time, he almost persuades me that I ought to be his supporter'.[42] Bevin spoke of his being 'held in very great respect by the Trade Unions',[43] and in the 1930s he developed a warm relationship with Citrine, the TUC secretary.[44]

Such attitudes had effects. Baldwin was usually presented by Labour and trade-union leaders not – as a different Conservative leader might have been – as a 'class enemy', but as an ordinary party opponent, exceptional only in his respect for labour aspirations. As such he became incorporated into their strategies in sometimes positive ways, as they sought to use him and his reputation to advance their own objectives. With the first Labour government creating an opportunity to supersede the Liberal party, Labour ministers contrasted Baldwinite considerateness to Liberal cantankerousness.[45] At the 1924 election he was praised on Labour platforms as an 'honest and admirable man'.[46] During

[39] Laski to Baldwin, 6 March 1933, SB 168/167. Cf. GMY pp. 54, 151, 155.
[40] Lord Snell, *Men, Movements and Myself* (1936; 1938 edn), p. 247.
[41] MacDonald diary, 18 May 1925 (among other pre-1931 indications of his regard).
[42] *The Diary of Beatrice Webb*, ed. N. and J. MacKenzie, vol. IV (1985), p. 309 (5 Aug. 1933); HCDeb 259, c. 106 (11 Nov. 1931).
[43] M&B pp. 483–4.
[44] Citrine, *Men and Work*, pp. 323–8, 353–4; Citrine to Baldwin, 8 June 1935, BF, congratulating him on becoming prime minister again.
[45] R. McKibbin, *The Evolution of the Labour Party 1910–1924* (Oxford, 1974), pp. 120–3; *Scott Diaries*, pp. 457, 460, 489 (3 Feb., 15 July 1924, 23 July 1927).
[46] Ramsden, *Balfour and Baldwin*, p. 203.

his 1925 phase of industrial conciliation, trade-union leaders had obvious reasons to declare confidence in him;[47] and it seems likely that such endorsements persisted in parts of the public memory as confrontation developed in 1926. If Baldwin helped corner the TUC leaders into a strike they had not really wanted, it is also true that his public reputation and their own faith in his word eased their eventual retreat. In Commons debates – even amidst the bitterness of the 1931 crisis – Baldwin was not an easy target, deflecting criticism and soothing tempers. When he spoke 'bitterness and anger vanished from the face of the Opposition'.[48]

Another of Baldwin's aims was to encourage the disintegration of the Liberal party, and to capture as many of its members and supporters as possible. In the mid 1920s he dismissed the party as an irrelevance, 'a relic of early Victorianism', and spoke of an 'effete Liberalism which has seen its day's work done in the world and has little now to live for'.[49] After its leadership fell into Lloyd George's hands in 1926, he declared that the party had 'lost its faith' and offered only diluted socialism.[50] Lloyd George's Liberal critics received or were offered peerages,[51] chairmanships,[52] or ministerial posts.[53] He developed friendly personal relations with leading Asquithians,[54] and in public tributes and valedictions laid claim to the Asquithian mantle.[55]

Plainly, such rhetorical subversion and practical enticements only assisted a process that was driven mainly by the party's internal difficulties and by Liberal anti-socialism. Yet Baldwin's

---

[47] E.g. Bromley, Cramp, Thomas, Clynes reported in National Union *Gleanings and Memoranda*, April 1925, pp. 411–13; Tillett and Cook in GMY p. 102.

[48] Cazalet-Keir, *From the Wings*, p. 104. For 1931 see Alexander and Addison, *HCDeb* 256, cc. 67, 1494 (8, 22 Sept. 1931).

[49] Liverpool, 3 Dec. 1923; Nonconformist Unionist League, 8 April 1924.

[50] Cambridge, 4 March 1927.

[51] For a peerage as inducement for defection to Conservatism, see Baldwin to Mond, 21 June 1926, SB 161/171–2. Inchcape, who remained nominally Liberal, received promotion within the peerage in 1929.

[52] Grey was first choice for the Coal Commission chairmanship – Jones *WD* I.328 (7 Aug. 1925) – eventually given to Samuel. Other chairmanships went to Hilton Young, Reading, and Simon.

[53] Most notably McKenna in 1923 and Churchill in 1924, but also what was presumably just a 'courtesy' offer of the foreign secretaryship to the aged and half-blind Grey, before the 1929 election: Jones *WD* II.165–6 (Jan. 1929).

[54] E.g. Oxford, *Memories and Reflections* I.273, II.194, 243–4; Dawson memo, 19 July 1928, Dawson papers 73/80–1.

[55] E.g. *OE* pp. 191–3 (13 May 1925); *OI* pp. 229–32 (16 Feb. 1928); Aberystwyth, 24 Oct. 1928.

leadership of the more successful anti-socialist party cannot alone explain his special place in the opinion of many Liberals, though hardly all of them. As in Labour politics, in part this arose because his reputation served an instrumental purpose, with attitudes towards him affected by the nature of Liberal divisions. Lloyd George's followers had particular reasons for disliking Baldwin. But Asquithians approved of him in ways which often expressed their disapproval of Lloyd George – who, according to Margot Asquith, was 'not fit to blacken Baldwin's boots'.[56] Even so, a view that Baldwin was a better Liberal than Lloyd George[57] or even, in the 1930s, that he provided a 'fuller & finer conception . . . of real Liberalism' than the party itself,[58] could arise only if he touched something wider and deeper. He seemed to conform to Liberal ideals of a public man: 'lofty character and purity of motive', 'clean and honourable and straight'.[59] He also gave fresh expression to values which had been common to Conservatives and Liberals before 1914: constitutionalism, ordered progress, social harmony, classlessness, self-reliance, voluntarism, service, active citizenship, international peace.[60] That he 'spoke like a Liberal' yet 'acted like a Conservative' seemed plain to a socialist critic,[61] but for many Liberals the resonances almost made policy differences forgivable. H. A. L. Fisher thought Baldwin 'not a Conservative but a Liberal with a heresy about protection'.[62] To *The Manchester Guardian*'s chief leader writer, he seemed to be turning the Conservative party into 'something like the Liberals of our youth'.[63] G. M. Trevelyan, the chief heir to the Whig historical tradition, thought him the best modern exponent of the Whig political tradition.[64] In 1934 Gilbert Murray, the League of Nations Union chairman,

[56] Lady Oxford to Reading, 12 March 1929, Reading papers F118/63/151–2.
[57] E.g. Sir H. Lunn, *Nearing Harbour* (1934), p. 198; A. Shaw to Bridgeman, 23 March 1929, SB 175/52–3.
[58] Lord Elgin to Baldwin, 17 Nov. 1935, SB 39/219–20.
[59] Maclean to Baldwin, 2 Aug. 1926, SB 161/154; Runciman in *The Methodist Recorder*, 18 Feb. 1926. Cf. Asquith in GMY p. 53; Grey to Baldwin, 5 Jan. 1929, in Jones *WD* II.166.
[60] For further Liberal responses to Baldwin and descriptions of 'what Liberals wanted' in the 1920s, see M. Bentley, *The Liberal Mind 1914–1929* (Cambridge, 1977), pp. 125–6 and *passim*.
[61] K. Martin, *Editor* (1968), p. 187.
[62] W. R. Inge, *Diary of a Dean* (1949), p. 136 (17 Feb. 1929).
[63] O. Elton, *C. E. Montague* (1929), p. 253 (26 Dec. 1924, and Nov. ?).
[64] Trevelyan to Baldwin, 17 June 1926, SB 161/227; D. Cannadine, *G. M. Trevelyan* (1991), pp. 160–1.

found it 'interesting ... how you from your Conservatism and I from my Liberalism come to so much the same conclusions about the present dangers of the world'.[65]

Baldwin made a notable impression within a further body of opinion, significant as an indicator of traditional, provincial Liberalism – that of Nonconformity. In 1925 his address to the National Free Church Council left its members 'spellbound', until its members felt moved to rise 'as one man to sing the National Anthem'.[66] For the rest of his career he was often praised across all the Free Church denominations, even the most working-class, the Primitive Methodists, as 'a Christian gentleman', commanding their 'respect', 'trust', and 'affection'.[67] Scottish Presbyterian leaders spoke of him as a 'co-worker with us for the Kingdom of God'.[68] Scott Lidgett, the Wesleyan Methodist leader, declared during the mid 1920s' industrial troubles that it was 'a providential mercy to this nation that at this time he was the master of their fortunes'.[69]

At the end of Baldwin's ministerial career the Conservative grandee Lord Crawford thought he had 'established a mystique in public esteem comparable only to that felt for Disraeli'.[70] Baldwin would have liked this verdict, but it caught only a part of his impact. Sympathetic Liberals and Free Churchmen reached for a different comparison – with Gladstone. In Free Church newspapers Baldwin's 1925 speeches on industrial peace were compared with 'Mr. Gladstone's Midlothian campaign'.[71] Even prominent Nonconformist supporters of Asquith and Lloyd George declared that he commanded their trust as no leader since Gladstone had done.[72] A Disraeli to some and a Gladstone to others: here was a politician creating a public appeal of unusual breadth, with significant effects for the Conservative party.

---

[65] G. Murray to Baldwin, 9 April 1934, SB 168/239.
[66] *The Yorkshire Post* and *The Hull Daily Mail*, 13 March 1925; Mrs Cadbury (NFCC President in 1925) recollection in *The Times*, 19 Dec. 1947.
[67] E.g. *Christian World*, 7 July 1925, 16 May 1929; *British Weekly*, 6 Aug. 1925, 15 May 1931; *Primitive Methodist Leader*, 14 Jan, 25 Feb. 1926; GMY pp. 198–9.
[68] The Revd J. White at Church of Scotland Assembly, and see United Free Church Assembly, both in *The Glasgow Herald*, 8 June 1926.
[69] *Methodist Recorder*, 18 Feb. 1926.
[70] *Crawford Papers*, p. 579 (5 May 1937).
[71] 'A new type of Conservative', *Christian World*, 19 March 1925; *British Weekly*, 19 March 1925.
[72] J. D. Jones to Baldwin, 19 May 1937, SB 152/225, and Jones, *Three Score Years and Ten*, p. 241; A. Peel and J. Marriott, *Robert Forman Horton* (1937), p. 357.

III

Baldwin's chief contribution to his own party was to ease its modernisation – helping to establish a successful Conservative position in new and potentially unfavourable contexts. There was nothing 'natural' about Conservatives becoming the 'majority party' in interwar Britain, as Baldwin himself proved in 1923 and as he found again in 1929.[73] The party's general election victory in 1922, after its disentanglement from the Coalition, had shown that it had structural strengths: socio-economic, organisational, and in the character of the electoral system. But these strengths seem impressive only in retrospect. In themselves they were inadequate and precarious; as historical conceptions they are more descriptive than explanatory. This is certainly so where they assume an identification of 'middle class' with Conservatism. Most obviously the 'middle class' was now greatly out-numbered by working-class voters; but in addition the various components of the 'middle class' did not necessarily have shared interests, and they were not automatically loyal to the Conservative party, as its organisers well knew – not least from the competition of middle-class interest groups and independent by-election candidates.[74] In any case, 'class' was not a simple, one-dimensional, motivation, nor was it the sole source of political allegiance. Within the new electorate, whose size was again increased in 1928, voting habits were still being formed. The Conservative share of the popular poll in 1922 was substantially lower than it had been before 1914. The three-fifths of the electorate which supported other parties might have increased in number, or might have become more consolidated behind one party to greater anti-Conservative effect. The Liberal party remained a substantial presence, capable of making significant inroads in 'middle-class' areas, and as was shown at the 1923 and 1929 elections posing a serious obstacle

---

[73] Emphasis on advantages from the electoral system and in party organisation in Ramsden, *Balfour and Baldwin* pp. 122–3; Ball, '1916–1929', in Seldon (ed.), *How Tory Governments Fall*, pp. 259–64, and Pugh, *Making of Modern British Politics*, pp. 243–50, should be compared with the more sophisticated understandings of the Conservative task in Cowling, *Impact of Labour*, pp. 419–21; McKibbin, *Ideologies*, pp. 259–93, 299–302, and D. Jarvis, 'The shaping of the Conservative electoral hegemony 1918–39', in Lawrence and Taylor (eds.), *Party, State and Society* pp. 131–52.

[74] McKibbin, *Ideologies*, pp. 265–6, 270, 276; Jarvis, 'British Conservatism and Class Politics', pp. 76–9, and 'Shaping of Conservative hegemony', pp. 144–6.

to Conservative success.[75] The particular fate it suffered, and the precise dispersal of its members and supporters, were not pre-ordained. The Labour vote was bound to increase to an extent which remained unknown, and the impact of the party's radical intentions – and its reassurances to nervous and 'liberal' voters – were uncertain. In these circumstances, even existing Conservative strengths needed to be made secure. Longer-term success required popular support to be expanded and new alliances of opinion to be formed.

Some form of Conservative adjustment would have occurred anyway, indeed the 1918 decision to perpetuate the wartime Coalition was a first attempt. But there were competing views on how adjustment was to be achieved, not all of which would have been equally effective. Some might have failed, or provoked such internal dissension as to retard the process. As it was, party tensions generated rebellion against the Coalition – a split which remained a problem when Baldwin became leader – and the revolt against himself from 1929 to 1931, as well as recurrent differences over major policies. The party might have reverted to its Edwardian position, divided and stuck in a parliamentary minority. Its interwar dominance only *seems* natural because of the success of its leading figures in creating appeals and alliances which outmanoeuvred both the party's opponents and their internal critics.

The Conservative party needed to capture large parts of the political middle ground, among new voters who had no previous Conservative allegiances and older voters who might earlier have opposed the party. It was not obvious that – or how – this could be achieved, nor was it an effortless process. The political centre was a fiercely contested place, which could be made to mean various things. With the rise of Labour, the Liberals found themselves occupying much of this ground, and Labour itself was making a strong bid for it. Against this competition any Conservative appeal faced problems of plausibility and definition, because new 'moderate' supporters had to be attracted while traditional Conservative supporters had to be reassured. Anti-socialism and anti-trade unionism provided the most obvious common denominators

---

[75] Cowling, *Impact of Labour*, pp. 227–8, 234–5; McKibbin, *Ideologies*, pp. 276–8; I. G. C. Hutchison, *A Political History of Scotland 1832–1924* (Edinburgh, 1986), pp. 312–18.

among these various groups, so all Conservatives made much of this aspect of their own elemental belief. To this extent, Ross McKibbin's argument about how the Conservative electoral coalition was assembled – by uniting the various parts of the middle classes and, crucially, also the non-trade-unionised working class in ideological opposition to a hostile stereotype of the Labour movement, the 'organised working class' – has considerable force.[76] It describes what many Conservatives said, especially at the 1924 and 1931 elections. It also describes some of Baldwin's statements: he was not 'moderate', 'consensual' or 'accommodating' towards socialism and 'political' trade unionism. Indeed he and other Conservatives took the rhetorical strategy still further, stigmatising these as 'foreign imports', alien to British character and culture.

Nevertheless, this is only a partial explanation of how interwar Conservative politics operated. It understates other dimensions of anti-socialism, and the range and richness of Conservative arguments. These are not reducible to 'class', nor even to 'languages' or 'stereotypes' of class. Even in private Baldwin was pained by such categorisation: 'we are not classes, but men'.[77] Nor did his rhetoric have a prominent 'gendered' appeal to women voters, significant though this was in Central Office propaganda.[78] As has been seen, other forms of identity and thinking remained important within early twentieth-century political culture. The Conservative position was not 'largely negative', nor were its stereotypes of the working class 'constantly hostile'. It did not always work by pitting 'the public' against organised labour.[79] If it had only been like this, the party could not have won so much 'middle opinion'. Liberals or quasi-liberals, and moderate, young, and female voters wanted something more than just blank resistance to Labour or crude appeals to material interest. When in 1922–3 – even before protection was raised – and again in 1927–8 Conservative governments could plausibly be presented as inert and socially divisive, there were significant Liberal revivals.

In reality any political party generates a spectrum of appeals

[76] McKibbin, *Ideologies*, pp. 270–5, 281–6, 299.
[77] Palmstierna, *Atskilliga Egenheter*, extract in Jones papers AA1/27.
[78] See esp. David Jarvis, ' "Mrs Maggs and Betty": The Conservative Appeal to Women Voters in the 1920s', *Twentieth Century British History* 5 (1994), 129–52.
[79] McKibbin, *Ideologies*, pp. 271, 275, 281–2, 292–3, 299.

and attracts support for various reasons; and success is bound to be a collective as well as a complex matter, not just that of its leader. In the mid 1920s few leading Conservatives supposed that an anti-Labour position alone could succeed. It seemed obvious that the 'leaders of thought in the democracy' were 'panting after ideals'.[80] Calculation fired belief to generate numerous forms of positive Conservatism, producing a mixture of negative and positive positions which had the potential to be either electorally powerful or internally destructive. As Baldwin said in other contexts, Conservative opinions varied from 'coal black to jet white' and from 'imperialists of the Second Jubilee to young advanced democrats'. In part his particular importance was that he acquired the stature to keep these different strands together, with the effect that a plurality of Conservative appeals worked to maximum effect. He ensured also that organised labour was treated in a more complicated and effective manner than stark opposition, one both more awkward for Labour leaders themselves and more acceptable to Liberal and moderate opinion. He did not present it as monolithic, but tried to distinguish between its various activities and to divide its diverse constituents. His ideological hostility was directed only towards particular types of labour action (strikes), arguments (socialism), and groups (socialist intellectuals). Otherwise his labour 'stereotypes' were positive, because his aim was to incorporate the Labour movement within Conservative definitions of the 'public': not to exclude, but to emasculate it.

Above all Baldwin was important because of his distinctive Conservative doctrine and 'non-political' reputation. These did much to enable the Conservative party to compete convincingly with Liberals and Labour on the moral high ground – the vital requirement for penetrating far into the political middle ground. As Steed wrote in 1930, for many non-Conservatives 'Toryism, expounded by him, lost many of its repellent features'.[81] His status as a sort of honorary Liberal was especially useful. During the General Strike the Asquithian leadership found it natural to declare unqualified support for Baldwin's Cabinet, which annoyed Lloyd George and Liberal 'progressives' so much that the party's splits were re-opened. He played some part not just in its internal con-

---

[80] Salisbury to Baldwin, 26 Jan. 1924, in Cowling, *Impact of Labour*, p. ix.
[81] Steed, *Baldwin*, p. 13.

fusion, but in its disintegration. Of the numerous Liberal politicians and publicists who from 1924 defected to or entered into
alliances with the Conservative party, some – like Churchill –
would have come anyway, for straightforward anti-socialist reasons
and to rejuvenate flagging careers. But for others Baldwin's brand
of Conservatism supplied a further factor: a constructive pretext
and guarantee against 'reaction'. All defectors feel obliged to
express tribute to a new leader, but these testimonials left no
doubt that 'recruits come over from Liberalism to support him',
not his Cabinet colleagues.[82]

Similar effects operated within the National government
alliance – the further accretions of Liberal and now even some
Labour elements which generated the huge Conservative dominance of the 1930s. After the crisis which precipitated its formation, its non-Conservative members found good reasons for
wishing to perpetuate the alliance, not least the desire to save
themselves from political obliteration. But Baldwin again lent self-
respect and public plausibility to potentially embarrassing
decisions. Not only his renunciation of his claim to the premiership but also the porous, 'national' qualities he had imparted to
Conservatism made it that vital bit easier for MacDonald and his
'National Labour' associates to join the autumn 1931 electoral
coalition against the Labour party, and during 1932 to be
unmoved by the departure of free-trade Liberal ministers. With
the National government cloaking Baldwin still more with the
mantle of 'national' leader, the remaining Liberal ministers had
little difficulty convincing themselves that he was 'an entirely
acceptable chief – he represents our general outlook completely
and there is nothing of the high and dry Tory about him'.[83]

What was true for some non-Conservative politicians was also
likely to have been so for many voters: negative anti-Labour and
positive Conservative appeals reinforced each other. With modern
electoral studies only now escaping from desiccated class assumptions, this is not yet easy to substantiate. Nevertheless there are
suggestive indications. Here Nonconformist opinion might stand
proxy for wider 'liberal' opinion. The 1924 election – amid not
just the anti-socialist 'scare', but also Baldwin's re-presentation of

[82] *The Observer*, 31 Jan. 1926.
[83] Simon diary, 14 Feb. 1935.

a high-minded Conservatism after the failure of protection – seems to have been the occasion when substantial numbers of Nonconformists voted Conservative for the first time.[84] The 1935 election is a still better instance. This did not turn mainly on matters of 'class' or anti-socialist allegiance, but on the direction taken by a broad swath of 'moral opinion'. At its core were Free Church and Anglican idealists, mainstays of the League of Nations Union and Peace Ballot organisation – their salience demonstrated by Lloyd George's attempted resuscitation of political nonconformity with his Council of Action. Ministers momentarily feared that there was 'every sign of the country being swept with the kind of movement that Gladstone started over Bulgarian atrocities'.[85] Yet the threat rapidly dissolved, as Baldwin exuded public reassurance over armaments and the League and spoke privately to a deputation of Free Church leaders.[86] The Council of Action all but collapsed as several of its leading members declared confidence in him, while others suffered criticism within their denominations.[87] By the election a substantial part of Nonconformist and wider moral opinion seems to have been attached or re-attached to the National government.

There is also much testimony from contemporary observers. Few doubted that Baldwin was a 'tremendous' electoral asset to his party. He 'holds the mugwumps and the clericals and the conscientious, earnest, theoretical Liberals as no one else in any party can'.[88] Gladstone's younger son, the vastly experienced Liberal organiser, thought after the 1924 election that the best hope for his party was that Baldwin might 'turn out [to be] another Peel & be beaten by Toryism'.[89] Another Liberal thought he removed 'the innate suspicion of [the Conservative party] from the minds of . . .

---

[84] *British Weekly*, 6, 20 Nov. 1924; Koss, *Nonconformity in British Politics*, pp. 175, 177–8; T. J. Nossiter, 'Recent Work on English Elections 1832–1935', *Political Studies*, 18 (1970), 527.

[85] Hoare to Drummond, 27 July 1935, in Parker, 'Britain, France and the Ethiopian Crisis', p. 298. Cf. Baldwin in Dawson diary, 12 June 1935.

[86] Jones diary, 18 Sept., 12 Oct. 1935; *The Times*, 2 Oct. 1935.

[87] Koss, *Nonconformity in British Politics*, pp. 196–211; P. Williamson, 'Christian Conservatism and the Totalitarian Challenge 1933–1940', forthcoming.

[88] N. Chamberlain to Irwin, 12 Aug. 1928, Halifax Indian papers C152/18/114a, and to H. Chamberlain, 17 Nov. 1935, NC 18/1. Cf. Jones *DL* pp. 155–6 (17 Nov. 1935).

[89] Gladstone to Maclean, 28 March 1925, Gladstone papers 46474/173. See, similarly, Lothian memo, late 1935, in J. R. M. Butler, *Lord Lothian* (1960), pp. 172–3.

working men and women'.[90] The 'man in the street' and 'hundreds of thousands of women' were understood to support him because of his 'un-political' qualities: he was 'honest', his broadcasts avoided 'personalities', he 'don't sling no mud'.[91] There was, a Conservative party organiser wrote, 'no one half so good at the business of getting the middle class and the working class to vote the same way'.[92] It seems probable that Baldwin's presentations of Conservatism eased the party's penetration across 'class' boundaries into new territory – into further layers of middle-class opinion; among working-class voters more familiar with chapel and friendly society than trade unions; and into former Liberal strongholds, including south-west and eastern England and parts of Scotland.

Contemporary belief in Baldwin's popular appeal explains how he survived for so long as Conservative leader, even when taking the party in directions many of its members and natural supporters disliked. From 1924 there was persistent grumbling among backbench MPs and constituency activists, stoked by the newspapers that most of them read. For those on the right of the party, statements of Liberal and Labour respect for him confirmed suspicions that he was really a Liberal or even a 'socialist'.[93] From an internal, party, perspective such discontent could appear to reflect poor leadership. But from an external, electoral position it was almost a measure of his success, in resisting a narrow, limited, conception of Conservative interests. This discontent – and the dissatisfaction at his executive style among colleagues – was containable as long as belief in his ability to win elections was sustained. His difficulties after the 1929 election were caused by a reaction against an excessive earlier expectation – that his reputation could offset a loss of party support to Liberal and Labour.[94] Even then he retained residual strength from a view that it had at least restricted the extent of the defeat, and remained vital if seats outside the Conservative heartlands were to be regained.

[90] G. Shakespeare, *Let Candles Be Brought In* (1949), p. 198.
[91] *Headlam Diaries*, p. 144 (30 March 1928); *Lockhart Diaries*, p. 230 (9 Oct. 1932); G. Lloyd to Baldwin, 8 Nov. 1935, SB 203/55–8; Stannage, *Baldwin Thwarts the Opposition*, p. 177.
[92] Linlithgow (former party deputy-chairman) to Lady Salisbury, 16 June 1936, Linlithgow papers F125/52.
[93] For a notable contrast to recent understandings of Baldwin's appeal, see John Green, *Mr. Baldwin* (1933).
[94] Williamson, 'Safety First', pp. 389–90, 409.

If, then, the 1924 election made it clear that Baldwin's 'function was to tie together the moral, industrial, agrarian, libertarian, Anglican and nonconformist bodies of resistance' to Labour,[95] this must be understood in constructive terms. As such it was not an easy matter, available to any potential leader. Other prominent Conservatives might have succeeded, but it is unlikely that any could have enabled the party to do so well. Salisbury and Halifax, whose Conservative idealism was closest to Baldwin's, were as landed aristocrats too distanced from industrial society, while the two Chamberlains, Birkenhead, Amery, Horne, and Churchill were in different ways too angular in their views or sympathies. Even allowing for changed circumstances, a comparison with Baldwin's successor is instructive. Neville Chamberlain had been a driving force in government policy since 1931, yet once he controlled its public presentation differences were soon widened and embittered. Labour MPs were repelled by his evident contempt towards them; conscious that his 'outspokenness and precision' were frightening 'the weak-kneed Liberals who felt safe with S.B.', he thought adequate compensation lay in 'greater enthusiasm in our own Party'.[96] The government's credibility in representing 'national' opinion was lost and disagreement developed within the Cabinet itself, tightening the domestic constraints on Chamberlain's conduct of foreign policy.

IV

Assessment of Baldwin's contribution to wider national life faces the difficulties that he was so deeply Conservative, seeking to preserve rather than to change; that on policy issues his leadership was highly collective; and that attitudes as well as circumstances changed so greatly just a short time after his ministerial retirement. The impact of the Second World War makes it impossible to know whether his part in adjusting Conservative attitudes towards the Empire, especially India, might have helped the Commonwealth to become a firmer international alliance. From almost any post-1945 perspective, Baldwin's governments are bound to

---

[95] Cowling, *Impact of Labour*, p. 421.
[96] N. to H. Chamberlain, 9 April 1938, NC 18/1/1046. For unfavourable comparisons with Baldwin's treatment of Labour, e.g. Halifax, *Fulness of Days*, pp. 228–9; B. Cartland, *Ronald Cartland* (1941), p. 129; *Reith Diaries*, p. 237 (10 Jan 1940).

seem inadequate in the face of Britain's economic difficulties –
though here, at least, it can be said that the record is better
described as mixed. The extent of attempted financial stabilisation, including Baldwin's American debt settlement and restoration of the gold standard, was misconceived in under-estimating
both changes in the international economy and the flexibility of
the British economy. On the other hand interwar 'economic ortho-
doxy' was not a rigid conception, and the version which developed
under Baldwin's form of Conservatism was more sensitive and constructive than the 'anti-waste', *rentier*, and business forms which
might have prevailed in the party. The rhetorical foundation he
had given to his 1924 government enabled it to resist harsher
pressures for retrenchment in social services, and allowed Neville
Chamberlain to begin a more genuine tradition of Conservative
social legislation than that ascribed to Disraeli. Unpleasant as
everyone knew the 1931 cuts to be, they were perhaps a necessary
price for sustaining confidence in the new monetary regime,
easing 'cheap money', the resumption of social reform, and
eventually the funding of rearmament. By the 1930s his Conservatism had also legitimated a more active conception of the state's
economic role.

Baldwin himself did not assess his career in terms of imperial
or economic policies. Given his modest public style, the claims he
did make were strikingly large. His main work had, he thought,
been in restoring public standards; preserving the constitution,
and more particularly integrating the Labour movement within
the parliamentary system; and 'the binding together of all classes
of our people in an effort to make life in this country better in
every sense of the word'.[97]

There is much contemporary testimony that Baldwin had a significant part in improving the character of public life, after the
atmosphere of lack of principle, even 'corruption', which had clung
to the Coalition. If the revulsion was in fact more widespread,
and if Baldwin had particular strategic reasons for stressing the

---

[97] *OE* p. 16, a text chosen at his memorial service in Westminster Abbey in 1948. Examples
of his own assessment of his career include 'Mr. Baldwin's Testament', 28 April 1937,
Crathorne papers; GMY pp. 246–7; AWB pp. 327–8. Given the priority he had placed
on political cohesion, at the end of his career he liked to compare himself to the seven-
teenth-century Lord Halifax, 'the Great Trimmer', if sometimes teasingly describing
himself as 'the Little Trimmer': Davies, 'Reminiscences', p. 413. Cf. Duff to Jones, 16
Nov. 1937, Jones papers A7/44; GMY p. 54.

contrast, it remains clear that he more than anyone else re-established moral authority as an element in political leadership – and that restored popular respect for parliamentary leaders and a revived ethos of service were undoubted public goods. So too was-defeat of 'press lords' who, irrespective of systems of political accountability, expected to impose their views upon a political party and shape a government's policy. On the main constitutional problem he faced, the Abdication, it is hard to imagine a different outcome, given the unanimity between the government and the opposition and Dominion leaders. Even so, Baldwin's command over constitutional and moral opinion avoided a messier and more protracted crisis, possibly with damaging complications for imperial relationships and foreign perceptions of British power.

More contentious are Baldwin's other claims, which reveal more about his Conservative fear than the actual threats to national cohesion. Constitutionalism was very deeply embedded: the Labour party and trade unions were not revolutionary bodies, and only a tiny proportion of their members looked to the methods of foreign 'bolsheviks' or syndicalists. Working-class consciousness was not 'class hatred'. There was no alienation from the political and social structures, but rather a desire to participate and share more fully in them. At one level, Baldwin understood this. Yet if his rhetoric of constitutional and social danger had evident parti-san purposes – the defence of a Conservative version of national order – this was not its sole source. The Labour movement's claims were such a challenge to the distribution of wealth and power that they could not easily be managed within the existing terms of industrial and political bargaining, and there was reason to fear unpleasant confrontations and an emergence of less 'liberal' atti-tudes on both sides. However the causes of the General Strike are assessed – and its intention was not 'revolutionary' – the threat had dangerous unintended implications, and for this reason it was disliked nearly as much by Labour and TUC leaders as the Con-servative Cabinet. After the 1931 crisis there was in some quar-ters a fashionable interest in communist or fascist ideas. Baldwin was – as Liberal and Labour admiration indicates – upholding a liberal and peaceful political culture which a majority of British people regarded as preferable to the alternatives. Here, as he in some sense again understood, his efforts to 'educate' were prob-ably less relevant to the Labour movement than to his own party.

He very deliberately set himself against the common Conservative assumption that 'Labour' was indistinguishable from 'bolshevism', and for all his own apprehensions checked a crude politics of class fear. If the Labour leadership had been excluded from government in 1924 or 1929; if Cabinet presentations of industrial disputes in 1925 and 1926 had been uniformly confrontational; if the General Strike had actually been treated – rather than described – as a revolutionary threat; or if the 1931 'National' election majority had been exploited still more ruthlessly for Conservative partisan policies, the temper of political life might have become more ugly. Baldwin's rhetorical commitments to 'democracy' and industrial peace, and calculated decisions to display parliamentary fairness – positions by no means agreeable to all his colleagues – imposed constraints upon Conservative party actions in ways which assisted national stability.

Assessments of Baldwin will always come back to the foreign and defence policies of the 1930s, and a comparison with Churchill. The National government did not ignore the danger from Hitler and Mussolini. It wished to avoid the horror of another world war, eschewed 'balance of power' policies and rhetoric which might have precipitated it, and hoped the dictators could be brought to serious negotiation. But under Baldwin it was not tempted to trust them: its strategy was rather to keep options open in uncertain conditions, in Keynes's words exercising a 'wise indecision'.[98] Over Abyssinia it had well-founded doubts about the practicality of collective security, and knew that while it could defeat Italy it would not then be able to defeat Germany as well. Since the late 1940s it has been known that Baldwin never 'confessed' to delaying rearmament in order to win the November 1935 general election. Since the 1960s it has been well understood that air rearmament began in 1934, and that as the election was called a general rearmament was in preparation. Even so it perhaps needs to be re-stated that in 1935 he had to defend the government chiefly against accusations that it was 'militarist' – not that its rearmament was insufficient – and that he committed his leadership unambiguously to greater rearmament: 'I will not be responsible for the conduct of any Government in this country at the present time, if I am not given power to remedy the deficiencies which

---

[98] Keynes, *Collected Writings*, XXVIII.49–50, 55.

have accrued in our defence services since the War.'[99] It has also become evident that Churchill and the Cabinet were not as far apart as was later claimed on his behalf, or as Churchill himself came to believe. In 1947 he wrote that 'it would have been much better if [Baldwin] had never lived'. Yet during 1935, when he was as conscious as Baldwin of the problem caused by peace opinion and equally concerned to avoid war with Mussolini, his attitude had been different: 'you have gathered to yourself a fund of personal goodwill & public confidence which is indispensable to our safety at the present time'.[100]

Rearmament was a complicated matter, facing financial and physical constraints, requiring decisions on priorities, and depending upon uncertain information about the German position. Cabinet ministers chose to plan for a possible war in the medium term (1939 and later) and in the short term to build a deterrent air force, while seeking to tie Hitler down to negotiated agreements. It cannot be assumed that if Churchill had been in their position from 1934 to 1937, his actions – rather than his words – would, or could, have been much different, or have produced better results. British policy, however inadequate, was after all not the only factor in the drift to war, nor in Hitler's early successes. Churchill in early 1940 no more expected the collapse of the Belgian and French armies, the major cause of the British retreat to Dunkirk, than Baldwin had done in 1935. Moreover, Churchill and Baldwin were equally mistaken in one crucial respect: whatever its scale or rapidity, air rearmament – the focus of both contemporary and historical debates – was never likely to have deterred Hitler, because the German military did not regard air power as a strategic weapon.[101] What can be said with certainty is that Baldwin early developed a language of ideological resistance to fascism, which in its appeals to traditions of 'ordered freedom' and to Christian values helped create a moral basis for rearmament in the mid 1930s, and to prepare the way for the national spirit of defiance after Munich.

[99] First election broadcast, 25 Oct. 1935.
[100] M. Gilbert, *In Search of Churchill* (1994), p. 106; Churchill to Baldwin, 9 July 1935, in *WSC Comp* V/iii.1210, and see D. C. Watt, 'Churchill and Appeasement', in R. Blake and W. R. Louis, *Churchill* (Oxford, 1993), pp. 199, 211, 214.
[101] Bialer, *Shadow of the Bomber*, esp. ch. 5; Watt, 'Churchill and appeasement', pp. 202–5.

Primary sources

BALDWIN SPEECHES AND NEWSPAPER COMMENT

Although the great age of political reporting was already passing, Baldwin's speeches and addresses nevertheless received a great deal of newspaper attention. They were normally printed verbatim in *The Times, The Morning Post*, and *The Daily Telegraph*; other national and regional newspapers, such as the *Manchester Guardian*, reported them in detail. Local, denominational, and institutional newspapers or journals almost always gave full reports of speeches delivered in their area or to their organisations.

For non-parliamentary speeches from 1923 to 1940 I have chiefly used the press cuttings in the Baldwin papers at Cambridge (volumes 205–14), as these consist of the fullest available newspaper transcripts, with secretarial corrections. They have been supplemented by *The Times* and by *House of Commons Debates*. For the period before May 1923 I have used *Berrow's Worcester Journal* and press cuttings in the Lloyd George papers. Where a speech or passage is reprinted in a volume of Baldwin's collected addresses, this is cited for ease of reference.

For newspaper comment, I have chiefly drawn upon the selected – and it should be admitted, largely favourable – press cuttings in the Baldwin papers (volumes 215–28).

BALDWIN PAPERS

1 The chief collection is the Baldwin political papers in Cambridge University Library, comprising 233 volumes.

2 Also in Cambridge University Library are A.W. Baldwin's correspondence about G. M. Young's biography and Tom Jones's obituary of Baldwin (MS Add. 7938); material assembled by D. Pepys-Whiteley (MS Add. 8770); letters from Baldwin to his eldest son Oliver, 2nd Earl Baldwin (MS Add. 8795); and other, mainly individual, items in MS Add.

3 Baldwin's personal and family papers – including letters to his mother and other relatives – together with the papers of his second son, Windham, 3rd Earl Baldwin, in the possession and by kind permission of the 4th Earl Baldwin of Bewdley.

4 Baldwin papers, Worcester County Record Office, seen by permission of Lord Baldwin. These consist of two large and one small deposits, mainly relating to Baldwin's parents: 6385, consisting of legal and business papers; 8229, containing Alfred and Louisa Baldwin's journals and correspondence, with other

family papers and additional business material; 8494, a few items of Alfred's political correspondence. (Other collections in the Record Office contain further material, notably 9338, the papers of the Revd. W. H. Cory, vicar of Wilden, and 9410, the records of Wilden church.)

5 Baldwins Ltd papers, previously at the British Steel East Midlands Regional Records Centre, Irthlingborough, but now at Worcester County Record Office as accession 12382, supplementing the business records in the 6385 and 8229 collections.

6 Baldwin papers relating to the Kipling family, University of Sussex Library. These contain only a little material on the Baldwins themselves.

FURTHER PERSONAL PAPERS
(UNPUBLISHED AND EDITIONS)

L. S. Amery	*The Leo Amery Diaries*, ed. John Barnes and David Nicholson, 2 vols. (1980, 1988)
W. J. Ashley	British Library
1st Earl of Balfour	British Library
	Whittingehame papers, Scottish Record Office
Lord Bayford	*Real Old Tory Politics. The Political Diaries of Sir Robert Sanders, Lord Bayford 1910–1935*, ed. John Ramsden (1984)
Robert Bernays	*The Diaries and Letters of Robert Bernays 1932–1939*, ed. Nick Smart (Lampeter, 1996)
5th Lord Brabourne	India Office Collections
1st Viscount Bridgeman	Shropshire Record Office
	The Modernisation of Conservative Politics. The Diaries and Letters of William Bridgeman 1904–1935, ed. Philip Williamson (1988)
R. A. Butler	Trinity College, Cambridge
Lord Carson	Public Record Office of Northern Ireland
Viscount Cecil of Chelwood	British Library
Sir Austen Chamberlain	Birmingham University Library
	The Austen Chamberlain Diary Letters 1916–1937, ed. Robert Self (Cambridge, 1995)
Neville Chamberlain	Birmingham University Library
Sir Henry Channon	*Chips. The Diaries of Sir Henry Channon*, ed. Robert Rhodes James (1967)
Sir Winston Churchill	*Winston S. Churchill, Companion* parts to vols. IV–VI, ed. Martin Gilbert (1976–94)
Lord Cilcennin (J. P. L. Thomas)	Carmarthen Record Office
Alfred Duff Cooper (1st Lord Norwich)	Churchill College, Cambridge
1st Lord Crathorne (Thomas Dugdale)	in the possession of the 2nd Lord Crathorne
27th Earl of Crawford	*The Crawford Papers*, ed. John Vincent (Manchester, 1984)
W. P. Crozier	John Rylands University Library of Manchester
	W. P. Crozier, Off the Record. Political Interviews 1933–1943, ed. A. J. P. Taylor (1973)

J. C. C. Davidson, 1st Lord Davidson	House of Lords Record Office
Joan, Lady Davidson (née Dickinson)	in the possession of Mr Richard Oldfield (extracts from some letters are published in *Memoirs of a Conservative. J. C. C. Davidson's Memoirs and Papers 1910–37*, ed. Robert Rhodes James (1969))
Archbishop Randall Davidson	Lambeth Palace Library
Clement Davies	'The Reminiscences of Clement Davies', ed. J. Graham Jones, *The National Library of Wales Journal* 18 (1993–4), 411–13
Geoffrey Dawson	Bodleian Library
17th Earl of Derby	Liverpool City Library
The Revd Alan Don	diary, Lambeth Palace Library
H. A. L. Fisher	Bodleian Library
Sir John Gilmour	Scottish Record Office
Mary Gladstone	British Library
Viscount Gladstone	British Library
Sir Arthur Griffith-Boscawen	Bodleian Library
H. A. Gwynne	Bodleian Library
Lord Haldane	National Library of Scotland
1st Earl Halifax (Edward Wood, later Lord Irwin)	Borthwick Institute, York
	Indian papers, India Office Collections
1st Lord Hankey	Churchill College, Cambridge
1st Lord Harvey	*The Diplomatic Diaries of Oliver Harvey 1937–1940*, ed. John Harvey (1970)
Sir Cuthbert Headlam	Durham County Record Office
	Parliament and Politics in the Age of Baldwin and MacDonald. The Headlam Diaries 1923–1935, ed. Stuart Ball (1992)
Bishop H. H. Henson	Dean and Chapter Library, Durham Cathedral
W. A. S. Hewins	W. A. S. Hewins, *Apologia of an Imperialist*, 2 vols. (1929)
Thomas Jones	National Library of Wales
	Whitehall Diary [1916–30], 3 vols., ed. Keith Middlemas (Oxford, 1969, 1971)
	Thomas Jones, *Diary with Letters 1931–1950* (Oxford, 1954)
Kathleen, Lady Kennet (Lady Hilton Young)	*Self-Portrait of an Artist. From the Diaries and Letters of Lady Kennet*, ed. Lord Kennet (1949)
Rudyard Kipling	University of Sussex Library
	The Letters of Rudyard Kipling, ed. Thomas Pinney, 3 vols. and continuing (1990–)
Andrew Bonar Law	House of Lords Record Office
2nd Marquess of Linlithgow	India Office Collections
1st Lord Lloyd	Churchill College, Cambridge
1st Earl Lloyd George	House of Lords Record Office
Sir Robert Bruce Lockhart	*The Diaries of Sir Robert Bruce Lockhart*, ed. K. Young, 2 vols. (1973, 1980)
7th Marquess and Marchioness of Londonderry	Public Record Office of Northern Ireland
11th Marquess of Lothian (Philip Kerr)	Scottish Record Office

J. R. MacDonald	Public Record Office
Malcolm MacDonald	University of Durham Library
William Mackenzie King	microfilm selections, Brotherton Library, University of Leeds (originals in National Archives of Canada)
Sir Donald Maclean	Bodleian Library
1st Lord Margesson	Churchill College, Cambridge
Gilbert Murray	Bodleian Library
Harold Nicolson	*Harold Nicolson. Diaries and Letters*, 3 vols., ed. N. Nicolson (1966–8)
J. B. Priestley	Humanities Research Centre, University of Texas, Austin
1st Lord Ponsonby of Shulbrede	Bodleian Library
1st Marquess of Reading	India Office Library and Records
Lord Reith	*The Reith Diaries*, ed. Charles Stuart (1975)
Lord Riddell	British Library
C. P. Scott	Manchester Guardian archives, John Rylands University Library of Manchester *The Political Diaries of C. P. Scott 1911–1928*, ed. T. Wilson (1970)
Sir Leslie Scott	Modern Records Centre, University of Warwick
1st Viscount Simon	Bodleian Library
Lord Somervell	Bodleian Library
Sir Arthur Steel-Maitland	Scottish Record Office
St Loe Strachey	House of Lords Record Office
1st Lord Swinton (Sir Philip Lloyd-Greame, later Cunliffe-Lister)	Churchill College, Cambridge
Lord Templewood (Sir Samuel Hoare)	Cambridge University Library Indian papers, India Office Collections
1st Lord Tweedsmuir (John Buchan)	National Library of Scotland (including microfilm of collection in Queen's University, Kingston, Ontario)
Beatrice Webb	*The Diary of Beatrice Webb*, ed. N. and J. MacKenzie, vol. IV (1985)
1st Viscount Weir	Glasgow University Archives
Sir Laming Worthington-Evans	Bodleian Library

OTHER RECORDS

Bowesfield Steel Co. Ltd: Cleveland County Archives, Middlesbrough

Board of Trade (BT) company files for A. Baldwin & Co. Ltd., and Wright, Butler, & Co. Ltd: Public Record Office

CAB 23 and 24 (Cabinet conclusions and memoranda): Public Record Office

Conservative Research Department: Bodleian Library

Foreign Office: *Documents on British Foreign Policy 1919–1939*

German Foreign Office *Documents on German Foreign Policy 1918–1945*, series C

PREM 1 (Prime Minister's Private Office): Public Record Office

Royal Archives (King George V): Windsor Castle

Worcestershire and West Worcestershire Conservative and Unionist Associations: Worcester County Record Office

Bibliographical essay

Publication details of all the secondary works used in this book may be found in the notes. The following describes the published works most directly relevant for understanding Baldwin, in an order intended to assist the interested reader and to indicate the development of the historical debate.

BALDWIN'S PUBLICATIONS

Baldwin is best approached through the volumes of his collected addresses:

On England and other Addresses (1926)
Our Inheritance. Speeches and Addresses (1928)
This Torch of Freedom. Speeches and Addresses (1935)
Service of Our Lives. Last Speeches as Prime Minister (1937)

All four volumes were reprinted in popular editions between 1935 and 1938; *On England* became a Penguin paperback in 1937. Extracts from the last three volumes were published as *The Torch I Would Hand to You*, ed. R. Bennett (1937). Several addresses, e.g. those to the Classical and English Associations, were published as separate pamphlets. Baldwin also wrote a number of prefaces to books, and a memoir of John Buchan, reprinted in *John Buchan by His Wife and Friends* (1947), pp. 144–6. Also important, in encapsulating Baldwin's message at the end of his career, are:

An Interpreter of England (1939): lectures delivered at the University of Toronto
The Englishman (1940): one of a series of British Council pamphlets by various authors, later collected as *British Life and Thought* (1941)

Together, his reprinted addresses and writings convey the tone and chief elements of his general doctrine, and in that respect are quintessential. Nevertheless they offer only a small selection – and a particular kind of selection – of Baldwin's public utterances, and do not indicate that most of his speeches dealt with economic, social, imperial, and international conditions and the specifics of government policies and party debate. Some of these party and ministerial speeches were published as pamphlets by the Conservative National Union, either individually or in groups. Significant examples of the latter are:

Employment, Trade and Empire Development (October–November 1923 speeches on protection)

Looking Ahead. Unionist Principles and Aims (May 1924 speeches)
Peace and Goodwill in Industry (March 1925)

FILM

There is a substantial quantity of surviving newsreel and party films of Baldwin, including filmed election statements. John Ramsden has produced a valuable video compilation: InterUniversity History Film Consortium, Archive Series No. 3, 'Stanley Baldwin'.

CONTEMPORARY PROFILES

These remain among the most interesting assessments of Baldwin. What they lack in access to private and government documents or in historical perspective they more than gain in their grasp of contemporary mood, and as reactions to Baldwin's speeches and public personality. One deserves special mention, because based on conversations with Baldwin and his close colleagues, and because it is unusually perceptive on his moral idealism and religious faith: 'Gentleman with a Duster' [Harold Begbie], *The Conservative Mind* (1924), pp. 13–32 (American edn, *The Windows of Westminster*, reprinted New York, 1970).
The most notable of the rest (listed chronologically) are:

Philip Guedalla, *A Gallery* (1924), pp. 117–25
Wickham Steed, 'Mr Stanley Baldwin. An Interpretation', *Review of Reviews*, May–June 1925, pp. 402–17
A. G. Gardiner, *Certain People of Importance* (1927), pp. 1–12
A. P. Nicholson, *The Real Men in Public Life* (1928), pp. 9–20
A. A. Milne, 'Portrait of a Good Politician', in *By Way of Introduction* (1929), pp. 63–9
Wickham Steed, *The Real Stanley Baldwin* (1930)
R. D. Blumenfeld, *All in a Lifetime* (1931), pp. 155–62
John Strachey, *The Coming Struggle for Power* (1932; 4th edn 1934), pp. 276–84: a perceptive Marxist analysis
John Green, *Mr. Baldwin. A Study in Post-War Conservatism* (1933): a reactionary Anglican, anti-democratic, English chauvinist, agrarian and protectionist Tory critique, arguing inter alia – and very much against the grain – that Baldwin was *insufficiently* English
'P. Q. R.' [Thomas Jones], 'Mr Baldwin', *The Spectator*, 7 June 1935, pp. 967–8
Bechofer Roberts, *Stanley Baldwin: Man or Miracle?* (1936): another hostile work, but with research on Baldwin's early life
Robert Menzies, 1936 profile in his *Afternoon Light* (1967), pp. 96–9
Sir Austen Chamberlain, 'Stanley Baldwin. An Appreciation', *The Daily Telegraph*, 28 May 1937: an interesting barbed profile, published posthumously
Algernon Cecil, 'Lord Baldwin', *The Quarterly Review*, 269 (1937), 1–23
Arthur Bryant, *Stanley Baldwin* (1937): written to help launch the National Book Association (the 'Baldwin book club') and drawing upon conversations with Baldwin and Lord and Lady Davidson. It out-romanticises

Baldwin himself, but usefully shows how far Baldwinism had been absorbed by some Conservative publicists.

Arthur Bryant, *Humanity in Politics* (1938), pp. 108–12

Beverley Baxter, *Westminster Watchtower* (1938): a forgotten but illuminating collection of weekly articles by a journalist-MP.

Philip Guedalla, *The Hundredth Year* (1939), pp. 80–92

See also the parliamentary tributes on Baldwin's retirement and death: *House of Commons Debates* 5s.324, cc. 682–6 (31 May 1937) and 445, cc. 1466–74 (15 Dec. 1947), and *House of Lords Debates* 5s.153, cc. 317–27 (17 Dec. 1947). Three obituary notices by close friends are of particular interest:

The Times [Thomas Jones], *Lord Baldwin* (1947, but first drafted in 1937): the fuller original of the obituary in *The Times*, 15 December 1947, published separately as a pamphlet

Lord Davidson, 'Stanley Baldwin', *The Cambridge Review*, 24 January 1948, pp. 260, 262

Thomas Jones, 'Stanley Baldwin', in *Dictionary of National Biography* (written 1953, published 1959)

For hostile sketches after Munich or Dunkirk, see:

Sir Arthur Salter, *Security* (1939), pp. 194–8

'Cato' [Michael Foot, Peter Howard, and Frank Owen], *Guilty Men* (1940, reprinted 1998)

A. L. Rowse, 'Reflections on Lord Baldwin', *The Political Quarterly* 12 (1941), 305–17, reprinted in *The End of an Epoch* (1947)

A rather different contribution, but reinforcing the impact of such writing was: Winston S. Churchill, *The Second World War.* I. *The Gathering Storm* (1948)

The first reassessment of Baldwin's record on rearmament was published shortly after his death: R. Bassett, 'Telling the Truth to the People. The Myth of the Baldwin "Confession"', *The Cambridge Journal* 2 (1948–9), 84–95, and see correspondence *ibid.*, pp. 237–42

MEMOIRS

Baldwin appears in many memoirs by contemporaries. The most illuminating references are in:

Thelma Cazalet-Keir, *From the Wings* (1967)

P. J. Grigg, *Prejudice and Judgment* (1948)

Lord Percy, *Some Memories* (1958)

Lord Templewood, *Nine Troubled Years* (1954)

Lord Vansittart, *The Mist Procession* (1958)

Memoirs of a Conservative. J. C. C. Davidson's Memoirs and Papers 1910–37, ed. Robert Rhodes James (1969), is important for extracts from contemporary letters and for general impressions. But Davidson's 'recollections' on specific episodes should be treated with caution, as they are not a wholly independent source: they include paraphrases from the memoirs, biographies, and private papers of other inter-war politicians available in the 1960s.

LATER ASSESSMENTS

The posthumous biographies are:

G. M. Young, *Stanley Baldwin* (1952)
A. W. Baldwin, *My Father. The True Story* (1955)
Keith Middlemas and John Barnes, *Baldwin. A Biography* (1969)
H. Montgomery Hyde, *Baldwin. The Unexpected Prime Minister* (1973)
Kenneth Young, *Stanley Baldwin* (1976)
Roy Jenkins, *Baldwin* (1987)

Though famously critical, G. M. Young's biography contains interesting snippets of Baldwin's conversation in the 1940s. The 3rd Earl Baldwin's riposte is illuminating on his father's early years and inner life, and has a still impressive analysis of Baldwin's presentation of rearmament. Middlemas and Barnes will remain important not just for interpretation of particular episodes but as a quarry of information. Hyde provides a more coherent portrait, and uses some evidence not easily available elsewhere. Jenkins's book is a popular but sometimes misleading gloss on previous biographies. The best short life is Kenneth Young's, making perceptive use of the published sources.

The following shorter accounts (in order of publication) have historiographical and in some cases interpretative interest:

D. C. Somervell, 'Stanley Baldwin', in Duff Cooper (int.), *British Prime Ministers. A Portrait Gallery* (1953), pp.154–67
D. C. Somervell, *Stanley Baldwin. An Examination of Some Features of G. M. Young's Biography* (1953)
C. L. Mowat, 'Baldwin Restored?', *Journal of Modern History* 27 (1955), 169–74: a review of the G. M. Young and Somervell books
R. T. McKenzie, *British Political Parties* (1955), pp. 38–42, 110–45
Anonymous review of A. W. Baldwin's biography in *Times Literary Supplement*, 10 Feb. 1956, p. 79
D. H. Barber, *Stanley Baldwin. Patriot Statesman* (1959), a pamphlet by an unusually enthusiastic admirer, but privately printed and rarely found in libraries
Robert Blake, 'Baldwin and the Right', in John Raymond (ed.), *The Baldwin Age* (1960), pp. 25–65: a landmark essay, still important
Francis Williams, *A Pattern of Rulers* (1965), pp. 5–59: a re-working of the Churchillian–Labour–G. M. Young view
John Grainger, *Character and Style in English Politics* (Cambridge, 1969), pp. 164–77
Barbara Malament, 'Baldwin Re-restored?', *Journal of Modern History* 44 (1972), 87–96: an important criticism of the Middlemas and Barnes biography
John Barnes, 'Baldwin after 50 years', *Crossbow* (May 1973), pp. 10–15
D. Southgate (ed.), *The Conservative Leadership 1832–1932* (1974), pp. 197–246
K. Middlemas, 'Stanley Baldwin', in Herbert van Thal (ed.), *The Prime Ministers* II (1975), pp. 247–69
John Campbell, 'Stanley Baldwin', in J. P. Mackintosh (ed.), *British Prime Ministers of the Twentieth Century* I (1977), pp. 188–218
David Cannadine, 'Politics, Propaganda and Art: The Case of Two Worcestershire Lads', *Midland History* 4 (1977), 97–122

David Dilks, 'Baldwin and Chamberlain', in Lord Butler (ed.), *The Conservatives.
    A History from their Origins to 1965* (1977), pp. 273–404
Andrew Jones and Michael Bentley, 'Salisbury and Baldwin', in Maurice Cowling
    (ed.), *Conservative Essays* (1978), pp. 25–40
John Ramsden, 'Baldwin and Film', in Nicholas Pronay and D. W. Spring (eds.),
    Propaganda, Politics and Film 1918–45 (1982), pp. 126–43
Bill Schwarz, 'The Language of Constitutionalism: Baldwinite Constitutional-
    ism', in *Formations of Nations and People* (1984), pp. 1–18: among the best of
    modern analyses
Philip Williamson, 'The Doctrinal Politics of Stanley Baldwin', in Michael
    Bentley (ed.), *Public and Private Doctrine* (Cambridge, 1993), pp. 181–208
Sian Nicholas, 'The Construction of National Identity: Stanley Baldwin,
    "Englishness" and the Mass Media in Interwar Britain', in M. Francis and
    I. Zweiniger-Bargielowska (eds.), *The Conservatives and British Society 1880–
    1990* (Cardiff, 1996)

Useful passages appear in a few more wide-ranging books. Most notable are the
Cowling volumes listed below, but see also:

Paul Addison, *The Road to 1945* (1975), pp. 26–9
Alan Fox, *History and Heritage. The Social Origins of the British Industrial Relations
    System* (1985), pp. 312–60
Bruce Lenman, *The Eclipse of Parliament* (1992), chs. 6–7

One argument of this book is that Baldwin cannot be understood adequately
without serious attention to the contexts of his life before 1918. The three main
Baldwin companies in the mid-Victorian period – Baldwin, Son & Co., Anglo-
American Tin Stamping Co. Ltd, and E. P. & W. Baldwins – received contemporary description in William Curzon, *The Manufacturing Industries of Worcestershire*
(Birmingham, 1883). For Baldwin's parents and his own early life there are, in
addition to the biography of his father by A. W. Baldwin:

Colin Baber and Trevor Boyns, 'Alfred Baldwin', in David Jeremy (ed.), *Diction-
    ary of Business Biography*, 1 (1984), pp. 116–18
A. W. Baldwin, *The Macdonald Sisters* (1960)

Baldwin's book contains much material not just on Louisa Baldwin (née
Macdonald) and her early milieu, but also on Alfred. It is to be preferred to
another book on the Macdonald sisters, Ina Taylor, *Victorian Sisters* (1987), where
extensive research cannot compensate for limited historical sympathy and understanding.

BALDWIN IN INTERWAR POLITICS

Baldwin in action as party leader and prime minister is best understood within
the full high-politics and high-policy contexts. For these see, in chronological
order of subject matter:

Maurice Cowling, *The Impact of Labour 1920–1924. The Beginning of Modern Brit-
    ish Politics* (Cambridge, 1971)
Philip Williamson, *National Crisis and National Government. British Politics, the
    Economy and Empire 1926–1932* (Cambridge, 1992)

Maurice Cowling, *The Impact of Hitler. British Politics and British Policy 1933–1940* (Cambridge, 1975).

The Conservative party during the Baldwin years is well described in: John Ramsden, *The Age of Balfour and Baldwin* (1978). Baldwin of course appears in the biographies of many other interwar public figures. Those of greatest interest are, in alphabetical order of subject:

Keith Feiling, *The Life of Neville Chamberlain* (1947)
David Dilks, *Neville Chamberlain*, vol. I *1869–1929* (1984)
Martin Gilbert, *Winston S. Churchill*, vol. V *1922–1939* (1976)
J. E. Wrench, *Geoffrey Dawson and our Times* (1955)
Philip Ziegler, *King Edward VIII* (1990)
E. L. Ellis, *T. J. A Life of Thomas Jones* (Cardiff, 1992)

In approximate chronological order of subject, further works with significant bearing on Baldwin are:

Cameron Hazlehurst, 'The Baldwinite Conspiracy', *Historical Studies* [Melbourne] 16 (1974–75), 167–91
David Jarvis, *Conservative Ideology and the Response to Socialism 1918–1931* (forthcoming)
Robert Self, 'Conservative Reunion and the General Election of 1923: A Reassessment', *Twentieth Century British History* 3 (1992), 249–73
G. A. Phillips, *The General Strike. The Politics of Industrial Conflict* (1976)
Philip Williamson, 'Safety First: Baldwin, the Conservative Party and the 1929 General Election', *Historical Journal* 25 (1982), 385–409
Stuart Ball, *Baldwin and the Conservative Party. The Crisis of 1929–1931* (1988)
Gillian Peele, 'St. George's and the Empire Crusade', in C. Cook and J. Ramsden (eds.), *By-Elections in British Politics* (1973), 79–107
Carl Bridge, *Holding India to the Empire. The British Conservative Party and the 1935 Constitution* (Delhi, 1986)
Tom Stannage, 'The East Fulham By-Election', *Historical Journal* 14 (1971), 165–200
Martin Ceadel, 'Interpreting East Fulham', in C. Cook and J. Ramsden (eds.), *By-Elections in British Politics* (1973), 118–38
Tom Stannage, *Baldwin Thwarts the Opposition. The British General Election of 1935* (1980)
U. Bialer, *The Shadow of the Bomber. The Fear of Air Attack and British Politics 1932–1939* (1980)
N. H. Gibbs, *Grand Strategy* I. *Rearmament Policy* (1976)

Index

Baldwin's concerns, themes and notable phrases are given separate headings.
His name is abbreviated to 'B.'.